Friendship & Politics

Friendship & Politics
Essays in Political Thought

Edited by
**John von Heyking and
Richard Avramenko**

*University of Notre Dame Press
Notre Dame, Indiana*

Copyright © 2008 by University of Notre Dame
Notre Dame, Indiana 46556
www.undpress.nd.edu
All Rights Reserved

Published in the United States of America

Library of Congress Cataloging-in-Publication Data

Friendship and politics : essays in political thought / edited by John vonÁ
Heyking and Richard Avramenko.
p. cm.
Includes index.
ISBN-13: 978-0-268-04370-4 (pbk. : alk. paper)
ISBN-10: 0-268-04370-1 (pbk. : alk. paper)
1. Political science-Philosophy. 2. Friendship-Political aspects. I. Heyking,
John von. II. Avramenko, Richard.
JA71.F65 2008
320.01-dc22
2008010164

Contents

Acknowledgments   vii

Introduction: The Persistence of Friendship in Political Life   1
John von Heyking and Richard Avramenko

I. Ancient Perspectives

1. Platonic *Philia* and Political Order   21
   James M. Rhodes

2. Taking Friendship Seriously: Aristotle on the Place(s) of *Philia* in Human Life   53
   Stephen Salkever

3. Cicero's Distinctive Voice on Friendship: *De Amicitia* and *De Re Publica*   84
   Walter Nicgorski

II. Christian Perspectives

4. The Luminous Path of Friendship: Augustine's Account of Friendship and Political Order   115
   John von Heyking

5. A Companionship of *Caritas:* Friendship in
   St. Thomas Aquinas   139
   Jeanne Heffernan Schindler

6. Friendship in the Civic Order: A Reformation Absence   163
   Thomas Heilke

III. Modern Perspectives

7. Plato and Montaigne: Ancient and Modern Ideas
   of Friendship   197
   Timothy Fuller

8. Hobbes on Getting By with Little Help from Friends   214
   Travis D. Smith

9. Social Friendship in the Founding Era   248
   George Carey

10. It Is Not Good for Man to Be Alone: Tocqueville
    on Friendship   268
    Joshua Mitchell

IV. Contemporary Perspectives

11. Zarathustra and His Asinine Friends: Nietzsche and
    Taste as the Groundless Ground of Friendship   287
    Richard Avramenko

12. Friendship, Trust, and Political Order:
    A Critical Overview   315
    Jürgen Gebhardt

Contributors   349

Index   353

Acknowledgments

The editors wish to thank the Eric Voegelin Society and the Society of Catholic Social Scientists for each hosting a panel at the 2004 Annual Meeting of the American Political Science Association, where several contributors to this volume were able to present their ideas. As one of the members of the audience observed, these essays demonstrate how the topic of friendship enables academics to move beyond their respective "sects." The editors also thank Barb Hodgson for her formatting and editorial work, and the editors of the University of Notre Dame Press for their support and assistance for this project.

Introduction

The Persistence of Friendship in Political Life

John von Heyking and Richard Avramenko

Throughout the greater part of the history of political philosophy, friendship has occupied a central place in the conversation. If we draw on conventional historical distinctions, friendship perennially figured as the sine qua non of discussions among ancient and medieval political thinkers regarding good political order and the good human life. As Horst Hutter explains, up to the end of the Middle Ages the idea of friendship was at the core of political thinking: "Western political speculation finds its origin in a system of thought in which the idea of friendship is the major principle in terms of which political theory and practice are described, explained, and analyzed."[1] It is only in the modern era that friendship has lost its prominence and been relegated to the backbenches of political philosophy. It simply has not been a central concern for political thinkers within the liberal tradition, or any other, in the past five hundred years or so.

This demotion has not gone unnoticed. Hans-Georg Gadamer, for instance, remarks that while justice needs only one book, friendship "fills two books in Aristotle's *Ethics* [but] occupies no more than a page in Kant."[2] Where friendship is actually afforded some attention in the tradition, liberal thinkers are, at best, lukewarm toward it. John Rawls, for example—contemporary liberalism's most famous expositor—regards it as a "nonmoral value," but at the same time he nonetheless recognizes that it helps to sustain justice.[3] There is, then, a shift in the history of political thought and in the practice of politics at the end of the Middle Ages. At the dawn of the modern state, the beginning of the scientific revolution, the outset of the spread of universal principles of rights and freedoms, and the advent of international truck and trade, friendship as a political concern nearly drops out of sight. However, as this book's essays on modern and contemporary political thinkers show, friendship does not drop completely out of sight. One notable example of a liberal for whom friendship was important yet ambiguous was Thomas Jefferson, who indicated in his First Inaugural that friendship may even be more important than liberty: "Let us restore to social intercourse that harmony and affection without which liberty and even life itself are but dreary things"[4] Yet, nearly out of sight has friendship dropped today.

So whither friendship? Commentators often observe that the modern era, and liberal democracies in particular, are so committed to liberty and autonomy—that the individual is emphasized to such a degree—that he perforce becomes isolated from other human beings. This is true as well for liberalism's critics including nationalists, socialists, and romantics who prize "the nation," "the people," the universal proletariat, and "the state" as an abstract entity that subsumes individuals and his intermediate relations, which is the predominant scope of his actions. So whereas liberalism and its offspring liberal democracy promise the individual liberty, the cost of this liberty is often isolation. Loneliness, or as Joshua Mitchell refers to it, "brooding withdrawal," therefore becomes one of the central experiences people have as liberal democratic citizens. This phenomenon is often recognized and painfully experienced by immigrants and visitors from outside North America and Europe, especially Muslims.[5] Homegrown accounts of life in liberal democracies also bear this out; one need only think of Robert Putnam's *Bowling Alone* and David Riesman's *Lonely Crowd* as testaments.

But not only have the bonds of friendship been eviscerated, the bonds between individuals generally have taken on a completely different hue. We commonly characterize the individual's relationship with others in terms of the contract. In fact, the liberal principle that society is grounded in a contract reaches into other areas of life to the point that we regard all our relationships in similar terms. We come to our private relationships, our loves and friendships, with the same desire to get a good bargain as we do when we purchase a car or a computer. We network, we schmooze, and we realize the "autonomous self," the ideal to which much of contemporary liberalism seeks. The autonomous self, however, while proudly asserting her independence, is forced to seek respite from her existential solitude in the companionship offered by her dog, the chitchat found on the internet, and the respite found in her lithium.[6]

If we seek less utilitarian, deeper, or more "authentic" relations, we almost naturally turn to romance, on the assumption that erotic attachments and bodily intimacy are the most profound expressions of connecting to another. Even if this is true, and there are good reasons to think there exist more profound expressions of love, romance fails to help us connect to the wider community, with those with whom we will not enter into romantic relationships. What we are left with is romance in private and contract in public, with the proviso that the contract will dominate one's private life once the heat of romance runs out of fuel. Romance fails to resolve the problem of how we can integrate our personalities into our political community. Moreover, romance does not apply to so-called Platonic relations, as evidenced by the confusion heterosexual males have regarding their relationships with other males. Beyond engaging in sports and women, modern society sheds little light on how they can share each other's company. Intimate conversation—which many thinkers in the Western tradition regard as the hallmark of friendship—is rejected as unmanly or "gay." This, combined with the widespread tolerance of homosexuality, does nothing to alleviate that sense of not knowing what to do with one's friend or, for that matter, how to be a friend. We seem unable to understand friendship and the act of sharing in terms that are neither romantic nor sexual.[7] We seem unable to be at leisure in the Aristotelian sense of activity, and, as he observes in the case of the Spartans, a people incapable of leisure becomes an imperial one.[8]

The confusion over friendship in the private realm is mirrored in the public when we seek relationships deeper, or more "authentic," than those marked by mere economic contract. Oft times when in search of this, compassion (and sympathy and pity) becomes the most likely mode of connecting and the surrogate for friendship. There is extensive suffering in our society and in the world at large, and we can identify with the plight of others because we share a common humanity with them. But compassion and its related emotions are unreliable precisely because they are emotions. Our compassion might lead us to help others, but it might simply make us feel good about ourselves, allowing us to indulge ourselves for feeling compassionate. We feel anger at the person, group, or party causing the suffering, but do we merely flatter ourselves for feeling indignation without seeking to alleviate suffering? Compassion as an emotion still depends on our ability to judge rightly about the justice of the case. This inclination toward self-indulgence, of viewing others and ourselves as tragic figures in the theater, is a constant danger in large societies where face-to-face encounters with fellow citizens are limited and replaced by media images meant to promote social cohesion as much as they purport to inform. With Aristotle, one may wonder whether our daily activity of guessing at the character and circumstance of our fellow citizens is in fact a daily act of injustice.[9]

Furthermore, to whom do we owe compassion? Who is our neighbor, as Christians ask? Should we prefer our fellow citizen to someone suffering (perhaps more severely) in a distant land? Why should a national border make a difference for a moral problem so serious? But if we practice "telescopic philanthropy," as Charles Dickens calls it in *Bleak House*, do we not neglect our own community and ultimately ourselves? What moral status does "our own" have anyway? As Alexis de Tocqueville found, liberal democrats find a distant solidarity with universal humanity because they lack an informed sense of "their own." The identity of "our own" shifts daily as alliances, affections, and friendships come and go. Many today attempt to anchor their identities in ethnicity, race, gender, or sexual orientation, but their violence, exclusivity, and their basis in the body make these allegiances suspect.

More promising for friendship is the recent attention political theorists have given "civil society," which consists of those voluntary institutions that include churches, unions, service clubs, interest groups, and others that mediate between the individual and the state, and that enable its members to enjoy each other's company while cultivating the virtues and habits necessary for democratic self-government. While this is true as far as it goes, most "civil associations," as Tocqueville calls them, are based on utility and do not devote themselves and their members to the life of virtue. In short, they are not what Aristotle calls "friendships of virtue" and their members do not live out their lives together, as "other selves," in those communities. Few groups today have such a thick sense of community, like Amish or Hutterite communities, and few suggest them as realistic political, economic, and social models for contemporary liberal democracies to follow.

Friendship in Politics, Politics in Friendship

Inquiries into civil society nevertheless recognize that those intermediary institutions form a bridge between the private and the public, between individual relations and politics. They show us how the personal becomes political, and back again. The essays in this collection demonstrate that what political thinkers say about friendship informs their views on political order, and, conversely, what they say about political order informs their views on friendship. In the case of premodern thinkers considered in this volume, including Plato, Aristotle, Cicero, Augustine, and Aquinas, the connection between friendship and politics is close; for many modern thinkers, including Montaigne, Martin Luther, John Calvin, Thomas Hobbes, John Locke, the American Founders, Tocqueville, Nietzsche, and various social scientists inquiring into "trust," the connection between personal friendships and politics can become tenuous, though never completely lost.

What then is friendship? If we take Aristotle's famous treatment as a starting point, friendship seems to involve reciprocated goodwill and some element of utility, pleasure, and moral and intellectual virtue.[10] The essays in this collection focus on one or a few thinkers in differing milieu, and each of them is in some agreement with this general description of friendship. They differ, however, in how they understand the character and quality of reciprocated goodwill, of utility, of pleasure, and of virtue. While some important thinkers—such as Jean-Jacques Rousseau, Adam

Smith, Immanuel Kant, Carl Schmitt, and Jacques Derrida—are not included, those here considered present a wide array of views of friendship found in the Western tradition of political thought. Many of Schmitt's and Derrida's post-Nietzschean ideas were anticipated by Nietzsche, whom Richard Avramenko covers; Smith and Kant have received a fair bit of scholarly attention elsewhere and, as representatives of the broad liberal tradition, their ideas overlap to a degree with the Hobbesian (by Travis D. Smith), Lockean (by Jürgen Gebhardt), Tocquevillian (by Joshua Mitchell), and American ideas (by George Carey) examined here; there is some question whether Rousseau supports a view of friendship, though his views on compassion have been documented extensively.[11] As part of the ambition of this volume to present a wide array of views on friendship in the history of Western political thought, three of the essays examine thinkers within the Christian tradition in order to uncover the complexities that Christian revelation introduces to politics.

All the thinkers whose works are canvassed in this collection treat friendship as an activity that engages the entirety of the human personality—including the rational, moral, and spiritual—and consider what the engagement implies for our sense of belonging in political society. The ways thinkers approach the great moral, intellectual, and political questions influence their understanding of friendship and the degree to which they account for the rational, emotional, and spiritual aspects of the phenomenon. For example, Thomas Hobbes, for whom human existence is best understood as a perpetual quest for power, writes of friends as patrons or cronies and seems to reject Aristotle's notion of friends of virtue (though he had friends of this type). Protestant Reformers Martin Luther and John Calvin treat ethics as a legalistic matter of duties and obligations, which limits the amount one speaks about friendly virtues including generosity. Other Christian thinkers, including Augustine and Aquinas, treat ethics in terms of virtue, and friendship plays a larger and more positive role in their thought than in that of the Protestant Reformers. Moreover, all the Christian thinkers treated in this collection confront the apparent conflict between preferential love suggested by friendship and Scripture's command to love all human beings as the image of God. Many in the Christian tradition regard friendship as too "pagan" because it prefers one's own to the stranger and enemy; eros and *philia* are rooted in love of self, while *caritas* is rooted in love of God and neighbor. Augustine and Aquinas regard friendship and *caritas* as harmonious because they consider the noetic consciousness of the ancient Greeks and Romans, as part of the created order, to be in harmony with pneumatic differentiation of Christianity.

The apparent conflict between Athens and Jerusalem, to use a trope favored by Leo Strauss, has important political implications for friendship. The hostility—or, at best, the ambivalence—toward friendship among various Protestant thinkers is one of the roots for the ambiguous place of friendship in liberalism. Both this stream of Christianity and liberalism throw suspicion on particular attachments, which is one reason why such political thinkers as Machiavelli and Rousseau regard Christianity as corrosive to patriotism and community. Comparing the Christian writers in this collection helps clarify these historical matters, but, more importantly, illuminates ways of thinking about friendship and particular attachments in ways liberalism fails to do on its own terms.

Four Epochs, Four Paradigms of Friendship?

For the sake of convenience, this volume of essays is divided into four sections, each devoted to a particular era in the history of Western political thought. The contributors, however, treat their respective thinkers in terms of how their thought can inform contemporary concerns instead of as products of their specific historical epoch.

Section 1 covers ancient Greek and Roman thinkers. In his essay "Platonic *Philia* and Political Order," James Rhodes considers Plato's approach to friendship as found in the *Lysis* as well as the *Symposium*, *Phaedrus*, and the *Seventh Letter*. Understanding Plato's view of friendship requires attending to the dramatic character of the dialogue because dialogue replicates the activity of friends and assists the reader to cultivate habits of insight and judgment. In short, the dialogue (among other things) helps one to practice friendship as much as it assists one to understand friendship. *Lysis* revolves around a discussion of what it is we love our friends "for the sake of." Interpreters often mistakenly attribute a utilitarian understanding of friendship to Plato, preferring instead that he should teach us to love our friends "for their own sake." Rhodes demonstrates the inadequacy of this kind of interpretation and argues instead that, by attending to the drama of the dialogue, one discovers it is the very "identity of the individual . . . to be an image of the divine." Participating in the drama of the dialogue, instead of viewing it as a tablet of propositions, enables the reader to understand, and thus to love, the friend for precisely whom he or she is.

Stephen Salkever, in his essay "Taking Friendship Seriously: Aristotle on the Place(s) of *Philia* in Human Life," demonstrates how Aristotle regards friendships of virtue as a "prohairetic" activity: "a philosophically informed *conversation* about our virtues and vices is the definitive activity of 'perfect' friends." Friends assist each other to gain self-knowledge and to become intellectually and morally virtuous. Just as for Plato, this activity primarily takes the form of conversation, of speaking with one another. This vision of friendship informs Aristotle's understanding of politics. The aim of politics is living well in a polity governed by justice, which justice is practiced by citizens in prohairetic friendship. Friendship and politics are mutually dependent.

In his essay "Cicero's Distinctive Voice on Friendship: *De Amicitia* and *De Re Publica*," Walter Nicgorksi shows how Cicero regarded friendship within reach of those less philosophical, and perhaps having a more direct impact on politics as a result. Unlike his Greek predecessors, Cicero's "dialogue" on friendship is actually a speech by Laelius on the virtues of his great friend, the Roman statesman Scipio Africanus. Yet, his praise is not without philosophical import, as Laelius provides a phenomenology of friendship while arguing that friendship is nature's highest gift. For Cicero, friendship and glory follow virtue, which in themselves implant "the seeds and sparks of virtue" in others. Friendship—and its related and more political concept, glory—are in a way the medium by which the virtues are communicated to others. The audience of Laelius' encomium includes the young, which illuminates how friendship can be extended across generations and influence the life of the Republic beyond the lifetime of the original friends. Nicgorski concludes: "Friendship is likely the most important instrument in the micropolitics of Roman life where constitutional development and leadership turn on political alliances and the give-and-take of personal interactions and relationships."

In section 2, we turn to thinkers in the Christian tradition, focusing on medieval and Reformation figures. John von Heyking writes in "The Luminous Path of Friendship: Augustine's Account of Friendship and Political Order" that Augustine agrees with Cicero's view of friendship as the microcosm of politics. He then focuses on politics as an analogue for friendship by considering Augustine's treatment of the role friendship plays as a "school for virtue." He examines the *Confessions* and *On the Trinity* for Augustine's treatment of how individuals encounter the mystery of another person, and the significance that our particularity and that of our friends plays in our lives. For Augustine, knowing another brings one outside oneself the moment one perceives oneself; friendship and self-knowledge are inseparable, which provides the basis for understanding the role of moral development in political community. The crucial role that friendship plays in inducing self-knowledge and moral development is one of the ways Augustine views Christian love and friendship as harmonious.

In "A Companionship of *Caritas:* Friendship in St. Thomas Aquinas," Jeanne Heffernan Schindler considers how Aquinas regards Christian love as harmonious and a consummation of Greek friendship. The transcendent dimension of *caritas* invigorates civic friendship instead of undermining it: "Charity, for Aquinas, not only strengthens justice, but perfects it, prompting the citizen to give his fellows their due 'spontaneously and joyfully,' even adding 'something in excess by way of liberality.'" In other words, *caritas* takes friendship out of the polis in order to situate it on more solid grounds. The result is a stronger and wider sense of common good than that found in Aristotle.

The Protestant tradition often expresses skepticism toward friendship because of its ancient and Roman Catholic associations. However, Thomas Heilke, in his essay "Friendship in the Civic Order: A Reformation Absence," demonstrates that Martin Luther and John Calvin lack a language of friendship, personal or civic. He notes that Luther treats friendly relations exclusively in terms of utility, and the closest Calvin speaks of friendship in a theological sense is by equating it with divine election. Instead, the ethical and political thinking of both Reformers is dominated by the language of duty and obligation, not virtue. The polis, as much as the ecclesia, is characterized by solitary individuals receiving God's grace (for they rejected the category of nature) in isolation from one another: "Concentrating on man's forensic status before God, Luther preached grace, but a grace taken up individually *in* the collective, not collectively for the individual; nor, more modestly, individually *amidst* the collective." The Protestant believer stands alone before God, and his loneliness would be amplified once the modern world sheared him from God.

In section 3, we turn to modern perspectives of friendship. Timothy Fuller's essay "Plato and Montaigne: Ancient and Modern Ideas of Friendship" documents the transition from so-called ancient to more modern understandings of friendship. While Fuller eschews "any simple dichotomy between ancients and moderns on this subject," he finds it useful to contrast Plato's view of friendship in the *Lysis* with that of Montaigne. *Lysis* ends with something of an aporia as to what precisely friendship is and whether it can be understood in terms other than utility (see James Rhodes's essay for further elucidation of this in Plato's own terms). Fuller turns to Montaigne to consider what friendship, freed from utility, consists of. For Montaigne, previous philosophers have deduced their views on friendship from general ideas instead of from the concrete experiences of their own lives. Montaigne's relationship with Etienne de la Boetie taught him that friendship, should one be so lucky to enjoy it, transcends the ability of philosophy to describe it. Philosophy, being reflective, impedes friendship. For Fuller, Montaigne introduces a Christian and a romantic element into consideration: "Christian because the encounter with a true friend is a kind of moment of incarnation, a revelation within human experience; and romantic because it is an adventure in which the ineluctable temporality of the human condition is challenged by the power of the human imagination to live as if it were eternal." Friendship therefore takes the form of conversation, an open-ended activity that is conducted for its own sake and expresses humanity's deepest freedom. Montaigne's emphasis on the freedom of friendship seems to lend itself to its privatization vis-à-vis politics, which is characterized by necessity and utilitarian relationships. However, Fuller observes that personal friendships, while not the direct substratum or micropolitics underneath civic friendship, would be sustained by an "association based on a framework of procedural rules that would permit the vast range of human possibilities to express itself." Political order depends on private spaces where people can reflect on the alternatives of friendship and on the self-knowledge that friendships ultimately help to sustain.

We see the dual rejection of ancient virtue teachings and friendship documented in Travis D. Smith's essay "Hobbes on Getting By with Little Help from Friends." Contrary to most of the premodern thinkers included in this volume, Hobbes regards all love a species of self-love. For him, the role of friendship in politics can be nothing more than the politics of patronage, which Smith maintains is Hobbes's primary political target throughout his writings. Hobbes seeks to replace the patronage system, characterized by partisan favors that political actors do for one another, with a neutral state. This requires recasting the meaning of friendship, as well as charity, for politics. Instead of seeing politics conducted by way of a web of face-to-face encounters and personal friendships, as Cicero sees it for example, Hobbes thinks politics must be centered on the neutral administration of the state and that individuals would practice a negative form of the Golden Rule and "complaisance," which one could regard as the virtue of "fitting in." Indeed, charity can only be administered by the state because individuals cannot be trusted to judge in their own case. It is enough that individuals leave each other alone. Even so, Smith notes the irony of a philosopher's depending so much on patronage while seeking an end to it. This irony seems to be blunted somewhat by the satisfaction Hobbes derived from serving as a benefactor for humankind who adopts his political system.

Comparing Montaigne and Hobbes demonstrates some of the limits of treating thinkers as "ancient" or "modern." Hobbes seeks to establish personal relationships on a low but reliable basis, while Montaigne attempts to surpass ancient and Christian conceptions of friendship by treating friendship as something ineffable. Even so, both treat friendship in terms of freedom, though from different perspectives. Yet both attempt to respond to similar conditions of modernity that are characterized by larger-scale political units and therefore extended human relations.

The United States is a unique hybrid of "modern" commercial (or Lockean) and premodern patriotic and religious principles that generate unique reflections on friendship. George Carey, in his essay "Social Friendship in the Founding Era," sees a streak of Hobbesian thinking in the ideas of the Federalists during the time of the American founding. However, even their language of self-interest on the part of the individual, and "aggregate interests" on the part of the nation, is not the same as Hobbes and his Fifth Law of Nature of "complaisance." Carey documents how the Anti-Federalists were the most likely to utilize the language of political friendship in their opposition to the extended republic. They thought such a system would make people too distant from one another, which would then undermine political friendship and liberty. Carey argues that the Federalists were more likely to invoke the interests and passions of individuals and of factions (who by definition are not friends with members of other factions) because a government based on those "lower" considerations of human nature is more reliable. However, Carey contends that theirs was also a matter of emphasis because they presumed the existence of "social friendship" and common customs among the people. Of the Federalist's explanation of checks and balances, Carey states: "To even contemplate such restraint suggests the existence of bonds of friendship to the extent, at least, of a framework of shared values that provides the basis for the meaningful exchange of views about what is best for the whole." They emphasized self-interest and ambition to promote economic activity that would enhance social cohesion. The small republics prized by the Anti-Federalists failed their own test of civic friendship because scarce resources divided rich from poor. In that sense, the Federalists' view of social friendship resembles that of Aristotle, whose polity must be a middle-class regime that mitigates the perennial factionalism between rich and poor.

Joshua Mitchell considers the paradoxes of this social friendship, or "mediational space between soliloquy and 'they say,'" in his essay "It Is Not Good for Man to Be Alone: Tocqueville on Friendship." Such mediational "gathering together" is the best that modern democracy can do in terms of political friendship because individuals relate to one another through sympathy (as members of humanity, not as fellow citizens) and money (having replaced honor as the measure of worth in society). Complicating matters is "self-referentiality," which refers to the characteristically democratic mode of knowing, including skepticism and pragmatism, in which the individual is his own authority, engaged in his own soliloquy about truth and falsehood, and right and wrong, and disengaged from others in their "they say." Self-referentiality lends itself to "equality in servitude," manifest in the centralized administrative state, because only the state constitutes what is public. Equality in freedom can be found in mediational spaces between individualistic soliloquy and the state, in civil associations in which citizens pragmatically carry out their corporate lives. Contrary to Plato and Aristotle, Tocqueville does not think philosophy can help democracy or the practice of friendship, though, unlike Montaigne's skepticism toward philosophy's ability to grasp the mystery of friendship, Tocqueville regards the utilitarian aspects of mediational space more conducive to friendship in democracy.

In section 4, we look at two present-day perspectives of friendship. Contemporary liberal democracies are experiencing the crisis of so-called foundationalism, which challenges their ability to justify their own practices and principles, including their communal identities and civic friendships. In his essay "Zarathustra and His Asinine Friends: Nietzsche and Taste as the Groundless Ground of Friendship," Richard Avramenko argues that Nietzsche's theory of the eternal recurrence of the same precipitates the need for a completely new kind of friendship. The vision of eternal recurrence moves man beyond both the nation state and Christian fellowship, which had hitherto been the ground on which friendship was predicated. By eroding this foundation the eternal recurrence establishes the need for a "groundless ground for friendship," which Nietzsche characterizes as "taste." Avramenko rejects the Derridean reading of Nietzsche of a "friendship to come" because it is messianic and not cyclic. Friendship, therefore, is possible only for those who wander freely and courageously outside the purview of the nation state and Christianity. What form that political unit might take is left unresolved, as necessitated by Nietzsche's insistence that one with taste embraces danger and welcomes both the exception and the unexpected.

Jürgen Gebhardt's "Friendship, Trust, and Political Order: A Critical Overview" concludes the volume. Even though the twentieth century severely challenged our confidence in the ability of rationality to sustain a just political order, as evidenced by the emphasis on enmity and domination among the writings of Carl Schmitt and neo-Hobbesians including Hans Morgenthau, Gebhardt finds an enduring reliance on trust among the ideas and practices of liberal democracy. Beginning in the Middle Ages with the concept of *fides* and finding major expression in John Locke, Scottish common sense philosophy, and analyzed by a series of social scientists including Samuel Huntington, Robert Putnam, and Francis Fukuyama, trust as an expression of political friendship endures at the core of liberal democracy. Few have analyzed trust as friendship in a philosophical manner, tending instead to apply uncritically the assumptions of American constitutionalism and theories of consent to their analyses without inquiring into the nature of the common world that these phenomena require. Gebhardt draws on Thomas Reid's and Eric Voegelin's formulations of common sense, as well as Hannah Arendt's neo-Aristotelian notions of political friendship, and finally Aristotle and Plato, to formulate what political friendship means within the parameters of modern liberal democracy: "[I]t refers to the public sphere of common meanings sustaining a common reference world that signifies common purpose, action, and aspiration of the members of society. They live together in virtue of the binding force of trust."

The Symbiosis of Personal and Political Friendships

The essays in this volume indicate that private friendships and political friendship are never completely detached. Moreover, as the essays on Plato, Aristotle, the American founding, and even Hobbes bring out, "lower" forms of friendship (for example, utility) require a "higher" form for them even to be intelligible. As Socrates in the *Lysis* argues, for every "use" there is something higher for which it is "for the sake of," whose nature dictates how those uses are to be understood. These two types of friendship, while separate, require one another; they share the same world and are, literally, symbiotic. All the essays demonstrate the ways that personal friendships inform and sustain the health of political society, which suggests how personal friendships are more authentic or satisfying than political society for human aims and aspirations for the good life. Even for a thinker like Montaigne, who perhaps separates private friendships from political society more drastically than the other thinkers included in this volume, the two realms inform and sustain each other. The persistence of the connection between personal friendships and the political society they sustain and that in turn sustains and protects them—as well as the variety of different forms that these thinkers express that connection—suggest the need for practical judgment in balancing political friendship with the recognition that political friendship can never be identified with the heights that personal friendship can achieve. We in the twenty-first century still grapple with Aristotle's insight that the political friendship of the polis is an analogy of the highest kinds of friendship, and that the city ceases to be a city the moment it attempts to obtain that highest form of friendship, as seen in his criticism of Socrates' (perhaps ironic) proposal for communism among the city's rulers.[12]

Insofar as the essays illuminate the relationship between a thinker's ethical teaching and friendship, each of them raises the question of how friends regard the mystery of the other's character. Is it self-projection, as Hobbes would have it? Do they experience their friend as an irruption of complete otherness, as Augustine, Montaigne, and Nietzsche seem to argue at times? While self-projection is normally associated with egoism, complete otherness seems an unintelligible ideal because one can hardly even know something without relating it to something one already knows. Or, as Socrates indicates in the *Lysis,* regarding friendship as a relationship of dissimilars implies that one would befriend one's enemy, thereby rendering "friend" and "enemy" meaningless.

The answer may be in recognizing that friendship consists of similarity and dissimilarity, and the key is to find the most appropriate conceptual language to describe it. The symbols of "conversation," "taste," and "image" of the divine or of God dominate the thinking of those who regard the practice of friendship as preeminent activity of human beings, and politics as secondary. The language of "law" and "duty" dominates the thinking of those distrustful of that view, and emphasize the necessity of the divine law, neutral state, or the market to restrain the propensity of friendships to operate as cronyism. The "law" and "duty" side considers the "conversation" side to be idealistic and overly reliant on people's virtue, while the latter regards the former as idealistic and depending too much on state power to sustain political society at the expense of the character of individuals and their relationships with one another. Whichever way the reader is inclined to think, the essays in this volume demonstrate the urgency of considering the problem of friendship's relationship with political life, and its intractability.

Notes

1. Horst Hutter, *Politics as Friendship: The Origins of Classical Notions of Politics in the Theory and Practice of Friendship* (Waterloo, Ont.: Wilfred Laurier University Press, 1978), 2.

2. "Gadamer on Strauss: An Interview," ed. E. L. Fortin, *Interpretation* 12(1) (January 1984): 9. See esp. *Nicomachean Ethics*, 1137a 31–1138a 5, 1155a 22–33. For Kant, see "Friendship," in *Lectures on Ethics,* trans. Louis Infield (Indianapolis: Hackett Publishing, 1981), 206–7; *Groundwork of the Metaphysics of Morals*, trans. and ed. Mary Gregor (Cambridge: Cambridge University Press, 1998), 215–17.

3. John Rawls, *A Theory of Justice* (Cambridge: Belknap Press, Harvard University Press, 1971), 434, 497–98.

4. Thomas Jefferson, "First Inaugural." Retrieved October 15, 2005, from http://www.yale.edu/lawweb/avalon/presiden/inaug/jefinau1.htm.

5. Recent novels from and about the Muslim world document the loneliness experienced in liberal societies. For example, the Muslim Turks in Orhan Pamuk's *Snow* (trans. Maureen Freely [New York: Knopf, 2004]) resist modernization, or "Europeanization," because it dissolves communal solidarity that is essential to their religious existence. The loneliness of Ka, the poet and main character of the novel, is exacerbated because he rejects Turkish society but cannot adapt to the individualistic sensibilities of Germany where he resides. Similar themes appear in Nahid Rachlin's *The Foreigner* (New York: Norton, 1999), which is about an Iranian biologist who leaves the United States to return to her homeland. Her stomach ulcer symbolizes the empty void in her soul caused by the restless but meaningless and solitary existence she led there (despite or because of being married to an American). Thus she chooses restrictive life in nonliberal Iran—where at least she can find meaningful friendships—over her prosperous and free, but withdrawn, existence in the West. Similarly, studies of jihadists demonstrate that loneliness and the desire for friendship play a crucial role in recruitment. Marc Sageman argues that friendship networks outweigh ideology as a factor to recruitment: "Relative deprivation, religious predisposition, and ideological appeal are necessary but not sufficient to account for the decision to become a mujahed. Social bonds are the critical element in this process and precede ideological commitment" (*Understanding Terrorist Networks* [Philadelphia: University of Pennsylvania Press, 2004], 134). Insofar as the war against jihadist groups is a war of political ideas and practices, the problem of friendship for liberal democracy must be regarded as being the most important factor to address.

6. Shortly after the fall of the Soviet Union, when victory for liberal democracy was fully apparent, a new wave of popular music burst on the American scene. The so-called Grunge Movement, which is closely associated

with Generation X, featured angst-ridden lyrics expressing anger, frustration, ennui, sadness, fear, depression, and, in general, the loneliness and alienation of the liberal democratic world. A leading band from this movement, Nirvana, recorded a very successful song titled "Lithium," which opens with and repeats sarcastically: "I'm so happy, 'cause today/I found my friends . . . /They're in my head." Nirvana frontman, Kurt Cobain, committed suicide not long after penning these lyrics.

7. See Jennifer Lee, "The Man Date: What Do You Call Two Straight Men Having Dinner?" *New York Times,* April 10, 2005. Retrieved October 15, 2005, from www.nytimes.com/2005/04/10/fashion/10date.html?ex=1129435200&en=f413d234ecb93439&ei=5070&ex=1128571200&en=5d5b6cc510345905&ei=5070&pagewanted=all&position.

8. Aristotle, *Politics,* 1271b5.

9. See ibid., 1326b15–20.

10. Aristotle, *Nicomachean Ethics,* 1155b30–1156a5.

11. On Smith, see Lauren Brubaker, "'A Particular Turn or Habit of the Imagination': Adam Smith on Love, Friendship, and Philosophy," in *Love and Friendship: Rethinking Politics and Affection in Modern Times,* ed. Eduardo A. Velásquez (Lanham, Md.: Lexington Books, 2003), 229–62, and Allan Silver, "'Two Different Sorts of Commerce': Friendship and Strangership in Civil Society," in *Public and Private in Thought and Practice: Perspectives on a Grand Dichotomy,* ed. Jeff Weintraub and Krishan Kumar (Chicago: University of Chicago Press, 1997), 43–74; on Kant, see H. J. Paton, "Kant on Friendship," in *Friendship: A Philosophical Reader,* ed. Neera Kapur Badhwar (Ithaca: Cornell University Press, 1993), 133–54; on Rousseau, see Pamela K. Jensen, "Dangerous Liaisons: The Relation of Love and Liberty in Rousseau," in *Love and Friendship: Rethinking Politics and Affection in Modern Times,* 183–228, and Allan Bloom, *Love and Friendship* (New York: Simon & Schuster, 1993), 39–156; on Rousseau and compassion, see Clifford Orwin, "Moist Eyes—From Rousseau to Clinton," *Public Interest* 128 (Summer 1997): 3–20.

12. Aristotle, *Politics,* 1261b7–9.

I

Ancient Perspectives

1

Platonic *Philia* and Political Order

James M. Rhodes

Recall the political life of Athens from the outbreak of the Peloponnesian War to the execution of Socrates. Democratic and oligarchic factions took turns ruling the polis, harming opponents, and enriching themselves. The leaders were notorious for power lusts, mendacity, fraud, diverting public moneys and war booty into personal fortunes and payoffs to cronies, and fanning the flames of toxic passions. Ordinary people were easily swayed by oratory that disguised the power libidos as noble ideals. These vices exacerbated a militaristic policy that arose out of popular anxiety for the safety of the city and private ambitions for profit; revived when Alcibiades deceived the Athenians about Sparta's aims; became a rhetorically celebrated imperialistic drive to dominate ever greater portions of the world; and ended fatally. Standing in the ruins, Plato judged Athenian politics incurable (Seventh

Letter, 326a4).[1] Looking back from our age to his, an American might be tempted to think that little has changed.

Plato diagnosed the disease of his civilization as an ethical failure. To treat the illness, he prescribed the practice of a *philia* (friendship) that inspires virtue. If it worked perfectly, this remedy would first produce small friendship circles and ultimately a just polity essentially constituted by *philia*. This would create necessary contexts for both the personal and political fulfillment of human nature. If the therapy could not cure the society as a whole, it still could generate friendship groups that nurtured philosophy, thus offering noble souls havens from the raging storms of evil politics and perhaps even chances to lead the best possible human lives—this depending on how one must answer Aristotle's question about the relative merits of action and contemplation. I argue here that, if America is in the same case as Athens, we would be well advised to heed Plato's advice.

An Objection to the Thesis

My suggestion will provoke an outcry. Many will deny the existence or knowability of virtue. They deserve a reply. The answer, however, would require volumes. For now, I beg leave to suppose that some insight into goodness is possible and to focus attention on the opposite objection to Plato, namely, that his idea of *philia* is morally reprehensible. I wish to concentrate on this charge because it resonates with a pervasive modern attitude and because it therefore has unduly biased scholars, becoming a major stumbling block to contemporary appreciation of Plato's wisdom.

Those who level the accusation are exemplified by Gregory Vlastos. In the last decades of the twentieth century, Vlastos was the acknowledged dean of American philosophy.[2] His interpretations of Plato were extremely influential. In the opening lines of his well-known essay "The Individual as Object of Love in Plato," Vlastos quotes Aristotle's notion of *philia*: "Let *philein* ["to love,"[3] as a friend or a parent loves] be defined as wishing for someone what you believe to be good things—wishing this not for your own sake but for his—and acting so far as you can to bring them about."[4] In the rest of the essay, he tries to prove that Plato fell far short of this understanding of loving.

Considering Plato's concept of *philia* broadly, Vlastos asserts that "[a] proper study of it would have to take account of at least three things about its creator: He was a homosexual, a mystic, and a moralist." The first of these attributes highlights the need for "a clinical study of the effect which Plato's inversion would be likely to have on one who saw anal intercourse as 'contrary to nature,' a degradation not only of man's humanity, but even of his animality." Presuming on the study, Vlastos comments that "[t]his thought would poison for him sensual gratification with anticipatory torment and retrospective guilt. It would tend to distort his overall view of sexual fulfillment, while leaving him with raw sensitiveness to male beauty and heightening his capacity for substitute forms of erotic response." Plato's mystical qualities, in turn, are striking for his coldness to the Hellenic gods and his strange love for the "severely impersonal Ideas," which make him speak "repeatedly of communion with Ideas as an act of blissful and fertile conjugal union." Coming to Plato's moralism, Vlastos concludes that his Freudian sublimation of homosexual desire into eros for the Ideas ends in a doctrine of *philia* that "is not, and is not meant to be, about personal love for persons" but, rather, about "love for placeholders of the predicates 'useful' and 'beautiful.'" Adducing selected proof texts from the *Lysis, Republic,* and *Symposium,* he claims that Plato has a utilitarian perspective on love in which both "good" and "beautiful" mean "useful." The utilitarianism that Vlastos has in mind is the sort that seeks socioeconomic advantage and pleasure at the expense of others, not the benevolent kind in which even sacrificing one's life for one's friends can be conceived as a means to personal perfection and happiness. For the purposes of this essay, utilitarianism is equated with the disposition to selfish exploitation that Vlastos dislikes. This said, Vlastos thinks that Plato intends to teach: "We are to love the persons so far, and only insofar, as they are good and beautiful [that is, useful, so that] the individual, in the uniqueness and integrity of his or her individuality, will never be the object of our love."[5]

The moral import of Vlastos's charge is that Plato violates the Kantian principle that people should be treated as ends in themselves. This renders Plato offensive to the apparent majority of moderns who adhere to Kant's ideal. Vlastos's finding will lead others to ask why I commend the friendship of a sexually repressed "invert" who needs psychotherapy, who loves not individuals but merely their utility, and who consequently is incapable of a friendship that cherishes a person for his or her own sake. In reply, I shall show two things as I proceed: that Vlastos was obtuse to the nature of Plato's writing and missed his intention, and that he either did not understand or rejected Plato's philosophic anthropology. We need better insight into Plato's *philia*.

Hermeneutic Assumptions

We cannot profit from Plato unless we know how to read him properly, as he himself wished. I need to outline some rules of interpretation that I think Plato wanted us to follow, relying for their defense on my analysis in another place.[6]

First, in his Seventh Letter, Plato warns that there never has been and never will be a writing of his treating that about which he is "serious," for "it is in no way a spoken thing like other lessons" (341c1–6). Further, in the *Theaetetus*, Socrates states that his function is that of a midwife. He has no wisdom and teaches nothing. However, by means of his art, all whom the god may have permitted have found themselves pregnant with beautiful things and given birth to them (150b–e). These remarks mean not that Plato's serious insights are esoteric but, rather, that they are ineffable. Thus, rather than look for propositional truths about ultimates in his texts, we should let the midwife Socrates help us bring forth our own beautiful things.

Second, Socrates argues the necessity of ascents to the acquisition of real virtues and to final visions. The visions of the beautiful itself (*Symposium*, 211d–e), the essence really being (*Phaedrus*, 247c), and the good (*Republic*, 506d–516c) are silent. So, the beauties that Socrates delivers are the real virtues and wordless visions that his words symbolize without essentially capturing. Plato expects us to open ourselves to mystical experience.

Third, Platonic dialogues are plays, not idiosyncratically ornamented treatises. The consequence of this is that we must read every section of a dialogue in dramatic context. We may not lift parts out of their wholes and recombine them as "theories." A prime corollary is that what happens trumps what is said. In the plays, a midwife attempts to deliver beautiful virtues and visions. He encounters different pregnancies with different complications. When he speaks to someone, he is ministering to a particular soul afflicted with a specific obstruction to the delivery of its "child," in order to facilitate its labor. He would say something else to another person who needed a different treatment.[7] Hence, Socratic dialectical arguments and myths are tailored to the requirements of the interlocutors. They must be analyzed relative to their specific therapeutic tasks and not taken for seriously proffered universal truths.

Fourth, we must ask how Socrates delivers the fair things. In the *Republic* (518), we learn that education is an art of turning the soul so that its eye gazes in the right direction and sees for itself. The method of the art is to break the holds that ruinous passions have on souls, freeing them to turn if they will. To smash these grips, Socrates tries to force his interlocutors to doubt that they know what is good for them. To raise the doubts, he ironically adopts the views of the interlocutors, reasoning from their premises to impasses that demand liberating admissions of ignorance. We must be on the lookout for irony and avoid construing Socratic statements as Platonic positions when they actually are the interlocutors' opinions.

Vlastos (perhaps with most modern exegetes) overlooks all these rules. He reads Plato seeking propositional theories that he can subject to logical and psychological criticism. He constructs these theories by disregarding Plato's drama, by cutting and pasting passages from different dialogues, by literalizing selected elements of Socratic myths, and by mistaking ironic dialectic for Plato's serious opinions. He does not cooperate with the midwife's art.

Philia in the Lysis: The Prelude

In a study of Platonic *philia*, it makes sense to begin with the *Lysis*, for this dialogue is the only one in the Platonic corpus with the subtitle "On *Philia*." However, we must notice that the full subtitle is "On *Philia*: Obstetric."[8] Plato, or an editor who appended the subtitle, wants us to be especially aware that, in this dialogue, Socrates is practicing the midwife's art. Socrates will not give us a propositional "theory of *philia.*" Rather, the "pregnant" characters in the play and we ourselves need to be delivered of the virtue of friendly love.

Other than Socrates, the persons of our drama are Hippothales, a silly *neanias* (young man) who wants to be the *erastes* (homoerotic lover) of Lysis and tries to win him by praising his beauty, pedigree, and riches; Ctessipus, a sensible *neanias;* Lysis, a comely, blue-blooded, philosophically promising *pais* (boy, about ten years old) whose wealthy father, Democrates, enters racing chariots in Greek games; and Menexenus, his equally gifted friend. Hippothales is too foolish to be counted among the "pregnant" souls. Thus, after the opening scenes, he is mentioned seldom. He never appears again in a Platonic dialogue. Ctessipus and Menexenus are pregnant. Socrates apparently delivers them of their nascent virtues of friendship, either in the *Lysis* or offstage, for they turn up again in the *Phaedo* among Socrates' dearest comrades who attend his execution. Menexenus also serves as interlocutor in the dialogue that bears his name.

Lysis is pregnant too. Like Hippothales, however, he appears nowhere in Plato's other dialogues. Although he surely is charmed by Socrates in this play, he is conspicuously missing from the *Phaedo.* His absence is one of Plato's many dramatic indications that Socrates does not always preside over successful live births. Lysis is not delivered of his incipient *philia.* At least, he is not delivered of a permanent friendship for Socrates. Inasmuch as he is also missing from the *Menexenus,* he may not be delivered of a lifelong friendship for his playmate either.

Ignoring Ctessipus in order to simplify matters, I am moved to inquire why two boys of approximately equal philosophic promise, Menexenus and Lysis, should have such different outcomes of their pregnancies. Plato has used dramatic signals to hint at a profound mystery: What explains friendship? Socrates also brings this question up explicitly in the *Lysis* (212a). Meditation on the mystery is prescribed to facilitate the births of our own healthy friendships.

Plato begins to examine the differences between the two boys' capacities for friendship with his character portraits. Lysis, unlike Menexenus, enjoys beauty, flattering suitors, family riches that include horses, and status (Socrates calls Lysis *kalos k'agathos,* "beautiful and good," an Athenian phrase that means "aristocratic" without necessarily connoting personal beauty and goodness). Lysis's blessings could be handicaps. His advantages and all the adulation may have turned his head too far to allow him to befriend anyone genuinely (a danger analyzed in *Republic*, 491a–e). Menexenus does not have these problems.

Now we may turn to a survey of the action and argument of the *Lysis*. As the curtain rises, Socrates is walking from the Academy to the Lyceum. He is hailed by Hippothales and invited to enter a wrestling school where good conversation and glimpses of beautiful boys are on offer. Socrates learns that the lad, smitten with Lysis, has been spoiling him with flattery, and he offers to teach the foolish *neanias* how to speak to the boy without making him haughty. Socrates and Ctessipus go into the school and talk. Menexenus and Lysis drift over to listen. Hippothales watches secretly. Socrates ascertains that the boys are friends and tries to open a discussion of justice and wisdom. This effort is thwarted when Menexenus is called away to participate in rites of Hermes, whose holy day it is.

Socrates starts to question Lysis. What ensues is a prelude to the main exploration of *philia*. In this preliminary exchange, Socrates intends to determine the nature of the child's character and to humble him if need be (206c, 210e). As the drama unfolds, he will find that Lysis is a utilitarian in Vlastos's sense of the word, so he will adhere to the program that he announced to Hippothales. Now, when we mean to take the wind out of a person's sails, we need not resolve that every word we utter be true. It suffices to contrive that our speech, true or false, will deflate our victim. I tender these comments in anticipation of Socrates' opening moves.

In his first gambit, Socrates asks Lysis whether his parents love him greatly. Lysis says yes. Socrates next asks Lysis whether his parents want him to be happy. The reply is "How not?" Plato has just pointed to something that we all know to be true. If we love a person we desire his or her happiness. I note in passing that Aristotle endorses the common conviction of all mankind that happiness is the supreme good (*Nicomachean Ethics*, 1095a1525). Plato may not agree with Aristotle's belief that loving essentially *is* wishing and striving for good things for the other, for the other's own sake, but he surely realizes that loving *entails* such wishing and working. Vlastos would have to infer that the stranger to true love, Plato, must have heard people opining that *philia* entails wanting good things for beloveds, for their own sakes, and that he inexplicably puts a condensed version of this alien concept into the dialogue here. However, it would seem more reasonable to assume that Plato is not quite so warped. Plato knows perfectly well that the opinion is true, regards the fact as so obvious that he can let Socrates slip it into a throwaway line, and makes Socrates use it as a safe starting point with Lysis, given that the dialectic always must begin with an agreed premise.

Things get interesting when Socrates makes his second move. Having induced Lysis to agree that his parents love him and therefore desire his happiness, Socrates asks him whether slaves who cannot do whatever they want are happy. Lysis answers no, with an oath by Zeus. Socrates then asks Lysis if his parents allow him to do anything he likes. The reply is that his parents forbid him to do many things. Socrates asks, What? Does Lysis mean that his father will not let him drive the chariots? Or the mule cart? And that he lets slaves do what he will not permit his son to do? Is Lysis saying that his mother will not let him play with her loom? How could these things be so if his parents love him and want him to be happy? Must we not deduce that they care little for him and have degraded him beneath the slaves? It will be clear to many that Socrates has just posed some perverse questions. To cast the affairs in a modern light, no parents would let their ten-year-old children drive race cars, take family automobiles out joy riding, or tamper with the controls of industrial machinery. Thus, it is surprising that Vlastos, in keeping with his hermeneutic proclivities, does not pounce on this text, interpret it literally as a Platonic doctrine, and decry "Plato's depraved idea" that parents who forbid their children to do whatever they like do not love them.[9] Certainly, the reason why he could not sound this alarm is that Socrates too obviously is being ironic as he pursues his maieutic aim.

To repeat, Socrates' intent is to test Lysis and shame him if need be. It will abash Lysis if he has to confess that his parents value him less than slaves. Socrates suggests this to Lysis ironically as a check and a medicine for pride. This stratagem would fail if Lysis were mature enough to see through it. A sensible child would answer: "Socrates, my parents forbid me to do some things that I wish to do just because they love me. They do not want me to injure myself or wreck property by trying to act in ways that are beyond my present capacity." But Lysis is not wise yet. He may be self-willed. Who has not heard a terrible child react to being forbidden something by screaming at its parents? The child's words are classic, nearly always the same: "You just want to control me! I am nothing but your slave!" Lysis may well believe what Socrates has said. To the degree that he takes this bait, he will be humiliated.

Lysis thinks fast and does not fall for the trick entirely. Retaining his good humor, he conjectures that his parents deny him things because he is not yet of age. We cannot quite tell from this what he grasps. His reply might signify everything that an astute *pais* should know. It also could mean that he thinks his parents loving but wrongheaded and expects them to stop interfering when he reaches majority. If he were giving the wise answer, Socrates could abort the exhibition and congratulate Hippothales for having found a boy who needs no deflating. In the opposite case, Socrates could judge that Lysis is determined to do what he pleases and too little mindful of the responsibilities of his parents' love. He would still have to humble a boy in the early stages of hybris. Also, his ruse of baiting Lysis by insinuating that his parents do not love him could still work.

Socrates already has two grounds for inferring that Lysis's reply has the wrong import. First, when Lysis swore by Zeus that slaves who are forbidden to do everything they desire are unhappy, he betrayed that he is agitated by the idea of being prevented from doing what he likes. To be sure, felicity does require freedom to make adult ethical decisions. Slaves are not happy. However, what Socrates suspects is that happiness for Lysis presupposes not only free moral choice but also an unfettered ability to gratify every libido he conceives. If this is how Lysis envisages happiness, he inevitably will misunderstand *philia*. He will assume that others "love" him only if they aid and abet, or at least do not resist, his endeavors. He will "love" others only if he can use them as means to his pleasurable ends. Second, while ticking off the list of activities that Lysis has been forbidden, Socrates suggested to him that he does "nothing" that he desires, derives no "advantage" from his family's property, is "enslaved" to others who "rule" him, and "rules nobody" (208e4–209a3). In speculating that his minority is the cause of all this, Lysis has not disputed Socrates' assessment. He evidently *does* want to do what his parents forbid, *does* believe that he is deprived of due advantage, *does* feel enslaved, and *does* aspire to rule others. Accordingly, the conception of happiness as the satisfaction of desire, maximization of advantage, freedom to do what one lists, and possession of power over others will infuse the subsequent arguments. We recall that Socrates refutes these accounts of happiness (and liberty) in other dialogues, especially in the *Republic,* where Glaucon, echoing Thrasymachus, extols them in his ring of Gyges story. Socrates clearly has been up to his old trick of arguing from his interlocutor's opinions here. Now he will undertake his third move, the validation of his diagnosis, that is, an attempt to verify his suspicions that Lysis's soul is infected with the indicated attitudes.

Socrates continues his maieutic examination by stating that Lysis's minority could not explain why his parents will not allow him to do what he likes. After all, they do not prevent him from reading, writing, or tuning his lyre, do they? There must be some other reason why they forbid him the race horses, the mule cart, and the loom. What could it be? Lysis replies that his parents probably decide on the basis of whether he has knowledge of the thing or not. If that is so, says Socrates, it follows that when Lysis has a "better *phronesis*"[10] than his father, his father will let Lysis rule him and all his household, right? Lysis answers: "I suppose so."

It should be evident for two reasons that Socrates has just said something exceedingly foolish. First, we should remember Plato's dramatic hint that the conversation is proceeding without a necessary prior investigation of the nature of wisdom. Lysis imagines that what he must acquire if he is to govern himself and his father is *episteme,* science (209c2). He is a little aspiring sophist who, like Phaedrus, would pay dearly to hear a Hippias expound his science, expecting to become "wise." Socrates, who is testing rather than teaching, ironically suggests a facile identification of *episteme* with *phronesis* (or *sophia*).[11] However, the science required to handle animals and tools is not the wisdom needed to live virtuously. Lysis will not be fit to rule his parents because he can manage horses, mules, and looms properly. Second, although a father might accept a son's advice in some area of the son's technical expertise, the father never would volunteer to surrender governance of himself and all his property completely into the son's hands. Adults need to make their own moral choices. Is Socrates (or Plato) asinine? I think that, far from being stupid, the midwife has been attempting to confirm the presence of a symptom. He has invited Lysis to betray the power fantasy of the rebellious child: "I should not have to obey my parents! They should obey me!" Lysis's answer is not a good omen.

Continuing along this line, the midwife encourages Lysis's *libido dominandi* to inflate to massive proportions. He suggests that the better *phronesis* will induce Lysis's neighbor to make him his household manager too, right? This picture is even more preposterous than the last but Lysis replies with a tentative yes. Socrates inquires whether the better *phronesis* will prompt Athens to put Lysis in charge of public affairs. We infer from the image of the ship in *Republic*, 488 that Socrates does not believe for a moment that this would occur.[12] However, Lysis says yes. Setting the seal of the joke on the matter, Socrates then asks whether the Great King would let us cook his stew, medicate his son's eyes with ashes, and govern his empire if we had the requisite skills. "Obviously," answers Lysis. Part of the diagnosis is confirmed. Callow, naïve power lust has taken root.[13] It is interfering with the pregnancy.

As mentioned above, Socrates has been pursuing his diagnosis and his deflation of Lysis simultaneously. Now his trap is ready and he arms the spring. Here is how things stand, he says to Lysis. If we acquire *phronesis* with respect to any matters, the Hellenes and barbarians and all men and women will entrust us with them. Then we shall "do what we wish" and we shall meet "no" barriers. We shall "rule" others and "profit" from them. They will be "ours," like chattel. If we do not become wise, the opposites will obtain. Does Lysis agree with these assertions (which are megalomaniac and worthy of tyrants)? "I agree," he cries (210a–c). Lysis is not wise or just. He wants to enslave and use other human beings for his own advantage, profit, and pleasure. This is strong evidence that his friendships fizzle because he is the selfish type of utilitarian and alienates people by trying to exploit them.

The trap snaps shut. Socrates makes his last move, asking whether anyone will regard us as friends or love us if we lack *phronesis* and are unprofitable. Certainly not, replies Lysis, who still does not see what is coming. Then, Socrates infers, Lysis's father does not love him, nor does anyone else, insofar as he is useless? Suddenly bereft of his confidence, Lysis answers hesitantly: "Apparently not." So, Socrates concludes, everyone will love Lysis insofar as he is useful and good but no one will love him insofar as he lacks these qualities, not even his father and mother. Socrates asks Lysis whether he can have a grand opinion of himself, in light of what he has been forbidden (210c–d). Lysis must answer no. He is ensnared in his affirmation of utilitarianism that now has been made explicit. Socrates looks at Hippothales and almost blurts out: See? This is how you should speak to your favorite to humble him.

Of course, it will be clear to nearly all that Socrates has made yet another monstrous statement in his effort to chasten Lysis. No adult with any ordinary human experience thinks that parents love or withhold love from their children depending on whether the youngsters are profitable or useful. Parents who are not unnaturally twisted love their children from the moments of their births, before they could be profitable or useful in Vlastos's senses of these words.[14] Socrates even indicates a bit later that he knows this (212e–213a). However, Vlastos adduces the outrageous lines (210c–d) as Exhibit A in his indictment of Plato as a utilitarian who cannot love others for their own sakes.[15] In reply, I may now recapitulate these points: Socrates' declaration that parents love only useful children occurs in the same context as his plainly ironic claim that parents do not love their children if they do not permit them to do whatever they want, and it is offered in aid of the same purpose. There is no good reason to think that the former remark is less ironic than the latter.[16] Vlastos unaccountably treats the two statements differently, taking one seriously and ignoring the other. Also, the offending comment is pitched to a boy's level, and it presupposes and concludes a long train of childish follies and sophisms that Socrates rejects elsewhere. Finally, Socrates effectively gainsays the proposition twice in the present dialogue, in assertions that Vlastos blithely disregards. The dramatic eye therefore can tell that the statement is what it purports to be, part of a campaign to humiliate the child. Far from being Plato's position, it is Lysis's own belief, dialectically elicited from him as a means to subjecting him to a salutary shame that prepares him for the next stages of the midwife's cure. What Vlastos has done by neglecting Plato's drama, tearing speeches out of context, and reading selected fragments with a wooden literalism, is to pervert Plato's intended effect into its opposite. He has turned Socrates' diagnosis of an ailment that needs to be cured into Plato's disease.[17]

Before passing to the next section of my analysis, I should note that David Bolotin, in his standard work on the *Lysis*, denies that Socrates' affirmations in these passages are either ironic or monstrous. He concedes that Socrates' remarks could be construed as libels on the parents.

However, he defends Socrates not by declaring that this would be to misunderstand him, but by justifying and celebrating Socrates' supposed intention to estrange Lysis from his parents. He says that Socrates needs to motivate Lysis to throw off all parental and religious authority so that he will be free to philosophize.[18]

Dramatic context and hermeneutic principle make this doubtful. In Plato's plays, the pious Menexenus, not Lysis, joins Socrates. In the *Apology,* no parents of Socrates' students agree that he has alienated their sons' affections or made them impious. Breaking up families seems to be neither Socrates' modus operandi nor philosophically necessary. Besides, Lysis was already irritated by his parents' governance before he met Socrates.[19] His resentment has loosed dangerous passions. What Socrates has done is to show that chaffing at just authority rapidly grows into the lust for power. I think that he would judge that inciting Lysis to rebel probably would do more harm than good.

By now, alert readers will have observed that Lysis resembles Alcibiades. The two are similar in their initial attraction to and later abandonment of Socrates; their fabulous inherited wealth; their horses; their beauty; their immense appeal to suitors who flatter them for their looks, noble births, and money; their tendencies to become haughty; their regal and imperialistic ambitions; and their Thrasymachean inclinations to use a technical "wisdom" in the service of profit and the *libido dominandi.* Given the example of Alcibiades, Socrates would have to be aware that he could not control the effects of exhorting Lysis to rise up against loving, sane, and prudent authority, do "what he wishes," and become scientifically "wise" to enable himself to "rule."[20] I think that, while applauding what Vlastos condemns, Bolotin makes the same mistake as Vlastos. He reads the *Lysis* as a compendium of serious "positive claims," ignoring Plato's warning in the Seventh Letter. This is evidence that the influence of Vlastos's analytic method of reading Plato has spread beyond his own school.[21]

Philia in the *Lysis:* The Main Inquiry

We must consider an objection to the diagnosis of Lysis's malady. When Menexenus returns from the Hermaea sacrifice, Lysis whispers to Socrates in a "most playful and loving" (*mala paidikos kai philikos*, 211a3) way, entreating him to repeat his discourse to Menexenus. Is the *pais* the little horror that I have made him out to be? I admit that Lysis is adorable and affectionate here, as all children can be when they wish. However, far from overturning the analysis, this episode confirms it. When Socrates comically declines Lysis's requests to debate with his comrade, pretending to fear Menexenus as a master of eristic, the exasperated Lysis reveals that he really wants Socrates to "punish" (*kolases*, 211c3) his friend. The boys have a history of quarreling over which of them is older and better born (and, thus, more entitled to precedence, 207b–c). Now Lysis has shown a powerful desire to drag Menexenus down too if he must be disgraced himself. His friendship is tainted with *philonikia*, a love of victory that craves superiority, domination, honor, and vengeance. Lysis has also proved that his sudden affection for Socrates is calculating. He has not begun to cherish Socrates for his own sake but because he regards him as an instrument of the suffering that he wants to inflict on Menexenus unjustly (a wish that Socrates never gratifies). His *philia* is both hybristic and utilitarian.

Having diagnosed the sickness of a boy pregnant with philosophic potential, Socrates will strive to cure him. Socrates' usual strategy is to liberate his patient from the appetites that enslave him by demolishing his convictions about what is good for him. Lysis's belief that he can exploit his friends sustains all the appetites to which he is in thrall. Hence, Socrates needs to undo his opinion that *philia* is for utility. The topic of the rest of the drama is not chosen arbitrarily. It should be stressed that Socrates will not proceed by delivering a sermon on true *philia*, expecting Lysis then to put the right principles into practice. Plato has already shown dramatically that this preachy cookbook approach to ethical edification fails. Earlier, Socrates attempted to quash the boys' dispute over rank by reminding them that friends have all things in common (207c). Lysis was not moved. He probably experienced the maxim as meaningless sound because his soul eye was not fixed on the ineffable realities that alone would attune him to the spirit of the words. Homilies proving fruitless, Socrates will try instead to throw Lysis into perplexity about friendship by any means fair or foul, freeing him to turn to the visions that constitute wisdom if he will. Accordingly, Socrates will conduct an aporetic inquiry into *philia,* often using bad, even sophistical, logic. He starts by addressing Menexenus.

Socrates tells Menexenus that he envies his friendship with Lysis, for he himself has no friends and does not even know in what manner two comrades become friends to each other (212a5–6). Thus, deviating from his usual procedure, Socrates asks not *what* friendship is, but *how* it arises. The experience of friendship is acknowledged as real even if we do not fathom its content. Socrates' allegation that he is friendless is an ironic pretense to need Menexenus's counsel.[22] His comment that he does not know how two people become friends may be true, if friendship ultimately is mysterious. It is important to observe that Socrates' question has a philosophic effect. It annuls the conclusion that crowned his conversation with Lysis in the prelude. If Socrates appeared to contend there that *philia* is inspired by expected utility, he now disavows that inference, together with all others. He is back to his normal condition of knowing nothing. By the end of the play, he still cannot say how *philia* comes to be (or what it is). The net effect is that Socrates affirms nothing in the dialogue, especially not the *philia*-utility nexus. This fact alone should have sufficed to make Vlastos more circumspect.

In his investigation of the topic, Socrates suggests several explanations of friendship but then immediately dashes them. His arguments deserve meticulous, line-by-line study, but I can present only ruthlessly compressed summaries here. Ironically seeking advice from Menexenus, Socrates asks him, in essence, whether love (friendship) is caused by love (loving), without inquiring further into the nature and origins of love. Affirmation of this tautology could be the most profound response of common sense to the mystery, for love might resemble existence in that it can be experienced but not explained. However, rather than profess something positive, Socrates complicates the analysis by guiding Menexenus through different versions of the causal relationship, asking whether *philia* results from loving without being loved, from loving and being loved, or from being loved without loving. Menexenus agrees to each hypothesis as it is advanced but is finally forced to reject all three, the first because friendship flags when love meets apathy or hatred; the second because we cannot rationally expect mutuality in friendship for animals, exercise, wine, and wisdom; and the third because it is absurd to suppose that foes are friends and friends foes (212a–213b).

Pretending that the alternatives are exhausted, Socrates asks where the argument can go next. Menexenus declares himself baffled. Our little "master of eristic" has not noticed that Socrates played fraudulently with the logic. Socrates first inquired how two persons become friends. As long as we are satisfied with a tautological answer of common sense, the thesis that *philia* between two human beings is generated by their mutual love is not refuted by the observation that there is no mutual love between people and nonhuman realities. Neither is the theorem that friendship for animals, exercise, wine, and wisdom is caused by a person's love for these realities refuted by the objection that friendship between human beings requires mutual love. The disproofs fail even if "love" has the same meaning in all these cases, which is debatable.[23] If Menexenus and Lysis reconsider the argument, bringing their embryonic philosophic ability to bear, they might see that the tautological mutual love thesis is still on the table.

Feigning desperation, Socrates now asks Menexenus whether they have been inquiring in the wrong way (213d1–2). Lysis says that it seems so to him. His involuntary interruption makes him blush, perhaps because he has made it too obvious that he thinks himself superior, or perhaps because disclosing his opinion has already gotten him burned once. Socrates replies that Lysis must be right, for a well-conducted analysis could not have gone so far astray. We must remember this. Sometimes, when we reach an impasse, the problem is not that our subject is illusory or completely inaccessible but that we have boxed ourselves in with our false questions, demands for impossible types of access, premises, methods, or reasoning.

Intimating that reliance on human reason has caused their troubles, Socrates suggests next that the group should turn to the poets, "our fathers and leaders in wisdom" (214a1–2). Homer has taught us that god makes people friends by drawing like to like. Sophists such as Empedocles concur in their secular way. Does Lysis agree too? He answers: "Perhaps." His reply makes two things clear. First, he has never been given to an uncritical piety. Expending effort to induce him to challenge religious revelation would be superfluous. Second, he is not awed by the majesty of science either. He bows to no authority, demanding to be persuaded by science.

Having found that Lysis rejects appeals to authority, Socrates reverts to the dialectic. Dismissing the idea that the wicked could be attracted to the wicked, he interprets the poetic saying to mean that the good are drawn to the good and that this is why two people love one another (214d). Lysis eagerly assents to this idea. We, too, could rejoice that we now have an explanation of friendship that is not tautological. However, the hypothesis really does not tell us very much, for we do not know yet what "good" is. We have not even considered what Lysis believes "good" is. We would be inexcusably remiss if we forgot that Lysis assumes that "good" equals "useful." To him, the poetic teaching now means that "the useful are attracted to the useful, thus causing friendship." He thinks that the poets have affirmed his opinion.

Socrates understands this, so he scrutinizes the thesis further. He asks how the like or the good (useful) could help each other. Lysis has a difficulty. If *A* needs a benefit that only *B* can supply, *A* is not competent to provide it, so he is neither like *B* nor good (useful) himself with regard to production of the benefit. To be sure of being a potential friend to any *B*, *A* would have to be unqualifiedly good (useful). To be unqualifiedly good (useful), *A* would need to be able to supply all benefits and, hence, be wholly self-sufficient. However, a perfectly self-sufficient being needs no help. Therefore, the good (useful) cannot be drawn to each other, either insofar as they are like or insofar as they are good (useful). They cannot be friends. Lysis agrees, so he and Socrates discard the hypothesis.

Clearly, Socrates' counterargument is unreasonable. Without being omnipotent, two individuals could be competent at their trades, alike in that respect, and good (useful) for each other in that their skills are complementary. In this commonplace scenario, they could forge a utilitarian friendship. Hence, Lysis's mutual attraction of the useful theorem could stand at least a while longer if he were able to resist the siren song of self-sufficiency. I believe that Lysis is blind to this possibility because his *philonikia* will not let him consent to be inferior to anybody in goodness (usefulness). His vainglory conflicts with his craving to use others by making him admire the absolute self-sufficiency that

Socrates dangles before his eyes. So now the good must be gods. This forces Lysis to yield to the conclusion that the good cannot love because gods have no needs. However, if we were to cater to Lysis's increasing megalomania, letting him transcend impossibility to become as self-sufficient a deity as ever he could desire, we would still have to inquire whether love's sole foundation is need. I do not see why a god or even a human could not love for another reason. In the absence of evidence or compelling logic that eliminates every other possible cause of love, it seems to be nothing but enslavement to one's appetites and the tendency to project one's habit of selfish calculation onto others that reduces all love to need. Like the tautological mutual love thesis, the mutual attraction of the good hypothesis could still be tenable if it prescinded from utility, want, and self-sufficiency.

Socrates takes up the reverse explanation. He claims to have heard someone maintain that opposites attract and supports this proverb with some misquotations from Hesiod. Lysis says nothing. Probably because he sees himself as "beautiful and good" (in both the honorific and literal senses), he cannot imagine being attracted to his opposites. However, Menexenus interrupts to approve of the idea. He probably views himself as the opposite of Lysis, at least insofar as he is not physically beautiful, so the maxim could account for his fondness for Lysis. His agreement is short-lived. Socrates observes that the saying would require us to admit the absurdity that the good and bad especially love one another, and that is the end of that.

Contemplating his next steps, Socrates becomes "dizzy," perhaps because the inquiry now will go round and round. Socrates lays down some new assumptions: that the beautiful is dear (or friendly) and that the good is beautiful. The beautiful is like something soft or sleek. This may be why it captivates us so easily. Socrates' stipulation of these premises seems pointless, for they play no apparent role in the logic of the ensuing analysis. However, the propositions have an essential dramatic function. Socrates is aware that his sophisms about self-sufficiency did not refute the thesis that utility causes *philia*. Lysis should realize soon that he renounced his opinion prematurely. Then he will want to renew it. Given his traits, it will occur to him that his beauty has a tremendous impact on men, who must find some use in it. Next he will think to maintain that an individual is good (useful) not insofar as he is a jack of all trades, but insofar as he and the benefits he confers are beautiful. He will infer that the good (useful) qua beautiful could still inspire friendship. By equating the good, the beautiful, and the dear, and by continuing to identify the good with the useful as a matter of course, Socrates anticipates this move, thus bringing the inquiry around to another examination of utility as the cause of friendship.

To finish setting the stage for this reconsideration, Socrates offers another hypothesis. Abandoning the poets and usurping their office, he "divines" that *philia* arises because those who stand between good and evil are drawn to the good. Beauty is not mentioned in this formulation because it has been subsumed under the rubric of the good to which those located between good and evil are attracted. The new thesis vaguely echoes Diotima's teaching in the *Symposium*, in which the Eros who exists between mortal and immortal, ugly and beautiful, evil and good, and ignorance and wisdom inhabits human souls, impelling us upward toward the highest realities (202e–204a). In a reflection not totally dominated by concerns for utility, the theorem would seem to be particularly suitable for explaining the purest sort of human friendship for the divine. However, in the *Lysis*, both boys will be delighted by the thesis for self-interested reasons: Menexenus because it elevates him from the lowest to the median status and Lysis because he can view himself as the good, godlike beauty to whom the in-betweeners gravitate.

Now Socrates illustrates his hypothesis by asking why someone becomes a "friend" to a physician. This example establishes the equation of the good qua beautiful with the useful so decisively that the argument can dispense with all explicit mention of beauty. Socrates states that no healthy individual is a friend to medicine (which functions as the good qua beautiful in this instance). Only a sick person, whose body qua body is "neither good nor evil" (a dubious notion) but has the evil of disease in it, seeks medicine. At this point, Socrates strains for a precise distinction between "being evil" and "having evil." He observes that blond hair powdered with a white substance is not white but has white in it. In the same way, something that is not bad in itself can have evil in it. This having been clarified at length, Socrates claims that whatever *is* neither bad nor good but *has* evil is forced to want the good. In other words, the accidental presence of an evil in a person will make him or her desire a utility that negates it. The individual will perceive and be attracted to something as good qua beautiful if it seems to be the required utility. This accounts for love and friendship. Presumably, if the evil is not present, the person will experience no need of the utility, will not perceive it as beautiful, and will not befriend it. This is why the healthy man will not be friend to the doctor.

Socrates does not spell out the implications of the medical example as I have just done. Instead, surprisingly, he changes horses in midstream, as it were, remarking that gods and men who are already wise no longer love wisdom. The comment extends the medical analogy and must be understood in this sense. In its context, it means that, like the man who has no illness in his body and therefore sees no beauty in medicine and is not attracted by it, the person who has no ignorance in his soul perceives no beauty in wisdom and is not drawn to it. Wisdom thus appears as just another possible utility whose beauty may or may not be in the eye of any given beholder. This unseemly insinuation echoes another argument in the *Symposium* (203e–204a) and therefore is interpreted by many as a Platonic doctrine. However, when Socrates reasons this way in the *Symposium*, he is moving from Agathon's premises to an aporia. The argument is contradicted by the account of the gods' ascent to the hyperuranian region in the *Phaedrus* (246e–247e). In our present dialogue, Socrates is maneuvering Lysis into one aporia after another. He repeats the defective idea of wisdom (which actually is beautiful in itself and always attractive even to those who have it) because it is Lysis's view, not his own. He wants Lysis's cavalier attitude toward wisdom to get caught up in the wreckage when all the utility explanations of *philia* have come crashing down. Perhaps then Lysis will seek true wisdom more receptively.

Both boys accept Socrates' illustrations and the thesis that they exemplify, namely, that people located between good and evil must befriend the good. Socrates is extraordinarily happy with his analysis. Once the theorem is approved, however, he abjures it. Returning to the example of the physician, which he never intended to abandon, he asks Menexenus whether someone befriends a doctor "for the sake of something" (health) and "because of something" (disease). In an argument dominated by the logic of utility, Menexenus has no choice but to answer yes. This leads straight to a double reductio ad absurdum. One is also a friend to that for the sake of which he befriends a friend, so there necessarily would be an infinite regress of things "for the sake of which" friendships are contracted unless the chain terminated in a "first friend." Therefore, Socrates infers, no person or thing called a friend is really such unless it is the first friend. What we really love is not the individual but the terminal "for the sake of which" in the chain of utilities. Further, the good that the needy individual befriends would be useless except for the presence of the evil because of which the good is sought. Thus, in all cases in which evil is absent, no friendship could arise. Owing to the double reductio, *philia* between persons has become impossible. However, Lysis should see that, like the mutual attraction of the good argument, the theory that in-betweeners are drawn to the good might have worked if utility had not been added to the calculus. There could even be friends whose existence is not threatened by a supreme first friend and who are loved despite the absence of an evil.

Socrates tries again. He asks whether morally neutral desires would remain if evil were abolished and whether they would love the desired objects. Menexenus thinks so. Then, says Socrates, desire might be the cause of *philia*. We could declare that what desires is deficient in that which it desires, that it loves that in which it is deficient, that it is deficient in that which has been taken away from it (a dubious proposition, for it might be deficient in that which it never had), and, thus, that the desirer loves what is "proper" to it. The boys agree both to this and to the inference that, as friends, they belong to each other by nature. Then Socrates adds that someone who loves or desires would not do so unless he belonged to the beloved. This does not follow logically from the preceding premises. Although Menexenus approves of the reasoning, Lysis is silent, perhaps because he has noticed the fallacy, or perhaps because he is loathe to admit that a lover whose attentions are unwelcome belongs to him. Socrates pushes harder, contending that a favorite must befriend someone who truly loves him.[24] Hippothales is delighted by this remark but the boys are decidedly unenthusiastic. One would not wager a lot on Hippothales' chances. What is worse for the silly *neanias*, Socrates promptly repudiates the argument. He says that if "like" and "belonging" are the same, we are back to the problem that likes cannot be friends because they are useless to one another. If "like" and "belonging" differ, good would have to belong either to bad, which is untenable, or to good, which would reduce to the previous difficulty. Utility has ruined yet another hypothesis.

The search has ended in aporia. Socrates laments that if loving, being loved, the like, the unlike, the good, the naturally proper, and all the other things he has forgotten fail to account for friendship, then he is baffled. This is the point at which we need to remember that, if an analysis has gone badly, our trouble might be that we have been inquiring wrongly. Everything that we have done must be suspected of having been erroneous: our formulation of the questions, our demands, our assumptions, our methods, our reasoning. Socrates expects the baffled boys (and us) to continue meditating on how the quest was bungled. This exercise should begin to purge souls of the blinkers that impede visions of the truth.

Socrates comments that he thought about engaging an older interlocutor to help him. This is a hint that we should retrace our steps, answering Socrates' queries in ways not colored by juvenile passions. This clue points in one direction especially. Given that every thesis that we examined broke down as soon as Lysis's childish *libido dominandi* introduced utility into the reasoning, I think that one of the chief lessons of the *Lysis* is that friendship *never* can be explained in terms of the useful (in Vlastos's sense). Selfish utilitarianism is the biggest blinker that the aporia removes.

Before Socrates can bring an older person into the discussion, the pedagogues of Lysis and Menexenus appear like some daimones, calling the boys to return home. Socrates and his group try to drive the pedagogues away but they continue shouting drunkenly in their foreign accents and acting menacingly until Socrates relents. His resistance to the tutors has been interpreted as an attempted blow at the authority of the boys' parents.[25] I think that Socrates' daimon simile means something different. The episode seems to cast Socrates in his usual role as Odysseus, alluding to the time when the hero wants to stay in Hades talking to children of the gods but is driven away by fear of what the guardian spirit of the dead might do (*Odyssey*, 11:630–34).[26] Plato is implying that Socrates had to leave the boys in a spiritual hell, at least for the time being. However, he makes one last effort to save them. As they move off, Socrates advises them that he and they have made themselves ridiculous. He remarks that he is willing to let the pedagogues say that he and the boys think themselves friends but he warns that they have not learned yet what a friend is. They should keep thinking.

Reflection on the *Lysis*

What have we learned from the *Lysis*? Chiefly, we have been taught that friendship is not a relationship of mutual utility. What is loved in such an association is not the other, but the benefits that the other supplies. No bond would arise at all if one or both parties were not needy. That is why the advantage-seeking Lysis cannot become a friend. This result is wholly negative. Have we gained nothing positive? Have we learned anything about why Menexenus *can* become a friend?

We might have some positive leads. Socrates' refutations of most of his theorems were sophistical. If we abstained from sophisms about need and utility, love (friendship) *could* be caused by love (loving), and various kinds or degrees of *philia* could be caused by the mutual attraction of the good, the attractiveness of beauty, the attraction of those who stand between good and evil to the good, and desire for what is proper to oneself. Suppose that we could be assured of the truth of these suggestions. Then, to obtain an adequate understanding of love and friendship, we would still have to ask what all those causes are. We would be on the right track but the ratio of our knowledge to our ignorance would be tiny. We would have almost everything left to learn. Sooner or later we would reach the limits of our ability to clarify the love that is mysterious insofar as we can experience it without being able to explain what it is.

It also could be the case that we would blunder by prescinding from need and utility in order to save the theses. I observed above that only thralldom to one's own appetites insists on tying *philia* to self-seeking. Many would object that this statement is facile. They would claim that no student of mankind could leave need and utility out of account because these are the roots of all human behavior. Friedrich Nietzsche, for example, maintains that all love is *Habsucht* (lust of possession). For him, this is both a psychological insight and an ontological necessity because being is will to power. Nature fashions us solitary. Thus, Nietzsche keenly feels the bitterness of the exclamation, "O friends, there are no friends!" (a remark attributed to Aristotle by Diogenes Laertius) even as he strives to transcend it.[27] Jacques Derrida adopts this cry as the thesis of his book on friendship, placing the *Lysis* at the head of a long tradition that equates love with *Habsucht* and calls selfless friendship impossible.[28] We need to inquire whether there is a metaphysical ground of *philia* that makes an unselfish love realistic. This question can be framed another way: Is there anything in human nature that allows people to cherish others for their own sakes, and to be loved in return for their own sakes, as Aristotle implies in his definition of loving and as Vlastos wishes?

Philia in the *Phaedrus, Symposium,* and *Gorgias*

With Plato's Socrates, I think that the answer is yes. We know that there is love that is not *Habsucht* because we experience it. Nietzsche's doctrine is not empirical but reductionist. Far from founding the tradition of Nietzsche and Derrida, Plato causes Socrates to expound on the unselfish love in the *Phaedrus, Symposium,* and *Gorgias.* However, Socrates does not provide a compelling propositional science of the ground of the true *philia* in these plays, for it is one of the serious things, a mystery that can be experienced but neither penetrated nor adequately captured in words. Instead, he symbolizes it mythically. His analysis requires a much more extensive treatment than I can offer here. I must be satisfied with a brief sketch.

In the *Phaedrus,* much of the talk concerns homoerotic love, which is pictured as the divine mania of a soul consisting of a charioteer and winged horses. The black horse lusts for savage sexual conquest and is resisted by his psychic yoke mates. When the black horse has been tamed and the *erastes* is on the verge of winning his *eromenos*,[29] the discussion of love suddenly changes from the language of eros to that of *philia*. Considering the immaturity of the young, and mindful of the element of human nature that undeniably covets advantage, Socrates comments that the *eromenos* is "by nature friendly to the one who serves" (255a3). Let us admit that, at least at first, the friendship of the *eromenos* for his *erastes* is utilitarian. However, this stripling is not the interesting partner in the relationship just now. The *erastes* whose charioteer has subdued his black horse, and who continues to deny sexual gratification to this steed forever in the *erastes–eromenos* union that has been called "Platonic love," is the epitome of the person who can love selflessly even as the voice of self-interest importunes him incessantly. This *erastes* becomes the "friend" par excellence (255b3–7). He gives "all service" to the *eromenos,* as if the youth were a god (255a1). He strives to give the boy a philosophic character and habits, in order to make *him* happy (253a–c). Socrates pointedly declares that his loving is neither "mortal" nor "illiberal" (*aneleutherian,* 256e5–6).[30] In a way, he agrees with Nietzsche that the human, all-too-human cannot love unselfishly but he thinks that we have a divine capacity for love that is free of the domination of the lower appetites.

Whence this divine, liberal love? In its erotic origins, it is a response to beauty (251a). As it becomes *philia,* it also is a response to good, "for it is determined by fate that evil cannot ever be friend to evil and that good cannot ever not be friend to good" (255b1–2). We see that, in the *Phaedrus,* Socrates advances some of the same theses as he does in the *Lysis* and that he does not repudiate them when the greedy anticipation of utility has been transcended.

Hearing this, the disciples of Vlastos will object that what Socrates loves in a person is beauty and goodness and not "the uniqueness and integrity of his or her individuality." But this merely raises a question: What *is* the uniqueness and integrity of a person's individuality? Who and what is a human being essentially? In what sense is the person unique and integral? Vlastos would reply in a Kantian way that makes individuals ontologically autonomous ends in themselves, but this would not be the indisputably correct thing to do. Socrates' *erastes* in the *Phaedrus* is a philosopher. In his mythical previous existence, his soul has made the ascent to the hyperuranian region, there to behold the essence really being and to partake of divinity that emanates from this ground, the divine consisting in "beauty, wisdom, good, and all such like" (246d8–e1). The wings of his soul are nourished by sharing in this divinity. Participating in it, they become like it. When the *erastes* gazes upon an *eromenos* whose soul once flew to the hyperuranian region (and all human souls have approached this height), what he sees and loves is an image of the divine goodness and beauty that became what it is by participating in the divine. It is true that the *erastes* loves the *eromenos* for this godliness. However, Vlastos fails to understand that the identity of the individual *is* to be an image of the divine. Socrates' *erastes* loves his *eromenos* precisely for who and what he is, in the uniqueness and integrity of his individuality, not in Kant's sense of the autonomous self, but in the sense that the lad is a particular instantiation of man's nature as an image of the divine beauty that is what it is by virtue of participation in the divine. This is the philosophic anthropology that Vlastos cannot understand or accept.

In the *Symposium*, virtually all of the conversation is again about homoerotic love. In the extraordinarily complex and subtle discourse of Socrates–Diotima, Eros is a daimon whose ontological status lies between mortal and immortal. He serves Aphrodite, the personification of eternal divine Beauty, by prompting human beings to beget in her presence. The erotic begetting can be biological, as in the case of male–female coitus that ends in reproduction, or it can be philosophic, as in the case of the generation of beautiful speeches and virtues in the soul of an *eromenos* by his wisdom-loving *erastes*. Diotima informs Socrates that, if he wants to be perfectly initiated into the mysteries of Eros, he will have to ascend a "ladder of beauty." He must start out by loving one particular human body, but then perceive the beauty that pervades other bodies and love them all, rising next through loves of ever higher beauties to a vision of the eternal divine beauty. It disturbs Vlastos and his followers that love of the first comely *eromenos* must be transcended. This distress is unwarranted, however. Diotima does not argue that the *erastes* must stop loving the original *eromenos* or give up a monogamous bond with him. Rather, she insists that, *if* one wishes to understand Eros, *then* one must open one's soul to all manifestations of the eternal beauty and love them too. Thus, symbolically, the ontological situation in the *Symposium* is the same as in the *Phaedrus*. The *erastes* loves the *eromenos* as the image of the eternal beauty that he *essentially* is and, hence, for his own sake, as his nature is understood in Plato's philosophic anthropology rather than in Kant's.

Theoretically, what is more relevant than the complaints of Vlastos is that, at a certain point in her speech, Diotima shifts from the language of eros to the language of *philia*, just as Socrates does in the *Phaedrus*. She argues that when an *erastes* meets a beauty, he undertakes the boy's education, speaking of the good man's character and acts. What follows is a mutual begetting of beautiful speeches and real virtues that bind the two in a community more perfect than any other. This community is friendship par excellence, the partners being much greater friends than parents and children (209c–d).

These musings permit a tentative, propositional conclusion, as long as we do not think that we fully grasp what we are saying, or that our assertion is serious knowledge. There is an ontological basis for selfless *philia*. Participation in the ground of being permits recognition in another of the particular image of the divine good and beauty that is the essential identity of the other, thus generating the friendship par excellence that propagates virtue in the friends.

In the *Gorgias*, Socrates expands this argument. He tells Callicles: "The wise say that community and friendship and orderliness and sane self-control [moderation, *sophrosyne*] and justice hold together heaven and earth and gods and men, and that is why they call the whole [the universe, *to holon*] an ordered world *[kosmon]*, O comrade, not a licentious disorder *[akosmian]*" (507e6–508a4). In the light of the *Phaedrus* and *Symposium*, he appears to mean that because gods possess the divine essence of good and beauty, and because people share in that same essence, there is a universal attraction of good to good and beauty to beauty that binds the whole of divine and human existence together. This attraction is the substance of a community and friendship that unite gods and men. It generates virtues (orderliness, sane self-control, and justice) that are the very being of cosmos, that is, of an order that embraces heaven and earth, directing divine life, human politics, and the myriad human loves to their proper fulfillment. Hence, it is not only true that *philia* has a metaphysical ground. *Philia* is itself the ontological ground of any politics worthy of the appellation.

Philia in the Regeneration of Political Order

Plato, speaking in his own name in the Seventh Letter, tells the story of his youthful aspirations to be a statesman. He was discouraged by the pervasive injustice of the Athenians and withdrew, concluding that it is impossible to act politically without friends (325d1). He did not mean that a politician can succeed only with the backing of a party or a constituency, true as that usually is. He meant that philosophers cannot make thoroughly corrupt political orders more just without the sorts of friends negatively adumbrated in the *Lysis* and positively symbolized in the *Phaedrus* and *Symposium*. When the government is depraved and a large majority of the citizens are either debased or deceived by clever rhetoric, justice can flow into these societies only from friendship groups organized by people who have seen the essence really being (the ultimate reality of the *Phaedrus*) and the vision of real beauty, recognized images of divine good and beauty in the young, fallen in love with the youths for the sake of the images of the divine that they are, and helped their beloveds give birth to visions of the highest truth and attain to the real virtues.

Plato's beloved Dion understood this. That is why he invited his teacher to Syracuse in aid of the project of reforming the politics of his country, reminding Plato that it was his life's work "to exhort young people to the good and the just and thus to bring them on every occasion to friendship and comradeship toward one another" (328d6–e1). Dion wanted Plato to befriend Dionysius II, the young tyrant who had just taken his father's place on the throne, together with a number of his nephews and other youths. Plato accepted the invitation to try to realize his philosophy in deed as well as word. His effort failed because Dionysius, perhaps like the child Lysis, was too far gone in his viciousness. This result contains an object lesson that Socrates articulates in the *Republic*. In most cases, reform must be viewed as a long-term enterprise that writes off the present dominant generation and works with the young, aiming at a better day in the future.

It is the model of the philosophic friendship circle that I envisage in recommending the practice of Platonic *philia* as a cure of the diseases of the United States. Genuinely philosophic souls—not ideologues who are fanatically certain that they know the truth but Socratics who are conscious of their ignorance—must befriend and deliver the young of the beautiful virtues and visions to renew the polity and preserve it for any decent length of time. If it be objected that there are not enough truly philosophic souls or equivalent types to shoulder the task, and if that is the case, I reply that it was ever so and that the cause of justice has typically been lost. The genuine philosophers and equivalent characters, if any there be, must keep trying, for no reform can be carried out by a depraved government that rules corrupted or duped citizens.

Notes

1. In-text citations of Plato in this essay refer to standard Stephanus page numbers. In-text citations of Aristotle refer to standard Bekker page numbers. Homer's *Odyssey* is cited by customary book and line numbers. For my purposes, readers may consult any good Greek or English editions of Plato, Aristotle, and Homer.

2. At various times in his career, Gregory Vlastos taught at Queen's (Canada), Princeton, Berkeley, and Cambridge. He was a holder of MacArthur and Guggenheim fellowships, a moving spirit in the creation of national fellowships and scholarships in philosophy, a founder of councils, a leader of philosophical societies, a prodigious publisher of books and articles on Plato, and a teacher of generations of doctoral students. In Donald Davidson and John Ferrari, "1992, University of California, In Memoriam: Gregory Vlastos, Philosophy: Berkeley," available on line, Vlastos is quoted as characterizing his chief contribution to scholarship as the application of the methods of analytic philosophy to the interpretation of Plato. In the same memorial, his disciples credit him with having restored the study of Plato to the curriculum of American philosophy departments (*Proceedings of the American Philosophical Society* 148(2) [June 2004]: 255–59, retrieved January 26, 2005 from www.aps-pub.com/proceedings/1482/480211.pdf).

3. In this essay, the word "love" refers to the Greek *philia* (noun) and *philein* (verb), unless otherwise noted. ("Love" also has to be used to translate *eros* and *agape*. The three Greek terms have different shades of meaning that lack exact English equivalents.)

4. Gregory Vlastos, *Platonic Studies* (Princeton: Princeton University Press, 1973), 3. Here, Vlastos is translating Aristotle's *Rhetoric*, 1380b35–1381a1.

5. Ibid., 24–25, 25, 26, 26, 26, 7–8, 13, 31. Vlastos's remarks about anal intercourse refer to the Athenian Stranger's comments on homoeroticism in *Laws*, 636b–e and 836a–e.

6. See James M. Rhodes, *Eros, Wisdom, and Silence: Plato's Erotic Dialogues* (Columbia: University of Missouri Press, 2003), particularly chaps. 1–3 and the opening pages of chap. 4.

7. This accounts for many of the contradictory expressions in Plato that certain of his readers mistakenly interpret as esoteric signals.

8. The traditional subtitles of the Platonic dialogues are recognized in the Loeb editions but not in the Oxford editions. Acknowledging the controversy, I must let professional classicists settle it.

9. A student of Vlastos might object that Vlastos himself asks whether the *Lysis* is a vehicle of Platonic doctrine and answers no, *Platonic Studies*, 35–37. However, what Vlastos means here is that the dialogue contains no teaching on the "theory of forms." In the broader sense of the word "doctrine" that I am using, Vlastos regularly interprets statements in the dialogues as Plato's serious teachings and he reads the *Lysis* as an exposition of Plato's early, Socratic theory of love.

10. *Phronesis* means wisdom, prudence, or practical wisdom in various contexts. It is a virtue associated with thoughtful reflection and understanding.

11. *Sophia* also means wisdom. It is a virtue associated with learning and sound judgment.

12. In this story, every sailor rejects not only the true *phronesis* of the navigator but also the ambitious claims of every other sailor to possess the requisite science. The big, stupid captain (the people) appoints as navigators sailors who have told him that there is no teachable art of navigation, who frequently have simply forced him to let them steer, and who hold their posts only as long as it takes their rivals to kill them. Evidently, in Athens, no claim to wisdom, be it true or false, legitimates political authority and power for long.

13. One could argue that the father, the neighbor, the Athenians, and the Great King *should* obey Lysis if he were wiser than they. However, this would be problematic even if one had true wisdom rather than technical ability in mind. The trouble resembles that which caused Aristotle to struggle with the question of what to do with godlike men. This aside, Socrates is arguing "would," not "should," so the boy's expectations are ludicrous. The neighbor would think that Lysis wanted to rob him. The Great King would suspect a good cook of wishing to poison him. If he met someone capable of ruling his empire, he probably would fear the man as a potential rival and have him murdered.

14. Someone might argue that parents have a utilitarian motive for loving their children even as new born infants, namely, that they see the babies as means to their vicarious immortality. This view contradicts experience. It is the worst kind of reductionism. Further, vicarious immortality means nothing to the thoughtful. It is utterly worthless.

15. Vlastos, *Platonic Studies*, 7–9.

16. It also should have bothered Vlastos that the comments are mutually contradictory, even if he attributed this fact to Plato's poverty as a logician.

17. Vlastos analyzes the proof texts that he selects from the *Republic* and *Symposium* with the same flawed methods, reaching similarly invalid results. I do not have sufficient space to show this here. See *Platonic Studies*, 11–23.

18. David Bolotin, *Plato's Dialogue on Friendship: An Interpretation of the Lysis, with a New Translation* (Ithaca: Cornell University Press, 1979), 83–103.

19. It seems that, long before he met Socrates, Lysis came close enough to tampering with his mother's loom to be threatened with a beating (208d). This, together with the boy's failure to object to Socrates' interpretations of his motives, seems to prove that Socrates has not been planting the seeds of rebellion but uncovering them.

20. The similarity between Lysis and Alcibiades is no dramatic accident. Lysis, whose name means "loosing" or "releasing," may be a fictitious icon of Alcibiades, the great looser of bonds of personal and civic *philia*.

21. Bolotin, *Plato's Dialogue*, 191. One also could cite evidence for the broader influence of Vlastos's Kantian sentiments. For example, with an eye toward the maxim that we should treat people as ends in themselves, Martha Nussbaum writes of Vlastos's critique of Plato that "[w]e feel that Vlastos must somehow be right." See *The Fragility of Goodness: Luck and Ethics in Greek Tragedy and Philosophy* (Cambridge: Cambridge University Press, 1986), 166–67. Nussbaum defends "Plato" by foisting the utilitarian sins off on Socrates and attributing generous love to Alcibiades, of all people.

22. Cf. Plato, Seventh Letter, 325d8–9, where Plato calls Socrates his friend. It appears to me that Plato was a good friend to Socrates indeed. Socrates had other excellent friends before he met Plato. However, Bolotin takes Socrates' claim at face value (*Plato's Dialogue*, 109). His reasons for doing so are unclear, especially inasmuch as students of Leo Strauss are supposed to be sensitive to irony.

23. As Aristotle knows, his concept of loving does not fit wine. One could not love wine by wishing good things for it for its own sake. The same difficulty exists in the cases of exercise, wisdom, and animals (other than pets). There are too many possible shades of meaning of "love" to permit us to approve of Socrates' logic without fuller consideration here.

24. Here, Socrates continues to use the language of *philia* but his meaning is skating on the edge of homoeroticism.

25. Bolotin, *Plato's Dialogue*, 65.

26. On Homeric imagery in Plato, cf. Zdravko Planinc, *Plato's Political Philosophy: Prudence in the Republic and the Laws* (Columbia: University of Missouri Press, 1991), and Planinc, *Plato through Homer: Poetry and Philosophy in the Cosmological Dialogues* (Columbia: University of Missouri Press, 2003).

27. Friedrich Nietzsche, *Die fröhliche Wissenschaft*, aphorism 14, in *Kritische Studienausgabe*, vol. 3, ed. Giorgio Colli and Mazzino Montinari (Munich: Deutscher Taschenbuch Verlag de Gruyter, 1999); Nietzsche, *Menschliches, Allzumenschliches I*, aphorism 376, in *Kritische Studienausgabe*, vol. 2.

28. Jacques Derrida, *Politics of Friendship,* trans. George Collins (New York: Verso, 1997).

29. In Greek homoeroticism, the *erastes* was an older lover on the giving side of intercourse; the *eromenos* was a younger beloved on the receiving side of the sex.

30. By "illiberal," Socrates means not the vice of illiberality later identified by Aristotle but, rather, something like "unworthy of a person who has been educated to freedom from the rule of the base passions."

2

Taking Friendship Seriously

Aristotle on the Place(s) of *Philia* in Human Life

Stephen Salkever

For present-day readers, Aristotle's discussion of friendship (in Greek, *philia*)[1] is both intriguing and perplexing—intriguing because of his unique emphasis on friendship as an essential topic for moral and political theory, perplexing because his lengthy discussions of friendship do not result in any clear moral or political principles. Anyone coming to Aristotle from modern philosophy must wonder why he cares so much about friendship, devoting much more time and attention to it than any modern philosopher. Friendship is the topic of a large portion of both the *Nicomachean* and the *Eudemian* versions of Aristotle's *Ethics* (books 8–9 of the *NE* and book 7 of the *EE*), and is central to the *Politics* (especially in book 3), the *Rhetoric* (book 2, ch. 4), and to his account of tragedy in the *Poetics* as well.[2] Our thoughts about friendship, shaped by the post-Aristotelian philosophical tradition, incline to the view that friendship should be treated as a relatively minor subject for philosophy, either as a sub-philosophic afterthought (as in Kant),[3] or as super-philosophic transcendence (as in Montaigne and Rousseau),[4] or as both (as in Heidegger).[5] For us, to think philosophically about ethics and politics is first of all to reflect on the individual, the family, the political community, and then, if we inquire more deeply, to turn our attention to more universal ways of being together, to communities of all believers in a certain faith, or of all human beings or of all rational or all sentient beings. The job of practical philosophy, we generally think, is to bring these various identities to our attention and to supply us with solid and clear principles that will tell us how to understand and to weigh the diverse and often conflicting claims such identities make on us. Against the general expectations formed by this background, Aristotle, undoubtedly a philosopher,[6] is an odd duck in two respects: he asks us to pay serious attention to a kind of relationship that appears on the surface to be much less important or much less intelligible than others we can name, and at the same time he fails to provide a clear and precise definition of what friendship is or of the principles he thinks should govern our friendships.

Aristotle's stress on the problem of friendship is out of step not only with modernity but with some of the leading ideas of his own time. Like Plato, Aristotle is writing against both the philosophical and the political current of his day, against what he calls the *endoxa* or the most widespread and influential opinions. No other Greek philosopher comes close to foregrounding *philia* as Aristotle does. As for political *endoxa*, the central moral questions facing his fourth-century BCE audience are more like the ones posed by Glaucon and Adeimantus to Plato's Socrates about the best, most choiceworthy way of life: which should I choose, the life of the good and just citizen, or the life of the all-powerful tyrant? In the *Republic*, Socrates tries to reorient his interlocutors away from the choice between citizenship and tyranny and toward the cultivation of eros and the attempt to understand the universal good; similarly, in the *Ethics* and *Politics*, Aristotle's project is to reorient his readers and auditors away from a focus on the choice between pleasure or power seeking on the one hand and good citizenship on the other, and toward a concern with their own friendships and an accurate perception of the human good.[7] For Plato's Socrates in the *Apology*, the unexamined life is not worth living for a human being; the Aristotelian equivalent is the *prohairetic* life, the life marked by thoughtful reflection on our goals and our ways of achieving them, a reflection that depends on an accurate conception of both the universal human species good and our own particular context.

Aristotle's substantive account of *philia* in particular is similarly counter- or transcultural. While his discussion does not follow in the footsteps of any previous philosopher, neither does he simply reflect or systematize standard non-philosophic Greek opinions about *philia*. As Lorraine Pangle notes, speaking of the Greek *endoxa* concerning friendship, "friendship was associated in the popular mind with courage, with republicanism, and with the spirited resistance to injustice and tyranny."[8] The standard endoxic characterizations of friendship included maxims like "the things of friends are in common" and "friendship is one soul in two bodies," both of which Aristotle disputes and revises, particularly by noting that true friends must be separate as well as other selves.[9] The typical Greek examples of great friendships are pairs of great male warriors or political heroes—Achilles and Patroclus, Hercules and Iolaus, Harmodius and Artistogeiton. But Aristotle associates this kind of friendship with spiritedness or *thumos*, with anger and yearning for revenge, and not with the desire for living prohairetically. The staunch preference for death over dishonor is central to the understanding of *philia* among Aristotle's contemporary Greeks, and it is something he wishes to open to critique in his *Ethics* and *Politics*. At the same time, it is the case that Aristotle seeks to preserve the "phenomena," the existing opinions about friendship, as much as he can, since it is no more his intention than it is Plato's to supply a new set of rules to replace those implicit in the culture. In particular, he wants to avoid clashing so much with the prevailing opinions that he will seem to be uttering paradoxes; his goal is to problematize the *endoxa*, not to overthrow them.[10]

For Aristotle, as for Plato, the goal and the task of practical philosophy is reorientation rather than systematic doctrine, an attempt to teach *questions* and a mode of inquiry rather than to supply definitive answers. While his emphasis on friendship is striking, it is equally striking that he gives us no separate treatise on friendship, no systematic account of what it is and of how friends should conduct themselves. But even though Aristotelian practical philosophy is not doctrinal or dogmatic, it would not be philosophy at all if he were not able to give good reasons for preferring the orientation he presents to others. We must ask why Aristotle cares so much about friendship and what he is telling us about how to understand it. The argument of this essay is that Aristotle's central message is that we need to care more about our friendships, to take friendship more seriously, to move friendship from the margins to the center of our moral universe.

But why should we reorient our practical reasoning in that way? Why isn't it enough to take seriously the life of the family, or of politics and the virtues of action or praxis, or of theoretical/philosophical reflection, or of erotic love, whether human or divine, and to treat friendship as ancillary to these more obviously central aspects of life? Why shouldn't we care most about our individual identity, or our citizenship, or our humanity, and treat friendship as subordinate to these other, better articulated concerns? Aristotle, in effect, has to argue for the centrality of friendship to human life in relation to the powerful claims of these other activities and communities. This, incidentally, was as true relative to Aristotle's immediate Greek philosophic and practical context as it is to our own time. We, as did Aristotle's immediate audience, need to know not only *why* we should take friendship as seriously as Aristotle wants us to, but also *how* to do so.

The answer to both these questions lies in Aristotle's discussion of the human good and the best way of life—friendship should be a central (though by no means an exclusive) concern because of the problems we confront in becoming good human beings, and the way to take friendship seriously is by following Aristotle in thinking about friendship through the lens of a particular conception of the human good, one that leads us to see not only the value of friendship but also the insufficiency of the other phenomena that push friendship aside. But before examining what Aristotle has to say about friendship, I need to sketch a general position concerning both the style and the overall content of Aristotle's practical philosophy as a whole. This approach is one that I and others have argued for elsewhere.[11]

Style and Substance in Aristotle's Practical Philosophy

There are two major points to be made about Aristotle's overall procedure in the *NE* and the *Politics*. The first, which concerns style, is that

Aristotle's presentation of his practical philosophy (his *politikê*) is protreptic, rather than deductive or inductive: a movement from, as he says, what is known to us to what is knowable simply—from, that is, opinions about the best life that are widely shared by his audience to those opinions that Aristotle holds. His style is also aporetic, in the manner of the Platonic dialogues, in that he seeks to move his students to pose certain questions for themselves rather than to persuade them of the truth of any clear answer to the question of the best life. The second point modifies the first: there is indeed a non-aporetic substantive basis for this aporetic teaching, and that is Aristotle's species teleology, his account of what it means to be a human being, of the problems and possibilities that, in his view, define humanity. Aristotle's approach to teaching *politikê* as a whole is justified and in part determined by his own theoretical understanding of human nature and the human good. Within that whole, the task here is to try to understand why Aristotle thinks we need to be persuaded to rethink *philia*—how taking friendship seriously in this way might contribute to making our lives better.

As a liberal educator of young Greek men, Aristotle speaks to us indirectly. We are, as it were, eavesdroppers on his lectures to his Greek audience, lectures in which he aims to move that audience to a point outside their own tradition, to partially and subtly liberate them from their Greekness in the interest of making them better human beings. His texts are in this respect not unlike Plato's dialogues, written dialectically and rhetorically, rather than as systematic demonstrations or deductions of propositions he holds to be true: dialectically in that they engage in conversation or dialogue with the opinions of others (sometimes named, sometimes not) on the questions they consider; rhetorically in that they want to influence their particular audience in a particular direction, rather than trying to measure up to a universal standard of deductive validity. For Aristotle, as much as for Plato, philosophical writing cannot be precise and systematic without distorting our understanding of the things that are. This is true not only of Aristotle's "practical" writing, but of at least some of his metaphysical and natural scientific writing as well. Much of what we can understand about nature has a sort of "thick and vague" character, to employ the phrase Nussbaum uses to characterize Aristotle's conception of the human good.[12] We can indeed know the human good, but only in outline. This is not only because of our difficulties in knowing relatively permanent and universal things, but because the good of composite beings, such as humans and other animals, will itself be less permanent and singular than the good of more fully actual beings, such as fixed stars and unmoved movers.

Aristotle's intention in the *NE* and the *Politics* is to move an audience that deeply honors public life, and that is interested in hearing that life celebrated, closer to the practice of philosophical inquiry about public life, understood as the repeated asking of questions that are never answerable once and for all.[13] He sometimes argues explicitly for the value of this shift (as at the end of book 6 of the *NE*); mainly, however, he tries to achieve his aim by guiding the audience of the *Ethics* and *Politics* on an extended tour of plausible answers—some endoxic, some more clearly his own—to the question of the most choiceworthy human life. One consequence of this way of reading Aristotle is that the meaning of any particular utterance in the text must be understood in terms of the intention of the whole work. Aristotle's lectures, like Plato's dialogues, must be read as wholes rather than as collections of self-standing systematic arguments or "proof texts" about a variety of ethical and political topics. To summarize the pedagogical movement of the *NE* briefly, prior to Aristotle's discussion of *philia* in books 8 and 9, Aristotle's survey of plausibly admirable lives provides "stops," in the *NE*, at the manly life (book 3), the great-souled life (book 4), the just life and the decent life (book 5), and the life of the *phronimos* (the practically wise person) and of *prohairesis* (thoughtful choice) as the most human of activities (book 6). Each of these ways of life involves an advance in human virtue beyond its predecessor, primarily an advance in the quality of the logos the way of life displays, logos having been specified in advance by Aristotle as the decisive human characteristic, the core of distinctively human virtue. Through book 6 of the *NE*, then, we are shown ever more comprehensive horizons of human excellence. Aristotle begins his survey of the virtues by praising the bravery *(andreia)* of the good soldier and the great-souled man *(megalopsuchos)*, both of whom live within the horizon of honor, an aspiration that draws us toward virtue but at the cost of overreliance on public opinion. The life linked to the virtue of justice in book 5 overcomes this dependence by replacing the horizon of honor and opinion with that of law *(nomos)*. But this horizon itself seems to demand a sacrifice of our *logos* capacity that is only partly remedied by the deepening of justice that Aristotle names "decency" or "equity" *(epieikeia)*. This new virtue allows us to understand the law more actively and to apply it thoughtfully rather than mechanically, but without any clear sense of the standard in terms of which our laws are to be interpreted and applied.

That standard is supplied by the account of the human species good provided in book 6, which opens with Aristotle's announcement that his discussion of the moral virtues—the virtues of character, including justice and *epieikeia*, that mark the human good in action (praxis)—has proceeded with a key term left unexplained. Such virtues incline good human beings to "choose a mean" that is determined as if by "right reason" (*orthos logos*, 1138b20). But what is a right reason or correct logos? The beginning of the answer he provides in book 6 requires a term that is not part of the endoxic vocabulary: correct logos is not an external law determining our choices but an internal mixture of reason and desire (*orexis*) that he calls *prohairesis: prohairesis* is "either desirous *nous* or thoughtful *orexis* and such a beginning *(archê)* is a human being" (1139b4–5).[14] This represents a substantial advance beyond the teaching of the previous books of the *NE;* we now have a way of describing what a human being and hence, given Aristotle's species teleology, a good human being is—not simply the practitioner of a variety of moral virtues, but someone who leads a prohairetic life. *Prohairesis* gives us a standard that goes beyond and incorporates the earlier virtue-horizons of honor and justice properly understood, but at the same time book 6 goes on to problematize the prohairetic life to make it quite clear that it cannot be the ultimate standard or horizon. The book ends by noting that there is a further perspective, that of wisdom or theoretical reason, that goes beyond *prohairesis* and the standard of the human good by recognizing the limits of humanity when seen from the perspective of the relatively divine and unchanging beings. This serious reservation about the adequacy of *prohairesis* as a standard is picked up once more in book 10 of the *NE* and again in book 7 of the *Politics.* This problematization of *prohairesis*, however, no more eliminates the need for both it and practical reason than the standard of the human good eliminates the need for honor and nomos.

Book 7 provides yet another new beginning, and contains yet another way of problematizing *prohairesis*, this time by way of the argument that true vice, as opposed to mere weakness of will or to incontinence, is also a product of thoughtful reflection (1151a6–7). Aristotle presents books 8 and 9, the books on friendship, as yet another new beginning. I argue in what follows that Aristotle's chief contention in these books is that *philia*, properly understood, is essential if we are to understand and enact a life of good prohairetic practice. In this respect, *philia*'s place in human life is, for Aristotle, similar to the role he ascribes to political practice and the life lived in accordance with *nomos* and justice in *Politics* 1 (1253a), that of shaping properly our inherited and quite plastic potential for logos in the direction of virtue rather than vice.[15] But not even the best or primary sense of *philia* can supply a perfectly sufficient solution to the human problem, and so the *NE* indicates certain internal perplexities of *philia* as well before moving to the discussion of the yet more-inclusive horizon of the theoretical life in chapters 6–8 of book 10. Yet this horizon too proves insufficient, and the *NE* concludes by announcing the need to supplement our thoughts about the superiority of philosophy to politics by a return to the horizon of laws and politics.

As a sequel to the *NE,* the *Politics* gives us critical accounts of a variety of ways of life: the master's life (book 1), the Spartan life (book 2), the life of the good male citizen (book 3), the life of the farmer of middling means (books 4–6), the theoretical life again (book 7), ending with consideration of the kind of political life that might accommodate recognition of the claims of the theoretical life (books 7 and 8). Aristotle uses this survey to demonstrate that *all* such univocal answers to the question of the human good are unstable and unsatisfactory, both theoretically and practically. But he supplies no approved formulation of just what human happiness really means to take their place. As a result, the *Ethics* and *Politics* are as aporetic, as perplexing, as any Platonic dialogue: they return us to the question with which we began. But like Plato's dialogues, these texts are not merely or aimlessly perplexing, but protreptic, designed to show that the question of the best life itself can be continually illuminating, if properly asked, in a variety of circumstances. Aristotle, like Plato, wants both to perplex his audience and to supply it with intellectual tools for capitalizing on the perplexity he hopes to induce. His primary goal in this educational project is not to turn his audience into either good citizens or good philosophers, or even to reconcile citizens and philosophers, but to produce deeper, more reflective, more serious, more prohairetic people. In other words, Aristotle's goal is not to set out a universally true *politikê*, but to contribute to the formation of an educated public.

What philosophy supplies is not a discipline for mastering the passions, but a set of questions and a way of inquiry that enable each of us to take passions, and the things that happen to us in general, seriously as parts of the whole that is our individual life. That is, the non-aporetic basis for Aristotle's aporetic philosophizing is his belief that the best (or the most) human life—and hence the central criterion by which any person or polis must be judged—is one lived *kata prohairesin* (*Politics*, 3, 1280a34), where *prohairesis* itself is neither nature-transcending choice nor reason cleansed of desire, but a uniquely and definitively human product of the mixture of *nous* and *orexis*, of mind and longing: "*Prohairesis* is either *orektikos nous* or *orexis dianoêtikê*, and such a beginning *(archê)* is *anthrôpos*" (*NE*, 6, 1139b4–5). In a wonderful moment illustrating the beauty of small distinctions between prepositions, Aristotle sums up his view of the virtue of the thoughtful life by saying that such a life is lived not *kata logon*, according to logos, but *meta logou*, with logos (*NE* 6, 1144b26–30).

This proposition comes as close as any single statement to qualifying as Aristotle's categorical imperative[16]—and yet, even here, in the immediate sequel in book 7 he makes it quite clear that logos and *prohairesis* can be wrong as well as right, just as well as unjust, and that someone whose *prohairesis* has led them astray will be both vicious, and thus unhappy, and prohairetic (*NE*, 6, 1148a16–17; *NE*, 7, 1151a29–35). Book 6 has told us that human virtue is an interplay of human logos and human desire within the souls of good human individuals. Aristotle's discussion of incontinence in book 7 immediately makes it clear that such an interplay of logos and desire is also true of vice. Vice is not the absence of reason in our decisions to act; such absence is better called "incontinence" or "weakness." Virtue, similarly, is not the triumph of reason over strong and base desire; such a triumph is continence *(enkrateia)* or strength *(karteria)*, but it isn't virtue: "So if the continent person must have strong and base desires, then the moderate person *(sophrôn)* will not be continent, nor the continent person moderate, for the moderate person has neither excessive nor base desires" (1146a9–12).

Let us pause here to note how remarkably at odds Aristotle is with both Hobbes and Kant, and perhaps with modern notions of virtue generally. A good Kantian is someone whose commitment to moral reason defeats the power of natural fears and temptations; a good Hobbesian's calculations of long-run advantage blunt the force of immediate desires and aversions. For both Hobbes and Kant, the work of either calculating (Hobbesian) or legislating (Kantian) reason is to protect the free self against the destructive consequences of naturally occurring pleasures and pains. For Aristotle, the practical work of logos is to reflect on our desires, to transform them from biologically inherited impulses to parts of a mature personality that we, along with the *nomoi* and the mentors of our childhood and—as he will argue in books 8 and 9—our friends, construct. Unlike the moderns, Aristotle acknowledges that there is no guarantee of success, even if fortune smiles, because vice, in this case immoderation, as well as virtue is "according to deliberative decision *(kata tên prohairesin)*" (1151a6–7)[17]—even though Aristotle has just said in book 6 that action based on the prohairetic interplay of logos and desire is what makes us human beings (1139b4–5), and even though he will say in book 3 of the *Politics* that human eudaimonia can almost be defined as living *kata tên prohairesin*, according to deliberative choice (1280a33–34). For Aristotle, serious reflection on what sort of life we want to lead may or may not result in a right *(orthê)* decision (1150b29–36), in spite of the fact that the central recommendation of the *Ethics* is that we take life seriously.

With friendship as with other topics, the project of Aristotle's practical philosophy seems to be paradoxical or contradictory: to clarify and make more accurate the endoxic view of *x* while at the same time complicating the endoxic view of *x*. His great enemy seems to be the idea that the path to clarification lies through simplification or reduction of differences to a single uniform and self-consistent thing. An aspect of this is his attempt to get us to hold more than one idea at a time about the subject at hand. For example, he wants to show his readers and auditors that the familiar idea of *nomos* embodies a paradox: it is both force against nature (as in the discussion of slavery in *Politics* 1) and nous without desire (in *Politics*, 3), something that completes and perfects nature understood as our biological inheritance.

Aristotle's project throughout his practical philosophy is not to set out systematic doctrine—either doctrine he derives from his understanding of nature or being, or doctrine that he systematizes out of the unsystematic raw material supplied by his culture, or the *endoxa*. Instead, his aim is to argue that in order to live as well as we possibly can as human beings,[18] we must treat certain questions and problems as central to our lives. His method is to *begin* with the *endoxa* or the tradition of what we would call his culture, but to take familiar concepts (like *philia* or friendship) and propositions (such as "the things of friends are in common") and subject them to a new and critical light, the light provided by what he takes to be his accurate and novel conception of reality, of the nature of the cosmos. His practical philosophy is thus in one way metaphysical or scientific, yet in another way not: that is, his goal is to show us that familiar concepts like justice and friendship take on a new meaning when seen from the perspective of nature and especially human nature, but he never claims that traditional moral and political concepts and ideas can be replaced by ones that are deduced from metaphysical starting points. His aim is not to legislate new principles of morals and politics, but to initiate a critique of morals and politics that prepares the way for context-sensitive practical reason.

Aristotelian Friendship and the Prohairetic Life

In *NE*, 8–9, Aristotle first expands and then immediately narrows, or rather organizes, the semantic range of *philia*. He begins by saying that *philia* applies to all instances of living together that involve some degree of reciprocity, enough equality to make reciprocity possible (master and slave qua master and slave cannot be friends, though qua human beings they can be), and some degree of *prohairesis*, which includes a measure of self-consciousness (*NE* 1155b34–1156a2). *Philia* thus includes relationships for mutual pleasure or mutual advantage, or for our mutual good (*NE* 1155b20), as distinct from pleasure and advantage. Thus understood, *philia* can include political, business, family, and many other forms of being together. But Aristotle immediately structures this broad range of meanings by saying that all the various kinds of *philia* take their meaning as forms of human living together from the paradigmatic or "perfect" or "complete" kind of friendship, the friendship of good people that aims at sustaining their virtues throughout the course of their lives (*NE*, 1156b7 ff.). What is the difference between "perfect" *(teleia)* friendship and the imperfect kinds, and what can Aristotle mean in saying that pleasure and advantage friendships *depend on* perfect friendship for their meaning? His point here is not that there is a single elevated standard of perfection that the best friendships achieve while the others fall short—it is not that "virtue" belongs to a higher order of being than pleasure or advantage. That would be Kant, not Aristotle. The key to Aristotle's claim about a "primary" sense of friendship is his distinction (that flows from his biology) between the *parts* or events that make up the life of any organism and its life as a *whole*. Friendships for mutual pleasure or advantage are partial friendships; they concern particular aspects of our life. What virtue friendships have that partial friendships do not is that they take seriously the problem of a life as a whole. Why, for Aristotle, are these friendships "primary" or perfect? Because, on biological or theoretical grounds, the whole of a life is more than the sum of its parts. The practical implication of his theoretical distinction between perfect and partial friendships is that we need friends to help us take seriously the problem of living a good life, a problem that is unique to human beings.[19]

Within this overall theoretical project, Aristotle treats friendship for the most part not as a virtue, but as a mode of human being together or interaction, similar to the polity or the family/household.[20] Friendship is a distinctly human mode of connection, as are, for example, political or family life—neither nonhuman animals nor gods can practice *philia*; nor do these other kinds of beings need to practice *philia* to achieve the goods proper to their kinds.[21] Aristotelian *philia* is various enough to include a variety of interactions, but it is not simply a synonym for human interaction, since not all human interactions involve *prohairesis* and mutuality. All of Aristotle's substantial accounts of the defining marks of *philia* (see *NE*, 8.2 and 9.4; *EE*, 7.2; *Rhetoric*, 2.4) stress mutuality and reciprocity as essential characteristics of true *philia*. Friendship is, in the language of the *Rhetoric*, "loving and being loved in return"—each person, in contrast to normal Greek erotic practice, is both the active and the passive partner in a relationship of true *philia*: "*philos d'estin ho philôn kai antiphiloumenos*" (*Rhetoric*, 1381a1–2). What interactions do not fit under *philia*? All those that lack any trace of self-conscious reciprocity, that do not require the partners to consider one another as separate selves toward whom they feel goodwill;

exploitative relationships are not instances of *philia*, and those human beings who are incapable of treating other selves with good will are incapable of *philia* at all.[22] Thus bad people, he says, cannot be friends because their badness is always driven by a *pleonexia*, a ceaseless and boundless desire for more and more instrumental goods that makes lasting good will to another self impossible (*NE*, 1167b9–16). The same is true for many old people who are driven by fear, as well as the young who are driven by unreflective affection, and also perhaps for both the very poor and the very rich who, because of their economic situation, are incapable of this kind of concern for others, or even for seeing others as separate selves at all, but only as potential or actual slaves or masters (*Politics* 4, ch. 11).

In speaking of *philia* in this way, Aristotle is not reporting facts about how Greek speakers use that word, any more than his definition of "polis" as a community of equals who rule and are ruled in turn with an eye to the laws in *Politics*, 1 is a report on ordinary or endoxic usage of that word. Rather, it is an evaluative and normative theoretical claim, telling us how we should conceive and use the term—but "should" relative to what? As with many of his normative definitions in the *Ethics* and *Politics*, it is not a categorical command, but one that presupposes a prior commitment, so that his claim is, in effect, "If you want to live well as a human being, then it is best to think about and use *philia* in this way." Aristotle's task is to redescribe and reconceive a familiar term in such a way that we understand it differently, and live better lives as a result—"better lives" meaning those that are better as *human* lives, not in terms of any other subjective or objective criterion. Aristotle's account of *philia* reflects his attempt to see this familiar relationship in the light of his teleological understanding of human nature. Given the unusually prominent position he gives *philia*, it is clear that part of what he wants to do in this account is to move *philia* from the margins to the center of Greek moral and political discourse.

All friendships, that is, all these relationships among separate selves who are aware of both their separateness and their similarity—advantage and pleasure friendships as well as virtue ones—emerge from self-interest. But once formed, they are no longer reducible to the self-interested motives from which they indispensably spring. In this respect, politics is indeed a kind of *philia*—it comes into being for the sake of living, but in its actual existence aims at living well. Nancy Sherman puts this aspect of *philia* as an emergent phenomenon[23] very well: "Apart from valuing the benefits and virtues related to being a friend, we prize the give-and-take of mutual exchange. We value creating a shared world and expanding self through a sense of mutuality defined by our interactions. The pleasure of mutuality and the expansion of self that comes with it is a core part of human development and flourishing."[24] We begin Aristotelian friendships (not counting relations of parents and children) with the desire for whatever shared activities give us pleasure, or for whatever material or intangible resources seem required for our success as particular individuals. But as such interactions persist, it is possible that these instrumental activities can become ends in themselves, constitutive conditions of our happiness rather than only instrumental ones. Of course, it is also possible (and even likely, given the strength of *pleonexia* and of human weakness and dependency in its various guises) that these interactions can become exploitative rather than friendly. *Philia* thus becomes both valuable for the end of human life (eudaimonia) and fragile, and is thus, for Aristotle, a— or perhaps *the*—central issue for political science.

Philia is thus in a way, as he says, even more important than law and justice: "If people are friends, they have no need of justice, but if they are just they need friendship in addition, and the most just sort of justice seems to be friendly *(philikon)*" (*NE*, 8.1, 1155a26–28). Not that friendship is an alternative to law and justice, but that they are mutually dependent: the perspective of justice and law enables us to see ourselves as others (relative strangers) see us (which is why even the best human beings require the discipline of law and justice to prevent us from rewarding our friends too much) (*Politics,* 3.16, 1287a32–b5, 6.4, 1318b38–1319a1), while *philia* enables us to see certain familiar others as we see ourselves (that is, as separate humans beings). Both *philia* and justice are thus universalizing elements in human life, though neither of them involves a move from selfishness to altruism either by way of utilitarian empathy or the Kantian transcendence of treating humanity as an end in itself. [25]

Advantage and pleasure friendships are intelligible only by reference to virtue friendships. This is because the useful things and the pleasurable things are not firm and separate categories of things; different people will regard different things or activities as useful, or useless, pleasant, painful, or indifferent. But Aristotle is not a relativist: the things that are truly pleasant and useful are those that appear so to the best human being by nature—the person who is living well as a human being. The measure *(metron)* of pleasant and painful, useful and harmful, is not any human being *(anthrôpos)* but a *spoudaios* (*NE* 10.5, 1176b15–16), someone who takes, and knows how to take, human life seriously. And getting pleasure and utility right means living prohairetically—with the reservation that living a prohairetic life as such does not guarantee that a person will live as good a life as is possible under the circumstances. To achieve this goal, our *prohairesis* has got to be as accurate as possible, both in our theoretical understanding of what it means to be a human being in general and in our understanding of the particular possibilities and limitations for human life that belong to our particular time and place.

To maximize prohairetic accuracy, both law-and-justice and virtue friendship are required, as is (at least) the degree of philosophical understanding we can obtain by engaging in something like Aristotelian political science as presented in the *Ethics* and *Politics*. This is what friendship is for in human life, according to Aristotle. Perfect friendship is not a comprehensive recipe for a virtuous life, nor a utopian community, but a kind of activity that, along with a number of other important factors, gives us the best chance at living well. Neither philosophy nor politics (ruling and being ruled in turn with a view to the laws) nor virtue friendship alone is adequate to constitute human flourishing. But in conjunction with good health, adequate material resources, and good luck, they can be the elements of a well-lived human life, one characterized not only by thoughtful and well-articulated choices, but by accurate ones. It is important to remember that Aristotle's god, the primary or focal instance of being and of good, neither philosophizes nor politicizes nor loves—all of these are specifically human activities. The important interpretive mistake to avoid is the conclusion that any one of these three supercedes the others, and makes them unnecessary—that politics is the supreme form of friendship (see *NE*, 8.11, 1161b), or that true friendship makes the political kind unnecessary, or that those who philosophize need neither laws nor friends (except as associates in theoretical inquiry). To the contrary, a successfully prohairetic life requires all three.[26]

Like *epieikeia* (equity or decency), *philia* seems to be both an enabling or necessary condition for justice and at the same time a commitment that points beyond justice. The going beyond is even greater here than with *epieikeia*. Of *epieikeia*, Aristotle says that it is a kind of justice: "[T]he nature of *epieikeia* is the correction of the nomos when it falls short of justice because of its universality" (*NE*, 5, 1137b26–27). Of friendship he says, "Where there is friendship there is no need of justice" (*NE*, 1155a26–27). But Pangle claims, correctly, that this requires perfect seamless friendship, and "Aristotle clearly considers the idea of a seamless union chimerical."[27] We cannot arrive at the proverbial condition of one soul in two bodies, nor should we try.

Aristotle's distinction between three kinds of friendship (for pleasure, for advantage, for virtue) reflects the multiple and partially conflicting goods that define humanity, and serves as a bridge between the political life and the life devoted to philosophy, to the activity of going beyond the human things altogether that is said to constitute the best human life in *NE*, 10.6–8 and in *Politics*, 7.[28] In *NE*, 8 and 9, friendship supercedes honor and justice as the motive for acting beautifully or nobly. For this reason, while "it is more necessary to have friends in bad times" than in good, "it is more beautiful to have them in good times," "for then we wish to act well *[eu dran]*" (*NE*, 9, 1171a20–25). This distinction brings into play Aristotle's contention that there are two orders of causality at work: necessary and constitutive conditions of a thing (the very same distinction between two orders of causality is set out by Plato in both the *Phaedo* and *Statesman*).[29] This distinction between instrumental and constitutive causality, derived from Aristotle's natural science in general and his theoretical account of the distinction between potentiality *(dunamis)* and actuality *(energeia)* in particular, comes into play in a number of crucial discussions in both versions of the *Ethics* and in the *Politics* as well. It is difficult to imagine Aristotle's *politikê* without it.[30]

Pangle argues persuasively that even the best Aristotelian friendship can be seen as an instrumental means, or necessary condition, to a philosophic life, rather than an end or a constitutive part of happiness or the human good in itself.[31] But Aristotle's discussions of friendship help us see that there is no bright line between activities instrumentally necessary for virtue and those that are themselves constitutive of virtue and happiness. The virtue-and-happiness constitutive aspect of friendship is that it allows us to see who we are—individual and distinct human beings, "composite" embodied beings, subject not only to mortality but also to unexpected and unpredictable events and passions of many different kinds. This is why Aristotle says that philosophically informed *conversation* about our virtues and vices is the definitive activity of "perfect" friends (*NE*, 9.9, 1170b10–12). Virtue friendship is not a merging of the minds, but a process of conversation about our perceptions among friends.[32] We share perception, but this does not mean that we see exactly the same things; rather, we transform individual perceptions into a shared understanding through the activity of articulate speech, of conversation. Friendships are the constitutive condition of the most human activity, the activity of logos and of a prohairetic life. As Frank says, "Rather than a 'primordial' sharing, concord among virtue friends is a sharing of perceptions or a coming to a shared perception via speech."[33]

Another way of getting at the work of *philia* in a human life is to consider the statement in *Politics*, 7.13, 1332a–b that human beings become good and excellent through three things: nature, habit, and logos. The *oikos*, the family or household, is concerned with all three of these, but primarily with nature; the polis with all three, but primarily with habituation. The work, or *ergon*, of the primary kind of *philia* is conversation/logos with another self about our lives—such friendships are the interactions within which we can best reflect on our habits and our goals, the meaning and quality of our prohairetic lives. Primary friendships are therefore to practical reason and prohairetic life what *epieikeia* is to justice and the political life, a mode of distancing (from our own best selves in the case of friendship and from the *nomos* in the case of *epieikeia*) that opens the possibility of the life-long self-reflection and critique without which human virtue, in political praxis and in philosophical inquiry, is a dream. The unexamined life is not worth living for a human being, and the primary form of *philia* is one of the constitutive conditions of such examination.[34]

Friendship allows us to see ourselves, keeps us from our strong tendency to hide from ourselves, and so allows us to be, in our actuality *(energeia)* and our work *(ergon)* more fully human. This makes *philia* more than simply a necessary bridge from politics to philosophy, since without self-perception and self-understanding even the most self-sufficient of human virtues are subject to decay without our noticing. How could virtue or primary friendship, a self-aware partnership of logos and mind (*NE*, 9.9, 1170b10–12), provide such a service? Aristotle, characteristically, sketches the general idea and leaves the examples up to us. The talking that friends do, at its best, must be devoted to making their lives more prohairetic by helping one another avoid self-deception. Perhaps we think we are being brave when we are merely stubborn; or we think we are being equitable and just when we are merely self-abnegating; or we think we are being great-souled when we are merely snobbish; or we think we are spending time with the immortal things when we are simply avoiding caring for our friends or our polis. More generally, we may think we are acting nobly, for virtue's sake, but without awareness that our actions are becoming more and more instrumental, *pleonexia* rather than *prohairesis*. This is not a problem that affects other animals, nor one that troubles gods or fixed stars. It is the uniquely human problem that calls for friendship even in the otherwise most self-sufficient human beings.[35]

Aristotelian Friendship in the Context of Modernity

Relative to modern views of friendship, Aristotle's two-part account of what friends are for seems to be located somewhere between two modern extremes. The primary instance of *philia* is a dialogue about how best to live our life *(bios)* as a whole that in itself constitutes a central aspect of human virtue. The other kinds of *philia*, for pleasure and for advantage, are connected to primary friendship in two ways: as necessary conditions for human virtue, indispensable parts of a whole that is choiceworthy in itself, and points of departure for perfect or complete friendship. For Aristotle, *philia* is not a merely "aesthetic" or prerational attachment of limited moral significance, as it seems to be for Kant in the part of the *Metaphysics of Morals* where he sets out his doctrine of virtue.[36] But neither is it an intimate relationship of soul mates, a kind of unity through and in which we achieve true humanity, as it is for Montaigne and for romantic writers in general. Nor is it the kind of friendship (*l'amitié*) that is the central idea of Rousseau's *Julie*, a calm yet all-absorbing and enlivening openness (an "ecstatic immobility") to a few well-known others, a feeling quite distinct from the frenzied passion of *l'amour*, which allows friends to escape from the falseness of ordinary society into a world of perfect and essentially wordless mutual transparency: "After six days wasted in frivolous discussions with indifferent people, we have today spent a morning in the English manner, gathered in silence, enjoying at once the pleasure of being together and the bliss of contemplation. How few people know the delights of that state!"[37] The work of Aristotle's friendship is not consolation and reinforcement, nor is it the way to avoid the worst of all evils, the feeling of being alone in the universe. Its function is to make us better prohairetic beings by giving us an opportunity for conversations of a kind that are indispensable, when properly informed by an accurate philosophical understanding of the powers and the limits human being, for a more accurate sense of who, and where, we are. Primary friendship thus completes nature in the way that law and politics are said to do in the *Politics*. Moreover, the significance of politics and family life is best understood as a series of imperfect or partial friendships, attempts to remedy the weaknesses of our biologically inherited nature and to capitalize on its strengths.

In a similar vein, David O'Connor, using examples from both modern philosophy and the *endoxa* of modern American popular culture, presents the relationship of Aristotelian and modern friendship as a contrast between the modern ideal of "intimacy," in which the true friend is the one who both knows us thoroughly and approves of us unconditionally, and the Aristotelian ideal of "partnership" in some humanizing activity.[38] In the modern ideal the activity is secondary to the value of sheer togetherness, while for Aristotle intimacy is a necessary condition for the most important kinds of shared activity and not an end in itself. From Rousseau and Kant to the present, we might say that modern philosophy is of two minds concerning the transformative power of sheer togetherness or identity. Susan Shell, in a discussion of Kant and Nietzsche on friendship, puts the matter this way: "The insistence on a certain 'pathos of distance'—even, and perhaps especially within the bonds of friendship—provides a certain anticipatory, democratic answer to Nietzsche's later animadversions against the 'last men,' who like 'to rub against one another for warmth.' Indeed, there is in Kant's and Nietzsche's common fastidiousness a curious aesthetic convergence; both are nauseously repelled by common intimacies—Nietzsche, in the name of 'aristocracy,'

Kant in the name of a nobility consistent with equality."[39] Shell's comment brings out two central aspects of the modern view about friendship and the human good, the first an opinion, the second a mood: first, the rarely examined two-part opinion that true human virtue involves overcoming our nature as animals, and that such overcoming requires participation in a community that goes beyond politics and ordinary society; and second, the deep modern anxiety that friendship of the wrong kind can easily entrap us in nature's amoral and essentially dehumanizing snares.

Kant wishes to align his thought with Aristotle, misquoting him—as do Diogenes Laertius and Montaigne—as saying, "My dear friends, there is no such thing as a friend." This is an evident corruption of Aristotle's "Those who have many friends and treat everyone they encounter as intimates seem to be friends to no one, except in a political way" (*NE*, 9.10, 1171a15–17), and where he endorses the common saying that "one who has many friends has no friend" (*EE*, 7.12, 1245b20–22), saying that it is true in a way, but that our prayer for many friends is also in a way true.[40] Derrida, in *Politics of Friendship*, tries to have it both ways, recognizing the misquotation but asserting that both the apparently genuine Aristotle and the corrupt pseudo-Aristotelian maxim share a defining commitment to undemocratic ("phallogocentric" and "fraternal") exclusion, something that the best understanding of friendship must first systematically dismantle and then replace by an unprecedented form of human being together, one that requires the voice of prophecy rather than philosophy: "Is it possible to open up to the 'come' of a certain democracy which is no longer an insult to the friendship we have striven to think beyond the homo-fraternal and phallogocentric schema? . . . When will we be ready for an experience of freedom and equality that is capable of respectfully experiencing that friendship, which would at last be just, just beyond the law, and measured up against its measurelessness?"[41] In effect, Derrida reenacts the modern ambivalence toward this oceanic intimacy, an ambivalence before which philosophy seems to dissolve into second-hand prophecy.[42]

To what extent can we bring Aristotle into conversation with these modern conceptions of friendship? Perhaps the closest counterpart to the unconditional and transcendent intimacy modernity both seeks and fears in the Greek *endoxa* to which Aristotle responds might be erotic *philia*. Such *philia* is always sexually charged, but not only sexual—some relevant examples are Thucydides' Pericles' Funeral Oration on the erotic longing that should characterize Athenian citizenship, Thucydides himself on the Athenians erotic longing to conquer Sicily, and the erotic longing for the beings cited by Plato's Socrates in the *Republic* and other dialogues. For Aristotle, the troubling feature about this kind of *philia* is not that it is about sexual activity, but that it seems to be essentially overwhelming and unconditional. Erotic *philia* knows no reasonable bounds and so overwhelms *prohairesis*, as in the case of the erotic relationships in which the lover foolishly thinks he must do everything for the beloved and disregard the claims of everyone else.[43] For Aristotle, the problem about erotic *philia* is that it is unconditional, a quality that blinds us to the inevitable imperfections of composite beings such as we. Even the best of us can have our virtue overturned by illness, age, sudden weakness, a series of mistaken judgments, or simply accident; and what is true of us is also true of our friends. There is nothing magical or permanently transforming about even the best friendship; given the natural limitations of our species, it is not surprising that unconditional loyalty is not an Aristotelian moral virtue.[44]

Until very recently, few theorists, whether Aristotelian or not, have attempted to develop anything that resembles an Aristotelian conception of friendship in the context of modernity. One exception to this absence of modern voices recalling Aristotle's is, perhaps surprisingly, Hannah Arendt, who in general appears as an Aristotelian only to those who know little Aristotle. Certainly Arendt dismisses without reflection the species teleological understanding of nature that colors every page of Aristotle's practical philosophy. Despite this, however, Arendt develops a very Aristotelian conception of the meaning of friendship in her essay on Lessing, "On Humanity in Dark Times." What is relevant here is Arendt's insistence on the importance of separating friendship from brotherhood, from a sheer togetherness that trivializes our separate individuality and can provide strength to "pariah" people and other outcasts in times of despair and alienation. For Arendt, the kinds of being together that humanize our lives—as opposed to the links that preserve and fortify those lives—consist primarily of conversations among friends: "Gladness, not sadness, is talkative, and truly human dialogue differs from mere talk or even discussion in that it is entirely permeated by pleasure in the other person and what he says."⁴⁵ The core of her argument is that human beings cannot live genuinely human lives without friendships involving continued conversation and thought. Neither citizenship nor ethnic solidarity can provide the context for the sort of humanizing friendship Arendt sees exemplified in Lessing's life and in his play *Nathan the Wise*, which dramatizes the superiority of virtue friendships to sexual love, religious community, and familial as well as political identity.

Arendt stresses the distance that separates the ancient and modern ideals of friendship:

> We are wont to see friendship solely as a phenomenon of intimacy, in which the friends open their hearts to each other unmolested by the world and its demands. Rousseau, not Lessing, is the best advocate of this view, which conforms so well to the basic attitude of the modern individual, who in his alienation from the world can reveal himself only in privacy and in the intimacy of face-to-face encounters. Thus it is hard for us to understand the political relevance of friendship. When, for example, we read in Aristotle, that *philia* friendship among citizens is one of the fundamental requirements for the well-being of the City, we tend to think that he was speaking of no more than the absence of factions and civil war within it. But for the Greeks the essence of friendship consisted in discourse. They held that only the constant interchange of talk united citizens in a *polis*. . . . We humanize what is going on in the world and in ourselves only by speaking of it, and in the course of speaking of it we learn to be human.⁴⁶

Arendt here connects virtue friendship with civic friendship more completely than Aristotle would, and more than she herself does in other places in the essay. But even here it is clearly friendship and not citizenship that matters, a friendship of separate selves, engaging in the essentially humanizing activity of continued dialogue about themselves and their surroundings.

But as close as Arendt comes to an Aristotelian account of friendship, her theoretical modernity is reflected in her claim that friendship, like citizenship, lives in a continual tension with truthfulness, given "the possible antagonism between truth and humanity."⁴⁷ What distinguishes Aristotle from Arendt is his commitment to the view that *philia* is a path, however indirect and complex, to a variety of contingent truths about ourselves and our world, truths that lead beyond us toward a more adequate and accurate theoretical sense of the beings, including those beings more perfect than we are. Aristotle's dialogic friendship understood in this way is thus both a constitutive element of a well-lived prohairetic human life and a framework for inquiry that goes beyond humanity.

For Aristotle, friendship is not a substitute for philosophy, for learning and inquiry and reflection, and in this his account is sharply at odds with later conceptions of friendship. The heart of Aristotelian friendship is neither consolation nor transcendent unity, but conversation about the way particular friends live their lives. The quality of a friendship thus depends on the quality of the conversation that constitutes it, and so a friendship that fails to involve some degree of shared philosophizing is a poor thing indeed. But Aristotelian friendship is also more than a mere stepping-stone from the moral virtues and politics to philosophy. True friendship can never be superceded by philosophy because no human being is immortal and all human beings are continually compelled to choose among a variety of options; at the very least, even the most accomplished and fortunate of philosophers will confront the problem of when it is appropriate to philosophize and when other matters should come first—we should not make all sacrifices to Zeus. A well-lived prohairetic life has two constitutive elements, neither of which is of any use without the other. The first is the critical illumination philosophic activity, time spent with the immortal things, supplies. The second is the reflection on our own individual relationship to immortality and mortality that requires the conversation of a few good friends.

Notes

1. In general, the Greek *philia* is more inclusive than the English "friendship," but it also involves slightly different implications. Martha Nussbaum is helpful on this: "*philia* is extensionally wider than friendship—it takes in family relations, the relation between husband and wife, and erotic relationships, as well as what we would call 'friendship.' It is also, frequently, affectively stronger: it is a requirement of *philia* that partners should be linked by

affectionate feeling; and, as we see, *philia* includes the very strongest and most intimate of our affective ties. We can say that two people are 'just friends'; no such thing could be said with *philia*" (*The Fragility of Goodness: Luck and Ethics in Greek Tragedy and Philosophy* [Cambridge: Cambridge University Press, 2001], 329n, 354). While Aristotle includes erotic relations within the overall category of *philia*, as Nussbaum goes on to note, "Aristotle's choice of a central word reveals something about what he values in human relationships. For the emphasis of *philia* is less on intensely passionate longing than on disinterested benefit, sharing, and mutuality; less on madness than on a rare kind of balance and harmony." Translations from the Greek in this essay are my own, though greatly aided by Carnes Lord's translation of the *Politics* (Chicago: University of Chicago Press, 1984) and the second edition of Terence Irwin's translation of the *Nicomachean Ethics* (Indianapolis: Hackett Publishing, 1999).

2. In *Politics*, *philia* among citizens is a necessary condition for avoiding stasis, without which political life proper (*Politics*, 2.4, 1262b7–9)—ruling and being ruled in turn with an eye to the laws *(nomoi)*—cannot exist. In the *Poetics*, he says that playwrights have discovered that the best way to achieve the tragic effect (moving the audience to fear and pity) is by having the dangerous interactions occur among members of the same *philia* in the sense of family.

3. "Friendship is not of heaven but of the earth; the complete moral perfection of heaven must be universal; but friendship is not universal; it is a peculiar association of specific persons; it is man's refuge in this world from the distrust of his fellows. . . . Friendship develops the minor virtues of life" ("Friendship," in *Lectures on Ethics*, trans. Louis Infield [Indianapolis: Hackett Publishing, 1981], 206–7, 209). See also Kant's brief discussion of friendship as a duty in *Metaphysics of Morals*, §§46–47.

4. See especially his depiction of the best kind of friendship in *Julie*, pt. 5, letter 3.

5. For an illuminating contrast between Aristotle and Heidegger on friendship, see Robert Dostal, "Friendship and Politics: Heidegger's Failing," *Political Theory* 20 (August 1992): 399–423.

6. That is, undoubtedly treated as such by authors in the Western philosophical tradition.

7. Plato's Socrates, in *Republic*, 7, 518b–d, asserts that philosophic education is not like putting knowledge into empty souls; instead, true *paideia* is the *technê* of turning the soul toward the things that are, and especially toward the good. In *NE*, 2, 1103b26–29, Aristotle says that the point of *politikê* is making us better, not providing knowledge simply.

8. Lorraine Pangle, *Aristotle and the Philosophy of Friendship* (Cambridge: Cambridge University Press, 2003), 1.

9. See *EE*, 7, 1245a35: "*autos diaretos ho philos.*"

10. The *NE* as well as the *EE* want to "save the appearances," to bring out the truths that are contained in widely shared opinions and maxims, but the *EE* is more obviously concerned to avoid paradox, a clash with prevailing *doxa*. (For "paradox" in this sense, meaning countercultural rather than self-contradictory, see Socrates' remark in *Republic*, 5, 472a2–6, that he fears his logos that there will be no rest from ills for cities until philosophy and political power coincide will be seen as "paradoxical"). See *EE*, 7.2, especially 1236b21–26 on why asserting that there is a primary instance of *philia* (that among good people) should not rule out treating other kinds of apparent *philia* as real *philia* nonetheless: "To call this [primary friendship] alone friendship is to do violence to the phenomena and to compel oneself to speak paradoxes *(paradoxa legein anagkaion)*."

11. See my "Aristotle and the Ethics of Natural Questions," in *Instilling Ethics*, ed. Norma Thompson (Lanham, Md.: Rowman & Littlefield, 2000), 3–16, and "The Deliberative Model of Democracy and Aristotle's Ethics of Natural Questions," in *Aristotle and Modern Politics: The Persistence of Political Philosophy*, ed. Aristide Tessitore (Notre Dame: University of Notre Dame Press, 2002), 342–74. See also Thomas W. Smith, *Revaluing Ethics: Aristotle's Dialogical Pedagogy* (Albany: State University of New York Press, 2001); Aristide Tessitore, *Reading Aristotle's Ethics: Virtue, Rhetoric, and Political Philosophy* (Albany: State University of New York Press, 1996); Susan Collins, *Aristotle and the Rediscovery of Citizenship* (Cambridge: Cambridge University Press, 2006); and two essays by Gerald Mara, "The Near Made Far Away: The Role of Cultural Criticism in Aristotle's Political Theory" (*Political Theory* 23 [1995]: 280–303), and "The *Logos* of the Wise and the *Politeia* of the Many: Recent Books on Aristotle's Political Philosophy" (*Political Theory* 28 [2000]: 835–59).

12. Martha Nussbaum, "Aristotelian Social Democracy," in Tessitore, ed., *Aristotle and Modern Politics*, 50.

13. In my discussion of Aristotle on *philia*, I treat the *NE* and the *Politics* as two parts of a connected series of lectures on *politikê*. Thus my focus is on the *NE* rather than on the *EE*. Nevertheless, I refer to the treatment of *philia* in *EE*, 7 for clarification. In general, I think Aristotle's substantive position in *EE*, 7 is much the same as in *NE*, 8 and 9—the primary difference between the two seems to be that the *EE* is more direct and more theoretical than the *NE*, perhaps indicating a less subtle and Platonic understanding of the relation between theory and practice than the greater richness and indirection of the *NE* embodies. While I am not persuaded by Anthony Kenny that the *EE* is more maturely Aristotelian than the *NE*, I do think he is right to notice it is closer in style to modern analytic philosophy than is the Nicomachean version: "As it happens, many of the features which scholars have noted as characteristic of the Eudemian books in contrast to the Nicomachean—a greater interest in the

rigorous presentation of argument and a lesser interest in the dramatic portrayal of character... these are features in which contemporary analytic fashion accords more closely with the interests and positions of the Eudemian than with the Nicomachean version of Aristotle's system" (*The Aristotelian Ethics: A Study of the Relationship between the Eudemian and Nicomachean Ethics of Aristotle* [Oxford: Clarendon Press, 1978], 4).

14. Aristotle's use of the word *prohairesis* to name the central activity of human beings is an innovation, though the word itself does appear occasionally in earlier Greek philosophic texts (for example, Plato, *Parmenides*, 143c). *Hairesis* by itself signifies choice; add the prefix *pro-* and you have a premeditated choice, choosing this rather than that. For a good discussion of "prohairetic activity" in Aristotle, see Jill Frank, *Democracy of Distinction: Aristotle and the Work of Politics* (Chicago: University of Chicago Press, 2005), 32–38.

15. In *Politics*, 1 Aristotle argues that we are political animals because we are the only animals to have the capacity to use language to articulate and reflect on what is good for us. Other animals have voice *(phônê)*, and so can indicate pleasure and pain to one another, but we alone have the reflective power he indicates by the word "logos." Owing to this power of articulate and rational speech human individuals can become either the best or the worst of animals. Such a power requires discipline if it is not to become a resource for tyranny and injustice, and the practice of politics, the activity of ruling and being ruled in turn with an eye to the laws of the city, is the humanly discovered remedy for our potential to abuse our rational power. The logos power that Aristotle identifies as human reason is thus quite distinct from Hobbesian instrumental reason, and also from Kantian reason, the capacity for transcending nature to give ourselves universal laws to follow.

16. The other leading candidate would be his statement in book 10 that we should "as far as we can, spend time with the immortal things [this is Arendt's rendering of Aristotle's *athanatizein;* I prefer it to "immortalize" or Irwin's "be pro-immortal"] and do everything we can to live according to the strongest of the things in us" (*NE*, 1177b33–34). This, to be sure, is also a question—just how far can we go toward living in the manner of the permanently actualized unmoved movers of Aristotle's cosmology? What are our powers? What other demands on us are there? The question, however, is as relevant for political people as for those not so fully involved in political life; Aristotle repeats it in book 7 of the *Politics* after setting out yet again the difference between *phronêsis* and theoretical reason: "For what is always most choiceworthy for each individual is the highest it is possible for them to achieve" (1333a29–30).

17. Note that Aristotle does *not* say, here or anywhere else, that the *prohairesis* that results in vice isn't really *prohairesis* at all. Bad people have

thoughtfully chosen badness just as good people have thoughtfully chosen goodness. What is crucial is that bad people are generally *unaware* that their thoughtful choice is bad: "as a whole, weakness of will *(akrasia)* and badness *(kakia)* are different kinds; for badness is unrecognized *(lanthanei)*, but weakness of will is not unrecognized" (*NE*, 1150b35–36). This statement in book 7 indicates, in advance, the human problem to which the primary kind of *philia* is a solution.

18. In saying live well *as human beings,* I stress Aristotle's way of framing moral or practical questions. For him, the moral point of view, the point of view that takes life seriously, is not that of empathic utilitarian altruists or of autonomous rational beings, but of people who want to live their lives as much in accord with specifically human excellence or virtue as possible.

19. As long as this priority of whole to part is established, it is not crucial (given his stated concern with making us better as opposed to theorizing as an end in itself) whether Aristotle establishes that priority, as in the *NE,* by saying that virtue friendship has the properties of all friendships to a higher degree than the others (1157a25–32), or by saying, as in the *EE,* that the other kinds of friendships all "point toward" virtue friendship in the manner of a *pros hen* or *pros mian* (toward one) equivocal (1236a15–20), in the same way that all beings point toward the primary instance of being, namely, perfectly actualized being. As in several other instances, Aristotle seems to opt, in the *NE,* to present his *politikê* in terms that are less dependent on knowledge of Aristotelian theory than he does in the *EE.*

20. In the *NE, philia* first appears in 4.6, as similar to a nameless moral virtue of social life or living together *(suzên),* a disposition to be neither ingratiating nor grouchy in the speeches and affairs of everyday life. By calling attention to this virtue's namelessness, Aristotle may be indicating that most Greeks take it less seriously than he thinks they should. He begins book 8 by saying that *philia* "is some virtue or with virtue, and moreover is most necessary for a way of life *[bios]*" (1155a3–5).

21. Speaking of the primary kind of *philia,* that of good people, he says in the *EE* that "this occurs in human beings only, because only human beings are aware of prohairesis; but the other kinds [of *philia*] also occur among beasts" (1236b5–7).

22. See Nussbaum, *Fragility of Goodness,* 355n.

23. "Emergent phenomenon" is a recent term for something well known to Aristotle and absolutely central to his understanding of nature, but dismissed by reductionist modern physics—wholes that are more than the sum of their parts.

24. Nancy Sherman, *Making a Necessity of Virtue: Aristotle and Kant on Virtue* (Cambridge: Cambridge University Press, 1997), 190. See also Stephen R. L. Clark, *Aristotle's Man: Speculations upon Aristotelian Anthropology*

(Oxford: Clarendon Press, 1975), 110: "We grow in community, partly because our friends assist us in the making of our identities, partly because having friends is to be introduced to a wider world."

25. Alasdair MacIntyre's commentary on the relationship of selfishness and altruism to virtue is sharply Aristotelian: "We do indeed as infants, as children, and even as adolescents, experience sharp conflicts between egoistic and altruistic impulses and desires. But the task of education is to transform and integrate those into an inclination towards both the common good and individual goods, so that we become neither self-rather-than-other-regarding nor other-rather-than-self-regarding, neither egoists nor altruists, but those whose passions and inclinations are directed to what is both our good and the good of others. Self-sacrifice, it follows, is as much of vice, as much of a sign of inadequate moral development, as selfishness" (*Dependent Rational Animals: Why Human Beings Need the Virtues* [Chicago: Open Court, 1999], 160). Glaucon and Adeimantus, at the beginning of *Republic*, 2, provide a wonderful example of this adolescent dilemma of the war between selfishness and altruism, and Plato's Socrates in the rest of the *Republic* represents one attempt at education of the kind MacIntyre describes.

26. Consider the differences between Aristotle's irreducibly complex prohairetic self and Hegel's conception of the irreducibly complex modern autonomous self, the man who has a foot in three camps—family, civil society, and state. Hegel's self requires no independent theorizing to be free (since the final results of this inquiry have been actualized and realized in the constitution of the modern state); the political community, the state, has become clearly the preeminent human community, thanks to its absorption of the theoretical truths implicit in Protestant Christianity. It is now possible to specify the boundary lines separating the three essential communities whose interaction in human souls gives rise to an autonomous life.

27. Pangle, *Aristotle and the Philosophy of Friendship*, 79.

28. See ibid., 197–98.

29. Aristotle introduces this methodological distinction very early in the *Eudemian Ethics*, while elaborating his thesis that everyone who is to live according to their own *prohairesis* should establish a telos at which to aim in the actions of their lives:

> It is especially necessary first to determine for oneself, neither recklessly nor lazily, in which of the human things living well consists, and without which of these things it is not possible for human beings to possess living well. For the things without which being healthy is impossible and being healthy are not the same, and this holds similarly with many other things. And it is necessary not to overlook these things, for they are the causes of the disputes about what being happy

is, and about the things necessary for becoming happy; for some people believe that those things without which it is not possible to be happy are parts of happiness. (*EE*, 1.2, 1214b11–27)

30. One of the clearest deployments of this distinction is at *Politics*, 3, 1283a14–22. Aristotle's distinction between necessary and constitutive conditions implies a continuum—some things are more like necessary conditions, others more constitutive of happiness—rather than a rigid dichotomy. This is very much in line with the way he uses his distinction between potentiality and actuality more generally.

31. Pangle, *Aristotle and the Philosophy of Friendship*, 197–98.

32. Jill Frank makes this argument using these terms in *Democracy of Distinction*, 160.

33. Ibid.

34. This point is made explicitly in the *Magna Moralia*, an incomplete Aristotelian (though perhaps not written by Aristotle) treatise on many of the same themes as the *EE* and *NE*. In the *MM*, 2.15, 1212b24–1213a26, the author argues that even the most self-sufficient human being will need virtue friends, since our self-awareness is inevitably distorted by our good will toward or strong feelings in favor of ourselves. Just as we need a mirror to see our bodies, so even the best and most self-sufficient of us need friends to help us understand ourselves as we truly are. For discussion of this passage, see John Cooper, "Friendship and the Good in Aristotle," reprinted in Cooper, *Reason and Emotion: Essays on Ancient Moral Psychology and Ethical Theory* (Princeton: Princeton University Press, 1999), 340–43. For discussion of the authorship of the *Magna Moralia* and its relation to Aristotle's practical philosophy, see Cooper, "The *Magna Moralia* and Aristotle's Moral Philosophy," in *Reason and Emotion*, 195–211.

35. In thinking through the question of how to fill in the gaps in Aristotle's argument in *NE*, 9.9, I have found Cooper's "Friendship and the Good in Aristotle" especially helpful. He argues there that, for Aristotle, the place of primary friendship in human life is twofold: to widen individual horizons and to make possible a level of self-criticism that individuals cannot achieve on their own.

36. See Immanuel Kant, *Groundwork of the Metaphysics of Morals*, trans. and ed. Mary Gregor (Cambridge: Cambridge University Press, 1998), 215–17.

37. This is from St. Preux's description of the small circle of intimates at Clarens in Rousseau's *Julie, or The New Heloise*, trans. Philip Stewart and Jean Vaché (Hanover, N.H.: University Press of New England, 1997), pt. 5, letter 3, 456.

38. David K. O'Connor, "Two Ideals of Friendship," *History of Philosophy Quarterly* 7 (April 1990): 109–22.

39. Susan Shell, *Embodiment of Reason: Kant on Spirit, Generation, and Community* (Chicago: University of Chicago Press, 1996), 160.

40. See Pangle, *Aristotle and the Philosophy of Friendship*, 193 and 240 n.24.

41. Jacques Derrida, *Politics of Friendship*, trans. George Collins (New York: Verso, 1997), 306.

42. Thus self-described postmodernity and post-Christianity dissolves yet again into a stale version of what it purports to have successfully deconstructed. On Derrida's debt to Christianity, see Pangle, *Aristotle and the Philosophy of Friendship*, 192. For the biblical traditions, the most important human interactions and communities are those that link human beings to God. The sense of transcendence and triumph over mortality is also present in those philosophers who spring from, though claim no reliance upon, Christianity—think of Kant's community of ends in themselves, of Marx's species-beings, of Nietzsche's ahistorical community of the great who recognize and "call to" one another across the centuries in *Advantage and Disadvantage of History for Life*. For these writers, a transcendently autonomous being slumbers in the lap of natural man, as it were, and the business of philosophy is to trace the path from nature to an entirely humanly created community and way of life, one that emerges from but goes beyond our merely biologically inherited nature. On the other hand, those philosophers who more clearly reject the authority of the Christian church as a guide to moral and political philosophy and build their systems on modern reductive physical science instead tend, like Hobbes, to treat all human communities as being fundamentally unstable and unreal, when compared with the power and reality of individual self-interest or, like Locke, to redescribe all human relationships as contracts made to enhance the length and security and freedom of individual human life and not to transform it. What these two approaches to friendship share is a belief that the worst of all human evils is death (and not, say, the danger of committing grave injustice, or of acting out of great stupidity or prejudice about the world, dangers the threat of which Plato and Aristotle are both at great pains to evoke in their audience), and all our efforts should be devoted to building a world in which death is somehow transcended; and if this is impossible or too dependent on unempirical mystery, then the best solution is to follow Hobbes and Locke (who proceeds by reimaging all communities as reducible without loss of meaning to contracts among individual members of the community) in attempting to design a regime in which life would be as far as possible protected from the internal fights that are life's greatest enemy.

43. As Aristotle puts it, "Those who give everything to their beloved (*eromenos*) are worthless" (*EE*, 7.11, 1244a19–20).

44. See Pangle, *Aristotle and the Philosophy of Friendship*, 137–41, especially on what she sees as the difference between Aristotle and at least some

versions of Christianity: "The most thoroughgoing rejection of Aristotle's teaching about the necessary conditionality of human love is found in the Christian injunction to 'love thy neighbor.'" In *NE*, 9.2, 1165b13–36, Aristotle discusses the problem of what to do when someone you have befriended for their virtue seems to have become bad. The first thing to do is to try to rescue them—that is, after all, what human friends are for. But if that fails, then it makes sense to break the friendship, though with regret and retaining the memory of past friendship sufficient to require that we "accord something to past friends because of our former friendship, whenever it is not excessive vice (hyperbolic *mochthêria*) that causes the dissolution." On Aristotle's rejection of an unconditional duty to one's political community, see Gerald Mara, "The Culture of Democracy: Aristotle's *Athênaiôn Politeia* as Political Theory," in Tessitore, ed., *Aristotle and Modern Politics*, 307–41, esp. 329–32.

45. "On Humanity in Dark Times: Thoughts about Lessing," in *Men in Dark Times* (San Diego: Harcourt Brace Jovanovich, 1955), 15.

46. Ibid., 24–25.

47. Ibid., 28. On the need to think very carefully about that "possible antagonism," see Arendt's "Truth and Politics" (arguing that a commitment to truth is a necessary condition for good politics, precisely because in political life the humanly created "world" matters more than the truth that is independent of human effort ["Truth and Politics," in Arendt, *Between Past and Future* (New York: Viking, 1977), 227–64]), and her "Philosophy and Politics" (arguing that a Socratic commitment to discover the truth in private is a necessary condition, or preliminary moment, for the emancipatory political life ["Philosophy and Politics," *Social Research* 57 (1990): 73–103]).

3

Cicero's Distinctive Voice on Friendship

De Amicitia and *De Re Publica*

Walter Nicgorski

Friendship was provided by nature as an aide to virtue, not an accomplice in wickedness; so it is that no solitary virtue but only one deeply allied with the other [friendship] can attain the greatest of goods. But if there be such a union, or if there ever was one or ever will be one, it must be regarded as the best and happiest alliance toward the highest good of nature. (*De Amicitia*, 83)

The model of friendship, so beautifully described in these words of Cicero,[1] could be seen as a rival to politics. Politics in the classical sense was especially oriented to "the highest good of nature." Aristotle, who systematically articulated the dominant classical understanding of political life, located his treatise of friendship in a richly significant way at the very heart of his practical philosophy. The obvious places to turn in pursuing how Cicero understands friendship and its relationship to politics is to his two writings explicitly devoted to friendship and politics or justice, *De Amicitia* and *De Re Publica*.² One can, of course, ask about this relationship from the side of politics. Does Cicero's teaching on friendship (assuming for now that there is one to be found) complement and enrich what might be learned from *De Re Publica*? Does it help to remove or does it contribute to difficulties that have at times posed obstacles to seeing Cicero as a coherent and worthy political thinker?

A notably fragmented work that was lost sometime during the fifth or sixth century, *Re Publica* was first recovered in that partial form early in the nineteenth century. It is the primary source for those important themes in the history of political theory often associated with Cicero's thought.³

Re Publica can be described as presenting the macropolitics of Cicero, the large question of right political form and the necessary moral underpinnings of a justice anchored in nature. Not only is Cicero's writing this work along with *De Legibus (Leg.)* broadly and consciously imitative of Plato's project in his *Republic* and *Laws*, but Cicero also confesses that he takes his fundamental principles about politics from Plato.⁴ *Re Publica* takes as its starting point the question of the best constitution, a topic at least suggested by a dominant motif of Plato's *Republic*. Yet if *Re Publica* is seen as moving the focus, in the light of the Roman experience of political development, from the large question of right form to the agents of that development and of potential development, a shift of attention occurs from a model or best constitution to the model statesman, and with that shift all that pertains to the preparation and education of such a statesman becomes centrally relevant.⁵ There are clear indications in what little remains of the missing books 4 and 5 of *Re Publica* that the kind of family life and education requisite for statesmanship was a major concern in these writings. What is missing here on education might plausibly be found in what we have on the education of the orator in Cicero's *De Oratore* and in the direction Cicero later gives his son and other young men in *De Officiis*.

It is less clear that friendship's role in nurturing statesmen—and thus friendship itself—received any specific treatment in the lost portions of *Re Publica*. Thus *Amicitia*, the explicit treatise on friendship that follows approximately a decade later,⁶ may be intended as a significant step toward the completion of Cicero's political theory. Though friendship may not have been a topic treated in the lost portions of *Re Publica*, the operation and example of friendship is everywhere in evidence in both these works under consideration. Furthermore there are ties between the works that invite an effort at interpreting each in the light of the other.

Affinities and Explicit Links

On the surface, there are notable affinities between *Amicitia* and *Re Publica* that suggest a special relationship between these works. Both are presented as conversations or dialogues that Cicero reports in the prologues as having been told to him by one of the minor figures actually present at the conversations. No other of Cicero's dialogues have this form of entrée into the reported conversation.[7] This form establishes Cicero's direct connection with Publius Scipio Aemilianus Africanus the Younger and Gaius Laelius, the principal figures in each work and that attractive pair of political leaders from the previous century. They were thought to have endeavored to bring Greek learning into relationship with successful Roman practice, an effort later associated with Cicero himself. Except for very minor roles assigned to them in *De Senectute*, written in the months immediately preceding the writing of *Amicitia*, Cicero uses the personas of Scipio and Laelius only in the two works under consideration in this essay.[8]

Besides their distinction for political leadership, Laelius and Scipio were also legendary for their exemplary friendship. While being the central figures and primary interlocutors in *Re Publica*, their friendship is explicitly noted there and shown in operation.[9] They are also, in a sense, the primary spokesmen in *Amicitia*. I must write "in a sense" because Scipio is present only virtually, having died or been murdered only a few days before the reported discussion takes place. He is present—though virtually—insofar as it is his legendary friendship with Laelius, a friendship now disrupted by his death, that provides the occasion within the dialogue for taking up its main topic. Scipio is present in the discussion in another more direct way, for at several points Laelius reports, as a friend would be inclined, what Scipio said in earlier conversations with him. So in effect, *Amicitia* presents a discourse of Laelius on friendship that likely is informed by his conversations as well as his experiences with Scipio and that explicitly incorporates certain views and observations of Scipio. Note must be taken also that the two younger men actually present with Laelius in *Amicitia* are his sons-in-law who have come in concern for his well being and to comfort him in these days after the loss of his dearest friend. These sons-in-law, Gaius Fannius and Quintus Mucius Scaevola, the augur, were also in the circle of friends gathered earlier around Scipio and Laelius in *Re Publica*.

Could it have been quite incidental that Cicero turned for his account of true friendship and all that entails to the same two historical figures utilized in his earlier account of the best or true constitution? Several major writings and approximately ten years intervened between his completing *Re Publica* and his writing *Amicitia*, which occurred in those prolific last years of his life. There are good Ciceronian grounds for his having selected the same spokesmen for what might be regarded as essentially distinct topics: his privileged spokesman or teacher on any topic is that person who has notable experience with what is to be discussed. That principle was brought forward strongly in both his prologue to and book 1 of *Re Publica*. As Cicero's own as well as Scipio's political experience gives them claim for attention, especially over against Greek talkers and theorists held suspect by Roman audiences, so when Cicero turned to treat friendship, these two historical figures, having the reputation of exemplary experience in friendship must have seemed the right ones.[10] Perhaps there is nothing more to be said about the fact of the central roles for Laelius and Scipio in these two works.

The affinity, however, between *Amicitia* and *Re Publica* seems to be drawn tighter and becomes more interesting when we notice their dramatic settings. It then becomes less plausible that Cicero's use of the same central figures is simple coincidence, as one might, in the context of the American republic, use George Washington in a story about truth-telling on one occasion and use him on another occasion as an exemplar of self-restraint with respect to the holding of power (for example, the two-term tradition). *Re Publica*'s discussion of the best constitution and all that entails is set in the year 129 before the mysterious death of Scipio; *Amicitia*, as already noted, is set just days after his death. What joins the two occasions in Cicero's narrative of that year is the final and long-treasured part of *Re Publica*, the Dream of Scipio.

Scipio's dream, which he shares with Laelius and other friends at the climax of his political inquiry, pictures his ascending from earth through heavenly spheres in the manner of one who has earned both liberation from this earth and reward above. In the course of this ascent and gaining of perspective, he is instructed by his ancestors in the way to eternal happiness and the nature of that happiness available in the afterlife. Beyond awe and delight, Scipio's understandable reaction to what he beholds is to want to move promptly from this world to the state now revealed to him. Even as earthly life and its achievements seem so small and insignificant, he is restrained by the image of his father with words about duty to the political community on this earth where Scipio and Laelius still live: "Thus Publius [Scipio] you and all good men *[piis omnibus]* must maintain the soul in the custody of the body, and only at the command of him who granted it to you, ought you be drawn away from human life lest the human duty *[munus humanum]* assigned by god be neglected."[11] It was then not long after and not through his own pious will but, it seems, in accord with his deepest yearnings that Scipio's life was ended. That this was to happen is, of course, a fact known to the reader of *Re Publica* and that it happened produces the looming physical absence as *Amicitia* begins.

Cicero does not leave the role of the Dream between the two works simply to the readers' noticing. He is explicit in bringing it to mind early in the first extended speech of *Amicitia*, what has fairly been called Laelius's "generalized encomium of friendship."[12] Reflecting on Scipio's death at a peak in a life of noble accomplishments, and expressing confidence that he has gone to join the gods rather than infernal beings, Laelius indicates that he cannot assent (using the terminology of the skepticism of the New Academy,[13] *Neque enim assentior . . .*) to the view, relatively new in the history of human experience, that the soul dies with the body, and this death brings total destruction (13). In the course of noting that the ancestral view of life after death is contrary to this clearly Epicurean view, Laelius mentions that he stands on the matter of immortality and reward and punishment after death with that man deemed wisest by Apollo's oracle. In *Amicitia*, this is already the second reference of three to Socrates, without direct mention of his name but in association with the oracle's assessment of him. Socrates' opinion was that of Scipio, reports Laelius, and he offers as some evidence of that claim the Dream of Scipio, which he specifically notes as following upon Scipio's discussion of the political community *(disseruit de re publica)*.

Shortly after this direct link to *Re Publica's* Dream of Scipio, at the end of Laelius's encomium though still at the stage when this "dialogue" is being set up and launched, there is a second explicit link to *Re Publica* (*Amic.*, 25).[14] The reference is to Laelius's defense of justice *(justitia)* as grounded in nature. It occurs in this way: Laelius's sons-in-law suggest there is something about his character that gave his encomium on friendship a special "feel" *(aliud quoddam filum);* his defense of justice in *Re Publica* is pointed to as having the same character that is then explained as being related to Laelius's being a just man.[15] Might not then a man who is an exceptional friend speak most wisely and effectively about friendship? Such a suggestion, already noted as a familiar theme in Cicero— namely the notion that experienced achievers in any realm of human endeavor are especially to be heard—hardly exhausts the tie between friendship and justice that is intimated. Laelius is in fact specifically praised for maintaining friendship marked by justice.[16]

What sense then might we make of these two explicit ties linking *Amicitia* to *Re Publica,* ties that entail direct references to Scipio's likely story or dream about immortality and Laelius's defense of justice? Is the prominence given those two important parts of *Re Publica* a strong suggestion or pointer that they are as important to the nature of true friendship as they are to a good constitution? And perhaps in addition, are justice and immortality critical concepts to integrating friendship with politics? This seems to be where we are left after an exploration of the surface affinities and explicit links between *Amicitia* and *Re Publica.*

A Notable Difference: Suppression of the Greeks

Besides affinities and links between these two works, there is a notable surface difference. In contrast to *Re Publica* and his other philosophical works, Cicero in *Amicitia* makes no direct reference to Greek treatments of its topic. No philosopher is named, much less explicitly engaged while being in an overall sense imitated and deferred to, as is Plato in *Re Publica*. There is no Carneades invoked, as he is when skeptical challenges are put to the very idea of justice in *Re Publica;* there is no Polybius or Panaetius singled out as a Greek teacher of or Greek source for the thinking of Scipio and Laelius as is done in *Re Publica*.

What we find in *Amicitia* is a form of suppression of the Greeks or, at the least in Powell's words "a diffidence about naming Greek sources."[17] This is not to claim that there is no evidence at all of the immense Greek learning and knowledge of the Greeks that Cicero possessed. Yet what is allowed to emerge in this work, aside from the indirect or nonexplicit references to philosophers and the philosophical schools of Greece, is clearly subdued or very limited, what would seem to be a minimum one might expect from an educated Roman, that is, some knowledge of Greek history, literature, and mythology.[18] In this respect, it is worthy of note that Cicero does not explicitly name the "three or four" legendary friendships into whose company he wishes to place that Roman exemplar of the friendship between Scipio and Laelius.[19] These other classic friendships are all those of Greeks, and when at another point in *Amicitia* (24) Cicero's Laelius wishes to illustrate a point with a tale about one pair of these legendary Greek friends, Orestes and Pylades, he does so by explicitly crediting for the tale the Roman playwright Pacuvius, identified as a friend of Laelius.

Given the subdued and, one might say, almost Roman character of *Amicitia*'s Greek references, one might indeed suspect, as Powell suggests with his comparison to Cicero's speeches,[20] that *Amicitia* is to have a public character somewhat different from Cicero's longer and more elaborate philosophical writings. Perhaps there is some reason for this work being even more sensitive than Cicero usually is to the apparent political liability and pedagogical obstacle caused by a manifest indebtedness to the Greeks.[21] At this point (the year 44), however, direct political ambition seems to have been displaced in Cicero's life by an intense dedication to writing and above all philosophical writing. What can certainly be concluded from this seeming suppression of the Greeks in *Amicitia* is that there is more evidence of it and apparent effort at it than in *Re Publica* written earlier and in *Senectute* and *Officiis* written at roughly the same time. Is there, then, something about the topic of friendship either in the capacity or need of Romans that has led to the more emphatic Roman character of *Amicitia?*

Left, perhaps, at the limits of reasonable speculation on the general treatment of the Greeks in *Amicitia,* let us look more closely at what must be considered the most remarkable type of the suppression of the Greeks in this work. This is with respect to Greek philosophers; the contrast of this dimension to *Re Publica* was already highlighted above. What makes this especially remarkable is that *Amicitia* takes the form of a philosophical dialogue focused on a classically formulated philosophical question: What is friendship? It is a question to which Greek philosophy at least as far back as Socrates/Plato to the schools of Epicurus and Stoa in Cicero's own day has spoken, usually directly. Though one recognizes in *Amicitia* points and observations that have appeared in the extant work of Plato and Aristotle,[22] and though some scholars speculate that *Amicitia*'s chief source is a lost work of Theophrastus, Aristotle's successor as head of the Peripatetic school, and some note his quite direct dependence on words from Xenophon's *Memorabilia,*[23] there is no naming of any Greek philosopher or source or school of thought in Cicero's text. There is neither direct engagement of any thinker nor explicit deference to any in any respect at all. Rather, indirection is always the mode used, even in those three distinct references (7, 10, 13) to Socrates. Each time, he is described as the man "judged the wisest of men" by the oracle of Apollo. In none of those instances is any direct Socratic/Platonic teaching on friendship involved.

What sense, if only provisional, can be made of this stand of Cicero on the philosophical heritage regarding the topic of friendship? Perhaps the Roman practice of friendship, manifest in various forms but exemplified at its peak by Scipio and Laelius and now by Cicero and Atticus, is being elevated over mere theorizing about friendship. Cicero then may be seeking to focus attention on the issues and level of achievement entailed in this practice. He may indeed find such a focus not only suits his audience particularly well, but also yields a more realistic and reliable teaching about friendship. Powell sensibly remarks that what is striking to him is *Amicitia*'s exemplification of Cicero's often-proclaimed independence of judgment: what matters to Cicero in the case of any philosophical idea about friendship is not whether it is Stoic or Peripatetic, but whether it will stand up to analysis and examination on its own merits.[24] Earlier, another student of *Amicitia,* Thomas Habinek, concluded a study of the dialogue by warning those hunting and scavenging in the writings of Cicero for sources in Hellenistic philosophy that "the characteristic feature and, I believe, greatest virtue" of Cicero's texts is "their deep engagement with Roman culture."[25] I proceed then from these initial investigations with every effort to be open to Cicero's distinctive voice, a voice not reducible to Greek sources or mindlessly eclectic in utilizing them. There is already ample reason to be expecting a voice reflecting Cicero's deep engagement with Roman culture and perhaps the peculiar needs as well as potential strengths of that culture. There is also the expectation of a voice that reflects Cicero's reputed allegiance to the New Academy, the school of Socratic Academic skepticism with its commitment to the testing of alleged truths, whether of Greek or Roman origins, at the bar of experience.

What Then Is Friendship?

Do the surface affinities, explicit links, and the notable difference between *Amicitia* and *Re Publica* amount to anything significant? Might they be leads to a larger thematic unity between the two works and thus to a greater understanding of the mind of Cicero respecting politics? These are the leading questions as I turn to the treatment of friendship in *Amicitia.* Here a methodological note is appropriate: whatever Cicero may have intended or not intended regarding the relation between these two works, a matter on which we can only speculate, reading the works together or, more precisely in respect to the case at hand, interpreting *Amicitia* against the background of *Re Publica,* becomes an occasion for a greater understanding of Cicero's thinking.

When asked directly to give his view of the nature of friendship and guidelines concerning it, Laelius (16) backs away from anything like a philosophical discussion or disputation—the characteristic approach, in his words, of learned men and Greeks. This move, along with the brevity and sweep of what immediately follows, warrants that first speech being called a "generalized encomium." Laelius clearly starts off in this direction, saying that all he is capable of doing is urging his listeners to put friendship first among all human things, nothing being more natural *(aptum naturae)* or more useful in both the favorable and unfavorable developments of life (17). These words and what follows in the next seven sections (18–24) might well be viewed as a phenomenology of friendship, that is, descriptions of ways in which it appears and thus a wholly appropriate approach—appropriate to entering on a philosophical inquiry—to the topic of friendship. Perhaps what is being undertaken is not so unphilosophical after all. Only two paragraphs after his initial refusal to undertake a philosophical discussion, Laelius is found offering a definition of friendship (20), thus responding directly to the key question (16) put to him and one in the form of a classic philosophical question, "What is this thing called friendship?"

Once Laelius launches forth, it is clear that we do not have in *Amicitia* anything like a philosophical disputation in the sense of an encounter marked by the pressing give-and-take of dialectic. Nor could we call what now unfolds a rhetorical dialogue in which opposing speeches are made, as in Cicero's *De Finibus.* Instead, Laelius speaks quite continuously to the end of *Amicitia.* The interventions by his sons-in-law are very brief and are not at all in the form of objections or challenges to Laelius. They are rather requests and exhortations for Laelius to go on and to say more, and in each case he responds positively at once. In effect, *Amicitia* can hardly be called a dialogue at all; it has some of the trappings but none of the substance of real exchange or conversation. The body of *Amicitia* can be seen as one long speech that in successive waves reveals ever more of what Laelius (and Scipio) thinks about the nature of friendship and the implications of striving to live in friendship. Thus, what is called the first speech or encomium might be regarded as the introduction or overview to a single long speech, an introduction in which the phenomenon of friendship as seen by Laelius is put before the reader to be further explored in the remainder of his discourse. The introduction or overview touches on all important aspects of what Cicero, through Laelius, has to say about friendship and thus becomes a convenient way, as in a prospectus, to overview the teaching that unfolds throughout the entire speech.

The definition of friendship (20), as indicated early in this overview, seems an appropriate ground from which to proceed. It is never abandoned or significantly revised in what follows in *Amicitia;* it is simply elaborated or "unpacked" as some might say. "Friendship," says Laelius, "is nothing other than an agreement *[consensio]* on all things human and divine, an agreement accompanied by good will *[benevolentia]* and affection *[caritate]*." Recalling at this point from *Re Publica* (1.39) the definition of the republic or political community *(res publica)* as a "joining of many people through an agreement on right and common interest" *(juris consensu et utilitate communione sociatus),* notice should be taken of the role of consent in both communities. Friendship clearly runs deeper and demands more in calling for agreement on the very nature of things. Justice plus ontology would apparently be most productive of good will and affection.

The second part of the sentence in which friendship is defined contains Laelius's observation that friendship is the greatest gift of the gods to humankind save for wisdom *(sapientia).* This observation in such a prominent position is especially notable in three respects. First, it echoes Cicero's affirmation elsewhere that philosophy is the greatest gift of the gods to humans.[26] Second, it seems to be the most fundamental statement by Laelius as to the ranking of friendship among human goods and should govern interpretations of other statements of praise for friendship. In one such observation already noted here, Laelius says friendship should be put first among human things, but this and other such statements can be seen to assume what is made explicit at this moment, that philosophy and wisdom are excepted and not among such merely human things. Third, it should be said that there is simply good sense in the exception for or elevation of wisdom. How could one possibly praise friendship among all human things if one did not reflect on friendship and in fact on the human condition? Wisdom in some form is the condition of any assessment of friendship. Laelius's praise for friendship does not entail a diminishment of philosophy.

Friendship is so elevated because it is said to be both in accord with nature and very beneficial in good and bad times. That it is natural in a sense of fulfilling and delighting rather than being useful or expedient in satisfying our ordinary human needs and wants is one of the great themes of this work as it is of Cicero's overall understanding of human sociality.[27] For Laelius and Cicero, good human beings seek to follow nature, and with respect to human relationships (19), nature, in the form of our elemental needs, brings us first into families and nations and appears to create a certain but infirm bond of friendship in these communities. Laelius remarks that these relationships will persist even if they are without good will and thus do not sustain the level of a true friendship. In accord with this view, Cicero in his *De Officiis,* indicates that friendship is the most satisfying of human relationships, but our most compelling human duties are those related to the familial and political communities in which we are embedded.[28]

It is nature, according to Laelius (26–27), that points from the beginning beyond our biological origins and need for physical security toward something deeper and nobler *(antiquior et pulchrior).* Nature's way apparently includes this more subtle and profound inclination. The truly first thing that brings people together is more an attachment or attunement of the soul to what is good than need or weakness *(imbecillitatem atque inopiam)* of any kind.[29] Laelius says it is love, after which friendship is named *(amor—amicitia),*[30] that primarily brings people together in a relationship of good will. Strikingly, he describes those who explain friendship solely or chiefly in terms of needs and utilities as taking the sun from our world (47). As for the stealers of the sun, Cicero has in mind in a special way the Epicureans, never explicitly named by him but experiencing a revival throughout Rome in his day.[31]

The parallelism with *Re Publica* continues, for there (1.39) the primary cause of humans coming together is not so much weakness *(imbecillitas)* as a certain sociality implanted by nature. At this point in *Re Publica,* just as the extant text fractures and some fifteen lines are lost, Cicero's Scipio is making the point, heard repeatedly from Laelius in *Amicitia,* that man is not a solitary being *(non singulare nec solivagum),* but rather is so born that even in great prosperity and with all needs clearly satisfied, he would seek out companionship. The delights of such companionship that could be called "friendship" are spelled out at one point by Laelius. His claim *(Amic.,* 22, 31) is that insofar as we find ourselves embedded in the mutual good will of friends, we have a capacity to live life to the fullest, to experience the sweet delight of talking openly with others who are, as it were, other selves, and to find the pleasure of sharing good fortune with such souls and having their support in adversity. Laelius later observes (87–88) that nature abhors the solitary, and he overall appears to give voice to what seems to be the teaching of Cicero that nature draws humans to delight in community and specifically in the goodness or virtue humans can share.

Friendship not only brings such delights and support but also serves in attaining all the ordinary things people deem useful, such as wealth and political office. Never does Cicero deny the powerful role that utility or mutual advantage plays in human relationships. Recall that as Laelius begins his discourse, the second reason he gives for ranking friendship highest among human goods—after saying it is in accord with nature—is that it is beneficial in good and bad times. Though denying that true friendship is rooted in deficiency and concomitant need, and though never denying that the occasion of friendship might be provided by association in mutual utility, Cicero's Laelius stresses that a true or genuinely grounded friendship does come to yield advantages, but a concern for these, a calculation focused on them or to maximize them, would undermine such a friendship.[32] As Laelius succinctly concludes at one point, "friendship does not spring from utility; rather, utility follows upon friendship" (51, 22).

This statement presumably includes low or crass utilities, our ordinary needs. This dimension of friendship and even of associations or alliances that are but pseudofriendships is no doubt the basis for the unanimous agreement on the value of "friendship" throughout mankind and across all schools of thought (86). The nature of this overwhelming agreement is made clear when Laelius indicates that it includes those who prefer "friendship" even to virtue. From this other side of "friendship's" range and, as it were, reminding us not to scorn our ordinary ways of dependency, Laelius observes (29) that even a good or true friendship not only yields benefits but requires nourishment through mutual presence and interchange of kind acts *(beneficio)*. Scipio, according to Laelius, claimed (33) that nothing was more difficult than to maintain a friendship to the very end of one's life.[33]

Beyond the difficulty of maintaining even a true friendship, it appears to Laelius that the coming to be of such a friendship is rare and its bond is usually quite limited in extent. In one sense, it seems to be Laelius's insistence that true friendship can exist only between good people, which limits its extent and makes it rare. It would be, then, the rarity of virtue in the world and the low incidence that virtuous people would encounter one another in circumstances favorable to friendship that limits the scope and instances of friendship.[34] Cicero's Laelius, however, also seems to resist too much selectivity and too narrow a range for friendship. He seems interested in bringing forward a flexible and potentially extensive model of friendship.[35]

Immediately after Laelius's assertion that friendship can only exist between or among good people, he is quick to raise a disclaimer that he does not mean "good" in that full and complete sense associated with the Perfect Wiseman of the Stoic tradition; in that concept, goodness and virtue are bound up with complete knowledge or wisdom. Laelius concedes that such refined analysis of human perfection may capture a certain truth *(fortasse vere)*, but it is not very useful for ordinary purposes and with human beings as we know them. Laelius draws attention to such Roman ancestors as Marcus Curius, commonly regarded as wise but not of course "wise" in the tradition of such philosophers as the Stoics. Let us, says Laelius (18), attend to such models of goodness as are part of common experience *(in usu vitaque communi)* and not fix on what is merely imaginary or hoped for *(quae finguntur aut optantur)*. If those we look up to need not be perfect models, and Cicero is constant throughout his writings in critiquing the unreality of the Stoic Wiseman, then of course friendships cannot be unions in perfect goodness but only at best unions of good people pointed to and striving for even greater goodness. For Cicero, both the models of human virtue and those of friendship are to be sufficiently proximate ideals that they can be seen as realizable.

Students of *Re Publica* will recognize a manifest parallel, in nearly exactly the same words, between the reasons for Laelius setting aside the Stoic model of human perfection and Scipio's explanation of his decision to turn from Plato's model city as merely imaginary and hoped for.[36] Scipio turns, of course, to the real and more proximate ideal of Rome, or, to be more precise, to Rome both developed in history and developing. Cicero, while learning from abstract analysis and pure models, is ever seeking an understanding of the good that might inform his models in a way that opens to ordinary patterns of development and levels of attainment. Friendships, persons, and cities, however good, are never complete *(perfecta)* and home free, as it were; those that are, are imaginary ones. The real ones need constant maintenance and nourishment. As suggested in large part by the opening segment of book 5 of *Re Publica*, and anticipating a dimension of the conclusion of this essay, there is an evident interdependence of persons, friendships and cities in the dynamic development that is moral development. Good persons make good friends and need good friends to remain in their virtue, and it is through such persons that the ways of good cities are progressively made. Such cities in turn nourish and support good persons and true friendships.

True friendship and good men are then not to be understood too restrictively. What limits genuine friendships to two persons or just a few seems for Laelius to be related to the inherent limits of the necessary affectivity, one of the conditions of friendship in the definition given, rather than to there being a shortage of good and worthy people for potential friendship (20). Love *(caritas)* is seen as necessarily intense and narrowly focused *(contracta res est et adducta in augustum)* on one or a few persons. Perhaps, one might add, this is especially so to the degree that it is true good or virtue rather than ordinary benefits and utilities that is drawing friends together. One can have many professional associates, be a great networker at academic conferences or in other heady venues, and still have at best one or a few good friends. One can have an extensive and extended family with multigenerational ties and responsibilities and still have at best one or a few friends. And in politics, of course, one can have a multitude of allies and be well connected and almost surely one will have no friends, save, perhaps, "man's best friend." This, I assume, is why observers have noticed the high frequency of dog lovers and owners in Washington D.C. and throughout and around the Beltway. Cicero's Laelius, though consistently intent on distinguishing relationships that have at least the spark of attraction to goodness as their primary cause from those that are primarily narrowly utilitarian, clearly does not want the standard of full friendship marked by *caritas* to delimit the range of the applicability of the idea of friendship to one-on-one relationships and mini-communities that are no larger than just a few. He talks of friendship, as has the tradition of classical political philosophy, as if it is in some way a helpful measure of a good citizenry, and he even draws attention (29) to how humans disposed to the good recognize it in others across the great divide of friends and enemies.

Cicero's Laelius sees possibilities of the requisite kind of attraction and hence of a sort of friendship horizontally throughout the world community as well as vertically with esteemed ancestors. Such a vertical affection Cicero clearly feels toward Scipio and Laelius, and also with those younger and potential successors marked by the necessary virtue. This "sort of friendship" is, of course, an attenuated one. Even for those acting in the light of Judaeo-Christian Revelation, it seems beyond our ordinary capability to have much affection *(caritas)* for distant sisters and brothers suffering in the Sudan or Bangladesh. It is, of course, also the case that whatever goodness attracts those well disposed across the distance of space or time, those relationships cannot be nourished and maintained by personal presence and mutual acts of kindness.

Where then has Cicero's Laelius left his listeners and us readers? He has offered a flexible and potentially extended notion of friendship after seeming to restrict friendship to the good and to those one-on-one or small-circle relationships that allow a sufficiently intense *caritas.* The more flexible and potentially extensive notion is clearly more applicable and hence useful in ordinary experience. Cicero has rendered the concept more applicable and useful by rejecting as "out of this world" and too restrictive a Stoic understanding of goodness as incorporated in the Stoic Wiseman. At the same time, he has recognized that the affective dimension of friendship can be more or less intense in the light of proximity and the opportunities proximity allows. In those cases of "less," one might say that a sort of or attenuated friendship is possible. Cicero's expansion of the concept of friendship makes it, of course, more politically applicable. As already emphasized, friendship's growth along with personal and community development toward justice and stability are always efforts in progress in the best of circumstances. Human experience and specifically Roman history serve to teach all this truth.

Progress in any meaningful sense always depends on a guiding sun, and because Cicero's Laelius is insistent on that orientation to the good rooted in human nature as the primary motivation for and hence form of true friendship, his teaching on friendship can be said to be not only practical but also ennobling. In a sense, Cicero provides a guide for uplifting Roman practices, such as political associations of various stripes including clienteles, in a philosophically informed Socratic direction. To note this is to recall Laelius's decisive rejection of any approach to friendship in which the calculation of benefits or utilities, whether in the form of quid pro quo or some kind of maximizing utility, is to be primary cause of a friendship. Such Epicurean approaches were said to steal the sun away while those of the Stoics assert that the sun's light is there only for a few—we can add, only for a hypothetical, perhaps simply imaginary, few. Neither of these approaches is adequate to the human experience of friendship. These potent schools of thought in Cicero's time, now largely in Roman garb but with a heritage of Greek founders and Greek teachers, represented dogmatic comprehensive systems that Cicero finds, throughout his writings, inadequate to experience.

Ever concerned with human things and the ordinary horizon—namely, philosophy brought into the homes and everyday lives of people—Cicero clearly has associated himself with the Socratic tradition as carried on in the school of the New Academy. It is in the larger fold of the Academy that Cicero learned from both the Platonic and the Aristotelian traditions. This appears to be reflected, if not explicitly acknowledged, in his treatment of friendship. It is, however, specifically in the tradition of Socrates that a more chastened approach to philosophy and its claims is found. Knowing one's ignorance and knowing well, if anything, love, love of the beautiful and the good: these hallmarks of Socrates are the inspiration for the practical yet ennobled view of friendship given by Cicero's Laelius. Three times in *Amicitia*, Socrates, unnamed but referred to as "the wisest of the Greeks," is cited favorably.

In the tradition of the limited skepticism of Socrates, Laelius, in rejecting the comprehensive Stoic claims to full knowledge and virtue, does not lose all ability to discern goodness and badness and hence to discriminate between good and bad in character as well as between genuine and pseudofriendships. It appears that Laelius's teaching, presented in his almost continuous discourse, has already assimilated an Academic critique (customarily given through dialectical exchanges) and is thus marked by appropriate, experientially based limits on the understanding of friendship offered. In *Re Publica*, book 3 presents openly, though for us in fragmented form, the Academic critique of a notion of justice rooted in nature. It is, of course, a critique where all of virtue is at stake. Laelius's defense there of the notion of justice appears to have been scaled back and adapted in the light of the critique, but it yet holds to a law of right rooted in nature and in doing so maintains the ability to discriminate between better and worse constitutions. In the *Amicitia*, Laelius cannot discriminate better or worse friendships without a reliance on a sense of the good and virtuous to which humans are drawn in the very nature of things. This orientation and rootedness in nature constitute a Socratic claim that allows moral and political inquiry to be potentially fruitful.

Students of modern political analysis and the history of political thought might especially notice that without anchoring friendship in humans' naturally given attunement to an objective good in the nature of things, two important passages we have considered in this essay's inquiry would likely draw readers in another direction. The very definition of friendship as "agreement on all things human and divine, an agreement accompanied by good will and affection" leaves open in one plausible interpretation the possibility that any bond of persons with a spirit of comradeship would fit the descriptive, value-free definition and hence be truly friendship. The definition would then encompass Epicurean friendship as well as a union of thieves who share a debased understanding of human and divine things yet a spirited internal comradeship and attachment to one another. One need not determine that such bondings are without all real good as part of their glue or just what capacity they have for persistence in order to recognize that the definition of Cicero's Laelius, if it is to capture genuine friendship moved primarily by the human good, must load the terms "good will and affection" in the definition in a way that implies that it is only a truly grounded good that can in any significant way elicit good will and *caritas*. Scipio's definition of the political community as an agreement in right and the common interest had the same potential to be read in a value-free descriptive way, and St. Augustine thought it would be best read that way rather than as an agreement in true justice that left all real political communities, even Rome at its best, falling short of meeting the definition of a republic.[37]

In another notable passage considered earlier in this essay and also paralleled in *Re Publica,* Laelius stresses that in judgments of human character we should look to our own and common experience and not to models merely imagined and hoped for.[38] Such passages in Cicero can be seen as clear anticipations, if not inspirations, of Machiavelli's famed injunction in chapter 15 of *The Prince* where he urges attention to the "effective reality" of political matters rather than resting "content with mere constructions of the imagination."[39] Cicero's turn, as opposed to Machiavelli's, does not entail the loss of the sun, the anchoring in the good of nature to which humans are drawn. Rather than abandoning such a good, his turn is to more proximate and realizable goals in friendship and political life, goals nonetheless made possible and illumined by the true good of human nature and its supportive communities.

Applications and Conclusion

The immediately preceding paragraphs focus on two instances in which Laelius's observations require the anchoring of the good in nature if something less than an ennobling view of friendship is not to emerge in *Amicitia*. The meaning of the very first claim of Laelius for friendship—namely, that it is in accord with nature—is progressively filled in as *Amicitia* unfolds. Friendship is not just a behavioral pattern, natural in the sense of a common and predictable way of acting, though it is surely this too. Friendship is presented as part of the very happiness or good we seek. Laelius says more about specifically how friendship works with virtue in their interaction as mutually supportive elements.[40] As the epigraph to this essay points out, virtue and friendship join within a bonding that constitutes human happiness. It is not, for Laelius, a union without precedence between the elements. Though Laelius explicitly acknowledges that there are those who put friendship even ahead of virtue in seeking happiness, his determination of precedence between the elements is decidedly the opposite. Friendship is to follow goodness; this is the right reading of nature (20, 61, 100, 104). This does not mean, however, that friendship is merely instrumental to virtue or simply an offspring of it, though it might appear in both these ways. The critical observation here is that it is not merely either of these. Laelius presents friendship as a constitutive element in a happiness that is truly human and rightly sought (83). Virtue's precedence is consistent with his statements that friendship is between good people and that the way to this true friendship starts by endeavoring oneself to be good (18, 81–82). That endeavor to be good includes self-examination and striving to understand the self in the context of the whole of nature, responsibilities Cicero addresses in other writings and that are especially laid on potential political leaders and assumed in an exemplary way by Scipio as portrayed in *Re Publica*.[41]

Friendship too, while being good in itself and a constitutive element of happiness, is not only elevated to true friendship in the company of virtue, but also assists the seeds and sparks of virtue toward their full development. Virtue again is always in progress; it is never simply there as in the case of the imaginary Stoic Wiseman. What friendship does for virtue is to give it encouragement of every form, and especially insofar as friends are alike, friendship facilitates self-examination. The epigraph to this essay, which first brought to attention the friendship or union between virtue and friendship, continues in *Amicitia* with Cicero's Laelius observing (84) that this union "contains everything humans regard as worthy of seeking—integrity *(honestas)*, glory, and a mind both at peace and in delight *(tranquillitas animi atque jucunditas)*. That glory is mentioned here reminds the reader what Cicero has said directly in another work and exemplified in *Re Publica* and *Officiis*, namely, that true glory follows virtue as its shadow.[42]

This essay began by noticing certain affinities and direct links between *Amicitia* and *Re Publica* and by letting these draw us into interpreting *Amicitia* in light of and in tandem with *Re Publica*. Perhaps at least a down payment on the fruitfulness of this approach has been made. There is, however, more that is suggested by the linking of these works to illuminate in important ways the political theory of Cicero. What follows is a sketch of where we seem to be led in this next step, a sketch presented under two topics: the special significance of friendship for politics and the importance of intergenerational friendship with respect to political development.

Cicero's Laelius highlights at one point (39–41) the alliances of wicked men, factions, we might say, which then as earlier threatened the Roman Republic. Later, he in effect comments on the capacity of such genuine friendships as that between himself and Scipio to counter such faction. Politics seems a real testing ground of friendships chiefly because it is a testing ground of character or goodness. Most are said to fail this test.

Politics then is a sphere where one rarely finds true friendships, and if they are ever budding there, they do not generally survive.[43] One senses a special poignancy in Cicero's writing these parts of *Amicitia* in what turned out to be the last year of a life so troubled, as we are especially reminded in his letters, by finding trustful relationships and appropriate alliances while he and events bounded from crisis to crisis in the late Republic.

Despite the almost insurmountable obstacles that the temptations and stresses of political life pose to goodness and to genuine friendship, Cicero seems to hold up such friendship as something of a last and best hope for securing and sustaining the type of leadership that might protect and further develop the Republic. This friendship is not, however, as tenuous as the diffusive good will or proximity to friendship alluded to earlier, which one might seek in binding any community's citizens and people together. This, rather, is specifically the more intense form of friendship exemplified in the unions of Scipio and Laelius and that of Cicero and Atticus. Such friendship seems to be a critical element in the micropolitics of Cicero's teaching about politics.

It is not just the horizontal friendship, above all that between Laelius and Scipio, that is witnessed to in both actions and words in the two texts under consideration, but there is also a highlighting of vertical intergenerational friendships. Recall that Cicero's Laelius specifically raises the possibility of attraction to the goodness of persons outside our time and thus to the idea of vertical friendships in some form. Such friendships might be something more than merely vertical ones. They might gain something of the intensity of the one-on-one friendship when there are personal links from present horizontal circles of friends to those exemplars of the past. They are called "friends," those younger men who gather with Scipio and Laelius for the discussion on the best constitution and the nature of justice. The account of the gathering has come to Cicero himself from one of the younger listeners in the circle. So it is, as we have noted earlier, that the discussion, more properly the discourse, in *Amicitia* gets started: it was brought to Cicero by Scaevola, one of the sons-in-law who heard Laelius speak, and within the speech of Laelius are the words of the late Scipio, now being heard by the two young men and later to be passed to Cicero.

A closing epilogue (100ff.) to Laelius's discourse specifically sings the praises of horizontal friendships, naming specific circles of friends and bringing to attention the ties of affection and friendship between the young and the old. This but sets the scene for Laelius's observing that the "law of our life and nature" is such that one generation follows on another, that generations do not in their entirety drop away at once and that rather they interpenetrate through the friendships of the young with the old. Immediately after those observations, Scipio's absence through his sudden snatching by death is recalled (102), and Laelius insists that for himself, Scipio yet "lives and will always live," for it is the "virtue of that man" that he loved and that remains alive and will be heralded into future generations. Scipio's Dream, earlier seen in this essay as possibly linking the two texts before us, brought Scipio into renewed contact with father and grandfather. The contact served both to fortify a virtue of dedication to the political community and its leadership and to impress Scipio and those who would hear his tale with the relative insignificance of politics and this world's affairs.

For Cicero, friendship's meaning is not exhausted in some kind of service to politics; it is a good in itself and a possible aid to even greater things. Yet friendship likely is the most important instrument in the micropolitics of Roman life where constitutional development and leadership turn on political alliances and the give-and-take of personal interactions and relationships. Those alliances and interactions seem to have become terribly corrupted in the late Republic into forms of servile clientelism, bitter factionalism, and outright conspiracies for power and control. Perhaps that is not peculiar to Rome but is an ever-present possibility and reality, especially where political life is essentially free. The mutual support of friends in such a politics and their cross-generational enrichment and sustenance seems for Cicero truly the last and best hope. Friendship then, as Cicero's life winds down, is to be praised and honored, but the nature of genuine friendship must also be understood. Above all, Cicero sought in *De Amicitia* to contribute to such an understanding.

Notes

1. I take responsibility for the English translations of Cicero used in this essay. With respect to the *De Amicitia (Amic.)* or *Laelius*, I have benefited frequently from J. G. F. Powell's fine translation in his bilingual edition, *Cicero: On Friendship and the Dream of Scipio* (Warminster, England: Aris & Phillips, 1990). Powell also provides an introduction and commentary. I have also consulted at times the earlier bilingual edition in the Loeb series: Cicero, *De Senectute, De Amicitia, De Divinatione*, trans. with introductions by William Armistead Falconer (Cambridge: Heinemann, Harvard University Press, 1959).

2. The Loeb bilingual edition is Cicero, *De Re Publica, De Legibus*, trans. Clinton Walker Keyes (Cambridge: Heinemann, Harvard University Press, 1959). Two translations have more recently appeared: *The Republic and The Laws*, trans. Niall Rudd, intro. and notes Jonathan Powell and Niall Rudd (Oxford: Oxford University Press, 1998); *On the Commonwealth and On the Laws*, trans. James E. G. Zetzel (Cambridge: Cambridge University Press, 1999).

3. These themes are the competing claims between the practical and theoretical way of life with the elevation of the practical life specifically in the form of the life of the statesman; a certain understanding of a mixed constitution or regime; the inevitable entailment of an understanding of justice in judgments of the goodness or badness of constitutions; a defense of universal justice grounded in natural law; an understanding of dynamic development in history, as illustrated in Rome, potentially toward stability and justice, a development critically dependent on political leadership or statesmanship; and political leadership exemplified in a model statesman/orator who is nurtured through the resources of tradition, appropriate education and an orientation to what is truly eternal.

Even over the centuries when largely lost, *De Re Publica (Rep.)* played—through its parts and concepts evident and acknowledged in the work of Saint Augustine and others—a role in associating Cicero with certain topics in political theory.

4. *Leg.*, 1.15, 2.14,16; *Rep.*, 2.52.

5. This interpretation of *Re Publica* is explored and defended in my essay "Cicero's Focus: From the Best Regime to the Model Statesman," *Political Theory* 19(2) (May 1991): 230–51.

6. Work on *Re Publica* seems to have started in the year 54 and was completed in the next two or three years. *Amicitia* was written in 44.

7. Whether historically true or not, Cicero chooses to give these conversations an aura of having actually occurred. In *De Senectute* (3), Cicero explicitly confesses to Atticus, to whom he dedicates this work as well as *Amicitia*,

that he has simply created this conversation and has sought to enhance the authority of its teaching by putting words in the mouth of an esteemed ancestor. *Amicitia* (see 3–4) appears to have more of a historical basis.

8. In *Senectute*, Scipio and Laelius say little and simply facilitate the elder Cato's beginning his discourse.

9. *Rep.*, 1.18, passim.

10. As he opens *Amicitia* (3–5) and addresses his lifelong friend Atticus, Cicero draws attention to his own experience with friendship. He is more forceful in *Re Publica* in asserting his record of experience in politics.

11. *Rep.*, 6.15.

12. Powell, *Cicero*, 12. Lorraine Pangle describes *Amicitia* in its entirety as "essentially Laelius's encomium on friendship." Pangle, *Aristotle and the Philosophy of Friendship* (Cambridge: Cambridge University Press, 2003), 106.

13. The philosophical school in which Cicero regularly places himself and which he finds the most representative of the Socratic way of approaching the search for truth.

14. The only direct or even indirect references to other writings of Cicero in *Amicitia* are these two links to *Re Publica* and several ties to his immediately preceding *De Senectute*. The relationship to *Senectute* is discussed in Paul MacKendrick, *The Philosophical Books of Cicero* (New York: St. Martin's, 1989), 220.

15. At this point in the text, it is claimed that Fannius was not present for the discussion in Scipio's garden related in *Re Publica;* this does not square with what is claimed in that work, *Rep.* 1:18. Though reported as present, Fannius does not speak in the extant portions of *Re Publica*. Powell (*Cicero*, 83–84) explores the state of scholarship on this discrepancy and offers an explanation.

16. It is in the context of treating the virtue of justice that friendship emerges for consideration in Cicero's *De Officiis*, a work he was likely writing either simultaneously with or around the same time as *Amicitia*. *Officiis* was apparently completed later in the year 44 than *Amicitia;* Cicero at one point refers the reader of *Officiis* to *Amicitia* for a more complete treatment of friendship (*Off.*, 2.31). *Officiis* presents friendship as a richer and better relationship than one that is merely just; yet it is to be ruled and thus constrained by justice (see esp. *Off.*, 1.55–58, 160; 3.43–44). It is reasonable to infer that the just man has the necessary perspective in which to discuss friendship.

In the *Pro Murena* (63 B.C.), nearly twenty years before writing *Amicitia*, Cicero discussed duty's controlling role with respect to friendship and cautioned against a Stoic perfectionism that would totally deny the claims of friendship (*Mur.*, 5–10, 65) when they appear to be in tension with what is right or just. Clearly throughout much of his life, as no doubt often the case with people in active political life, Cicero struggles with just where to draw the line between the claims of right and duty and those of friendship. *Officiis*, 3.43–44 reveals him confessing that this is especially difficult matter for most people bound up in ordinary friendships. It is no problem where perfect Stoic Wisdom is assumed. Pangle properly notes the seeming inconsistency in Laelius's handling of the sometimes opposing claims of justice and friendship (*Aristotle and the Philosophy of Friendship*, 119, 225–26 n.50). However, it seems wrong to suggest that Cicero is trying to highlight weakness in Laelius as a thinker, for the issue is a difficult one in political practice and the irresoluteness and ambiguity in the words of Laelius seem to reflect Cicero's own thinking that appears to come, in *Officiis*, to a somewhat settled view on the limited preference allowable to a friend. P. A. Brunt indicates that there was a general expectation in Cicero's time that friendship yield to the public good. "*Amicitia* in the Roman Republic," in *The Fall of the Roman Empire and Related Essays* (Oxford: Clarendon Press, 1988), 368ff., 380–81.

Though there are overall clearly differences of emphasis between Cicero's Scipio and Cicero's Laelius in *Re Publica* as well as in *Amicitia* where Pangle's interpretation brings them to the fore (*Aristotle and the Philosophy of Friendship*, 121, passim and 222, n.3), perhaps the distancing of Laelius from Scipio and thus from Cicero himself is not so convincing when one considers that these two exemplary friends might both be speaking for Cicero and reflecting tensions in his own thinking such as that between the attraction of speculative inquiry and the dutiful attention to more practical and pressing questions and that between different emphases on how important friendship is to happiness. Scipio with the greatest enthusiasm of all present approves Laelius's defense of justice (*Rep.*, 3.42), and in *Tusculanae Disputationes (Tusc.)*, 5.54–56, Cicero apparently in his own voice praises Laelius as a model of decency and calls him wise (*sapiens* cf. Pangle, 108). Earlier I explored Leo Strauss's endeavor to distance Cicero from the views of Laelius; see "Cicero and the Rebirth of Political Philosophy," *The Political Science Reviewer* 8 (Fall 1978): 93–94.

17. Powell, *Cicero*, 18.

18. What is to be found are seemingly stock references to instructive aspects in the lives of Themistocles (42), Neoptolemus (75), and Timon of Athens (87). The acts of Themistocles and Timon are specifically not approved. An observation of Bias (59), one of the ancient seven sages, is met with objection from Laelius, and one of Archytas of Tarentum (88) is cited as apparently true.

19. *Amic.*, 15. The legendary friendships are commonly identified as those of Theseus and Pirithous, Orestes and Pylades, Achilles and Patroclus, as well as Damon and Phintias; the last is given explicit and extensive attention by Cicero in book 3 of *Officiis*. Powell, *Cicero*, 85.

20. Powell, *Cicero*, 16, also 7. At least with respect to overt Hellenism, *Senectute* is more like Cicero's other philosophical writings than *Amicitia*. In the pages of the former, the reader will find Greek sources, such as Xenophon, cited openly and with approval along with approving citations of Socrates, Pythagoras, and Hesiod. Greek exemplars of a happy and productive old age are brought before the reader.

21. Plutarch, in treating Cicero in his comparative lives, makes note of the hostility directed at Cicero because of his being perceived as a Graecophile. Plutarch, "Cicero," in *Eight Great Lives*, ed. C. A. Robinson Jr. (New York: Holt, Rinehart & Winston, 1960), 145 (5.2). The much larger work from which this selection is taken is generally titled *Parallel Lives* or simply *Lives*.

22. Pangle (*Aristotle and the Philosophy of Friendship*, 104), quite rightly it seems, observes that much of Cicero's treatment of friendship is in "a thoroughly Aristotelian spirit."

23. Powell, *Cicero*, 2–3; Falconer, 106; MacKendrick, *The Philosophical Books of Cicero*, 220; Brunt, "*Amicitia* and the Roman Republic," 355.

24. Powell, *Cicero*, 20, 5.

25. Thomas N. Habinek, "Towards a History of Friendly Advice: The Politics of Candor in Cicero's *de Amicitia*," in *The Poetics of Therapy*, ed. Martha Nussbaum, *Apeiron* 23(4) (1990): 185. Yet earlier and writing specifically about *Amicitia*, Brunt ("*Amicitia* and the Roman Republic," 355) observed that this work "is constantly illustrated from Roman life and it should be taken seriously as an expression of Roman experience."

26. *Leg.*, 1.58ff.; *Tusc.*, 1.64–65 where Cicero attributes to Plato the statement that philosophy is the gift of the gods; see also *De Finibus (Fin.)*, 2.45, 4.33ff., 5.11; *Off.*, 1.153, 2.5; *Academica (Ac.)*, 2.6.

27. See *Rep.*, 1.39; *Off.*, 2.30–31.

28. See note 16 above. The truth that family are not necessarily the same as friends is evident on one occasion (*Ad Atticum [Att.]*, 1.18), where Cicero indicates that his brother Quintus is a potential friend not simply as brother, but in the light of certain qualities he possesses.

29. On the natural attraction of the good, see later in *Amic.*, 35, 48–49, 100; *Off.*, 1.55–56, 58; see also Cotta the Academic speaking in Cicero's *De Natura Deorum*, 1.121–22.

30. See Brunt, "*Amicitia* and the Roman Republic," passim, for the range of use of *amicitia* in Cicero's time. *Caritas*, rather than *amor*, is used at times by Cicero to describe the affection that marks friendship as in Laelius's definition of friendship above, where it seems a necessary element or effect of friendship. It seems that friendship rooted in the good may have an erotic dimension, for in overall Latin usage of the time, as indicated in the *Oxford Latin Dictionary*, *amor* but not *caritas* appears often but not always to suggest

sexual and passionate love. It does not appear that Cicero intends such a distinction between *amor* and *caritas,* especially in the light of both instances of his use of that latter at *Amic.,* 20. Note, however, that *caritas* is used to characterize the disposition of the people to the fathers *(patres)* from whom Romulus was said to have fashioned the first Senate. *Rep.,* 2.14. In the famous passage of *Officiis* (2.24), later turned around in Machiavelli's admonition to princes, Cicero says the way to power, influence, and popular support is through *caritas* rather than fear.

31. Note the claim of Cicero (*Off.,* 1.5), directed primarily at the Epicureans, that friendship, justice, and generosity are not consistent with certain understandings of the supreme good. The most direct and thorough consideration by Cicero of the Epicurean understanding of friendship is found in *Fin.,* 1.65–70; 2.78–85. A full discussion of Cicero's encounter with the Epicureanism, including interpretive debates on the fairness of his treatment of this school, is found in my essay "Cicero, Citizenship and the Epicurean Temptation," in *Cultivating Citizens,* ed. Dwight Allman and Michael Beaty (Lanham, Md.: Lexington Books, 2002), esp. 12 and nn.59, 75, 76.

32. A strong and Stoic statement along these lines is found in the mouth of Cato in Cicero's *De Finibus,* 3.70–71: "Justice and friendship can in no way be present unless they are sought for themselves." This view in essence is also put by Cicero in the mouth of Cotta the Academic, speaking against the Epicureans at *De Natura Deorum,* 1.122.

33. Consider the glow this at once puts upon the friendship of Scipio and Laelius in the light of the dramatic circumstances of *Amicitia.*

34. Since Cicero has Laelius confess (35) the role of fortune or luck in sustaining a friendship over various obstacles that usually arise, one supposes that he would readily acknowledge luck's role in finding a true friend, a "soul mate," as current dating services say in their self-proclaimed effort to replace good fortune with the control of computer-aided data collection and matching.

35. Some are said to need many friends; others but a few (*Off.,* 2.30).

36. *Rep.,* 2.3, 52.

37. Augustine, *The City of God,* 19.24; also 19.21 and 2.21.

38. *Amic.,* 18.

39. The phrasing here is from the translation by A. Robert Caponigri. Machiavelli, *The Prince* (Chicago: Henry Regnery, 1963), 84.

40. With respect to friendship, Laelius seems to say that humans are needy but not in the ordinary sense of "need." As Scipio says with respect to political community (*Rep.,* 1.39), it arises not from weakness or "need" but from the human being's very communal nature. The human is said not to be a solitary being.

Laelius's treatment of the relationships between humans' need, friendship, and the virtues requires the kind of charitable interpretation that Pangle (*Aris-*

totle and the Philosophy of Friendship, 195–97) brings to Aristotle in concluding about his teaching that friendship is "an important and integral part of the happy life," that friendship's "intrinsic goodness is augmented by its goodness as a means," and that Aristotle, addressing himself especially to statesmen and educators, focuses on the things of solid worth in friendship that readers should cultivate and build upon." Cicero's Laelius does seem in these important respects "thoroughly Aristotelian."

41. *Rep.,* 2. 69; also see "Cicero's Focus," 243ff., esp. n.46. Cicero might be viewed as extending to politics (specifically to circles of potential statesmen) the practices among friends in the philosophical schools, practices with which he was surely familiar. Referring to "the Aristotelian school" in antiquity, Pierre Hadot writes, "Such a community of research, discussion, care for oneself and for others, and mutual correction could also be found in other schools; we have seen it in Epicurean friendship, as well as in Stoic and Neoplatonic direction of conscience.... Another exercise of the philosophical way of life is meditative discourse—a kind of dialogue which philosophers carry out with themselves. Dialogue with oneself was a widespread custom throughout antiquity." *What Is Ancient Philosophy?* trans. Michael Chase (Cambridge: Harvard University Press, 2002), 179.

42. *Tusc.,* 1.109–10; see also *Pro Archia,* 14–15; *Pro Sestio,* 143.

43. *Amicitia* opens by Cicero reporting that the occasion for his hearing the discourse of Laelius from Scaevola was a widespread concern over the falling out in the heat of politics between Publius Sulpicius and Quintus Pompeius; they fell into bitter enmity from the closest and dearest friendship one might imagine (2–3).

II

Christian Perspectives

4

The Luminous Path of Friendship

Augustine's Account of Friendship and Political Order

John von Heyking

Cicero was Augustine's principal ancient teacher and interlocutor about politics and Augustine knew he had to go through his teaching, as it were, in order to demonstrate the superiority of the Christian contribution to political life over the ancient.[1] Yet, as much as Augustine thought that he had surpassed Cicero, he depends on Cicero's identification of, as opposed to answers to, the perennial questions of political order, including those concerning justice, law, religion, and rhetoric. Among Augustine's "Ciceronian" identifications—after all he too was Roman—is the attention he gives to friendship, and it is Cicero's teaching that provides the backdrop for his understanding of its political dimension. Commenting on Augustine's understanding of the "love thy neighbor" commandment, Carolinne White observes that Cicero's view "actually helped him in his understanding of this commandment which he set at the center of his thought."² Even though Augustine revised elements of Cicero's account of political justice, the macropolitics of Rome as it were, one senses profound agreement with Cicero on how networks of friends form the micropolitics of political society and how the highest friendships cultivate the virtues. In this sense, both Augustine and Cicero inherited the Aristotelian insight that political community is somehow analogous to friendship—it is both like and unlike friendships among the virtuous: like because both exhibit a form of love, and unlike because only smaller friendships exhibit the highest possibilities of love.³ Augustine's lifelong quest to form contemplative communities of friends, which forms the basis of medieval monasticism, was meant to find an extrapolitical space for peace, for that proximate peace of the city of God that would serve as the exemplar of community and inform the ecclesia and, more distantly, the polis. The formative role of friendships on the ecclesia has been well documented⁴ but their thematic connection to political life has not. This essay examines the analogy—analogate relationship between Augustine's views on political community and friendship. I show how his view of friendship as an expansive communion of souls experiencing the fullness of their friendship guides his reasoning about politics. Political friendship is inferior yet supportive of the higher types of friendship, and, paradoxically, political friendship is impossible without the prior experience of the fullness of friendship. Augustine's analogical approach captures the "unrolling" circularity or dialectic between friendship and political friendship. It enables us to understand how the face-to-face encounters of friends inform, and are informed by, political community. To guide this inquiry, I draw from Augustine's method of analogical reasoning in *On the Trinity,* of knowing unknown things "from those things which are known."⁵

This analogy—analogate relationship between political friendship and the highest type of friendship is itself predicated on their relationship with the highest human good. Cicero and Augustine were part of the ancient tradition that regarded friendship in light of the highest good humans experience, of which James Schall remarks: "[C]ontinuity appears in intellectual history in connection with the issue of immortality and the proper life of man, also including, as directly related, the classic questions of friendship and its destiny, of truth and its source."⁶ Cicero in his *De Amicitia* looks to the friendship of the virtuous as that place in society where it is most open to the eternal, where it is most luminous to the order of nature or the gods. Thus, friendships among the virtuous are said to be eternal, not because Cicero seeks valiantly for some consolation to sustain his stoicism, but rather because such friendships are the completion of nature, a microcosm of nature. And the memory of such friendships emits their glory to form the moral and spiritual substance of political order.[7]

The question concerning friendship and its relationship with political community and the eternal is perennial as much as it is pressing in our own time. For instance, Adam Smith and Alexis de Tocqueville notice the danger that modern politics pose to the personality, and the temptation to extinguish oneself in exuberant ideological and religious movements.[8] These movements provide a purpose to life when liberal politics seem unable to, and this apparent lack of purpose of the modern state negates the transparency between friendship and eternity one finds in Cicero's and Augustine's reflections on politics. Modern politics destabilizes traditions and places and so destabilizes one's sense of identity as well as time, which are both the basis and fruit of friendship. Identity and time, or soul and providence to use Augustine's symbols, motivate my analysis, and I return to these problems of modern politics in this essay's conclusion. First, I turn to consider how political community is an analogy of friendship before turning to friendship as the analogate.

Political Community as an Analogy of Friendship

The general view of Augustine is that while he had high regard for friendship, in a sense baptizing Cicero's account of it, he rejected any analogy between friendship and political society. An entire generation of scholars, including Robert Markus, Herbert Deane, and Oliver O'Donovan, have read Augustine as regarding politics as *propter peccatum*, a holding tank to protect the virtuous from the predations of the wicked. Hannah Arendt has identified love as the core of his account of social life. She argues that Augustine undermines what could be a rich account of social life by postulating a self with no existence of its own except insofar as it is created by God and stands in isolation in God's presence. The neighbor is thus a mere occasion of love because the self's otherworldly attention overlooks the neighbor who stands in proximity of it.[9] Such understandings are due in part to the general perception that Augustine's love of God eclipses love of earthly things.

While avoiding the opposite extreme of attributing utopian aspirations to Augustine, more recent scholarship has tended to consider his attitude toward politics as more continuous with those of friendship, virtue, and the world. Because of the imperfection of our knowledge, the city of God and earthly city view each other more through a looking glass than understanding themselves as distinctly defined categories. Both are mystical allegories rather than geometrically precise categories drawn from discursive reasoning (see CD, 15.1). Thus, I have argued for the need to distinguish Augustine's *theory* about the human good of political life, which includes a positive sense of civic virtue connected to common objects of love, from its usual *practice*. O'Donovan similarly finds it useful to distinguish his *theoretical* treatment of transcendental representation from the fallen *condition* that characterizes the communication of such signs.[10]

This new emphasis on the role theory plays in Augustine's political thought can only make sense when the perspective of Augustine the theorist is grounded in conversation that is friendship, because friendship is the analogate from which theorizing about political community proceeds. The perspective of the political thinker is a perennial problem for political theory whether it is Socrates' erotic turn toward the Agathon or Machiavelli's synoptic perspective from the mountain and from the plain that enables him to be the true prince. Augustine's practice of friendship enables us to see his appreciation for the manner in which friendship ripples throughout the political order. Discussing how analogical reasoning is appropriate for friendship, David Burrell states that "analogous terms need to be anchored to a primary analogate, so that other uses can be related proportionally to that central use. Otherwise, they will appear and be employed in a merely 'abstract' manner, and prove unable to lead us on to an understanding beyond that connatural to us.... [T]heir proper use will require a mode of inquiry and of life which privileges certain paradigm instances over others: 'spiritual exercises,' if you will."[11] Augustine's analogical reasoning toward political community is predicated on the practice of friendship, which itself is predicated on a philosophical anthropology that takes its form and content as a spiritual exercise. Augustine regarded several of his texts as spiritual exercises, including *Confessions*, *On the Trinity*, and the extremely long *City of God*, which he states must be read repeatedly before its meaning is fully discerned.[12]

Augustine's analogical reasoning about political community from the basis of friendship is seen in various places. The examples he uses to demonstrate the fallen condition of politics are often treated as deformations of friendship. For instance, he provides Cicero's example of Alexander's capturing a pirate who points out to the emperor that his empire is simply a large-scale version of the pirate's activities (CD, 4.3). He uses the example of a deformed friendship, the gang of pirates, to reason analogically about political community.

Augustine's positive treatments of political community also proceed analogically from friendship. He compares political order to the beauty and arrangement of the Psalms: "For the rational and moderate harmony of diverse sounds insinuates the compact unity of a well-ordered city" (CD, 17.14). The order that the city represents is a harmony of its parts: "[F]or each single human being, like one letter in a discourse *(sermon)*, is as it were the element of a city or kingdom, however wide is the occupation of land" (CD, 4.3). Our face-to-face encounters reveal each individual, with his own goodness, as a part that helps to constitute the whole, but who, conversely, contains the "whole" within him. Augustine chooses to compare the whole to a discourse, which becomes senseless and incomplete when it lacks its parts, just as a Psalm would lack harmony if it lacked the full amplitude of notes and words that constitute it.[13] John Milbank and Gilbert Meilaender observe that as participants within this *ordo*, we encounter others—who are also microcosms of the common objects of love—serially, one at a time, which means that the "whole" is never fully present but rather refracted or intimated by each of us who serve as analogues.[14] This gives political society, like friendship, the character of a conversation that resembles a harmony and discourse. Moreover, in this conversation we are embedded in a social web of customs, language, and friendships, which means that others, most noticeably notables, serve as *exempla* whom we recognize and imitate, as imitation of *exempla* for Augustine is the primary manner in which we learn from one another.[15] Referring ourselves to the analogate, not to abstract rules drawn from discursive reasoning, is the starting point, and eventual end point, of our spiritual exercises. As Arendt observes, the "relatedness of human existence is actualized in imitation."[16]

One sees this analogy—analogate relationship directly in comparing Augustine's definitions of friendship and of political community *(populus)*. Following Cicero, friendship is "agreement on things human and divine combined with goodwill and love" and a *populus* is agreement about common objects of love.[17] A *populus* is better or worse depending on what it agrees to love, while friendship is anchored in friends' perceptions about highest things. There are numerous types of friendships, but Augustine simultaneously recognizes that anything less than friendship in virtue is not really friendship. Even so, utility friendship, like his own that helped his career, can be called friendship as well.[18] Human societies are largely bound together by "mutual give and take."[19] Moreover, political communities exhibit a wider diversity of personality types because they seek to obtain a wider variety of goods, ranging from the cultivation of virtue, to securing bodily necessities, and battling the "fornications of phantasy" (DT, 12.9.14) of internal and external enemies. Coercion and power relationships play a greater— though not determining—role in political life, that Augustine, like Cicero, hopes can be tempered and formed by friendships among the virtuous. One should note too that the city of God is also included in the definition of *populus*, which at this apex coincides with Augustine's definition of friendship. What this seems to imply is that friendships and political communities themselves are analogues in differing degrees of the city of God, and that friendship and *populus* are defined in a fairly inclusive manner to include, potentially, everyone.

Oliver O'Donovan advances our analogical understanding of *populus* in his lectures on the Trinitarian structure of common objects of love that form the definition of political community:

> Simply in loving them, we become part of a community that is not constructed to accomplish some task but is given in the very fact that we cannot but love them. . . . Loving is the corporate function that determines and defines the structure of the political society; it is the key to its coherence and its organization. Loving things, not loving one another. Augustine also affirmed that members of a community

loved one another; but that is a second step. The love that founds the community is not reciprocal, but turned outward upon an object.[20]

For Augustine, political society resembles friendship in that it has a givenness whereby its members participate within it. O'Donovan observes the relationship of the experience of givenness with Augustine's notion of *ordo amoris:* whatever we know we necessarily love in some form (in order to know it), and vice versa. The "second step" of friendship that follows one's love of common objects does not mean fellow citizens are an afterthought or a mere "occasion" (Arendt) of one's love. Rather, a political community embodies its common objects of love in the face-to-face interactions, customs, and habits of its citizens. In other words, we love those common objects through loving others because, in a sense, those others "are" those objects. Similar to how our personal friendships develop, we enter relations for utilitarian reasons by identifying common interests. Our love of common objects transforms into love of each other as our habits and predispositions intermingle to the point where we cannot conceive of those common objects of love independently of those we share them with (depending on the degree to which those objects can be shared).

Augustine provides a pneumatically differentiated account of friendship that enables us to reconsider it as the analogate of *populus*. Two texts, *Confessions* and *On the Trinity*, illuminate this differentiation most clearly because they show how divine love moves people in their lives, in their communities, and in the deepest recesses of their souls. These texts illuminate the nature of friendship in such a way as to show how friendship serves as the analogate of political community. Two insights regarding friendship, noticed by Gilbert Meilaender, guide this treatment of these texts. First, friendship is a "school" for virtue, a spiritual exercise to learn the love that is open to loving all neighbors. Preferential love is thus luminous and open to love of all. Second, our natural experience of friends is random. That is, friends enter our lives; we do not choose them, but rather discover them "as if by lot."[21] "Lottery" is a symbol of that experience on the level of the reflective light of truth—natural reason as one might say. It is the way Augustine, the speaker as opposed to the narrator of the *Confessions*, experienced reality up to his conversion at the end of book 8. It expresses our openness toward those who might be our friends, which openness is the basis of decent political community. This randomness is not the meaningless and self-negating randomness of the time of modernity, however, because Augustine shows us how friendship constitutes luminous, yet mysterious, irruptions of meaning in our lives. In pointing beyond politics, such irruptions sustain the analogate of friendship that sustains, in its analogue, a more decent political community.

Friendship as Analogate I: *Confessions*

The *Confessions* provides a reflection about providence and displays how Augustine's friends serve as those luminous irruptions of divine love that point him toward, away from, and again toward God. For instance, Frederick Crosson notices that Augustine only begins to name individuals he knows personally in book 5, mostly friends (and most notably Monica), because it is then that they turn him toward God. Even the exception to this rule of naming his "dear friend" Nebridius testifies the importance of friendship.[22] This act of naming perhaps says more about Augustine's turn of soul than of the friends he names or does not name. Who does not have vivid memories of those who have taught us or those with whom we have sighed in common perception of truth? Naming is an act of glorification and praise, and it plays a role in the development of oneself as much as it does in the history of a political community that sets up monuments and memorials for its benefactors. Cicero has Laelius do this in remembrance of Scipio Africanus in *De Amicitia*.

The structure of the *Confessions* reflects the framework on which friendship operates. William Stephany shows how the first nine books are organized according to pairs of books that exhibit mirror-image treatments of themes.[23] In the case of friendship, the "friendship unfriendly" pear-theft episode of book 2 corresponds with book 8's abundance of friends who unwittingly direct him and themselves toward God. Alypius is of course present at the conversion, and whether or not they both were converted there as Eric Plumer suggests, the text indicates friendship as the literal place of conversion, which corresponds to the garden as its symbolic place.[24] Book 4's episode of the death of his friend in which he proclaims the "madness that knows not how to love men as men" (Conf., 4.7) corresponds with book 6's focus on his friends who share a more proper practice of friendship in their common quest for truth.

In light of our hermeneutical principle of viewing friendship as a school for love, let us consider a few passages in which Augustine treats friendship as a moment of illumination toward the divine ground.

One of the characteristic features of his discussions of his friends is how he understands them as vessels that unknowingly point him toward his conversion (and he for them). Alypius is present at his conversion and in a way completes the movement of Augustine's conversion because, just as Augustine takes up the book to read and applies the text of Paul to his own life, so too subsequently does Alypius interpret the book as telling him that he must be Augustine's guide in faith (Conf., 8.12).

Earlier in book 8 we hear the story that Ponticianus, a Roman courtier, tells Augustine about his own conversion, where he gave up the empty and fragile friendship with the emperor for the satisfying and secure friendship with God. This story sets Augustine off into the anxiety that leads to his conversion (Conf., 8.7). If Ponticianus could transcend his love of the imperial court, then Augustine should be able to transcend his inordinate love of the body and of the world. Further, Ponticianus' conversion was chanced upon by his reading of the life of Antony, who had also been a Roman official. Ponticianus and Augustine began their discussion when Ponticianius happened upon the book by the apostle Paul in Augustine's possession. So we have these friends chancing upon books, upon the struggles of holding imperial office, and upon their respective accounts of transcending those struggles. Similarly, earlier in book 6, we hear of Alypius' love of shameful gladiator shows. Augustine tells of the episode one day when, apparently without having Alypius in mind, he used an example of the gladiator shows to illustrate a text he was teaching (Conf., 6.7). Alypius took the example to heart and applied it directly to himself and was "cured of that disease." Unfortunately, Augustine does not inform the reader of the example or the text he was using.

Augustine had once been interested in astrology and related matters like fate and chance because, like the ancients, they provided an account whereby one can make sense of disparate and contingent events, situating those events within a broader context of meaning. The theme of texts reorienting friends toward truth in inadvertent ways moved him away from this "ancient" view, dominated by chance and fate, and toward symbolizing order in providential terms. Even so, he was prepared for a providential understanding by a conversation with a proconsul who was pagan, and who warned him away from astrology by pointing out that chance explains why predictions happen to turn out true from time to time:

> Thus if one happened to consult the pages of some poet, who was singing (and thinking) of quite other matters, the eye often fell on a verse quite extraordinarily relevant to the matter in one's own mind; and, he said, it was not more extraordinary if from the mind of man—by some higher but quite blind instinct, not by art but merely by chance—things should sometimes emerge that should seem to have a bearing upon the affairs and actions of the inquirer. Surely it was You who from him or through him procured this for me and gave my memory the hint of the answer that I was later to arrive at for myself. (Conf., 4.3)

The narrative between books 4 and 8 traces Augustine's movement from seeing contingent events governed by fate to seeing them governed by God. Further, while he originally looked to fate to discover the course of the future, he now looks to providence to discover meaning in the present. The turn to providence is not a turn toward a more sophisticated or pious foresight. Rather, it gives up its attempt to know the future by becoming a function of memory, that ultimate faculty whereby we understand ourselves and the meaning of the present. The turn to providence is thus a turn toward living in the eternal present and seeing one's past life as a movement toward it. Even so, as seen in the lesson Augustine drew from the Roman proconsul, his insight that friendship arrives "by the lot" is accessible both to the Christian with faith and providence, and to the non-Christian, because both are equally open to that human truth that friendship is a gift and sparks meaningful direction to our lives.

In the very next sentence after the one just quoted, Augustine mentions Nebridius by name, which is to my knowledge the first personal relation he names in the *Confessions*. The subsequent chapters deal with the loss of Augustine's unnamed friend. We learn that his all-consuming love for his friend, whom he loved as if he were immortal, was in fact manipulative and deformed. Yet, as Carl Vaught observes, the ultimate concreteness of death snapped him out of his youthful and indeterminate attitude of being in love with the idea of being in love, which spurred him toward a more determinate Manicheanism that would then lead to greater maturity.[25]

The episodes featuring Alypius and the gladiator bouts, Augustine and the proconsul's discussion of chance and texts, Ponticianus, Antony, political ambition, and the death of his friend—all these fragments are gathered together in the conversion scene in the garden at the end of book 8. That is the point where Augustine's mind focuses all those fragments, as a reader's mind collects the fragments of text and of his life, in a single epiphanic moment of realization that he has been led to the point all along. Robert McMahon demonstrates that Augustine the author knows this providential ordering all along while Augustine the speaker only learns this after the conversion: "In this [providential] vision, and in the *Confessions,* sin leads to redemption, digressive wanderings become directed movements in an ascent, disorder is founded on and informed by order."[26] The conversion is the epiphany of *ordo,* and Augustine's friends were primary vehicles that pointed him toward it. Neither the *Confessions* nor human life in general has a strict mathematical structure, as digressions and adventures throw a degree of randomness into our existence as we experience it from within, yet that randomness plays a crucial part in the overall *ordo.* Friendship is thus the luminous path of *ordo* (Conf. 2.2). As McMahon observes, Augustine symbolizes his friends as the angelic messengers who deliver God's word.[27] However, they are only such if they are first open to truth; and their friendships are only "by the lot" when they allow them to enter into their lives that are devoted to seeking truth.[28] *On the Trinity* clarifies the nature of this highest kind of friendship as an analogy of *ordo* and analogate of *populus.*

Friendship as Analogate II: *On The Trinity*

The luminous path of friendship that the *Confessions* presents dramatically receives its meditative account in the form of a spiritual exercise in books 8–15 of *On the Trinity*. He characterizes the mind's ascent to wisdom, in conversation with friends, as an act of memory, understanding, and love, at first "rolled up" into one as the pregivens of soul, then "unrolled" *(involuta evolvi)* in an expansion and differentiation of meditative ascent (DT, 9.4.5). There we find an account of the unfolding of love characterized as a unity of erotic love and friendly love. Augustine characterizes the relations of the Trinity—which are imaged in the soul as memory, understanding, and love—as friendly love (DT, 8.10.4, 9.4.5). Friendly love refers to simultaneous unity and separation of substances, as the members of the Trinity are three in one.

The Socratic symbol of midwifery and begetting is also central to this text in that one finds completion in having truth drawn from one's soul. Because love is prior to understanding and memory (DT, 9.12.18), and in loving another we necessarily love love, all of us live our lives with souls pregnant with the desire to seek truth in the company of friends (for example, DT, 9.7.12, 11.9.16). If friendship is primarily conversation (DT, 11.8.14), then conversation is deep-down an erotic activity that speech begets upon the souls of one's conversation partners: "[I]n conversing *(loquimur)* with others we add the service of our voice or of some bodily sign to the word that remains within, in order to produce in the mind of the listener, by a kind of sensible remembrance, something similar to that which does not depart from the mind of the speaker" (DT, 9.7.12, 11.8.14). This is no protomodern mind–body dualism because the very nature of sensible images, whether visual or auditory, is to beget the forms of those images in the recesses of memory (DT, 11.2.3, 11.9.16, 14.7.9). The form is in its instantiation and the instantiation is in the form, just as "common objects of love" are instantiated in fellow citizens who, in turn, constitute those objects. The soul is not autonomous and set off against the external world and against friends because it is in a state of pregnancy, awaiting the midwife. In Jean Bethke Elshtain's words, "Mind is embodied; body is thought."[29] The midwifery of friends and their images makes them "adventitious" *(adventia)* to the mind (for example, DT, 14.8.11). The will brings the mind's attention to the words and images created by friends in an act of uniting those images with the memory and, moreover, with the mind of the friend: "For that species [of image] touches the mind, which knows and thinks; it reveals the beauty of minds that have been brought together in fellowship by listening to and answering questions through signs that are known" (DT, 10.1.2).

Thus, there exists a unity of image and mind, mediated by the will, that explains how our friends help to determine not just what we know, but who we are (DT, 11.4.7). The relationship among friends is reciprocal and, in instances of intellectual superiority, where one is in a position possibly to dominate, let us not forget Augustine's central insight in *On the Teacher* that the centrality of memory and recollection implies that there is, strictly speaking, no such thing as a teacher, except for Christ who is the foundation of memory.[30] Conversation climbs an epistemological ladder beginning with sensible images acting on the imagination, memory, understanding, and will, and back down again. Augustine symbolizes each rung of the ladder as an "incorporeal conversion" (DT, 14.6.8) because of the mysterious process of change from material to intellectual substance, an everyday miracle that he regards as more miraculous than even the Resurrection of the body.[31]

Yet conversation is an incomplete trinity (11.8.14), which explains why we encounter others *in seriatim*. Speech with others operates on those universal ideas we share interacting with the specific "historical" images that differ with each individual and that beget those ideas. Augustine observes that while we know ideas, the details of a friend's life that are communicated as images are matters of belief (for example, DT, 10.9.12). In the same way are the facts of history objects of belief and not of knowledge.[32] The ignorance we have of those details explains the tragic quandary of the judge who cannot know for certain whether the accused is guilty (CD, 19.6). It further explains why deliberation is indeterminate, as Aristotle notes, because we can never have perfect knowledge of historical events, which means that politics is necessarily factional, as each side of a debate has a reasonable claim to its opinion.[33]

However, there are limits to how much we can converse with some types of people. Ignorance and sin impede communication. Ignorance and the occasion for sin increase as one broadens one's scope from friendships to a political community: "The larger the city, the more is its forum filled with civil law-suits and criminal trials" (CD, 19.5). Thus, Augustine preferred a small to moderately sized political community (CD, 4.3, 15). Is it any wonder that globalization aggravates experiences of exile and alienation that promote the formation of extremist groups, and verify Nietzsche's observation that people prefer faith in nothing to having no faith? In the worst case, how do we know whether the other person is even capable of conversation? How do we communicate with someone seduced by "fornications of phantasy" that go beyond simple intemperance by engulfing him in an imaginary dreamworld—whereby, for example, one believes one is the hand of God or that one's own religious conversion will usher in the apocalypse, perhaps by using commercial airliners as weapons of mass destruction? The fact that we necessarily lack knowledge in the details of another's life, not to mention the recesses of their soul, forces Augustine to ask how it is at all possible to love someone one cannot fully know (DT, 13.20.26).

Augustine's answer to how we cope with the mystery of another's personality is to restate the thesis of *On the Trinity:* "when unknown things are said to be loved, they are loved from those things which are known" (DT, 13.20.26). Signs, which are adventitious to the mind, draw us out erotically to understand them. The faith that we put in friends also constitutes the spur to conversation whereby the conversants circle around the good they share but that is only partially glimpsed in each act of their conversation with one another. It also enables us to regard the friend as wholly other—like the Trinity, of the same substance but other. One discovers that a friend is also another self when one remembers that his act of begetting is one of returning to your own memory *(redis in memoriam)* (DT, 14.13.17), when one cannot conceive of oneself one's identity, and one's happiness without your friend, in God.

Augustine characterizes the act of recognizing one's friend, with whom there is one heart and one mind, as the act of recognizing oneself because one cannot conceive of oneself in isolation of the other. Augustine does not believe in a simplistic "melding of minds." He meditates on the mystery of two (or more) individuals loving one another with unique souls and histories. The intellectual act of knowing another, essentially the subject of the entire treatise *On the Trinity,* has a complicated ecstatic structure that brings one outside oneself the moment one also perceives oneself. The conversation of friendship is a reciprocal expansion or "unrolling" of this ecstatic perception of oneself and the other that moves outward into a shared life of friendship with all its contingencies, as well as the recognition that it is oneself and one's friend or friends who live it. Paul Wadell puts the matter succinctly when he observes: "So much of our life *is* a history of friendships."³⁴ One sees this dialectic in Augustine's argument that in loving one's neighbor, one loves love, which is God: "When we love our brother from love, we love our brother from God; nor can it happen that we do not love above all else that same love by which we love our brother. From this we conclude that these two commandments cannot be without one another.... For he who does not love his brother is not in love; and he who is not in love is not in God, because God is love" (DT, 8.8.12).

Augustine in these pages provides scriptural evidence to show that the first two commandments imply one another, and that one is often used to cover the other. Even so, Augustine's lengthy spiritual exercise on friendship in *On the Trinity* is summarized in his observation in *Confessions* book 4 that friendship truly exists when God binds friends together (Conf., 4.4.7); *On the Trinity* provides the way *into* that statement because it begins with the nature of the soul, from the things we know. The reciprocally constituting nature of that love can further be seen in Augustine's observation that the mind knows and loves others by the same knowledge and love of itself (DT, 9.4.5). David McEvoy refers to this dialectic of unrolling when he observes that while Augustine needed solitude, "it had to be the solitude of interior recollection practiced within a community of love."³⁵ Moreover, we see this dialectic at work in Augustine's understanding of *populus*, as when it forms the substance of O'Donovan's insight that common objects are "givens": they form the starting points and end points of the conversation of friendship as much as they do the self-definition of *populus*.

This unrolling also provides the basis for enabling us to regard political community, inasmuch as it is a given, as one of those proximate goods in which we can have a proximate delight. Augustine generally claims God to be the only thing that we delight in, while everything else, including friends, are used. The meaning of *usus* and *fruitio* has been subject to much interpretation, including my own, but I'll let Augustine draw his own analogy:

> But we speak of the will at rest as an end, when it is still referred to something further, in the same way as we speak of a foot at rest in

> walking, when it is placed whence another may tread in order to follow a man's steps. But if something so pleases us that the will rests and finds some delight in it, yet this is not yet the end for which it is striving; but this too, is referred to something further, so that it may be regarded not as the rest of the citizen in his native land, but as it were the refreshment, or even the lodging of a traveler. (DT, 11.6.10)

Delighting in the friend, rather than using him, is possible because it takes the form of continuous conversation, through which God is refracted in those flashes of insight and illumination that come along and surprise us.

We turn now to the identity of our friend. Augustine states in *On Christian Doctrine* that our friend can be just about anyone who enters our lives. Our friend is potentially anyone, as seen in his treatment of justice in book 8 of *On the Trinity*. Augustine provides three definitions of justice that correspond with friendship. Justice is "certain beauty of the soul *[quaedam pulchritude animi]* through which men are beautiful, even though the body of very many is misshapen and deformed" (DT, 8.6.9). Justice is a quality of the soul and the just person is a kind of microcosm of the just and therefore beautiful *ordo* of creation. Justice also entails giving to each his or her due. What is each person due? We "owe no one anything except to love one another," which is ultimately expressed in offering our life to the other. The willingness to offer up our life depends on loving the soul over the body, which is learned by those few readers willing to engage in the spiritual exercise that Augustine calls the second half of *On the Trinity*.

Even so, we are mortal; because we experience reality *in seriatim*, we cannot be friends with everyone. Instead, we are friends with those we happen to be in proximity with, which does not mean whoever happens to walk down the street. Rather, we are friends with those who are our "givens," those we dwell with and who compose the web of our memories. Augustine provides the analogy of the lover of learning who wishes to learn all languages, but since that is impossible, "strives to become particularly proficient in that of his own people" (DT, 10.1.2). He states this principle of preferential love more forcefully in *City of God* when he refers to 1 Timothy to characterize one who does not love his own as worse than an infidel.[36] To deny one's own is to deny the "givens" of our existence. It is to deny ourselves and our own (and our friend's) historical particularity and individuality.

Moreover, "our own" is not simply our clan, tribe, ethnic group, fellow citizen, or parishioner. Rather, Augustine has a generalized sense of "our own" whereby those who spur us on to the good life are most truly our own, and they can dwell with us every day, even should they live afar, remaining present in the form of letters and emails. Carolinne White observes that letter writing was central in the early Christian period as a way of maintaining the presence of friends across vast distances of the empire. Augustine characteristically puts the problem into context in Epistle 40 to Jerome: "For if the reason I do not know you is that I have not seen your actual face, then by the same argument you do not know yourself, for you do not see it either. But if you are only known to yourself because you know your own mind, then I too know it quite well through your writings and I bless the Lord for giving a man of your caliber to yourself, to me and to all the brothers who read your works."[37]

The placement of those most significant is random, which has the effect of mixing up and stratifying our allegiances. Our allegiance to our polis is tempered by our allegiance to our ecclesia, and both might be tempered by our friend who belongs to neither one but in whom, through the spiritual exercise of conversation, we recognize a deeper "agreement of things human and divine combined with goodwill and love" than either polis or ecclesia can represent. Contrary to Arendt's view that Augustine's understanding of love is a recipe for homelessness so characteristic of the modern age, Augustine's account of friendship, based on a philosophical anthropology of *ordo amoris*, locates one's home in the "incorporeal conversions" that compose conversations and that bind friends with one another.

On the Trinity presents a meditative ascent whose swirling sets of trinities attempt to see God in whose image we are made. We do not see God even though we have reached the stage of being able to discern the love that structures our own souls and that conjoins us with others. This seems to be a far cry from the confident Augustine of book 13 of the *Confessions* who, as Robert McMahon observes, takes on the voice of the prophet who knows God's will as seen retrospectively in his life.[38] But perhaps the two voices are not so far apart if we consider that both *Confessions* and *On the Trinity* detail how those "givens" create us and how we respond to them. They become arranged in memory as the soul is moved toward its origins.

Conclusion

For Augustine, the "luminous path" of friendship consists of a process of differentiation or unrolling that begins with a perception of *ordo*, experienced as the trinity of memory, understanding, and love in the soul and as glimpsed in the other, that then unrolls in a common life of loving, learning, and recollecting. For mature souls, this unrolling also includes the perception that their act of loving is predicated on a formative love whereby they love their neighbor in the act of loving love. Friendship is a continuous spiritual exercise that moves between specific acts of love and the analogate love that founds it. If we recall Augustine's criticism of the Academics—that they cannot refute the certainty that we have of our existence, our knowledge of our existence, and our love of our existence—then the love that is friendship consists of the fullness of that certainty. Augustine shows us that our desire for happiness, and of friendship, is implied in the three preconditions of existence, knowledge of existence, and love of existence: "But if they do not will not to be blessed, they undoubtedly do not will that their blessedness be destroyed and come to naught. But they can only be blessed if they live and, therefore, do not wish that their life should perish. Consequently, whoever are either truly blessed, or who desire to be so, will to be immortal" (DT, 13.8.11). Augustine's meditations show us that friendship intimates the eternal love that sustains existence. This claim does not contradict his lament that sin, ignorance, and the vicissitudes of life illuminate the fallenness and uncertainty of existence. Rather, it reinforces the damage we do to ourselves in sinning, and how friendship is an appropriate human response to coping with our fragility.

The argument of this essay has been that political community is an analogue of friendship. This means that the fullness of friendship cannot be found in politics. Or rather, the *populus* is incomplete because its common objects of love differ and cannot be ascertained with the same firmness or clarity as those of friendship. Even so, without the practice of friendship and the fullness of love that it comprises, people will face the temptation to seek that fullness in politics. Augustine's observation that in friendship many become one (Conf., 2.5) will be transposed to politics without the qualifications and moderation that the slogan *e pluribus unum* has found in the American regime.

Generally, modern political thinkers try to make this transposition from friendship to politics without the qualifications characteristic of liberal constitutionalism, which hinders one's ability to find the fullness of friendship. In so doing, it eclipses those irruptions of the good that friends bring, and along with it the experiences of transcendence that compose the growth and communion of souls. As the great diagnostician of modern individualism and its terrible loneliness, Tocqueville shows us the spiritual sources of this modern problem that allow an Augustinian entry point into contemporary discussion. Tocqueville's account of the problematic of friendship in modern democracy is closer to us than Cicero's because it is even more egalitarian and because modern loneliness is its core experience. For Tocqueville, the seemingly providential march of the worldwide historical process toward equality is experienced as meaninglessness on the individual scale, which inverts the Augustinian notion of time in which individual lives are unwittingly guided by particular providence and nations by general providence. In modernity, the Augustinian lottery of friendship is degraded to blind fate, and the pleasure of learning to love is lost because, even if possible, it is seen as pointless owing to the inability of modernity to integrate the individual personality into the political community's "common objects of love." Despite the grandeur of his soul, Tocqueville himself was not immune to this meaninglessness and his sufferings are representative for us. He wrote in a letter to Mme. Swetchine that reading the *philosophes* drove him into melancholic despair because of the implications of their skepticism. However, "strong passions drew me out of this state of despair; they turned me away from the sight of these intellectual ruins and led me toward tangible objects [*objèts sensibles*]."[39] Tocqueville does not specify the *objèts sensibles* that restored his hope, but one may surmise that they included his love of the active life and his engagement in the world, the activity of civil associations he praises in *Democracy in America,* in which he took greater comfort than he did in friendships, especially later in life. Even so, even the active life was limited, as he confessed his alienation from people: "Whenever there is nothing in a man's thoughts or feelings that strikes me, I, so to speak, do not see him. . . . I have never been able to fix in my memory the forms that those features take in each particular case."[40]

From Augustine's perspective, Tocqueville is not open to the "incorporeal conversion" that turns the loving soul toward the friend in truth. As a modern, he seeks the fullness of friendship in political and civil relationships better characterized by utility, which blinds him to the true location of that fullness. Like the Laputians of *Gulliver's Travels*, Tocqueville has one eye pointed down, toward the self, and the other eye pointed up, to the infinite, leaving him no eye to consider the intermediate, the human perspective where friendship resides. Tocqueville recognizes this blindness toward the intermediate as the fundamental existential problem of friendship in democracy, but, from an Augustinian perspective, he fails to go far enough in confronting it. Little wonder then of the uncertainty of his existence, of regarding himself as nothing in the face of the infinite, and incapable of friendship in its fullest.

Augustine's account of friendship enables us not only to diagnose the crisis of modern democratic friendship, but also to move toward a way of transcending it because he tells us where to look, in the intermediate, "from those things which are known." He states in *On the True Religion:* "For on whatever place one has fallen, on that place one must find support so that one may rise again."[41] From that statement we may conclude that we identify whom the "lottery" has given us, and begin with the friend in front of us.

Notes

Earlier versions of this essay were presented in October 2004 at the conference "A Legacy of Provocation: Augustine Reconsidered," sponsored by the Center for the Study of Religion at Princeton University, and in October 2003 at the "Formation and Renewal" conference, sponsored by the Center for Ethics and Culture at the University of Notre Dame. I thank Walter Nicgorski for his comments on a previous draft.

1. Augustine, *City of God against the Pagans*, trans. R. W. Dyson (Cambridge: Cambridge University Press, 1998), 19.21, 24. Hereinafter cited as CD.

2. Carolinne White, *Christian Friendship in the Fourth Century* (Cambridge: Cambridge University Press, 1992), 195.

3. Aristotle, *Nicomachean Ethics*, trans. Joe Sachs (Newburyport, Mass.: Focus Publishing, 2002), 1160a30–1162a30.

4. James McEvoy, "*Anima una et cor unum*: Friendship and Spiritual Unity in Augustine," *Recherches de Theologie Ancienne et Medievale* 53 (1986): 80–91.

5. Augustine, *The Trinity*, trans. Stephen McKenna (Washington, D.C.: Catholic University of America Press, 1964), 13.20.26. Hereinafter cited as DT. Augustine reflects more on the nature of signs than on analogy (see *De Doctrina Christiana*, trans. R. P. H. Green [Oxford: Clarendon Press, 1995]). The meaning of analogy is more restricted than that of signs because signs can signify things as well as other signs (and treat things as signs), whereas analogies express the relationship among things.

6. James V. Schall, *Reason, Revelation, and the Foundations of Political Philosophy* (Baton Rouge: Louisiana State University Press, 1987), 17.

7. *De Amicitia*, 6.23, 9.32, 21.76. See also 9.29, 14.49, 14.28. See also Walter Nicgorski's essay in this collection, "Cicero's Distinctive Voice on Friendship."

8. Adam Smith, *An Inquiry into the Nature and Causes of the Wealth of Nations*, vol. 2, ed. R. H. Campbell et al. (Indianapolis: Liberty Fund, 1981), 795; Alexis de Tocqueville, *Democracy in America*, trans. Harvey Mansfield and Delba Winthrop (Chicago: University of Chicago Press, 2000), 510.

9. R. A. Markus, *Saeculum: History and Society in the Theology of St. Augustine* (Cambridge: Cambridge University Press, 1970); Herbert Deane, *The Political and Social Ideas of St. Augustine* (New York: Columbia University Press, 1963); Oliver O'Donovan, "Augustine's *City of God* XIX and Western Political Thought," *Dionysius* 11 (1987): 89–110; Hannah Arendt, *Love and Saint Augustine*, ed. Joanna Vecchirarelli Scott and Judith Chelius Stark (Chicago: University of Chicago Press, 1996), 97.

10. John von Heyking, *Augustine and Politics as Longing in the World* (Columbia: University of Missouri Press, 2001); Heyking, "From a Wooded Summit: Learning to Love Through Augustinian Meditation at Ascona," in *Pioniere, Poeten, Professoren: Eranos und der Monte Verità in der Zivilisationsgeschichte des 20. Jahrhunderts*. Eranos — Neue Folge Nr. 11, ed. Elisabetta Barone, Matthias Riedl, Alexandra Tischel (Würzburg: Königshausen & Neumann, 2004), 83–96; Oliver O'Donovan, *Common Objects of Love: Moral Reflection and the Shaping of Community* (Grand Rapids, Mich.: Eerdmans, 2002), 36. Other scholars who see greater continuity between politics and other goods include Jean Bethke Elshtain, *Augustine and the Limits of*

Politics (Notre Dame: University of Notre Dame Press, 1998); Peter Burnell, "The Status of Politics in St. Augustine's *City of God*," *History of Political Thought* 13(1) (Spring 1992): 13–29; Catherine Pickstock, "Ascending Numbers: Augustine's *De Musica* and the Western Tradition," in *Christian Origins: Theology, Rhetoric, and Community*, ed. Lewis Ayres and Gareth Jones (New York: Routledge, 1998), 185–215; Todd Breyfogle, "Augustine and the Politics of Friendship," paper presented to symposium on "The City of God," Vancouver, September 1997. See also Michael Oakeshott, *On Human Conduct* (Oxford: Clarendon Press, 1975), 324.

11. David Burrell, *Friendship and the Ways to Truth* (Notre Dame: University of Notre Dame Press, 2000), 27.

12. Augustine, *Confessions*, trans. F. J. Sheed (Indianapolis: Hackett, 1970), 6.10. Hereinafter cited as Conf. See also DT, 13.20.26; Lewis Ayres, "The Christological Context of Augustine's *De trinitate* XIII: Toward Relocating Books VIII–XV," *Augustinian Studies* 29(1) (1998): 111–39. Augustine told Firmus, his "literary agent," that *City of God* should be read repeatedly to understand its meaning (cited in Peter Brown, *Augustine of Hippo* [London: Faber, 1967], 304). See also CD, 11.24, 22.24.

13. John von Heyking, "Disarming, Simple, and Sweet: Augustine's Republican Rhetoric," in *Talking Democracy: Historical Perspectives on Rhetoric and Democratic Deliberation*, ed. Benedetto Fontana, Cary J. Nederman, and Gary Remer (University Park: Penn State University Press, 2004), 182–83. Elsewhere, Augustine calls individual human beings the elements and seeds (*elementa et semina civitatum*) of cities (*Nicene and Post-Nicene Fathers*, vol. 8, *Expositions on the Book of Psalms*, trans. A. Cleveland Coxe [Grand Rapids, Mich.: Eerdmans, 1989], 9.8). See also *City of God*, 22.30.

14. Milbank, *Theology and Social Theory* (Oxford: Blackwell, 1993), 405; Gilbert Meilaender, *Friendship: A Study in Theological Ethics* (Notre Dame: University of Notre Dame Press, 1981), 21.

15. Augustine, *De Doctrina Christiana*, 4.151; DT, 8.6.9; CD, 5.14. In general, see Heyking, "Disarming, Simple, and Sweet," 169–70.

16. Arendt, *Love and Saint Augustine*, 53.

17. *Ancient Christian Writers*, vol. 12, *Against the Academics*, trans. John O'Meara (New York: Newman Press, 1951), 3.6.13; *The Confessions and Letters of St. Augustine*, trans. J. G. Pilkington and J. G. Cunningham (Grand Rapids, Mich.: Eerdmans, 1994), Ep. 258; CD, 19.21, 24. Augustine modifies Cicero's definition by placing human before divine, which is first in Cicero's definition. Maurice Testard argues that Augustine reverses the order to make friendship more theological, to emphasize the process of the human to the divine (cited in McEvoy, "Anima una et cor unum," 79).

18. See, e.g., *Against the Academics*, 2.2.3; *Fathers of the Church*, vol. 59, *The Teacher, the Free Choice of the Will, Grace and Free Will*, trans. Robert P.

Russell (Washington, D.C.: Catholic University of America Press, 1968), 1.15.31.

19. *On Various Questions to Simplicianus*, I, 16, quoted in Arendt, *Love and St. Augustine*, 101 n.12.

20. O'Donovan, *Common Objects of Love*, 19.

21. *On Christian Doctrine*, 1.61–62; Meilaender, *Friendship*, 19; Heyking, *Augustine and Politics as Longing in the World*, 204–5.

22. Frederick J. Crosson, "Book Five: The Disclosure of Hidden Providence," in *A Reader's Companion to Augustine's* Confessions, ed. Kim Paffenroth and Robert P. Kennedy (Louisville, Ky.: Westminster/John Knox Press, 2003), 84.

23. William Stephany, "Thematic Structure in Augustine's *Confessions*," *Augustinian Studies* 20 (1989): 129–42.

24. Eric Plumer, "Book Six: Major Characters and Memorable Incidents," in Paffenroth and Kennedy, eds., *A Reader's Companion to Augustine's* Confessions, 97. Augustine states that friendship is the place where divine love is found (DT, 9.4.6).

25. Carl G. Vaught, *The Journey toward God in Augustine's* Confessions: *Books I–VI* (Albany: State University of New York Press, 2003), 94.

26. Robert McMahon, *Augustine's Prayerful Ascent: An Essay on the Literary Form of the* Confessions (Athens: University of Georgia Press, 1989), 149.

27. Ibid., 88; Conf., 6.9.15, 13.20.26.

28. "No one can be a true friend of man unless he is first a friend of Truth; if friendship does not come into being spontaneously, it cannot exist at all" (Ep. 155).

29. Elshtain, *Augustine and the Limits of Politics*, 55.

30. Augustine, *On the Teacher* 11.36.

31. "If we consult sober reason *[sobria ratione]*, however, we surely find that the more miraculous *[mirabilioris]* of the two divine works is the interweaving, as it were, rather than the coupling of earthly things with heavenly, which, though different, are nonetheless both corporeal" (CD, 22.4).

32. *Fathers of the Church*, vol. 70, Augustine, *Eighty-Three Different Questions*, trans. David L. Mosher (Washington, D.C.: Catholic University of America Press, 1982), 48.

33. "Deliberating is present in things that happen in a certain way for the most part, but are unclear as to how they will turn out, and in which this is undetermined. And we take others as fellow deliberators for large issues, not trusting that we ourselves are adequate to decide them" (Aristotle, *Nicomachean Ethics*, 1112b10–11).

34. Paul Wadell, *Friendship and the Moral Life* (Notre Dame: University of Notre Dame Press, 1989), 7.

35. McEvoy, "*Anima una et cor unum*," 89.

36. "In the first place, then *[Primitus ergo]*, he has the care of his own household, inasmuch as the order of nature or of human society provides him with a readier and easier access to them for seeking help. Wherefore the Apostle says: 'Whoever does not provide for his own, and especially for those of his household, he denies the faith, and is worse than an infidel (1 Timothy 5:8)'" (CD, 19.14).

37. Quoted in White, *Christian Friendship in the Fourth Century*, 7.

38. McMahon, *Augustine's Prayerful Ascent*, 134.

39. Letter dated February 26, 1857, *Correspondence d'Alexis de Tocqueville et de Francisque de Corcelle et Correspondence d'Alexis de Tocqueville et de Madame Swetchine, Œuvres Complètes* XV, ed. Pierre Gibert (Paris: Gallimard, 1983), 2:315, quoted in André Jardin, *Tocqueville: A Biography,* trans. Andre David and Lydia Davis (New York: Farrar, Straus & Giroux, 1988), 61.

40. Alexis de Tocqueville, *Recollections: The French Revolution of 1848,* ed. J. P. Mayer and A. P. Kerr (New Brunswick, N.J.: Transaction Publishers, 1987), 82–83.

41. *On the True Religion,* in Augustine, *Early Writings,* ed. J. H. S. Burleigh (Philadelphia: Westminster Press, 1953), 24.45. Translation altered.

5

A Companionship of *Caritas*

Friendship in St. Thomas Aquinas

Jeanne Heffernan Schindler

"When friendships were the noblest things in the world," Jeremy Taylor observed, "charity was little."[1] So begins Gilbert Meilaender's thoughtful examination of the theological significance of friendship. Meilaender features Taylor's observation because he thinks it captures an important shift in Western culture, specifically the shift from a classical period in which friendship commanded a high degree of respect and attention from statesmen and philosophers alike to a modern period in which friendship has a much-reduced place, meriting little attention from intellectuals. Rather than claiming a central place in political and moral philosophy, friendship has been relegated to the private sphere, becoming so much sentimental grist for the commercial mill.

How did such a state come to pass? Meilaender offers a few suggestions. The modern world, he notes, is one increasingly focused on work. The categories of the working world dominate our self-understanding, and we, unlike the ancients, are far more apt to identify ourselves with our occupation than with our circle of friends. The modern world is also marked by an extraordinary mobility, partly demanded and reinforced by the pressures of the workplace. We go where the jobs are. Such a setting, Meilaender observes, is hardly hospitable to cultivating the kind of friendships cherished by the ancients, which only develop through time spent together. Friends, Aristotle reminds us, must eat the required pinch of salt together.[2]

Yet for Meilaender economic changes alone cannot account for the decline of interest in friendship. Philosophical changes also play a role. He notes that the preoccupation of modern ethics, so dominated by Kant, is with obligations. In such a schema, friendship, which Meilaender calls "a personal bond entered freely and without obligation,"[3] finds no place.

Most relevant for our purposes, however, is Meilaender's claim that theological factors share in the responsibility for the displacement of friendship. Citing Taylor's observation again, Meilaender appeals to a New Testament passage that lends it support. Jesus did say to the disciples, "If you love those who love you, what reward have you? . . . And if you salute only your brethren, what more are you doing than others?" (Matthew 5:46–47). For Meilaender this text reveals the general tendency in Christian thought for *philia* to be superseded by *agape*.

That this shift should occur is no mystery, given what Meilaender takes to be the fundamentally different character of the two. *Agape* love is nonpreferential, like the love of the Father who sends the rain on the just and the unjust, whereas *philia* is precisely "a preferential bond in which we are drawn by what is attractive or choiceworthy in the friend."[4] Moreover, *philia* is a bond marked by reciprocity, while *agape* extends even to our enemies. The love of *agape* is not only broader in scope than *philia*, it is also more constant. The bond of friendship can change, but *agape* should reflect God's enduring faithfulness to the covenant.

The tension Meilaender describes is the starting point for this essay, which seeks how friendship is regarded in Thomistic theology. Mindful of Jeremy Taylor's charge ("When friendships were the noblest things in the world, charity was little"), I will focus attention on one question: Does Christian charity eclipse friendship? To consider this question in the context of Aquinas' encounter with Aristotle seems especially promising, for on the one hand, in Aristotle we find a supremely high estimation of friendship, and on the other, in Aquinas we find a celebration of charity as the highest theological virtue.

Friendship in Aristotle

Before examining Aquinas' discussion of charity, we should recall Aristotle's extensive treatment of friendship in the *Nicomachean Ethics*. From the very start of book 8 we are impressed with the seriousness of the topic, as Aristotle calls friendship "most necessary for our life" (*Ethics*, 1155a2), noting that "no one would choose to live without friends even if he had all the other goods" (*Ethics*, 1155a5–6). Rich and poor, powerful and weak, young and old—all stand in need of friendship. Yet friendship is not only a necessary thing, but also a fine thing, having to do with love.

As Aristotle observes, we love a variety of objects, for instance, what is pleasant, useful, and good. And each of these characterizes a type of friendship. "[F]riendship," he maintains, "has three species, corresponding to the three objects of love" (*Ethics* 1156a5). What they have in common is "reciprocated goodwill" (*Ethics*, 1155b34). Each species of friendship involves conscious, "mutual loving" (*Ethics*, 1156a5) and the wishing of goods one to the other.

While they enjoy certain commonalities, the three species of friendship are not equal in quality. Those who love for utility love the other not for his own sake or in himself, but for the sake of some good he provides. Older people with a keen eye for what is useful are especially inclined to this sort of relationship. Likewise, friendships of pleasure are grounded not in the partners themselves, for themselves, but in the pleasure each takes in the other. Young people, motivated principally by their feelings, are prone to this sort of relationship.

Now while Aristotle classifies friendships of utility and pleasure as friendships, he contends that they are incomplete. Their limitation and fragility is not hard to recognize, for what is useful or pleasant to a person changes, sometimes rapidly; hence the raison d'être of the bond disappears. To call these relationships "friendships," Aristotle explains, is to do so by way of similarity. They partake to some degree in the character of the highest form of friendship, the friendship of the virtuous, which is at once useful, pleasant, and good.

True friendship for Aristotle is a rare and precious thing. Its rarity stems from the fact that it can only be found among the virtuous—virtue itself is rare—and from the fact that it requires face-to-face companionship over time. (As Aristotle reminds us, "Though the wish for friendship comes quickly, friendship does not" [*Ethics*, 1156b32].) At the heart of complete friendship, that is, "the friendship of good people similar in virtue" (*Ethics*, 1156a7), is reciprocated goodwill "for each other's own sake" (*Ethics*, 1156b10). This provides the stability lacking in friendships of utility and pleasure: a true friend loves the other in himself, not conditionally. And he does so from a firm disposition; "loving," Aristotle is quick to point out, "would seem to be a feeling, but friendship is a state" (*Ethics*, 1158b30). But while the hallmark of this bond, unlike the others, is a common life of virtue based in decision, complete friendship is also pleasant and useful. Good people, Aristotle insists, are good and advantageous and pleasant in themselves and for the other. It is no wonder that such a form of friendship is highly praised and is desired even by "blessedly happy people [who want for nothing]" (*Ethics*, 1157b22).

Friendship in the Christian Dispensation

Now in the terms of the Gospel, Christians should be accounted the most blessed of all. But if Meilaender's initial suggestion is right, there would seem to be little room for friendship, at least as classically understood, in the life of beatitude. Charity eclipses *philia*. Meilaender's observation finds support in various Christian writers throughout the ages, from the New Testament to the modern period. As David Konstan argues in his survey of early Christian texts, the classical conception of friendship, if endorsed at all by antique Christian writers, underwent significant modification. That the elevated status of friendship found in Rome and Greece would lose its place of primacy in the early Christian period is anticipated by the fact that friendship receives relatively little attention in the New Testament—recall, by comparison,

Aristotle's and Cicero's extensive treatment of the topic. Noting the rarity of the terms *philo* and *philia* in these texts, Konstan observes that "the Christian writers themselves place small emphasis on friendship among the faithful."[5] Instead of appeals to friendship to characterize the distinctive bonds between the followers of Christ, the Scriptures draw on familial and kinship metaphors; the disciples are brothers to one another, adoptive sons of the Father. Such usage abounds in both the gospels and epistles. In one of the post-resurrection narratives, for instance, John recounts Jesus' instruction to Mary Magdalen: "Do not hold on to me, for I have not yet returned to the Father. Go instead to my brothers and tell them, 'I am returning to my Father and your Father, to my God and your God'" (John 20:17). The motley crew assembled by Jesus, including such unlikely associates as tax collectors and sinners, fishermen and a Pharisee, becomes a family, united by their common adoption by the Father—they have received "the Spirit of sonship"—and their fraternal bond to Christ.[6] Thus, the early Christian community employed familial terms far more often than the language of friendship to describe relations among the followers of Jesus.

Konstan suggests several reasons for this choice, evident not only in the biblical texts but also in antique Christian writings up to the fourth century. First, he recalls that the sine qua non of classical friendship was equality—and this of several kinds. In the era of the city-states, Konstan observes, friendship was understood to obtain among men of equal social standing, participants together in the democratic life of the polis.[7] Friendship, in other words, presupposed citizenship and its activities. More importantly, however, the great distinguishing mark of friendship was equality in virtue. As is clear in Aristotle's description of the most complete friendship, friends are men who have attained that rare and estimable condition of character, *arête*. In such men one finds an internal harmony among the parts of the soul; reason is at the helm, directing the will and cultivating the proper passions. Possessed of such inner order, they engage the world oriented by a firm disposition toward goodness and a correspondingly strong will to choose it.[8] Only men of such high character, whom Aristotle describes as friends of themselves (*Ethics*, 1166a2, b28), are fit for complete friendship. In these relationships alone, unlike friendships of utility or pleasure, "reciprocal regard for the virtue of the other is what excites the amicable feelings in each of the parties."[9]

According to Konstan, for many early Christian writers this mutual regard for one another's excellence at the heart of classical friendship ran contrary to the great Christian virtue of humility. Surveying a set of texts from Paulinus of Nola, which Konstan considers typical of a main stream in Patristic thinking, he observes that Paulinus most often substituted Christian *caritas* for *amicitia* when characterizing his relationship to other believers. For Konstan, this stems from Paulinus' humility; he cannot assume the role of friend in the classical sense, for his modesty prevents his claim to equality in virtue with his peers, let alone those more advanced in the Christian life. When writing to Augustine's companion Alypius, for instance, Paulinus begins his letter with the following address: "To his lord, deserving and honored and most blessed, father Alypius, from the sinners Paulinus and Therasia."[10] Paulinus thus characterizes the relationship as that between saint and sinner and exhibits a kind of self-effacement that would be foreign to the terms of classical friendship; hence his appeal to a different kind of response from Alypius—namely, one resembling the gratuitous love of God, *agape*, not a gesture of friendship based on a positive assessment of the other's virtue. Taking Paulinus' texts as illustrative of an important current in early Christian thought, Konstan contends that Christian humility "disrupts the classical ideal of friendship based on a consciousness of virtue" and concludes that, in turn, "Christians writing in this vein present themselves to one another not as friends and equals, but as brothers united in the body of Christ, thanks to their common faith."[11]

The tension between *philia* or *amicitia* and *agape* underscored by Meilaender finds evidence in early Christian texts, but it is not limited to this period. A brief look at Søren Kierkegaard will suffice to show that this tension endures into the modern period, though different dimensions of the tension are accented. As Paul Waddell points out, the problematic feature of classical friendship for a thinker such as Kierkegaard was not its basis in equality of social standing or excellence; rather, it was the preferential character of such love that most distinguished it, indeed separated it, from Christian love. Celebrated by pagans, *philia* belongs to a world unenlightened by Gospel truth; hence it remains worldly and earth bound, in dramatic contrast to the sublimity of Christian *agape*. As Kierkegaard declares, "Christianity has thrust erotic love and friendship from the throne, the love rooted in mood and inclination, preferential love, in order to establish spiritual love in its place, love to one's neighbour."[12] Everything about *philia*—its origin, nature, and end—stands in opposition to Gospel love. Rooted fundamentally in self-love, friendship rests on attraction to a particular person deemed worthy of one's attention and affection; it is by its nature preferential and exclusive and serves to benefit the self. "Consequently," Kierkegaard insists, "Christianity has misgivings about erotic love and friendship because preference in passion or passionate preference is really another form of self-love.... Therefore," he continues, "what paganism called love, in contrast to self-love, was preference. But if passionate preference is essentially another form of self-love, one again sees the truth in the saying of the worthy father, 'The virtues of paganism are glittering vices.'"[13] As Waddell summarizes, friendship is thus conceived as erotic, preferential, selfish, and exclusive, whereas *agape* is spiritual, obedient, other-regarding, and inclusive. With Christianity, there dawns a new kind of love that forever eclipses that most celebrated of pagan relationships.

Friendship in St. Thomas Aquinas

Evidence from the New Testament, Patristic, and modern periods indicates that Christian writers across the centuries have perceived a basic and irreconcilable tension between friendship, at least as classically understood, and Christian love. *Agape* supercedes *philia*, which the ancients prized so highly. Yet, not all Christian thinkers have held such a stark view. As David Konstan notes, while the substitution of *caritas* and *agape* for *amicitia* and *philia* was common in the early Church and Patristic eras, renowned Christian theologians, such as Gregory of Nazianzus, John Chrysostom, Basil, and Augustine, favorably appeal to the terms of classical friendship, transforming them in distinctively Christian ways. This suggests that the soil of *philia* might not be inhospitable to the root of Christian love as it might first appear.

A turn to the medieval period and an examination of Aquinas on this point is illuminating and somewhat surprising, for we find in Aquinas neither a rejection nor even a diminution of friendship; rather we find friendship elevated and transformed by the order of grace. It is elevated insofar as it takes on a supernatural character foreign to classical friendship, while it is transformed by divine power into a means of enjoying eternal beatitude.

The first clue that indicates the enduring value of friendship in the Thomistic schema is in Aquinas' treatment of the passions of the soul in the Prima Secundae Q. 26 of the *Summa*.[14] Here we see that friendship is an important category for Aquinas, for it exemplifies a particular kind of love. In contrast to concupiscent love or desire, which loves something or someone instrumentally, for the sake of something else, friendship reflects what Aquinas calls the primary "movement of love"[15] (directed only toward human beings and not to inanimate goods or to animals, which by their nature serve human uses). In this primary movement of love, we love someone, wishing good to him *for his own sake*. Indeed, it is insofar as relationships display the second movement of love, borne of concupiscence, that they defect from the love of friendship. Clearly referencing Aristotle, Aquinas deems friendships of utility and pleasure as defective in this way.

Having introduced the category of friendship, Aquinas proceeds to describe it in quite favorable, even extravagant, terms. The friendship is unitive, bringing lover and beloved together physically and emotionally; friends enjoy the presence of the other and share in affection.[16] So intimate is true friendship that it effects a "mutual indwelling" of persons, by way of the apprehensive power and the appetitive power. On account of the first, the beloved abides in the mind of the lover, who "strives to gain an intimate knowledge of everything pertaining to the beloved, so as to penetrate his very soul."[17] On account of the second, the beloved dwells in the affections of the lover, who wills the good of the beloved, takes pleasure in his presence, and longs for him in his absence. Friendship, then, entails the action of both the heart and the mind and is marked by a particular kind of intensity—Aquinas calls it "zeal"—which "causes a man to be moved against everything that opposes the friend's good."[18]

Now each of the characteristics described above might also be said of Aristotelian *philia*. Indeed, Aquinas makes explicit his debt to the Philosopher's treatment of friendship numerous times throughout his analysis, appealing to such texts as Aristotle's *Nicomachean Ethics, Politics,* and *Rhetoric*. Thus, the preceding discussion shows only that Aquinas is attentive to the category of friendship and considers it important. I have yet to show what a distinctively Christian understanding of friendship would be, or to put it differently, how charity in Aquinas relates to friendship.

Aquinas himself makes the link for us, and quite dramatically at that. First, in II–II, q. 23 Aquinas appeals to a startling passage in the Gospel of John, which serves as a counterweight to the Matthean text Meilaender cites in which Christ seems to place the universality of Christian charity in tension with the particular bonds of friendship (*agape* over against *philia*). By contrast, the Johannine passage, which is authoritative for Aquinas on this question—"I will not now call you servants . . . but my friends" (John 15:15)—indicates that human beings can, through the theological virtue of *caritas,* enjoy a bond of friendship with God, the very source of *agape* love. Aquinas puts it most straightforwardly when he says, "charity *is* friendship."[19] Now one might suspect that he is using the term "friendship" in an equivocal sense. But as if to head the objection off at the pass, Aquinas immediately invokes Aristotle's definition of friendship as that particular kind of love marked by mutually reciprocated goodwill for the sake of the other, communication, and fellowship. Each of these conditions obtains—however imperfectly—in the friendship of man and God in charity. As Anthony Keaty observes, Aristotle's categories of benevolence and communication furnish a taxonomical scheme according to which Aquinas identifies the genus and species of charity friendship.[20] But when he identifies the substantial good shared between friends in charity, Aquinas moves beyond Aristotle's categories onto qualitatively different ground.

To gauge how significantly Aquinas' *caritas* transforms the Philosopher's *philia,* we must turn to Aristotle's treatment of friendships between unequals. After noting that friendships resting on "superiority" (1158b)—such as those between father and son, men and women, and rulers and subjects—entail a proportional equality, he observes that great disparities impede the formation or maintenance of friendship. Among such disparities is that found between gods and men. So removed from the human estate, the gods enjoy, in Suzanne Stern-Gillet's words, "complete autarky," self-sufficiency to the highest degree. Immune from fortune and appetitive desires, "the divine nature constitutes its own, uniquely suitable, cognitive object." Unlike human beings who gain self-understanding through relationship to others, the divinities need no friends: "divine autarky is total."[21] Not surprisingly, Aristotle proceeds to question whether a friend really wishes the greatest good, namely, to be a god, to his fellows, since "[if he becomes a god], *he* will no longer have friends" (1159a8–9). Betwixt god and man is affixed an unbridgeable gulf—not even proportional equality is possible here; hence neither is divine—human friendship.[22]

Christian charity, by contrast, is precisely friendship between God and man. How is such a thing possible when Aquinas, no less than Aristotle, recognizes the radical disparity between the divine and the human? The answer lies in the action of the transcendent God himself. Having created man in his own image, capable of knowledge and love, God invites him into a *communicatio,* a sharing of "God's beatitude," what Paul Waddell describes as "the friendship love that is God, the perfect love relationship that is Trinity."[23] Human beings are by nature incapable of effecting such a relationship. As Aquinas insists:

> Charity, as we have said, is our friendship for God arising from our sharing in eternal happiness, which is not a matter of natural goods but of gifts of grace, according to St. Paul, "The free gift of God is eternal life." Consequently charity is beyond the resources of nature, and therefore cannot be something natural, nor acquired by natural powers, since no effect transcends its cause. Hence we have it neither by nature, nor as acquired, but as infused by the Holy Spirit, who is the love of the Father and the Son; our participation in this love . . . is creaturely charity itself.[24]

So gifted by grace, human beings are "elevated *by God's power* to a state of *actual* similitude with God, i.e., to a state of participation in the blessedness of God's own life."[25] God alone initiates charity friendship. It is "the Holy Spirit," Aquinas explains, who "constitutes us God's friends, and makes Him dwell in us, and us dwell in Him."[26] But this friendship commences only when man freely accepts the divine invitation. And it grows only as he becomes "the sort of person who embodies God's perfection," that is to say, only as he becomes more like Christ.[27]

It is in light of this primary friendship with God that Aquinas understands human friendship for one another. *Philia* has thus been given a new foundation; the source of friendship has been taken out of the bounds of the polis.[28] But while friendship finds its origins outside the polis, according to Aquinas, it returns to it in a new way, for the supernatural virtue of charity transforms every natural relationship. Recalling Jesus' articulation of the Great Commandment,[29] he explains that, "God is the principal object of charity, while our neighbor is loved out of charity for God's sake."[30] Christian friendship finds its source in God and its sustenance in grace, but it extends beyond God to our neighbor. Human friendships are not lost under the Christian dispensation. Making an explicit appeal to Aristotle's definition, Aquinas takes care to note that the Christian wishes good things for his friend, does good things for him, takes pleasure in his company, and enjoys with him a communion of sorrow and joy.[31] What adds leaven to this list, however, is the character of the goods he wishes for his friend, for the primary good he wishes for his friend—one that informs all of the others—is not to be found in the city. It is the "fellowship of everlasting happiness."[32] Above all, heaven is what we wish for our friends, and we foster this end in ways that evince the distinction between classical and Christian friendship. For instance, Aquinas notes that friends imbued with the love of charity share spiritual goods with one another through the mystical connection they enjoy. Through activities such as prayer and fasting, instruction in the faith, and heroic material sacrifices, "the good of one is communicated to the other."[33] Such acts of *caritas* bear both temporal and eternal fruit, a fitting yield for a natural relationship that, once elevated by grace, becomes "a means of salvation for those involved."[34]

We have seen how the source and end of friendship is transformed in the Christian life, but for Aquinas its scope is also changed. Herein lies the greatest challenge to the classical definition. Christians are commanded to love their enemies, but friendship presupposes reciprocal goodwill. Mindful of this tension, Aquinas explains that friendship extends to a person in two ways. First and most directly, we love our virtuous friend; second, we love those belonging to the friend, whether virtuous or no. "Indeed," Aquinas maintains, "so much do we love our friends, that for their sake we love all who belong to them, even if they hurt or hate us; so that, in this way, the friendship of charity extends even to our enemies, whom we love out of charity in relation to God, to Whom the friendship of charity is chiefly directed."[35] The circle of friendship is dramatically extended.

But is it so extended that the concept is stretched beyond recognition? Do we assume that Christians have to spend as much time in the company of their enemies as they do with their friends? Must they have the same sentiments toward them? Is *caritas* blind to virtue and vice? Aquinas sheds some light on these matters when he considers the question "Ought we to love one neighbor more than another?" The recurring claim found in the three objections he entertains is from Augustine's *On Christian Doctrine*: Christians are called to love all men equally. Now some, he notes, interpret this to mean that we ought to have the same inward affections, ties of the heart, to all men equally, including our enemies, but that for obvious reasons of human finitude, we ought to confer more "outward favors" on those with whom we are most closely associated. Interestingly, Aquinas rejects this view and vindicates particular attachments not only on account of the constraints of time and space, but also, it seems, in principle. He argues that "one's obligation to love a person is proportionate to the gravity of the sin one commits in acting against that love" and adds that "it is a more grievous sin to act against the love of certain neighbors [such as father and mother], than against the love of others." And so Aquinas concludes, "[W]e ought to love some neighbors more than others."[36] The universal scope of charity is not contradicted thereby, he insists, since we love all men equally according to charity, that is, we wish them all the same good, eternal life. But as to our beneficence, we have differentiated obligations; there are "those to whom we ought to behave with greater kindness."[37]

For Aquinas this differentiation applies not only to our actions, but also to our affections, which would seem to leave more room for expansion. Aquinas accounts for this by appealing to the particular way in which the order of grace relates to the order of nature. Grace builds upon nature, for both the inclinations of grace and the natural appetite "flow from the Divine wisdom."[38] As Robert Sokolowski expresses it, friendship is "a natural substrate that can be elevated by grace into the Christian theological virtue of charity. It is the point of contact between nature and grace." Friendship is thus a "natural anticipation" of the graced love of charity.[39] And, for Aquinas, just as we are called to express our love more intensely for some than for others, so too ought "the affection of our charity" reflect the same proportion.[40]

Aquinas' treatment of friendship, then, provides some resolution of the tension to which Gilbert Meilaender has alerted us. Friendship retains a high place in the Christian life, but it has a new source, end, and scope. *Agape* and *philia* meet in the companionship of *caritas*.

Political Meaning of Thomistic Friendship

As evident above, charity complements natural human love, a fact that illustrates one of the central tenets of Thomistic theology cited earlier—namely, grace builds on, not destroys, nature. Those ends that Aquinas identifies as natural are not denigrated for being temporal; rather, earthly happiness and the virtues requisite to it are given their due as reflective of God's design of creation and providential care for man in history.[41]

In the Thomistic schema, the most auspicious context for achieving such happiness is the polis; it is here that man can develop his moral and intellectual faculties most fully. Political authority plays an indispensable role in this development, for it attends to the character of its citizens, employing law to habituate them in virtue so as to flourish as human beings. Insofar as the statesman is concerned with the good of his people, he enjoys a kind of friendship with them. As Aquinas describes in his *Commentary on Aristotle's Nicomachean Ethics*, a king worthy of the authority vested in him acts not for his own interest "but rather for the benefit of his subjects."[42] This other-regarding orientation is precisely what distinguishes a good regime from its corruption and provides the basis for the friendship between ruler and ruled. Reflecting again on Aristotle's account of political systems, Aquinas notes that each form of government involves a type of friendship founded on justice and that in the best regime, namely, kingship, there exists "a superabundant friendship" between a king and his subjects as between a benefactor and beneficiaries. "It is proper to a king," Aquinas explains, "to confer benefits on his subjects, for if he is a good ruler he takes care that they perform good deeds, and strives to make his subjects virtuous." He continues, "Hence, inasmuch as he leads his subjects as a shepherd his flock, he is even given the title. Thus Homer called King Agamemnon shepherd of his people."[43]

Law is the most prominent staff of statesmanship for this shepherd. It is an instrument by which he communicates concern for his flock; it is, as it were, a means of expressing his friendship. Such a notion likely sounds foreign, at best, to modern ears; at worst, it strikes us as clever propaganda deployed by a ruling class. Schooled in the terms of liberalism and postmodernism and accustomed to viewing law through a suspicious hermeneutical lens, we are apt to conceive of law as Thrasymachus cynically described justice: "the advantage of the stronger."[44]

Aquinas disagrees. Though no stranger to unjust regimes and bad legislation, he nevertheless insists, "Law is nothing else than an ordinance of reason for the common good, promulgated by him who has the care of the community."[45] Self-interested statutes imposed by an elite on a vulnerable public hardly qualify as law—in Augustine's famous formulation, "a law that is not just seems to be no law at all."[46] It is striking, in fact, to recognize the many ways in which Aquinas thinks particular laws can deviate from their proper form. As he explains at length, laws may be unjust:

> Either in respect of the end, as when an authority imposes on his subjects burdensome laws, conducive, not to the common good, but rather to his own cupidity or vainglory; or in respect of the author, as when a man makes a law that goes beyond the power committed to him; or in respect of the form, as when burdens are imposed unequally on the community, although with a view to the common good. Such are acts of violence rather than laws.[47]

Nor could such measures be considered acts of civic friendship.

By contrast, genuine law in its promulgation and reception is always a reflection of civic friendship. Guided by reason, the ruler articulates an ordinance designed to benefit the citizenry and promote the common good; lawmaking is thus beneficent. Its beneficiaries, for their part, reflect the friendly goodwill they have toward their sovereign by obeying his just commands; in so doing, they not only honor the authority of his office but also express friendship toward one another, since the law is directed toward the good of the whole.[48]

As Aquinas notes in his *Commentary on Aristotle's Nicomachean Ethics*, the particular friendship citizens share—namely, "concord" or "political friendship"—entails a particular kind of agreement. It is not agreement over speculative matters, but practical ones that rise to a certain level of importance. Aquinas explains that for Aristotle, "citizens of a state are said to have concord among themselves when they agree on what is useful, so that they vote for the same measures and work together on projects they consider for their interests."[49]

Civic Friendship and Charity

But does the natural good of civic friendship relate to the supernatural virtue of charity? It does and in several ways. Recall that for Aquinas the particular grace of charity perfects temporal loves, including the bonds between citizens. As Aquinas affirms in *De Caritate*, "[C]harity embraces in itself all human loves, those alone excepted that are supported on sin. So that love for relations and fellow-citizens and companions voyaging together or for anybody, however associated, can be from charity and worthy of heaven."[50] As Michael Sherwin explains, charity has a special unifying effect among human beings, and when citizens are bound to one another not only by a common political tie, but also by charity, their civic communion is enhanced. In the first place, the individual endowed with charity enjoys an inner union of heart, mind, and will that "is an invaluable asset to the community and safeguards its good,"[51] for it enables him to promote peace in the community. In addition to fostering tranquility, charity causes the citizen "to desire and actively promote the good of every other member of the community," manifested most clearly in the alacrity with which he exhibits the cardinal political virtue of justice. Charity, for Aquinas, not only strengthens justice, but perfects it, prompting the citizen to give his fellows their due "spontaneously and joyfully," even adding "something in excess by way of liberality."[52] The interior order of its citizens' souls, animated by *caritas,* thus profoundly affects the common good of the city.

That the bonds of civic friendship are assimilated for Aquinas into the love of charity becomes more readily understandable when one considers that he views life in political community as natural, an outgrowth of man's God-given sociability. So, too, is political authority. Aquinas rejects the view found in some strains of political theology that government was simply remedial of sin, "a necessary evil," as Reinhold Niebuhr put it, "required by the Fall of man."[53] To the contrary, Aquinas held political authority to be natural, part of the created order from the beginning. As his treatment of the state of innocence makes clear, both the welfare of individuals and the community would have required the "office of governing and directing."[54] This seems implausible to a modern audience accustomed to seeing political authority primarily as an agent of coercion and punishment. For Aquinas, though, the punitive function of government, made necessary by sin, is secondary and accidental to its main function: ensuring the conditions for the fullest moral, intellectual, and spiritual development of persons. In other words, political authority is charged with care for the common good.[55]

The directive function of this authority, for Aquinas, whether in Eden or east of it, must always reflect God's own design of creation found in the eternal law. Human law, in other words, is derived from the wisdom of God evident in the intelligible structure of the created order and mediated to human consciousness by natural and divine law; it ought to remain faithful to that order, for it is precisely the conformity of human law to the eternal law that furnishes its obligatory force. "If they be just," Aquinas insists, "[laws] have the power of binding in conscience from the eternal law whence they are derived."[56] Thus, to recall the description of civic concord described above, the reception of law by the citizens is a mark of their friendship toward their governors, but it is more than that. Given that government is providentially appointed for human perfection and that legislators share some part of the divine activity of lawmaking, obeying human law can be seen as a manifestation of charity, that is, of friendship with God.[57] This becomes more evident when we note that Aquinas recommends disobedience of any law that is "opposed to the divine good,"[58] whether because it is idolatrous or offends some portion of the divine law.

Civic friendship on the part of the citizen, then, reflects the supernatural virtue of charity insofar as it springs from his love of God and the things God has ordained, including political authority and law. Yet, as demonstrated earlier, friendship in the Christian dispensation finds its origins from above and returns to the polis on a new footing; it is precisely this foundation that provides a standard for judging the limits of civil obedience. The friendship a man enjoys with God dictates the terms of his friendship within the city. Since he "must obey God rather than men,"[59] the requirements of charity supersede the claims of political authority when it transgresses the divine law. But it is important to note that the disobedience required in this instance is itself borne of friendship, both for God and man; it is not anarchistic in inspiration. The Christian citizen who disobeys such a law publicly testifies to friendship with God and instructs his fellows in the right ordering of love.

While acts of genuine civil disobedience afford an opportunity for this kind of witness and instruction, they are occasioned by a failure of charity and civic friendship. Any law that opposes the divine good, for Aquinas, is an affront to charity; the lawgiver has failed to respect the dictates of the eternal, natural, and divine law. He has also offended against charity in promulgating an act that jeopardizes the spiritual welfare of his citizens, with whose good he has been entrusted. Now for Aquinas the immediate direction of individuals to their eternal end, their ultimate good, is vouchsafed to the Church and its ministers through the proclamation of the Word and the performance of the sacraments.[60] But while the statesman does not directly govern the spiritual life of his subjects, he should nevertheless advance it. At a minimum, he should never enact a statute that would offend against the divine law, but more is required. Prompted by charity to be concerned about their ultimate end, he habituates his citizens in the natural virtues, which enable them to live out the infused virtues with greater ease. He likewise prohibits those vices that would threaten their temporal, as well as eternal, well being.[61] Civic friendship and charity require attention to both ends.

Caritas and a Companionship of Earthly and Heavenly Cities

As the preceding discussion makes clear, friendship retains an elevated status within the political theology of Thomas Aquinas. Unlike other Christian thinkers such as Kierkegaard, Aquinas denies an irreconcilable tension between *philia* and *agape*. The two converge, in fact, in the virtue of *caritas*—the new foundation of friendship and the highest of the Christian virtues. United in the bond of charity, Christians enjoy a tie of friendship with God that informs and infuses all of their other relationships, including their political bonds. Mindful of their primary friendship with God through which they love one another, Christian citizens enjoy a distinctive kind of concord, desire and promote one another's good, and obey the just ordinances of their rulers as deriving from God's wise ordering of the cosmos. Christian rulers, in their turn, govern in friendship with their subjects, taking care to promote not only the temporal but also the eternal good of the citizenry. In the political theology of Thomas Aquinas, then, *philia* and *agape* have met in the companionship of *caritas* that finds a home in both the earthly polis and the heavenly city alike.

Notes

1. Quoted in Gilbert Meilaender's *Friendship: A Study in Theological Ethics* (Notre Dame: University of Notre Dame Press, 1981), 1.

2. Aristotle, *Nicomachean Ethics,* 2d ed., trans. Terence Irwin (Indianapolis: Hackett, 1999), 1156b28. Hereinafter cited as *Ethics.*

3. Meilaender, *Friendship,* 2.

4. Ibid., 3.

5. David Konstan, "Problems in the History of Christian Friendship," *Journal of Early Christian Studies* 4(1) (1996): 96–97.

6. Romans 8:15. The familial metaphors used to describe Christian solidarity are voluminous. In addition to those noted above, representative passages can be found in Matthew 5:45, 23:8; Luke 22:32; Acts 11:29; and Galatians 4:6.

7. In light of the primacy placed on equality in the classical ideal of friendship, it is not surprising to see that Aristotle carves out a special category to describe the relationship that obtains between persons who are in one respect or another unequal. Fathers and sons, men and women, and rulers and ruled fall into this category. In these relationships, ones that "rest on superiority" (*Ethics,* 1158b25), a kind of equality is effected by proportional love in which the proper acts of love are differentiated according to station. Parents and children, for instance, owe different things to each other and do not exhibit the same kind of love as that found between peers. Nevertheless, they achieve a kind of equality required of friendship: "when the loving accords with the comparative worth of the friends, equality is achieved in a way, and this seems to be proper to friendship" (*Ethics,* 1158b27–29). Aristotle cautions, however, that if the friends become separated by an unbridgeable gap, the friendship

cannot endure, and in this vein he notes that "far inferior people" (*Ethics*, 1159a1–2) cannot expect to enjoy the friendship of a king. Aristotle does not specify the nature of this gulf or the way in which these persons are "far inferior." But since he mentions it in the context of his discussion of unequal friendships—among which political friendships receive specific mention—it should be seen as an *exception* to the type of friendship enjoyed between ruler and ruled; it should not be seen to undermine the category per se. This exception indicates that Aristotle is working with an implicit distinction between those among "the ruled" who are fit for this kind of friendship and those (including, slaves, perhaps) who are not.

8. Aristotle vividly contrasts the integrity of soul found in the virtuous man with the divided soul of the vicious: whereas "the excellent person is of one mind with himself, and desires the same things in his whole soul" (*Ethics*, 1166a14–15), actively exerting himself for the good, the vicious man experiences conflict in his soul, being ever "at odds with [himself]," having "an appetite for one thing and a wish for another" (*Ethics*, 1166b7–8). At the most basic level, then, the vicious man lacks the dependability required for those ongoing acts of goodwill demanded by friendship.

9. Konstan, "Problems in the History of Christian Friendship," 100.

10. Ibid.

11. Ibid., 101.

12. Paul Waddell, *Friendship and the Moral Life* (Notre Dame: University of Notre Dame Press, 1989), 75.

13. Søren Kierkegaard, *Works of Love*, trans. Howard and Edna Hong (New York: Harper & Row, 1964), 58, quoted in Waddell, *Friendship and the Moral Life*, 76–77.

14. Several of Aquinas' reflections on friendship have been helpfully collected in *Other Selves: Philosophers on Friendship*, ed. Michael Pakaluk (Indianapolis: Hackett, 1991). I have made use of this collection here.

15. *ST*, I–II, q. 26, art. 4.

16. *ST*, I–II, q. 28, art. 1.

17. *ST*, I–II, q. 28, art. 2. In his argument concerning friendship and justice in Aquinas, Daniel Schwartz Porzecanski contends that the intensity of this desire to know the friend intimately does not yield a perfect knowledge of him; all human friendships, even those deeply rooted in charity, are subject to the constraints of human finitude and fallenness. "Aquinas's friendship," Porzecanski maintains, "coexists with conflict, disputes, and mutual uncertainties between friends (which are ineliminable features of the personal relationships we can experience in this world). For this reason, whatever the closeness present in a relationship, justice never becomes redundant." Thus, in reflecting on Aquinas' assertion that "a thing is loved more than it is known; since it can be loved perfectly, even without being perfectly known" (*ST*, I–II,

q. 27, art. 2, ad 2), Porzecanski concludes that "the effect of the union of love (as to apprehension) is a *desire* of cognition of everything related to the beloved, not that the effect is the actual and complete cognition of it" ("Friendship and Justice in Aquinas," *Review of Politics* 66(1) (2004): 35, 41).

18. *ST*, I–II, q. 28, art. 4.

19. *ST*, II–II, q. 23. (Emphasis added.)

20. Anthony Keaty, "Thomas's Authority for Identifying Charity as Friendship: Aristotle or John 15?" *Thomist* 62 (1998): 585.

21. Suzanne Stern-Gillet, *Aristotle's Philosophy of Friendship* (Albany: State University of New York Press, 1995), 123, 129.

22. L. Gregory Jones reflects on this paradox of the divine *autarkeia* and human happiness by noting that for Aristotle "what it means to be human is to be more than human; it is to attempt to become divine, to resemble (if we can) the gods. Yet," he continues, "Aristotle's account is limited by its inability to find a way to make what is necessary for human happiness possible. Human happiness is dependent on becoming like the gods. Yet on the basis of his understanding of the gods' relation (or lack thereof) to the world, as well as the gods' being so unlike us that friendship with them is impossible, Aristotle had no means to envision how human happiness could be possible" ("Theological Transformation of Aristotelian Friendship in the Thought of St. Thomas Aquinas," *New Scholasticism* 61 [Autumn 1987]: 380). Jones argues that Aquinas' theological resources provide the grounds for a resolution of this problem; I offer a similar argument here.

23. Waddell, *Friendship in the Moral Life*, 122–23.

24. *ST*, II–II, q. 24, art. 2.

25. Joseph Bobik, "Aquinas on *Communicatio*: The Foundation of Friendship and Caritas," *Modern Schoolman* 64 (November 1986): 7.

26. *Summa Contra Gentiles*, IV, 22 (3).

27. Jones, "Theological Transformation," 385. Jones persuasively argues that Aquinas' account of *caritas* presupposes a Christological and sacramental context, for it is only through the merits of Christ that human beings experience redemption from sin—a prerequisite to the life of friendship with God. Moreover, it is only by the grace continually offered to the disciples in the sacrament of the Eucharist that they are transformed into friends of God who imitate the works of God.

28. This contrast with the polis is meant to underscore the supernatural origin of Christian friendship, not to suggest that the highest form of friendship for Aristotle is civic friendship. As his fuller description of eudaimonia in *Nicomachean Ethics* book 10 makes clear, the highest human activity is contemplation; thus, the practical virtues most associated with the active life of the polis are secondary to the cultivation of the contemplative capacity. The best form of friendship, then, would have a more comprehensive field than civic

friendship. In addition to the practical political concerns shared by citizens, those who enjoy complete friendship also share a commitment to the life of study. These friends recognize that exercising the "divine element" (1177b28) of the human soul, the understanding, gives rise to the fullest happiness, and so they assist one another in this activity; together they "do philosophy" (1172a5). Underscoring the importance of this companionship, Aristotle notes that while the wise person is able to study by himself, "he presumably does it better with colleagues" (1177b1).

29. "'Love the Lord your God with all your heart and with all your soul and with all your mind.' This is the first and greatest commandment. And the second is like it: 'Love your neighbor as yourself'" (Mt. 22:37–40).

30. *ST*, II–II, q. 23, art. 5, reply obj. 1.

31. *ST*, II–II, q. 25, art. 7.

32. *ST*, II–II, q. 25, art. 3. The way in which this primary good orders all others might actually jeopardize the attainment of certain natural goods pertaining to the city in the interest of securing supernatural ones. An example from contemporary American politics comes to mind. During the 2004 election, several Catholic bishops decided to withhold communion from pro-choice politicians within their dioceses. In light of Aquinas' schema, this is properly viewed as an act of Christian friendship, for the bishops are concerned in the first place with the spiritual welfare of the politicians, who have placed their salvation in jeopardy. The tension with the immediate temporal good at stake becomes clear when one considers the probability that had the politicians in question changed their public stance on abortion and returned to full communion with the Church, they would very likely have imperiled their reelection. Insofar as political office is a natural good, it would thus be forfeited for the sake of a supernatural good. (The fact that these conflict in this case indicates, of course, that the context within which reelection would be forfeited is itself a fallen one. There should be no conflict per se between exercising political authority and enjoying full Christian communion; only the circumstances of sin pit the one against the other, that is, only in a broken world is it the case that a candidate feel pressure to contradict Church teaching in order to secure political office.) At the same time, at a deeper level the bishops' actions can be seen as contributing to the natural good of the polis, insofar as their interventions encourage its improvement in justice. By reminding their flock of the impermissibility of abortion, by potentially changing the policy stance of Catholic officials, and by alerting the broader public to the gravity of the issue, their actions might well decrease the prevalence of the injustice.

33. *In Symbolum Apostolorum*, 13 (135), quoted in Michael Sherwin, O.P., "Charity as Friendship in the Promotion of the Common Good in the Thought of Saint Thomas Aquinas" (unpublished master's thesis, Graduate Theological Union, 1991), 101.

34. Ibid., 103.

35. *ST,* II–II, q. 23, art. 1, reply obj. 2.

36. *ST,* II–II, q. 26, art. 6.

37. Ibid.

38. Ibid.

39. Robert Sokolowski, "Phenomenology of Friendship," *Review of Metaphysics* 55 (March 2002): 470.

40. These passages in Thomas bring to mind a vignette from Boswell's *Life of Johnson* recounted by Gilbert Meilaender. In this scene Dr. Johnson is conversing with one Mrs. Knowles who suggests that friendship is a Christian virtue, to which Johnson responds, "Now Christianity recommends universal benevolence, to consider all men as our brethren; which is contrary to the virtue of friendship, as described by the ancient philosophers." Mrs. Knowles, in turn, appeals to the biblical injunction to "do good to all but *especially* to those of the household of faith." Johnson counters that "the household of faith is wide enough." And the quick-witted Mrs. Knowles reminds her interlocutor that though Jesus gathered twelve apostles "we are told that there was one whom he loved." And Boswell records that Johnson ("with eyes sparkling benignantly"), conceded, "Very well, indeed, Madam. You have said very well." Boswell: "A fine application. Pray, Sir, had you ever thought of it?" Johnson: "I had not, Sir." (Meilaender, *Friendship,* 7).

41. A passage in John Paul II's *Evangelium Vitae* (Boston: Pauline Books and Media, 1995) expresses this perspective well: "Man is called to a fullness of life which far exceeds the dimensions of his earthly existence, because it consists in sharing the very life of God. The loftiness of this supernatural vocation reveals the greatness and the inestimable value of human life even in its temporal phase. Life in time, in fact, is the fundamental condition, the initial stage and an integral part of the entire unified process of human existence. It is a process which, unexpectedly and undeservedly, is enlightened by the promise and renewed by the gift of divine life, which will reach its full realization in eternity (cf. 1 John 3:1–2). At the same time, it is precisely this supernatural calling which highlights the relative character of each individual's earthly life. After all, life on earth is not an 'ultimate' but a 'penultimate' reality; even so, it remains a sacred reality entrusted to us, to be preserved with a sense of responsibility and brought to perfection in love and in the gift of ourselves to God and to our brothers and sisters" (3).

42. *Commentary on Aristotle's Nicomachean Ethics,* trans. C. I. Litzinger, O.P. (Notre Dame: Dumb Ox Books, 1993). When appealing to this commentary, I am operating with the assumption that Thomas is in substantial agreement with Aristotle on the question of civic friendship. I have not found anything in the text itself or in Thomas' political writings to suggest otherwise.

43. Ibid., para. 1688–89. See also *De Regno*, trans. Gerald B. Phelen (Toronto: Pontifical Institute of Medieval Studies, 1949), I [10]. It is important to note that Thomas sees the task of the statesman as including not only the promotion of the temporal end of natural virtue for his citizens, but also their supernatural end. He explains in *De Regno*, for instance, that "through virtuous living man is further ordained to a higher end, which consists in the enjoyment of God, as we have said above. Consequently, since society must have the same end as the individual man, it is not the ultimate end of an assembled multitude to live virtuously, but through virtuous living to attain to the possession of God" (III, 1, 14 [107]). How the statesman directs his subjects to this higher end is discussed in the following section on "Civic Friendship and Charity."

44. Plato, *Republic*, I, 344 c.

45. *ST*, I–II, q. 90, art. 4.

46. Augustine, *On Free Will*, I, 5, cited in *ST*, I–II, q. 96, art. 4.

47. *ST*, I–II, q. 96, art. 4.

48. Aquinas describes this appropriate receptivity as a virtue. "Now the virtue of any being that is a subject consists in its being well subordinated to that by which it is regulated; and thus we see that the virtue of the irascible and concupiscible powers consists in their being obedient to reason. In the same way, *the virtue of every subject consists in his being well subjected to his ruler*, as the Philosopher says" (*ST*, I–II, q. 92, art. 1).

49. *Commentary*, para. 1836, 1832.

50. *De Caritate*, 7, quoted in Sherwin, "Charity as Friendship," 61.

51. Ibid., 97.

52. *Summa Contra Gentiles*, III, 128 (8), quoted in ibid., 99.

53. Reinhold Niebuhr, *Children of Light, Children of Darkness* (New York: Scribners, 1944), 91.

54. *ST*, I, q. 96, art. 4.

55. See also Thomas' discussion of the necessity of political authority in *De Regno*, I [2–10].

56. *ST*, I–II, q. 96, art. 4.

57. Likely following Thomas's political reflections, the late pope John Paul II underscored the dignity of the legislative office in his *Jubilee of Government Leaders, Members of Parliament, and Politicians* (November 4, 2000) (retrieved October 15, 2005 from www.vatican.va/holy_father/john_paul_ii/speeches/documents/hf_jp-ii_spe_20001104_jubil-parlgov_en.html). After recognizing what the pope called a "a true and genuine *vocation to politics*" (emphasis in original), he reminded his listeners of the nobility of their charge, noting that "the very delicate task of formulating and approving laws" is, in fact, a "task which brings man close to God, the Supreme Legislator" (1, 4).

58. *ST,* I–II, q. 96, art. 4.
59. Acts 5:29, quoted in ibid.
60. *De Regno,* III (I, 14 [108–13]).
61. Thomas' much-discussed treatment of the role of the state in punishing heretics is relevant here. See, e.g., Marie Nicholas, "St. Thomas and Religious Liberty," *Papers on the History of Religion* (L'Institut Catholique de Toulouse, 1972); Takashi Shogimen, "From Disobedience to Toleration: William of Ockham and the Medieval Discourse on Fraternal Correction," *Journal of Ecclesiastical History* 52 (2001); and Michael Novak, "Aquinas and the Heretics," *First Things* 58 (December 1995). For our purposes, what deserves emphasis is the statesman's concern for the souls of his subjects; it is not simply a question of concern for public order. Those who remain obstinate in heresy, Aquinas contends, should be subject to capital punishment by the state: "For it is a much graver matter to corrupt the faith which quickens the soul, than to forge money, which supports temporal life. Wherefore if forgers of money and other evil-doers are forthwith condemned to death by the secular authority, much more reason is there for heretics, as soon as they are convicted of heresy, to be not only excommunicated but even put to death" (*ST,* II–II, q. 11, art. 3).

Not only does heresy jeopardize the individual's eternal standing, it has the potential to corrupt others, wreaking religious and social havoc; a movement of spiritual rebellion against Church authority, heresy was thought to undermine respect for temporal authority, as well. As noted by David Abulafia in *Frederick II: A Medieval Emperor* (New York: Oxford University Press, 1992): "Heresy, indeed, is presented as treason. Those who deny the articles of the Catholic faith implicitly deny the claims of rulers to derive their authority from God. They are enemies not merely of God and of the souls of individuals, but of the social fabric. Their questioning of religious truth involves a questioning of the monarch's command over the law; as enemies of the law, they are its legitimate targets, and the position of primacy accorded to legislation against heretics is thus entirely proper" (quoted in Novak, "Aquinas and the Heretics," 34). Thus, for Aquinas, the statesman's severe punishment for heresy reflects his concern for both the spiritual and temporal good of his subjects.

6

Friendship in the Civic Order

A Reformation Absence

Thomas Heilke

In Michael Pakaluk's anthology of the key writings in the Western literary and philosophical tradition concerning friendship, which begins with Plato and Aristotle, there is a major lacuna. So, too, in several recent collections of scholarly treatments of the topic in the self-same tradition, or even in wider comparative context.[1] Missing in every case are *all* of the sixteenth-century Reformers. This gap seems not to be from arbitrariness or capricious ideology: we look in vain for a treatise or even a brief, consolidated treatment concerning friendship, especially civic friendship, among *any* of them—Zwingli, Luther, Calvin, Bucer, Menno Simons. Their biographers tell us of friendships, so the problem is not that the phenomenon or its experience was personally alien to them.[2]

This essay focuses on the problem of friendship in two of these Reformers: Martin Luther and John Calvin. Both explicitly rejected

Aristotelian teleology, and we might imagine that this dismissal disabled them from thinking about friendship in specifically teleological Aristotelian terms. Both, however, were heavily influenced by Augustine, who had a good deal to say about friendship,[3] leading us to expect that their anti-Aristotelian handicaps would not have hindered them from understanding the importance of the topic. This topical gap is widened by the absence or abbreviation of friendship in modern accounts of political life,[4] but that is reading backward: Luther and Calvin did not set out to be "modern" in our sense of the word, and both were raised in the cultural context of a waning medieval period in which friendship had been a core experience and a key element of political life.[5] It may be the case, then, that these two Reformers provide a clue to the curiously thin treatment and understanding of friendship in the modern period. Given the centrality of these figures to our modern religiopolitical landscape, what are we to make of this friendship gap, both in the original writers and in subsequent scholarly treatment? What, if any, are its implications for us?

If my reading of Calvin and Luther is correct, an evaluation of their notions of friendship becomes a report on an absence. Like the problem of counterfactuals in historical writing, such a report must refer to what *could* have happened, what *could* have been said, but was not. It is a report in the subjunctive mood. Therefore, to highlight what is both present and missing in Calvin's and Luther's treatments, I will conduct a brief excursus that maps out a few mythic, literary, and biblical aspects of civic friendship before returning to these two Reformers. Since they both rejected the Aristotelian tradition of inquiry, I deliberately consider examples of pre-Socratic, non-Greek sources to indicate the basic structure of questions found even in myth that could have been available—not in specific *content*, but in general structure—to Calvin and Luther, but seemingly were not or were considered to be unimportant. In the same way, I consider briefly some biblical examples that Calvin and Luther did know, but did not exegetically or theologically exploit. The role of this contrast is to point briefly to neglected options and missed opportunities (that do not require the acquaintance with Aristotle that both Reformers actually had), which then permits us to ask why such omissions occurred.

Friendship and Philosophical Analysis

Friendship is portrayed as a vital part of civic life—and therefore as a central problem of human life together—long before Greek philosophy. The Mesopotamian *Epic of Gilgamesh,* for example, includes an extensive treatment of friendship in the medium of epic myth, and we know that this epic existed in various forms in a number of diverse cultures in the wider Mesopotamian region.[6] Gilgamesh is the ruler of a city, a great doer of deeds, physically perfect, wise, but arrogant and demoniacally energetic. His worn-out subjects plead with the gods to create a companion for him who will redirect his energy away from them and their sons and daughters to more worthy pursuits. The gods find/create Enkidu, a "natural man," who "was innocent of mankind and knew nothing of the cultivated land." Seducing him by means of a woman, the gods civilize him, thereby alienating him from the wild animals and filling his heart with a longing for civic companionship. Enkidu finds and enters Uruk, the city of Gilgamesh. During an ensuing battle—over access to a woman some versions of the myth imply—the two discover their mutual qualities of great strength and other god-like attributes; they "embrace," and their friendship is sealed. The two heroic friends now engage in a project of urban renewal: Enkidu reports of a great pine or cedar forest inhabited by a ferocious "evil" giant, Humbaba; conquering this giant and bringing back the lumber to build great walls and temples for the city will win them honor among the subjects.

Humbaba and his forest, we may suggest, represent in conventional mythic form the natural world in all its unruliness ("evil") against which the ruler of the city and his friend(s) must do battle in order to found and maintain the city. It is also out of this unruly nature and its destructive forces that the friends extract the raw resources to build and maintain the city over against that nature. No doubt we see reflected in this episode of the myth the experience of early city building and the experience of salvation to be found in the city that is the refuge and sure defense against a nature that is hostile and yet benevolent at the same time.[7] It is in the context of establishing and preserving a city that the friendship of the two heroes—which began in an associational conflict—finds its meaningful purpose. Humbaba's defeat is the clear work of partnership, of a cooperation of companions in arms. It is in the context of contest, not civic order, however, that a friendship of equality is first formed.[8]

In a subsequent episode, the question of friendship turns in a much different direction. Heroic poetry inevitably includes in its depiction of the structure of society "a conception of the human condition as fragile and vulnerable to destiny and to death, such that to be virtuous is not to avoid vulnerability and death, but rather to accord them their due."[9] Having subdued the guardian of the forest and having refurbished the city with its natural treasures, Gilgamesh glories in his deeds. With the arrogance of accomplishment, he insults a goddess. His punishment is the death of his companion. The unheroic death of Enkidu from illness is a loss of true friendship built on equality and reciprocity of heroic deeds, but Enkidu's demise also reminds Gilgamesh of his own mortality: "[W]hat shall I be when I am dead?" he asks. As in later epics of quest, Gilgamesh undertakes a long and ultimately futile journey to discover the answer to this deepest question. This spur to reflection is bound not merely to death as such, but to the expiration of a friend. The great warrior Gilgamesh had previously seen and dealt death, as is implied in the complaint of the citizens of Uruk to the gods, but this death is different because it is the departure of a friend.

It is surely not stretching the interpretation of the mythic narrative to suggest the following conclusions: friendship is central to the foundation and internal maintenance of the city; friendship redirects the spirit in constructive, civically salutary pursuits; friendship is a source of and perhaps even a spur to reflection; friendship arises among equals. While the epic contains nothing of a typology of friendship, one may suppose that the heroic friendship of Gilgamesh and Enkidu would have shone forth as a highest kind of friendship in the minds of the epic's audience, in contrast to other, "lesser" kinds of friendship with which the listeners would have been acquainted. Accordingly, great friendship is likely rare, and it takes root in mutual recognition, which may originate in conflict and contest,[10] but it produces harmony that flows beyond the immediate relationship of the friends.

Betrayal and neglect of friends do not appear in the Gilgamesh epic—it is the arbitrary gods, not Gilgamesh, who kill Enkidu as punishment for Gilgamesh's dishonoring speech—but treachery and carelessness among friends were known to the inhabitants of the ancient world as they are to us. In the well-known third-millennium lament of the Egyptian poet who contemplates suicide with his soul, one of the several signs of societal breakdown is that one either has no friends or one cannot face them honestly:

> To whom can I speak today?
> (One's) fellows are evil; . . .
> To whom can I speak today?
> Faces of disappeared;
> Every man has a downcast face toward his fellows.
> To whom can I speak today?
> There is lack of an intimate (friend);
> One has recourse to an unknown to complain to him.[11]

The complaint has a positive inversion: friendship and trust—meeting one another's eyes with no injustice to hide—are constituents of an orderly society.

These mythical and poetic accounts remind us that friendship can be a primary experience, not a derivative one. Indeed, one may argue that notions of politics arise out of experiences of friendship, and not the reverse. That is to say, "Western political speculation finds its origin in a system of thought in which the idea of friendship is the major principle in terms of which political theory and practice are described, explained and analyzed."[12]

And so to the Greeks, where the two most important epic poems that survive from the cycle of epics surrounding the Trojan War and its aftermath are laden with well-known treatments of friendship. The *Iliad* is a story of the rage of Achilles, a rage that brings much destruction to Achilles' friends, the Achaians, and that results in the death of his best friend (dear comrade) Patroclus. This epic, and Homer's other surviving epic, the *Odyssey*, contain multiple accounts of friendships gained, kept, lost, or betrayed. Surprisingly, but importantly for our considerations of how to understand the Protestant Reformers, Homer does not use the later standard Greek term for friendship, *philia*. He does use *philos*—friend—and, less surprisingly, there is considerable unresolved etymological and philological debate concerning its origin and its precise meaning in his poems.[13] And again of importance for how we should approach the friendship topos in Calvin and Luther, the "uncertainty about this issue [concerning "the original and Homeric meaning of *philos*"] should not obscure the fact that the *idea* of friendship is clearly present in the Homeric epics."[14]

A thorough study of Homer reveals that there exist a variety of friendships in his world, and one is led to the conclusion that Homer and Homer's time may have lacked or only partially possessed "a specific vocabulary of friendship," so that "the practice of friendship thus precedes its precise definition."[15] That *practice* in its varied forms and meanings, however, is made clearly visible in Homer's works.[16] Homeric friendship of whatever kind requires, for example, a "oneness of mind," or "unity of mind and purposes."[17] Homer's epics also treat specific friendship problems, including especially the nature of guest friendship, the death of friends, and alienation (and reconciliation) between friends.[18]

This illustrative excursus, already far afield from the topic of Reformation Europe, could be extended into a multivolume treatment of the specifics of friendship in the Greek and wider Mediterranean world. It delivers several matters of importance for our concerns. First, there is no instance in any treatment of this story of friendship in which friendship is a purely private matter. None. In all cases, from the myth of Gilgamesh to the epics of Homer, through the poems of Theognis, to the tragedies of Sophocles and all points between, friendship always has public, political connotations and implications. Indeed, as Fitzgerald claims, "the history of Greek friendship is thus intertwined with Greek political history, and the one cannot be written without a knowledge of the other."[19] More strongly, perhaps, we may argue that it is not only the case that, as in the *Eudemian Ethics,* the political art consists in the production of friendship, but that for the Greeks, practices of friendship were what first informed their practice of politics, or that politics was understood "as the means for the exercise of friendship."[20] To put it yet a third way, friendship leads to deeds, and deeds—heroic, legislative, tyrannicidal, marshal, and so on—are public,[21] to be seen not only by foe, family, clansman, and stranger, but especially by friends. It is perhaps this central role of friendship in public life that raises the immediate question of its potential destructiveness in Homer's epics and the plays of the Greek tragedians, a question that also lurks in the background of Plato's *Republic.*

Second, friendship is not only intertwined with politics generally, but specific *kinds* of friendship and specific problems concerning friendship only make sense within specific political or sociological contexts. Indeed, this may well be an extension of the argument that any systematic account of a particular ethics demands a specific social embodiment in order to be intelligible.[22]

Third, friendship is an old story and does not require philosophy to make it work. What philosophical analysis *does* do, however, is to make available to us a clear understanding of the various alternatives concerning types, uses, and roles that friendship could play or does play in various contexts. Philosophical analysis differentiates the various kinds, qualities, contexts, possibilities, or shortcomings of friendship, thereby providing us with more or less useful philosophical maps by means of which we make sense of the world even as we act in or into it.[23] Just as importantly, it is not possible to crawl back into the womb of the cosmos, the compacted articulation—pardon the *contradictio in adjecto*—of the myth, once philosophical analysis has had its way with the phenomenon. Certainly, it is possible to continue to tell and enjoy illuminating stories, but we now know their shortcomings.

Arriving at Aristotle's encyclopedic philosophical treatment, we can dispute whether his discussion reflects an essentially Homeric (or more widely "Greek") understanding of friendship *(philia)* or if it "reflects the specific concerns and values of the democratic polis of the classical period."[24] Perhaps Aristotle was specifically and flatly wrong about some aspects of friendship.[25] Corrections to apparent Aristotelian errors and elaborations of contextual meanings can be absorbed into an account of friendship that is still fundamentally Aristotelian, just as Homer's heroic account can be rendered intelligible to a Midwestern, middle-class, high-school student: insofar as our lives take narrational form and insofar as human experience across time and space contains substantive and structural similarity, if not to say equivalence, we can imaginatively reenact the substance and structure of past experience based on present experience, including the alien sociological structure within which these experiences are rendered intelligible. While that same youth may understand what it might mean to take vengeance on one's widowed mother's spendthrift suitors, he is unlikely to do so because the sociopolitical strictures of his middle-class society indicate otherwise, offering a different, perhaps more or perhaps less just and satisfying set of options for action. Beyond equivalences of this sort, we may suggest more strongly that it is only some kind of account like Aristotle's that will allow for a coherent account of a life of virtue that includes friendship.[26]

Aristotle's context for friendship is the polis, but this context is at least in part a retrospective. The polis as Aristotle describes it—autarkic, a site for the final administration of justice and the determination of what is just, for example—no longer existed when he wrote his *Politics* and *Ethics*. Indeed, Aristotle was tutor to the boy who in manhood brought about its demise. In his inimitable, encyclopedic fashion, Aristotle lays out for us some of the possibilities and qualities of friendship that allow us to extend his categories of friendship beyond the context of a Greek polis. There are three kinds of friendship, distinguished one from another by that which attracts the friends to one another: pleasure, utility, and virtue. For friendship to come into being, the mutual attraction must result in activity, centered in one of these sources of attraction. Friendship of any kind must include an element of "mutual liking" or "well-wishing and well-doing out of concern for one another." While Aristotle's "central case"—namely, "friendship based on the recognition of moral goodness"—most clearly requires such mutual concern, he holds this requirement to be true for all three species of friendship.[27]

The upshot of this extra-polis context is twofold for our purposes. First, no polis is necessary for at least certain kinds of friendship, although some varieties of friendship may be necessary for a certain sort of polis. Second, it is therefore the case—and so, it seems to me, Aristotle argues—that everyday *political* friendships are not, in fact, virtue friendships, but utility friendships. While it may be the case that the best sort of polis is a partnership in virtue, it is also that case that all "lesser" sorts of poleis, as well as the best sort, require partnerships in utility in order to be preserved. While utility relations are necessary for the preservation of political order, are they sufficient? Are partnerships in virtue a constituent part only of the best regime?[28] Civic concord [*homonoia*] as Aristotle describes it requires agreement in utility, but does the well being of a less-than-best regime also require the friendship of moral excellence for at least a few of its inhabitants? On this question, which is open to interpretation in Aristotle, we will hear a steady silence (or perhaps an implicit denial) in Calvin and Luther.

Luther, Calvin, and Friendship

To begin with the unremarkable observation that Luther and Calvin reject Aristotelian philosophy is scarcely a preface to what we might expect from their account of friendship; friendship is prior to Aristotelian philosophy and Aristotle's work was essentially unknown to the medieval era in which specifically Christian notions of friendship developed. These medieval practices, however, were informed by other classical accounts of friendship, especially that of Cicero. His notion of ideal friendship as a disinterested bond cultivated among the virtuous was strongly civic-minded in the tradition of other classical modes of friendship: such friendship was to serve a public good, which was for Cicero the preservation of social order of the administrative machinery of the (Roman) imperium. As with Aristotle, Cicero's account of friendship was "based on virtue, not private emotion."[29] The theologian of the medieval West, Aurelius Augustine, too, had an elaborated account of friendship, and it, too, was arguably linked to a conception of political justice. Augustine, like some heroes of ancient mythical accounts, experienced the loss of a friend as a devastating occasion for reflection.[30]

Beyond the common experiences that myths, epics, and philosophical analysis share and which we could therefore anticipate as available to the Reformers, we might also look to the New Testament writings, a source that was key for them. The topos of friendship is not missing there. Indeed, as Mitchell shows in his review of recent New Testament scholarship on this question, the friendship topos plays an important role in the Pauline correspondence and in Luke's writings. While Paul rarely uses the usual Greek friendship terms—*philos* and *philia*—he does appeal consistently "to conventions associated with friendship," and he uses the topos of friendship to describe both his relations with his correspondents and to prescribe the kinds of relationships that should be occurring within the communities to which he writes.[31] Luke, on the other hand, uses *philos* frequently, including, it seems, as a title for Christians.³² Luke has specific interests revolving around reciprocity and (social) obligation in friendship that he appears to highlight in his Gospel and his church history accounts.³³ These, too, would have been available to the Reformers. Similarly, the Old Testament stories of Jonathan and David—a friendship set in a wholly political context—or of Job and his friends could have served as points of departure for reflection and extended comment.³⁴

Luther

We might imagine that Luther's explicit rejection of Aristotelian teleology disabled him from thinking about friendship in Aristotelian teleological terms.³⁵ However, while friendships based on pleasure and utility may form the substructure of virtue relations for Aristotle (by administering necessities, for example), they do not require a teleologically informed philosophical anthropology in order more or less to make sense of themselves. Perhaps Luther would admit of pleasure and utility friendships even if sharing in virtue, as contrasted with sharing in pleasures or utility, is excluded.

In the Small and Large Catechisms, undoubtedly Luther's most-read works, we find several possible topoi in which a discussion of friendship might take place: the discussion of the Seventh and Eighth (by Luther's count) Commandments; the Lord's Prayer, and the final article of the Apostles' Creed, for example. Friendship and friends are mentioned in several instances. He who "trusts and boasts," in contradiction to the prohibitions of the First Commandment, "that he possesses great skill, prudence, power, favor, friendship, and honor," "also has a god." Friends, like neighbors, exist for aid; like other external goods, they can be treated as resources.³⁶ On the other hand, "good friends," along with neighbors and servants *[Gesinde]* "from whom I expect good . . . defraud me most of all."³⁷ Resources can be two-edged.

In Luther's exegesis of the Eighth Commandment, we receive a hint of virtue friendship, a hint, indeed, that most clearly distinguishes him from his classical past. This commandment, Luther argues, forbids us to speak evil of our neighbor, but "the civil authorities *[weltliche Obrigkeit]*, preachers, father and mother" are exempted from this rule;

otherwise this commandment would imply that evil should go unpunished. While no one "has a right in his own person to judge and condemn anybody," there are divinely sanctioned offices *[Ämter]* in society that require those who hold them to speak necessarily "of the evil, to lay charges, to serve affidavits, to interrogate, and to testify":

> Indeed, the procedure here is no different than with a physician, who must sometimes examine and touch in hidden parts the one he is supposed to heal. In the same way, political authorities, father and mother, indeed, even brothers and sisters and other such good friends are obligated among one another to punish evil where it is necessary and useful.[38]

But what is "useful" *[nützlich]*? In what ways do the seemingly disparate members of this large category of entities and persons, each playing an apparently distinct role with regard to the beloved malefactor in question, in fact belong to this self-same category? We see here an instance of Luther's self-assigned imperative to simplify both the politics and the theology of medieval Christendom.[39] Friendship implies the making of distinctions—friend and not friend (how to decide?); worthy of friendship and not worthy (how to know?); and the creation of corresponding hierarchies (to know on what basis?). In Luther's flattening of distinctions and hierarchies, the roles that political authority, parents, kin, and friends play are not identical, but they are of one category—the useful. Moreover, none should be understood as aids to virtue. Rather, both spiritual and secular authority exists to restrain evil, no more. Accordingly, friendship cannot be understood as a mutual aid to virtue, since no such end exists.

As another instance of this simplification, doing good merely to friends is a "heathen virtue," but Luther takes no pains to resolve the Christian dilemma of having love for all while also holding to select friends.[40] Our "neighbor" *[Nächsten]* may be either friend or foe, and we are obliged to "help, support, and lend" to both alike.[41] To extend such kindness, regardless to whom, is to do these acts out of "friendship."[42] There is in these writings no effort whatsoever to identify various kinds of friendship and to distinguish them from each other. Luther's explicit rejection of Aristotle's *Ethics*, which he read and had taught,[43] does not issue in an effort to replace Aristotle's account of friendship with another. So, too, Luther elides friendship not only with other kinds of relationships, but with other kinds of objects and forces. In his "Treatise on Good Works," he lists friends, along with "body, property, honor . . . or whatever they have," as those things in which we can suffer, and he lists friends as one of the possessions, along with "body and life and property" that people will sacrifice to gain glory, which he considers the worst of vices.[44] Possessions, honor, favor, and friendships are, in converse, the list of goods we must be willing to give up in favor of defending the truth.[45] If friendship were a good that led to virtue or if the practice of friendship were itself a virtue, we could imagine either of these lists, so they alone do not distinguish Luther from his classical predecessors. Nor does his explication of Jesus' words that "You shall be hated by all men for My Name's sake" with the observation that "here we must provoke to anger father, mother, and the best of friends" imply such a distinction. After all, it is precisely in the determination of what is our highest good that friendships are made and broken. Rather, it is in the failure to distinguish various kinds of such relationships or their ends that Luther flattens the idea of friendship and renders it essentially useless for any work in political, social, or personal ethics.

We may ask the question yet another way: What do friends do? For Luther, they bring material advantage or the practical advantage of prosperity and stability, as do a multitude of other external goods. The list includes "food and drink, clothing, house, and home, and health of body," good harvests, a household of "godly wife, children, and servants," success in trade or business, and "faithful neighbors and good friends." It also includes wise, strong, and successful "emperors, kings, and all estates, . . . counselors, magistrates, and officers," alongside "obedient, peaceful, and socially harmonious common people."[46] Friends are a favor from God, a favor of utility like "faithful neighbors," which in turn are a part of the material and organizational requisites for prosperity and success. Luther's list makes no substantial distinctions between any of these God-given goods. So, too, in the *Small Catechism*, where "daily bread" means:

> Everything that nourishes our body and meets its needs, such as: Food, drink, clothing, shoes, house, yard, fields, cattle, money, possessions, a devout spouse, devout children, devout employees,

devout and faithful rulers, good government, good weather, peace, health, discipline, honor, good friends, faithful neighbors and other things like these.

For this reason, unlike in Aristotle's conception of friendship, even the wicked can have friends,[47] and our acts of friendship are from "feeling" or from divine command, not an estimation of virtue.[48] None of this should take away from the possibility that friendship can be understood as a kind of blessing, even a spiritual one. Certainly, Luther shows a recognition of friendship in pleasure and utility. Friendship even of a utilitarian kind requires work, and Luther could give personal advice on how such work should proceed:

> Although we are moved to suspicion and displeasure, we should beat these back and remember not to allow them to sever the bond of love and extinguish its fire; but we should cling firmly to our friendship in the face of them. And if perchance displeasure and disagreement arise, we should renew and improve our love and friendship. For to begin to love is not so great, but to remain in love (as Christ here says) is a real task and virtue.[49]

To continue such friendship is a practical activity of securing spiritual goods negatively, which is to say, to avoid loss or a fall from grace:

> Throughout life a faithful friend is a very great blessing and a very precious treasure. This is true not only in view of the ordinary dangerous difficulties in which he can offer help and consolation but also in view of spiritual temptations.
>
> For even though your heart is thoroughly confirmed by the Holy Spirit there is nonetheless a great advantage in having a friend with whom you can talk about religion and from whom you may hear words of comfort.[50]

To know precisely what to make of this advice requires a glimpse into Luther's ecclesiology.

It has become virtually a commonplace that Luther tended from early in his reformist career to "minimiz[e] the political character and ecclesiastical power of the Church," which logically "opened the way for a temporal monopoly on all kinds of power."[51] The effect that this move had on his ideas of friendship is less immediately clear, but we have now observed its results. Since the political realm is not a realm of virtue, but of "repressive power, law backed by coercion," whose role it is to suppress evil,[52] one can hardly imagine much of a positive role for friendship in such a realm of activity. And, for Luther, there is not one. The community of believers, on the other hand, seems not to have any features that would give us much more. Luther's exegesis of the third article of the Apostles' Creed stresses the role of the Holy Spirit in the life of the individual believer and its accumulation of such individuals into a "flock," where the Word of God is preached and whereby individual faith is instilled and nourished.[53] Reading this exegesis, one is persuaded that Luther understands faith as entirely individual. Outside of the collective nouns—"church," "assembly," "flock"—Luther mentions the collective of believers as a mutually supportive group only once: "Because we live in Christianity *[Christenheit]* in which there is all forgiveness of sins, in the double sense that God forgives us and that we forgive, carry, and help one another."[54] Luther adds no explicit details for what these three activities should look like; indeed, he adds no elaboration whatsoever. Friendship, if these acts constitute it, is not articulated. This absence should not surprise anyone who reads "The one who does much 'work' is not the righteous one, but the one who, without 'work,' has much faith in Christ," or "The work of Christ shall rightly be called an active work, and ours that which is worked, so the one which is worked is well-pleasing unto God, thanks to the active work,"[55] and who finds nowhere a communal context for either human faith or the work of God.[56]

Luther's famous *Table Talk*, a large collection of sayings and quotes on various topics taken down by several of Luther's students in informal settings over a fourteen-year period, renders nothing further than what we encounter in his formal publications. Friends, friendship, neighbors, and fellowship appear in this collection, but in the same occasional manner and with the same emphases. While one should not expect a systematic treatment in such a context, neither does one find a hint that such a treatment might be useful or that friendship deserves it.[57]

Luther was heir to a long medieval tradition in which "innumerable medieval anthologies and encyclopedias frequently included a chapter on friendship,"[58] but he does not avail himself of this inheritance. Concentrating instead on man's forensic status before God, Luther preaches grace, but a grace taken up individually *in* the collective, not collectively for the individual; nor, more modestly, individually *amid* the collective. Sheldon Wolin well articulates the aftermath: "The pressing problem confronting Luther, Zwingli, and Calvin was to bring Protestant man back to a consciousness of community after first having encouraged his individualism."[59] How to restore harmony and order around a governing principle in what had come to be conceived forensically as a highly individualistic collectivity? Apart from advocating authoritarian forms of rule within and without the church, Luther furnishes little by way of an answer and friendship played no significant role in that minimum. Can we find more in the work of the greatest representative of the "second generation" of the Protestant Reformation, John Calvin?

Calvin

If Calvin's theology has been accurately described as in part a kind of hyper-Lutheranism,[60] then we may, in fact, expect to find little more concerning friendship in Calvin's work than in Luther's. We will hardly be disappointed. Calvin uses "friend" and "friends" for the most part in a casual associational mode without further comment. In his commentary on Hebrews, he equates "concord" with "friendship," arguing that we cannot be friends with "the wicked" to the point of having such relations "defile or pollute" us: concord is limited by conscience.[61] Friendship has no special qualities here, being reduced to a kind of civil association of the most basic sort that includes no common aim aside from a desire for peace, but without moral compromise, whatever that may mean. Friendship is for Calvin, as for Luther, a utilitarian association. It may call us to make compromises we should not make, and so we must resist its siren call at that boundary.

In his booklet "On the Life of the Christian Man," which he extracted from his *Institutes,* Calvin has almost nothing to say of friendship; he appears to see no important role for friendship as such in his description of the "Christian Life." Indeed, he calls on his readers to have "courteous and friendly" relations with all, exhibiting "moderate and modest" behavior toward everyone, but no more is said. Concerning the death of friends, Calvin enjoins an attitude adopted from Stoicism (with which, his first publication having been a commentary on Seneca's *De Clementia,* he was closely familiar): our tears are the payment due to nature at the death of our friends, and such occurrences, along with disease and poverty, are but one variant of adversity in life. In all three kinds of adversity, "the Lord so wills it, therefore let us follow his will" is the recommended response. Insofar as friendship is mentioned at all in Calvin's *Institutes,* its qualities and features remain unanalyzed and Calvin treats it as an instrumental function of social cohesion.

People have friends, and so does God, who can make people His friends. How people become friends with one another and why, Calvin does not say, nor does he distinguish with any precision between friends within and without the body of Christian believers, the organization that most concerns him. Insofar as Calvin does comment on it, friendship is, like all other human relationships, prescribed by duty:

> Our Savior having shown, in the parable of the Samaritan, (Luke 10:36,) that the term *neighbor* comprehends the most remote stranger, there is no reason for limiting the precept of love to our own connections. I deny not that the closer the relation the more frequent our offices of kindness should be. For the condition of humanity requires that there be more duties in common between those who are more nearly connected by the ties of relationship, or friendship, or neighborhood. And this is done without any offense to God, by whose providence we are in a manner impelled to do it.[62]

Like Luther, then, Calvin recognizes the tension in Christian doctrine between particularity and love of all and, like Luther, he makes no effort to resolve or even clearly address this tension, nor does he care to analyze the important potential differences between "neighbor" and "friend." He tends strongly toward treating them as the same:

> But I say that the whole human race, without exception, are to be embraced with one feeling of charity: that here there is no distinction of Greek or Barbarian, worthy or unworthy, friend or foe, since

all are to be viewed not in themselves, but in God. If we turn aside from this view, there is no wonder that we entangle ourselves in error. Wherefore, if we would hold the true course in love, our first step must be to turn our eyes not to man, the sight of whom might oftener produce hatred than love, but to God, who requires that the love which we bear to him be diffused among all mankind, so that our fundamental principle must ever be, Let a man be what he may, he is still to be loved, because God is loved.[63]

Calvin perceives or acknowledges little difference between neighbor and friend with regard to obligation, nor does he entertain the possibility that there may be nuances or differences in what is meant by "love" in different circumstances. Missing almost entirely from the *Institutes*, for example, are references to the friendship tropes of such New Testament passages as Acts 4; John 17:26; 20:2; 21:7, 20.

In what would become the hallmark of Protestant theology, Calvin rejects the Roman Catholic distinction between professional religion and laity regarding what the practice of loving the neighbor should be. His vituperative prose against this distinction does not, however, lead him to offer any practical advice concerning love of neighbor. Indeed, the *context* of the brief discussion cited above is an exegesis of the Tenth Commandment, and Calvin is largely at pains to demonstrate the inviolability of God's law and the work of divine grace in making it possible to both keep the dictates of that law and to obtain pardon when human weakness subverts our efforts. Love of neighbor is love of God, and love of God is understood by means of reference to divine edicts and as exhibiting in action what is commanded,[64] not by means of a growing maturity in practice: "It is certain that, in the law and the prophets, faith, and whatever pertains to the due worship of God, holds the first place, and that to this charity is made subordinate; but our Lord means, that in the Law the observance of justice and equity towards men is prescribed as the means which we are to employ in testifying a pious fear of God, if we truly possess it."[65] Possession of this pious fear and of God's grace is of paramount importance for Calvin, and its individuality seems to undermine any elaboration of the possibility of friendship. In this light, consider Calvin's exegesis of the third article of the Apostles' Creed.

The creedal claim that "I believe in the holy catholic and apostolic church" reminds the speaker first and foremost of his or her duties: "every one of us must maintain brotherly concord with all the children of God, give due authority to the Church, and, in short, conduct ourselves as sheep of the flock."[66] Calvin's focus, after all, is on the "Government, Order, and Power" of the church. Having recovered a political vocabulary after Luther jettisoned it in his radical simplification and dichotomization, Calvin approaches the question of church community:

> [S]aints are united in the fellowship of Christ on this condition, that all the blessings which God bestows upon them are mutually communicated to each other. This, however, is not incompatible with a diversity of graces, for we know that the gifts of the Spirit are variously distributed; nor is it incompatible with civil order, by which each is permitted privately to possess his own means, it being necessary for the preservation of peace among men that distinct rights of property should exist among them. Still a community is asserted, such as Luke describes when he says, "The multitude of them that believed were of one heart and of one soul" (Acts 4:32); and Paul, when he reminds the Ephesians, "There is one body, and one Spirit, even as ye are called in one hope of your calling" (Ephesians 4:4). For if they are truly persuaded that God is the common Father of them all, and Christ their common head, they cannot but be united together in brotherly love, and mutually impart their blessings to each other.[67]

Having made this approach and having hinted at a possibility of mutuality, if not outright friendship in a common project, Calvin immediately turns without further comment or elaboration of its particulars to the individual and the relationship between that individual and divine command:

> Then it is of the highest importance for us to know what benefit thence redounds to us. For when we believe the Church, it is in order that we may be firmly persuaded that we are its members. In this way our salvation rests on a foundation so firm and sure, that though the whole fabric of the world were to give way, it could not

be destroyed. First, it stands with the election of God, and cannot change or fail, any more than his eternal providence. . . . so long as we continue in the bosom of the Church, we are sure that the truth will remain with us.[68]

Like Luther, so Calvin reduces church community to a minimum, a relation between a divine Sovereign and individuals who are bound together chiefly to receive an assurance of grace, mediated through church rulers who themselves possess considerable authority:

We see that God, who might perfect his people in a moment, chooses not to bring them to manhood in any other way than by the education of the Church. We see the mode of doing it expressed; the preaching of celestial doctrine is committed to pastors. We see that all without exception are brought into the same order, that they may with meek and docile will allow themselves to be governed by teachers appointed for this purpose.[69]

Either Calvin does not know what to make of the *community* of saints, or it is of insignificant account for him, since he leaves it aside, shifting instead to an authoritarian model in which he depicts teachers of "heavenly doctrine" standing before compliant, imbibing listeners: "Let us hold, agreeably to the passage we quoted from Paul, that the Church can only be edified by external preaching, and that there is no other bond by which the saints can be kept together than by uniting with one consent to observe the order which God has appointed in his Church for learning and making progress."[70] Progress is understood, it appears, as largely related to understanding of doctrine, not maturity in prudence, wisdom, or other virtues, all of which are peripheral to Calvin's vocabulary and none of which are understood, or at least articulated, in the context of some kind of mutuality, that is, of friendship. The blessings that are "mutually imparted" appear to be material or utilitarian ones, and brotherly love seems not to include a kind of friendship that would be required in the constitution and maintenance of a community. That resource is supplied instead by individual obedience to divine command. In their aggregate, these obedient atoms constitute the community.

More strongly still, Calvin gives second place to this visible, concrete community in which friendship could conceivably take root. Rather, this manifest institution points us to the invisible church, to an apprehension of the unknown, and to an inward assurance of divine election that Calvin clearly and deliberately distinguishes from the visible community that houses it: "we are not enjoined here to distinguish between the elect and the reprobate (this belongs not to us, but to God only), but to feel firmly assured in our minds, that all those who, by the mercy of God the Father, through the efficacy of the Holy Spirit, have become partakers with Christ, are set apart as the proper and peculiar possession of God, and that as we are of the number, we are also partakers of this great grace."[71] This grace is known not primarily in its visible manifestation, but in its invisible assurance, "a unity into which we feel persuaded that we are truly ingrafted," and that, Calvin argues, is of primary importance over the more "external Church," the visible community of saints.[72] In this invisible realm of truth, human friendship, as it is commonly understood and concretely practiced, is unimaginable.

It is not the case that Calvin denies friendship any place at all in human life. We have seen instead that he acknowledges friends and friendship, and that he does so not only in his personal references, but also in some references to Scripture. For example, Abraham is "called by the command of God," Calvin reflects, by which "he is torn away from friends, parents, and country, objects in which the chief happiness of life is deemed to consist, as if it had been the fixed purpose of the Lord to deprive him of all the sources of enjoyment."[73] Rather, like Luther, Calvin understands this relationship in utility terms, and he, like Luther, is unclear what place to give it in his theology generally and in his political theology or ecclesiology specifically, even though both had deep and sustained friendships. Like Luther, Calvin appears unable to conceive of friendship as something more than a relation of pleasure or utility in the course of a life in which we move not toward moral excellence and maturity in that excellence, but toward the overwhelming experience of the grace and election of God that descends on the solitary individual.[74]

To be sure, friendship, like justice, temperance, fortitude, and prudence, are means by which God preserves society, even through the unbeliever, but these "good works" can all be executed through bad motives, and none are worthy of regard apart from the grace of God. In what way friendship preserves order Calvin does not say. His recovery of a language of politics from its Lutheran demise is a recovery toward authoritarian forms of rule, both in his ecclesiology, as I have noted, and in his account of civil government in the final chapter of the *Institutes*. The vocabulary of that chapter includes rule and magistracy, law and obedience, sovereign decree and individual conscience, but rarely concord and never friendship.[75] Government may exist to promote piety,[76] but this promotion is doctrinal and institutional, not convivial, effected through "common peace and security," and laws that safeguard public manners.[77]

It is possible, finally, to be "admitted to [the] friendship" of God, but not by any action that we may undertake. "On the contrary, though we may be redeemed by Christ, still, until we are engrafted into union with him by the calling of the Father, we are darkness, the heirs of death, and the enemies of God."[78] What the substance of friendship with God—once we are elected to it by God—consists of Calvin does not say. Indeed, Calvin leaves his readers with the distinct impression that friendship is nothing other than that status of election itself. It is in its motives, not its outward appearance, that a deed of virtue—including friendship—is distinguished from one of vice.[79] The friends and family of God are the church, which has this status by dint of God having elected each individual member individually to divine grace.[80] The substance of such friendship is exhibited in specific acts of obedience,[81] but these acts do not bring us closer to a sovereign, omnipotent, and omniscient God in the way that common experience tells us acts of mutual kindness, support, or understanding can deepen or solidify friendships.[82] We cannot be fellow workers of God except in the sense that God imputes to Himself any acts of His people that display His benevolence.[83]

The Friendship Gap

"The practice of friendship which was characteristic of the medieval centuries," writes James McEvoy, "can be illuminated strikingly by means of the theories, ideas and images which lent it consistency and afforded it at the same time a generous measure of moral guidance. The ideas which helped to shape the experience of friendship themselves require, in their turn, to be elucidated."[84] It should hardly need pointing out that to be able to *say* what we are doing helps (or hinders) in the doing of it. To say, then, what friendship is and is not aids in the practice of it. To clarify may mean to affix, or change, or even to transform an activity, but the phenomenon or activity on which the analysis rests exists *prior* to the analysis. If the Protestant Reformers did not talk about friendship, that does not mean that they did not practice it. Did Calvin and Luther have friends? Certainly. But their articulated understanding of friendship, however they may have practiced it in "real life," was rule and duty bound, not virtue bound. And since those rules were of no avail for their ultimate aim, namely justification before God,[85] the contents of those rules, too, were relegated to second place in the theologies of these two Reformers. Included in that displacement was any serious engagement with the problems and possibilities of friendship.

Politically, too, friendship played a negligible role in their thinking. When he thought about government, Luther had in mind some kind of tyranny, strong monarchy, or at least territorially centralized authority. To have friends is difficult for authoritarian rulers and impossible for tyrants.[86] Friendship, in either case, is not an important category for understanding such rule—except negatively—so it is not surprising that he did not employ it in thinking about government. For Calvin, political possibilities included a republic, but a republic founded in laws, rules, and decrees, not the give-and-take of deliberation in political association.[87] More disconcerting is the absence of same in thinking about ecclesiastical polity. Here again, however, the authority of divine grace (Luther) or divine command quickened by divine grace (Calvin) seems to have overtaken any consideration of a polity informed by friendship, even God-centered and God-directed. In neither case does the fragility of community that is apparent in epic myth and whose self-same quality is not hidden from the Reformers[88] appear as a problem that friendship and not merely disciplinary force can help to solve.

These remarks cannot yet be the full measure of the friendship gap in the writing of these Reformers. On the one hand, Calvin and Luther were focused on problems in many ways alien to the Western and pre-

Western tradition in which thinking about friendship begins. Of paramount importance to them, instead, was the juridical/forensic status of the individual before God. All other concerns were subsidiary. Their experience of politics did not raise to the first rank question of the origins of political order as we see in the *Epic of Gilgamesh* or in Homer's epics or other ancient literature concerned with friendship and social order. Government is a mandate of God, an ordinance of the Divine that seems to be largely unproblematic in its genesis and whose maintenance and sustenance are based on an exercise of power, juridically defined, not in the bonds of friendship.[89] The medieval experience of a fragile political and social order that required the bonds of friendship to sustain itself and the much more distant Mesopotamian and Greek experiences of political founding and political intimacy along with an ongoing fragility prior to the emergence of empire were far behind these Reformers. Although all three problems were of foremost importance to their Italian contemporary, Machiavelli; although Calvin, at least, had extensive experience in a small city-state; and although Luther's harsh response to the Peasant's War indicates a strong awareness of the problems of political and especially a linked ecclesiastical stability, these political problems were secondary, not primary for Calvin and Luther, and, in any case, neither Reformer saw friendship as a source of remedies for either (political or ecclesiastical) set of concerns.

On the other hand, while neither took their philosophical cues from Aristotle, this need not have disqualified them from a more intense engagement with the problem of friendship, since Aristotle was unknown to the European Middle Ages, but careful thinking about friendship, based in the writings of Cicero (with which Calvin was familiar) and others was extensive. So, too, we find considerable material for thinking about friendship in the writings of Augustine, which had a formative influence on both Reformers. Neither were Calvin or Luther ignorant of yet other classical writings, especially of the so-called Church Fathers, whom both liked to cite, and where they should have found in abundant measure the topic of friendship.[90] It is therefore insufficient to say that, because both Reformers, recurring to Augustine and dealing with a scholastic legacy after Aquinas, explicitly rejected Aristotelian or Thomistic scholasticism, they were left without a closely articulated version of a human teleology, thereby disabling them from placing friendship in the same context that Aristotle and Aquinas's teleological frameworks of philosophical anthropology and concomitant analysis of political life could. They knew several other possibilities that all included a rich tradition of friendship.

A teleological conception of friendship, which, in my view and as indicated earlier, reflects basic friendship notions to be found in the epic myths of Mesopotamian and Greek civilizations alike, "embodies a shared recognition of and pursuit of a good," and "this sharing . . . is essential and primary to the constitution of any form of community."[91] Friendship is here, to speak most crudely, the "dependent variable," and whatever project it is that friendship embodies is the "independent variable." The independent variable for both Luther and Calvin—be it the construction and maintenance of either a secular polity or a church—does not require the support of friendship understood in this manner. The church is made up of individuals who are converted to faith by one or another means that occur "in an intimate sphere of relations between man and God, . . . entirely unmediated by anything except Scripture."[92] Scripture, where it does not point directly to God, points, especially for Calvin, to practical obedience in lawlike fashion, by which it points indirectly to God. Recognizing and pursuing a common good that conforms to either mutual or God-given human ends is simply not part of this picture, so that human friendship, too, can only be a utilitarian good, but not a communally formative one. A model of magisterial supervision—both within (church) and without (saeculum) the gathering of believers—provides a paternalistic frame that does not and perhaps cannot require friendship. The church, for example and especially for Calvin, is constituted by law and a correspondingly authoritarian discipline that together admit of trivially few "adiaphora" for friends to discuss and resolve.[93] Discipline, whose threefold purpose is to maintain order, to isolate "sinners" so as to "prevent contagion," and to prevent "dishonour, infamy, or insult to the name of God,"[94] replaces the friendship of a less legalistic and more teleologically constituted community.[95]

Recall that one might summarize the Protestant sociopolitical and ecclesiastical problem of this period by suggesting that it reduces to determining how, after having strongly promoted their individualism, one could return Protestant human beings to an awareness of community.⁹⁶ In this return, Luther himself was not especially successful, but some of his successors and especially Calvin were. With his conception of a "triangular relationship of ruler, people, and the law," Calvin was able to reestablish "the idea of the institutionalized community,"⁹⁷ but, in my estimation, this idea never recovered the substance of the friendship idea that had animated so much of earlier political conceptions. Perhaps we cannot lay this loss entirely at the feet of the Reformers: perhaps, as Brian Patrick McGuire reports, it was already appearing in the late medieval period, when "an expectation of the fruits of friendship in the life of those who seek Christ" was replaced by "fear or hesitation about the worth of bonds of friendship in a Christian context," and by a "loss of faith in the place of friendship in human and Christian life."⁹⁸ In the example of such loss in the life and thought of Jean Gerson, McGuire suggests that we first see "the terrible aloneness of the person in receiving God's unpredictable gift of grace," made more prominent by authoritarian churches and a "rejection of nurturing human bonds of equality that lead to Reformation dilemmas of conscience."⁹⁹ Perhaps the Reformers inherited a problem that they only amplified.

Regardless the efficient cause for their theological moves, with the Reformers we have lost something. In the conceptions of political friendship that take their cue from Aristotle and even the Stoics, the best kind of friendship is understood to be an activity of improvement—friends make each other better, more complete in virtue. For Calvin, and especially Luther, the sphere of politics can play no such role; oddly (at least until we note their theologies of divine grace), the church cannot or does not play such a role either. In the accounts of friendship that Aristotle and Aquinas have left us, "the quality of our friendships and the quality of our moral lives are inseparable."¹⁰⁰ Calvin or Luther appear not to have believed such a claim. Their estimation of the quality of a moral life was bound up in the terms of duty, law, command, and grace, not in accounts of a friendship with God or of human beings one with another in which one could give a narrative account of the constitutive elements of one's own or another's good and in which that good is understood as something attained in the ongoing development and practice of virtue. Absent an account of human telos that contains a developmental narrative and not merely grace-infused, rule-bound acts in response to commands, the "quality" of a friendship may be judged in utilitarian terms, but not under the terms of its effects on the moral quality of a moral life. That is a modern absence to which Calvin and Luther contributed much.

Notes

1. Michael Pakaluk, ed., *Other Selves: Philosophers on Friendship* (Indianapolis: Hackett Publishing, 1991). Examples of extensive collections of recent treatments include Thomas A. F. Kelly and Philipp W. Roseman, eds., *Amor Amicitiae: On the Love That Is Friendship* (Leuven: Peeters, 2004); Luigi Cotteri, ed., *Il concetto di amicizia nella storia della cultura europea* (Meran: Tip Hauger, 1995).

2. For an explicit treatment concerning Calvin, for example, see Richard Stauffer, *The Humanness of John Calvin*, trans. George H. Shriver (Nashville: Abingdon Press, 1971), 47–51. Nearly any biography of Calvin or Luther, on whom I focus here, includes comment on their friendships. Luther, in particular, is noted to have been "warm-hearted," not a term generally associated with Calvin. Nevertheless, Calvin, too, was held in great affection by his friends.

3. See John von Heyking, *Augustine and Politics as Longing in the World* (Columbia: University of Missouri Press, 2001); and von Heyking's essay in this collection.

4. Cf. Steven Salkever, *Finding the Mean* (Princeton: Princeton University Press, 1990), 243.

5. See, e.g., Gerd Althoff, "Friendship and Political Order," in *Friendship in Medieval Europe*, ed. Julian Haseldine (Phoenix Mill: Sutton Publishing, 1999), 91–105.

6. Cf. N. K. Sandars, "Introduction," in *The Epic of Gilgamesh: An English Version with an Introduction*, ed. N. K. Sandars (London: Penguin Books, 1972), esp. 13–20; and Stephanie Dalley, "Gilgamesh: Introduction," in *Myths from Mesopotamia: Creation, the Flood, Gilgamesh and Others*, trans. and ed. Stephanie Dalley (Oxford: Oxford University Press, 1989), 39–49.

7. For an account of the modern version of this state myth, see William T. Cavanaugh, "The City: Beyond Secular Parodies," in *Radical Orthodoxy: A New Theology*, ed. John Milbank, Catherine Pickstock, and Graham Ward (New York: Routledge, 1999), 182–200, esp. 186–94.

8. The strong romantic (perhaps wistful) overtones of his treatment notwithstanding, it seems to be something of this sort that Nietzsche has in

mind in his understanding of friendship. Cf. "Sternen-Freundschaft": Aph. 279 of *Die Fröhliche Wissenschaft*, and his early essays "Der Griechische Staat" and "Homers Wettkampf," in *Friedrich Nietzsche: Sämtliche Werke, Kritische Studienausgabe*, vol. 1, ed. Giorgio Colli and Mazzino Montinari (Berlin: de Gruyter, 1980), 764–77, 783–92.

9. Alasdair MacIntyre, *After Virtue: A Study in Moral Theory* (Notre Dame: University of Notre Dame Press, 1984), 128–29.

10. Which is an equality that is not the same as Hobbes's equality in the ability to kill one another (*Leviathan*, ed. C. B. MacPherson [New York: Penguin, 1981], XIII).

11. "A Dispute over Suicide," trans. John A. Wilson, in *Ancient Near Eastern Texts Relating to the Old Testament*, ed. James B. Pritchard (Princeton: Princeton University Press, 1969), 406.

12. Horst Hutter, *Politics as Friendship: The Origins of Classical Notions of Politics in the Theory and Practice of Friendship* (Waterloo: Wilfrid Laurier University Press, 1978), 2.

13. John T. Fitzgerald, "Friendship in the Greek World Prior to Aristotle," in *Greco-Roman Perspectives on Friendship*, ed. John T. Fitzgerald (Atlanta: Scholars Press, 1997), 13–34, at 15–21.

14. Ibid., 19.

15. Ibid., 20.

16. Ibid., 21.

17. Ibid., 22, 23.

18. Ibid., 24–26.

19. Ibid., 27. Accordingly, Fitzgerald argues that "in a very concrete sense, the *Iliad* is not so much about the 'wrath of Achilles' (1.1) as it is about the loss and restoration of friendly relations between Agamemnon and Achilles" (25). It is only the reconciliation of the two rulers that can reestablish communal harmony and a concomitant winning military strategy among the Greeks camped on the shores of Ilion.

20. Hutter, *Politics as Friendship*, 25.

21. Ibid., 26.

22. MacIntyre, *After Virtue*, 22, 23.

23. For a brief discussion of "philosophical maps" that is particularly critical of modern versions and sympathetic to classical epistemological arguments, see E. F. Schumacher, *A Guide for the Perplexed* (New York: Harper & Row, 1977), 1–14.

24. Fitzgerald, "Friendship," 14.

25. Alasdair MacIntyre, "What Both Bad and Good Bring to Friendships in Their Strange Variety," in *Amor Amicitiae: On the Love That Is Friendship*, ed. Thomas A. F. Kelly and Philipp W. Roseman (Leuven: Peeters, 2004), 241–55.

26. Cf. MacIntyre, *After Virtue*, 109–20.

27. John M. Cooper, "Aristotle on Friendship," in *Essays on Aristotle's Ethics*, ed. Amélie Oksenberg (Berkeley: University of California Press, 1980), 303–5.

28. For a thorough discussion of this point, see Edward W. Clayton, "Aristotle and Political Friendship," 1997 (unpublished manuscript, cited with permission of author).

29. Julian Haseldine, "Friendship, Equality and Universal Harmony: The Universal and the Particular in Aelred of Reivaulx's *De Spiritali Amicitia*," in *Friendship East and West: Philosophical Perspectives*, ed. Oliver Leaman (Richmond: Curzon, 1996), 192–214, at 192; cf. 197–98; James McEvoy, "The Theory of Friendship in the Latin Middle Ages: Hermeneutics, Contextualization and the Transmission and Reception of Ancient Texts and Ideas, From *c.* AD 350 to *c.* 1500," in Haseldine, ed., *Friendship and Medieval Europe*, 3–44, at 13.

30. Augustine, *Confessions*, 4.4.

31. Alan C. Mitchell, "Greet the Friends by Name: New Testament Evidence for the Greco-Roman *Topos* on Friendship," in Fitzgerald, ed., *Friendship*, 225–62, at 226.

32. Mitchell, "Friends," 236.

33. Ibid., 237.

34. Since neither Calvin nor Luther wrote extended commentaries on the "historical" books of the Old Testament, this possibility is muted from the outset in any direct way, but it does remain available for treatment in other homiletic or exegetical contexts.

35. See esp. "An Appeal to the Ruling Class of German Nationality as to the Amelioration of the State of Christendom," in *Martin Luther: Selections from his Writings Edited and with an Introduction*, ed. John Dillenberger (Garden City, N.Y.: Doubleday, 1961), 470–71; and "Disputation against Scholastic Theology, 1517," in Helmut T. Lehman, ed., *Luther's Works*, vol. 31, *Career of the Reformer: I*, ed. Harold J. Grimm (Philadelphia: Muhlenberg Press, 1955), 9–16, esp. §34, §§41–53.

36. Martin Luther, *Der Grosse Catechismus* (Munich: Siebenstern Taschenbuch Verlag, 1964), 22 (my translation). For an English version, see *Dr. Martin Luther's Large Catechism* (Minneapolis: Augsburg Publishing House, 1935).

37. Luther, *Der Grosse Catechismus*, 70 (my translation).

38. Ibid., 76 (my translation).

39. Sheldon Wolin, *Politics and Vision: Continuity and Innovation in Western Political Thought* (Boston: Little, Brown, 1960), 143.

40. Cf. Eoin C. Cassidy, "'He Who Has Friends Can Have No Friend': Classical and Christian Perspectives on the Limits to Friendship," in Haseldine, ed., *Friendship in Medieval Europe*, 45–67.
41. Luther, *Der Grosse Catechismus*, 72.
42. Ibid., 72; cf. 79.
43. Luther, "Appeal to the Ruling Class," 471.
44. Martin Luther, *A Treatise on Good Works* [1520], I.xxi, I.xxxiii. Cf. *Luther's Works*, vol. 44, *The Christian in Society*, ed. Helmut T. Lehman (Philadelphia: Muhlenberg Press, 1955).
45. Luther, *Good Works*, I.xxx.
46. Ibid., II.ii.
47. Ibid., X.ii.
48. Ibid., II.xii.
49. Martin Luther, *What Luther Says*, vol. 1, ed. Ewald Plass (St. Louis: Concordia Publishing House, 1986), lecturing on John 15:9, xxx.
50. Ibid., lecturing on Genesis 13:5–7, xxx.
51. Wolin, *Politics and Vision*, 148.
52. Ibid., 151.
53. Luther, *Der Grosse Catechismus*, 98, 104.
54. Luther, *Der Grosse Catechismus*, 161. Luther also calls it a "holy congregation" *[heilige Gemeinde]*.
55. Luther, "Theses for the Heidelberg Disputation," in Dillenberger, *Martin Luther*, 503 (theses 25, 27).
56. One may also consider Luther's exegesis of Isaiah 42:3, in which he notes that "[The church] is a hospital, where there are the strong and the weak, bones and flesh. One bears another's burden. The Christian life, therefore, is a mixture of strength and weakness. One supports the other. This is indeed a comforting situation" (*Luther's Works*, vol. 17, *Lectures on Isaiah, Chapters 40–66*, ed. Hilton Oswald [St. Louis: Concordia Publishing House, 1972], 66). Luther sees no reason, however, to exploit this opportunity for more extensive practical advice or explication concerning friendship. This promising beginning, moreover, should be contrasted with his exegesis of John 15:13–15 (*Luther's Works*, vol. 24, *Sermons on the Gospel of St. John, Chapters 14–16*, ed. Jaroslav Pelikan [St. Louis: Concordia Publishing House, 1961], 251–58), in which friendship does not reach even this minimal position.
57. Martin Luther, *Table Talk* (Albany, Ore.: AGES Software, 1997). See, e.g., §§623 and 82, in which friends are treated as external, utilitarian goods, or §102, in which friends, again, can become a source of betrayal and suffering. In the *Table Talk*, as elsewhere, friendship is a social form and a kind of utilitarian convention that is worthy of high regard because of what it can accomplish for us, but not worthy of analysis; it is a form of relationship that offers neither resources nor impetus for theological, ethical, or political reflection.

58. McEvoy, "Theory of Friendship," 29.
59. Wolin, *Politics and Vision*, 240.
60. Ralph C. Hancock, *Calvin and the Foundations of Modern Politics* (Ithaca: Cornell University Press, 1989), 33–34; Harro Höpfl, *The Christian Polity of John Calvin* (Cambridge: Cambridge University Press, 1982), 22.
61. John Calvin, *Commentary on the Epistle of Paul to the Hebrews*, ed. and trans. John Owen (Albany, Ore.: AGES Digital Library, 1996), 265. This is *not* the *homonoia* of the Apostle Paul.
62. John Calvin, *Institutes of Christian Religion*, trans. Henry Beveridge (Grand Rapids, Mich.: Eerdmans, 1983 [1945]), II.viii.55.
63. Ibid.
64. Ibid., II.viii.51.
65. Ibid., II.viii.53.
66. Ibid., IV.i.3.
67. Ibid.
68. Ibid.
69. Ibid., IV.i.5.
70. Ibid. "Still everyone who listens with docility to the ministers whom God appoints, will know by the beneficial result, that for good reason God is pleased with this method of teaching, and for good reason has laid believers under this modest yoke."
71. Ibid., IV.i.3.
72. Cf. ibid., IV.i.7–10, 21.
73. Ibid., II.x.11.
74. Even his most sympathetic commentators are not, it seems to me, able to move beyond this boundary. See, e.g., Stauffer, *Humanness*, 47–71; and Fritz Büsser, *Calvins Urteil über sich selbst* (Zürich: Zwingli-Verlag, 1950), 67–83, who summarizes Calvin's practice of friendship with the observation that "Freundschaften mit Calvin waren konzentrierte Nächstenliebe" [Friendships with Calvin were concentrated love of neighbor] (76).
75. See, e.g., Calvin's summary at *Institutes*, IV.xx.2. Höpfl's splendid study *(Christian Polity)* of Calvin's political thought is unable, in a careful and thoughtful reading of Calvin's work, to move beyond such language.
76. Calvin, *Institutes*, IV.xx.9.
77. Ibid.
78. Ibid., III.xiv.6.
79. Ibid., III.xiv.5, 7.
80. Ibid., III.xxii, passim; III.xv.6.
81. See, e.g., ibid., III.xviii.6.
82. See, e.g., ibid., III.xxiv.3; Calvin says nothing of such common experiences of friendship except with reference to the command to give alms.
83. Ibid., III.xviii.6.

84. McEvoy, "Theory of Friendship," 3.//
85. Calvin, *Institutes,* III.xix.2.
86. See Plato, *Republic,* 567a–569c; Xenephon, *Hiero,* VI.1–16.
87. See Höpfl, *Christian Polity,* 152ff.
88. See W. D. J. Cargill Thompson, "The 'Two Kingdoms' and the 'Two Regiments': Some Problems of Luther's *Zwei-Reiche-Lehre,*" in *Studies in the Reformation: Luther to Hooker,* ed. C. W. Dugmore (London: Athlone Press, 1980), 42–59, esp. 57–58. Surely Luther's ethical bifurcations, well analyzed in this article, are in part animated by the perception of an inescapable social necessity that stands in uneasy tension at best with the demands of ecclesial purity and separateness as he understands these.
89. Calvin, *Institutes,* IV.xx.9.
90. See esp. Cassidy, "He Who Has Friends," 45.
91. MacIntyre, *After Virtue,* 155.
92. Höpfl, *Christian Polity,* 23.
93. Ibid., 86, 102, 106–15, 146. For Calvin, as for Luther, civil order, too, begins with commands from the top (ibid., 153), even though, for Calvin, such a conception does not imply monarchy as the best form of rule. The centrality of "discipline"—an authoritative call to obedience—can hardly be understated in any review of Calvin's thought. Luther, too, increasingly became entrapped in this model as the antinomian, or at least anarchic, possibilities of his reformation made themselves felt.
94. Ibid., 116–19.
95. Which replacement should not belie the important but subordinate place of laws and rules even in the latter. Cf. MacIntyre, *After Virtue,* 150–53; E. A Goerner, "On Thomistic Natural Law: The Bad Man's View of Thomistic Natural Right," *Political Theory* 7 (1979): 101–22.
96. Wolin, *Politics and Vision,* 240.
97. Ibid., 189.
98. Brian Patrick McGuire, "Jean Gerson and the End of Spiritual Friendship: Dilemmas of Conscience," in Haseldine, ed., *Friendship and Medieval Europe,* 229–50, at 230.
99. Ibid., 244.
100. MacIntyre, "Both the Bad and the Good," 255.

III

Modern Perspectives

7

Plato and Montaigne

Ancient and Modern Ideas of Friendship

Timothy Fuller

My aim in this essay is to reflect on ancient and modern ideas of friendship by considering Plato's dialogue on friendship, the *Lysis,* and Montaigne's essay "Of Friendship." In so doing, I must pass over many other significant reflections on friendship, especially those of Aristotle, that equally should claim our attention. With due apologies to the authors of those works, I reason that the ones I have chosen already offer plentiful food for thought. What I have to say about ancient and modern friendship is well illustrated in these two thinkers. Between them, they should help us become more thoughtful about friendship. At the same time, I find no simple dichotomy between ancients and moderns on this subject. We shall encounter both persistent themes and changes of emphasis. But I believe it to be perfectly plausible that Plato and Montaigne can engage each other in reflective conversation, perhaps in friendship, and try to see them that way in what follows.

What I want to suggest is that friendship may be understood as the discovery of what is most truly human. What this means I hope to make clearer as we proceed. It will also become clear, I hope, that both these thinkers consider friendship as a key to gaining insight into the human situation, yet each has a distinctive way of stating the matter. What puts the Platonic Socrates and Montaigne on a common ground is, first, reflection on the human being as the intersection of the compulsory and the free, of nature and the intellect, or, to put it differently, the human is the dialectic between the unchosen and the chosen. Second, each addresses the question whether friendship is a matter of utility—usefulness—or is an end in itself. These two considerations must be addressed somehow in every worthy reflection on friendship. In these respects, there are neither ancient nor modern, but differing emphases in considered reflection.

The idea that friendship is a relationship constituted in mutually acknowledged utility or advantage is inherent to our experience of life and to reflection on the subject. But this idea, even if it is unavoidable, has often seemed inadequate on serious consideration. There is, of course, a good reason for the intrusiveness of the utilitarian view. The realm of the useful, of advantage and disadvantage, is a mixture of compulsion and choice, standing between the unsought and unavoidable on the one hand, and the unexpected and freely chosen without ulterior motive on the other—between iron necessity and the romance of poetic flight. Consider, first, the following observation of Machiavelli in *The Prince* on the question whether it is better to be feared or loved:

> [I]t is much safer to be feared than loved, if one has to lack one of the two. For one can say this generally of men: that they are ungrateful, fickle, pretenders and dissemblers, evaders of danger, eager for gain. While you do them good, they are yours, offering you their blood, property, lives, and children . . . when the need for them [to be offered] is far away; but, when it is close to you, they revolt . . . for friendships that are acquired at a price and not with greatness and nobility of spirit are bought, but they are not owned and when the time comes they cannot be spent . . . men have less hesitation to offend one who makes himself loved than one who makes himself feared; for love is held by a chain of obligation, which, because men

are wicked, is broken at every opportunity for their own utility, but fear is held by a dread of punishment that never forsakes you.[1]

Let us note that Machiavelli's passing acknowledgment of a possible friendship based on greatness and nobility does not qualify his advice on the iron necessities of the human condition. That there could be a higher friendship is small consolation if the world cannot be transformed by its possibility, and Machiavelli tended to think that the necessities of the world were everything.

On the other hand, according to Thomas Merton, love is not a "deal" but a sacrifice of self, "a positive force, a transcendent spiritual power . . . the deepest creative power in human nature . . . love flowers spiritually as freedom . . . a living appreciation of life as value and as gift."[2] Montaigne experienced what Merton describes when he insisted that friendship can be only with one other, and said of the one he found to be that friend that their relationship flowered "[b]ecause it was he; because it was I."[3]

The realm of the useful is an impure and ambiguous realm, encouraging, sometimes guiltily, Machiavellian thoughts; it is the ordinary condition of human existence; the useful occupies the middle ground of everyday life. When I say that friendship holds out the hope of discovering the truly human, I mean that the human is to be found in the direction of poetic flight, not in that of iron necessity. What seems obvious in experience to most is the usefulness of friendly relations, but within this world of advantage and disadvantage there is another possibility awaiting us over which the philosophers dispute and about which poets sing.

Toward the end of this essay I consider political community, philosophy, and liberal learning as modes of the freely chosen that can transcend the useful, offering, in distinctive ways, experiences of friendship as the disclosing of the truly human. First, I turn my attention to Plato's dialogue, *Lysis*.

Ancient Ideas of Friendship

In the *Lysis* Socrates recounts his dialogue with several boys who are seeking, driven by various motives, to understand friendship. A philosophically satisfactory understanding of friendship is not achieved in the dialogue. Although a number of compelling ideas about friendship are considered, they apparently are incompatible with each other, and each achieves its coherence by excluding some part of the experience of friendship. If, for example, we say that friendship is always a matter of utility or advantage, we may be able to assign defining purposes but no single meaning to friendships, but in so doing we exclude the friendship that arises out of simple affinity, the friendship for its own sake, which has no practical purpose strictly speaking. If, on the other hand, we focus on friendship as the desire to realize an affinity, the concreteness of practical purpose eludes us.

Yet both sorts of friendship are reported among human beings. Even though friendship is a feature of everyday life, it seems to be something that we can know up to a point, through experiences of various sorts, but that we may not be able to grasp entirely or without qualification. We can see also that affinity does not guarantee that utility will not intrude, nor does utility ensure that the practical disadvantage of becoming devoted will not override practical purpose. Socrates voices all the possibilities that emerge in the dialogue, thereby embodying comprehensiveness in the sense of simultaneous awareness of the alternatives. In his attentiveness to the range of experiences, he is the touchstone of reflection on friendship. As he says to Hippothales near the beginning, "I am inferior and useless in other things, but this has somehow been given to me from a god — to be able quickly to recognize both a lover and a beloved."[4]

Hippothales is besotted with Lysis, and he bombards his companions with his thoughts and praises of him. When Socrates hears this he asks Hippothales to tell him what he has been displaying to his companions "so I may know whether you understand what a lover needs to say about his favorite to him or to others" (205a). Socrates, in asking Hippothales what one is to say about the one you love, is implicitly asking what love is about. To know what to say is to know what love is, or to have knowledge. What must then follow is an exploration of what we know about the relationship of love or friendship, the difference between the two being itself ambiguous, just as the basis of such relationships, as we will discover, is also ambiguous: there is utility and there is attraction or affinity. Socrates goes on to say to Hippothales that what he really wants to know is the *thought* behind Hippothales' songs of praise for Lysis (205b).

Here and later in the dialogue, the image is of the lover as "hunter" stalking the beloved as his "prey." This is powerfully erotic. But hidden in what Socrates is saying is the hunt for wisdom about love and friendship. Is the hunt for wisdom a transcending of utility (philosophy often appears to be this to the practical minded) or is it the ultimate form of utility because it is what we most need? Already it is intimated that the explicit object of one's quest may not reveal adequately what we are really looking for, what would really satisfy us. It is understandable that we should want to get what will satisfy us, but what actually will do that? Is it another person? Is it something else that others may point to but not themselves provide? This is the issue Hippothales needs to confront. Suppose, for instance, that his poetic efforts bring harm to him rather than fulfillment, suppose he gets what he wants only to regret it? It would be bad to use poetry or song if it harms the singer.

Hippothales asks Socrates to advise him about what to say (206c). First, Hippothales must maneuver Lysis into conversation with Socrates so that Socrates can demonstrate what should be said. A strategy is hatched whereby Socrates will engage several of the young men within the sight of Lysis, and, because Lysis likes to listen to conversations, he will be drawn into the discussion. The plan works and soon Socrates begins to question Lysis (207d).

Lysis is young and still under the direction not only of his parents but their servants and thus he is not permitted freely to conduct himself. Socrates wonders how he feels about a situation in which these people show their love by imposing restrictions. But it turns out that Lysis is not entirely constrained. He is free to conduct himself in those matters his parents know he understands. Lysis, though young, appears to understand both others and himself. He and Socrates agree that people will trust you in those matters where you are sensible, and not in those where you are not, and that is a good thing. Trust seems to be given where those who give it expect a benefit in return. If this applies to Lysis' family and neighbors, then friendship and affection are determined by what is useful and useless, the principle of utility. Socrates universalizes this by saying, "therefore, not even your father loves you, nor does anyone else love anyone else insofar as he is useless" (210c). If Lysis were to become competent in every important matter, in principle everyone might be his friend.

At this point, Socrates tells us that he began to reflect on what he had been doing so far with Lysis. Hippothales has been observing this whole discussion. What Hippothales should see is that Socrates has been humbling Lysis, not flattering him. In the meantime, Lysis urges Socrates to have the same discussion with Menexenus, who is mentored by Ctesippus, that he has had with Lysis, so that Lysis can enjoy seeing Menexenus chastened too. Ctesippus asks Socrates and Lysis what they have been talking about. Socrates tells him that he wants to ask Menexenus something that he and Lysis think he knows and they do not. Ctesippus urges Socrates on.

Socrates then, professing a passion for friends, asks Menexenus about friendship, for he sees that Menexenus and Lysis have easily become friends, while he, Socrates, "does not even know the manner in which one becomes a friend of another, but these are the things I wish to ask of you, since you are experienced" (212a). But in the effort to sort out what the experience might teach, complications and confusion arise along the following lines: If one loves another, who is the friend? The one who loves or the one who is loved? Or is there no friendship unless both love each other? Yet we know that we can love someone who does not love us, just as we know that we can be loved by one we do not love. Depending on how we answer the questions posed, we are left with the following problems: suppose the friend is the beloved, not the lover. If one's beloved hates one, then the beloved is a friend who is an enemy. Suppose the friend is the lover, not the beloved. Then the friend is the hated one. And so on.

Among the things this tells us is that much of life is confusion and mismatch. The human situation is full of unrequited affections. We can see how grounding relations such as friendship in utility can circumvent some of the difficulties by relating people in terms of mutual advantage where affection is not needed, and, indeed, where different people can fulfill the same function for us, thus depersonalizing our desire for friendship. But we can also see that the grounding in utility, as essential as it is to the maintenance of social life, cannot complete us or bring us final satisfaction. For needs can proliferate, the satisfaction of one desire opening the way to others not yet satisfied. A true friend might be one who is, so to speak, an inexhaustible resource. Have we thus reached an impasse, a disjointedness, irreparably at the heart of humanity?

At this point in the dialogue, Lysis breaks in to turn the conversation in a different direction, apparently rescuing us from the disheartening path we have been treading (213c–d). He and Socrates agree to consider what the poets can teach us. One poetic teaching is that like is attracted to like. But the problem is that this does not work if the parties are evil, because then they make each other worse and they cannot trust each other. To be alike and to be good, then, seems the answer. But this requires us to know who or what is good. Attraction without knowledge is evidently a problem.

Beyond that, if those who are good are self-sufficient they do not need anything. So how can the attraction take place between the good and self-sufficient if the good and self-sufficient are not in need? If they are really good, what benefit do they need to acquire? If to be good is to be self-sufficient, then friendship is not needed. Friendship seems to go with being partly good or incomplete. This conclusion reminds us of why so much importance is attached to the argument based on utility. Can there be a friendship that does not fill a need?

So let us try the argument the other way: suppose opposites attract. Opposites can supply something to each other that each otherwise would not have (216a). But opposites are still opposites. So even if opposites need each other, they will resist if they are not good. After all, the bad reject what they need. But if they are good, as we have already seen, they do not need each other. Let us then retreat to the thought that what is neither good nor bad may become a friend of the good (216c). We seem to have established that friendship is not between good and good, nor between bad and bad, nor between bad and good (the perfect opposites who cannot combine). But the in-between can relate to the good (217a).

The in-between beings are actual human beings who are neither simply good nor simply bad, but a mixture. A human being who became completely bad could no longer seek completion, having fallen away from all awareness of the good. A human being completely good would transcend the need of friendship, being in a state of completion. The actual human being—the in-between being—seeks the good as an antidote to its sense of the danger of the bad. This shows us that friendship is a distinctly human phenomenon and why the argument from utility is always present. The human being appears as situated between the perfectly good and the perfectly bad. Consider how this is stated in the dialogue:

> Because of these things, then, we might say also that the ones who are already wise, whether these are gods or human beings, no longer love wisdom [because they already have it]. Nor, on the other hand, would we say that those love wisdom who have ignorance in such a manner as to be bad. For we wouldn't say that anyone bad and stupid loves wisdom. There are left, then, those who while having this evil, ignorance, are not yet senseless or stupid as a result of it, but still regard themselves as not knowing whatever they don't know. And so, therefore, the ones who are not yet either good nor bad love wisdom; but as many as are bad do not love wisdom, and neither do those who are good. . . . We have now, then, discovered that which is the friend and that which isn't. For we assert—regarding the soul, and regarding the body, and everywhere—that whatever is neither bad nor good is itself, because of the presence of an evil, a friend of the good. (218a–c)

Knowing what we do about Socrates from the *Apology* and other places, we see that what has just been described is Socrates himself, the one who knows he does not know, and he is, as the exemplar of the human condition, the touchstone of friendship.

Before a sigh of relief is uttered, however, Socrates suspects something is still wrong. For example, we are a friend to the medical art because it contributes to health, which is a friend, and health allows us to pursue many other things that are friends. If we befriend something in order to get something else, after all the purpose of friendship is in doubt because we might be going on forever seeking things beyond those we have befriended. In short, even if utility explains our attachments, it is possibly open-ended and leaves us in doubt as to what is really useful. None of these friendships seem to be ends in themselves, but always point beyond themselves to other possibilities (219c–d).

We must find out what is the end served by all these friendships if we are not to be trapped in an endless series of limited relationships without a meaningful outcome. Friendship as we know it in experience is practical, it seems, but it points toward the "true friend" that does not itself point beyond itself. The true friend is the end we seek. But in connecting it to the good, it appears that the true friend is not another person: "What is really a friend is that itself into which all these so-called friendships terminate" (220b).

Now we stumble onto another difficulty: Does something that helps us cease to be a friend when we have acquired the help it provides? This is implied in the utility argument: friendship is, because based on helping, temporary and contingent, and it only remains important so long as we remain in the in-between condition of human existence. We are forced back to the question whether there could be a friend even if we did not need anything. More particularly, could we have a friendship that is pure—not merely useful for something else—while remaining in the in-between state? To anticipate, we may remark that Montaigne would say yes to this. Even if there are no lacks in our lives could we not have a passionate desire for someone? Could there not be a positive love when no deficiency is at stake? But on the basis of what we have considered so far, how could that be? Could there be another kind of desire based on affinity of souls? Could there be a relationship that is not like to like or attraction of opposites, but of "kinship," a kind of meeting of the minds, so to speak?

If being akin and being alike are not the same thing, then perhaps there can be a friendship not based on need. However, another problem now comes into view. Having this kinship relativizes relations because bad can be akin to bad, and we had ruled out a possible friendship between those who are bad. This seems to suggest that the friendship between humans, not based on utility, has no clear purpose; it would always be between particular people and we could not generalize from such relationships; and thus we do not know how to judge their value. It becomes private, one might say—insulated from assessment by observation and thus inaccessible to rational understanding or philosophical judgment.

The limit of utility is that it has no place for friendship that comes purely from desire to be at one with someone, no place for what we might call a "directionless" relationship, or a human relationship that is an end in itself. But without utility, we find that purpose, aim, evaluation, and judgment all seem thwarted. This friendship is in a private realm that bars the way to philosophical inquiry, perhaps even shows us a limit to what philosophy is competent to understand. Investigation and explanation are foreclosed. At the dialogue's close, Socrates, Menexenus, and Lysis—who certainly seem to have been getting along—are left to wonder if they are friends since they do not yet know what friendship is.

Modern Ideas of Friendship

The question who or what is a friend is a philosophical abstraction for Montaigne, who finds whatever answer there is to be found in the experience of a specific, real, and unanticipated human being. The incompletion of the philosophic understanding that ends Socrates' dialogue with Lysis is asserted in a new way in Montaigne's great essay "Of Friendship."

Montaigne discusses friendship from the perspective of his experience of an actual, real friendship he enjoyed for several years with Etienne de la Boetie. The fact that he cannot explain it philosophically certifies for him the genuineness of the friendship. The rest of his life, by comparison to the four years of his association with his friend, is "nothing but smoke, nothing but dark and dreary night."[5] Moreover, Montaigne finds the ancient writers on friendship to be "weak" because the facts of friendship "surpass even the precepts of philosophy."[6] Discussion of what friendship is tends to abstract one's reasoning from the experience of friendship itself, and the abstraction from the experience is a kind of disease of the mind in which we go in search of what we cannot have while abandoning the enjoyment actually possible for human beings.

The universal elements of friendship that can be identified analytically are transcended by every true friendship. A true friend, if anyone should be so lucky as to have one, could never be deduced from the philosophical description of the relationship of friends. The actuality is greater than any intellectual description of it. It is as if Montaigne might have been present when Socrates, Lysis, and the others discussed friendship, and then went away to draw his own conclusion.

The reflectiveness of philosophy, Montaigne seems to say, is an impediment to an act of faith or commitment to another, and that act of faith or commitment is outside philosophy. The conversation of friends need not be the Socratic dialogue. It can be the enjoyment of self-disclosure in an open-ended adventure of mutual self-discovery. In these respects, Montaigne introduces a Christian and a romantic element for our consideration: Christian because the encounter with a true friend is a kind of moment of incarnation, a revelation within human experience; and romantic because it is an adventure in which the ineluctable temporality of the human condition is challenged by the power of the human imagination to live as if it were eternal, while remaining creatures of time that sweeps everything away. Philosophic sobriety is challenged by romantic immediacy. The experience challenges the reflection for primacy.

Montaigne's *Essays* are the language of conversation transferred to a book. As Plato's dialogues are the attempt to write down without loss the vividness and drama of dialectical inquiry, so Montaigne's essays are the expression of self-disclosure in a conversation that remains concrete and real rather than recast in systematic abstractions. A common aim, in a way, but different temperaments. His book, the *Essays,* invites the reader to respond conversationally, to befriend the man revealed there. In writing his essays, Montaigne was first thinking of his own true friend, Etienne de la Boetie, whose death inspired this essay "Of Friendship."

In reflecting this way on friendship, Montaigne allows the reader to take the place of his beloved conversational partner, offering us the possibility of friendship by way of his self-disclosure. We can achieve this relationship to Montaigne because, in his self-revelation, we find both the man himself and something human altogether. Friendship that for Montaigne is between two unique human beings, and exclusive, nevertheless opens out into the human condition insofar as every friendship is an impermanent moment of stability in the passing of all human things. To have gained and to have lost Etienne dramatizes this. The unique and unrepeatable experience nevertheless reveals something to us about what we can and cannot hope for within the human sphere.

Montaigne sees the limits of unaided human reason and of all claims to transcend by reason the human condition. He knows that the range and complexity of experience must outstrip every scheme to systematize, order, and control it. The conclusion of the *Lysis* would also allow or suggest this. But within the constraints of being human, for Montaigne, the happiness that is open to human beings may be found, especially that attained in friendship. The relationship of friends makes our world, which is beyond our control, a little of what we want it to be.

Friendship is devotion, not a rational ordering. There is an arbitrariness in every person's way of knowing the world, but the coalescence of two minds in friendship establishes an artful beauty amid the grotesqueries of life. It is, and can only be, a specifically human achievement, real enough even if its life is "rounded with a sleep." Reason, the distinguishing human trait, is also the source of the disease of man. In reasoning, we overreach—like Icarus we soar only to plunge into the depths. We are bodies as well as souls and thus we must make our bodies and our souls friends if we are to offer any semblance of unity to another. There is an internal friendship, requiring us to acknowledge our earthen ways, without which we jeopardize a relationship to another. To be a friend, then, is first an internal achievement, moderating the prideful aspiration to live by standards too high for humanity, which would logically exclude friendship. Human reason is embodied, and if we cannot be angelic, we can still find the satisfaction of companionship within the limits of human possibility.

There is, for Montaigne, no single way of being human and no obvious way of ranking the many ways of life. Friendship is not an association in service to an abstract ideal, but a mutual recognition of a distinctive beauty accessible without entry into some imagined, alternative world. Friendship is between two individuals who unexpectedly find each other; it is neither complacent nor covered over with goals and strategies. It can neither be planned in advance nor is it an emblem of an ideal relationship of which it is an inferior imitation. It is unique, and, while to know of it in others may inspire us, it is not a model we can imitate. It is what it is, and to look beyond it for something more is to abandon a truly human relationship for the sake of what can only be guessed at.

Friendship, then, is a relationship lived in the present moment in poignant awareness of the inevitability of past and future. Friendship is a release from utility into mystery that illuminates what I understand myself to be through connection to another's self-understanding. Conversation is the central act in which friends regard each other through self-disclosure, not ceasing to be individuals but reaching out as selves beyond themselves, receptively, and without anxiety for their identities.

Montaigne begins his essay with a mind to imitate a painter he knows who chooses the best spot on each wall to put a skillful picture, which he then surrounds with "grotesque and monstrous bodies, pieced together of divers members, without definite shape, having no order, sequence, or proportion other than accidental."[7] He directs us to the thought of an enclave of stability within the confusion and mismatch of life. In Plato's *Lysis,* Socrates is the beautiful picture surrounded by the chaos of opinion and argument. Here it is the friendship of Michel and Etienne. It is worth considering the difference.

Montaigne fears, however, that the skillful picture eludes him, perhaps only misshapen images are within his range. His friend, had he lived longer, would have done better. Such works as he did produce brought him to Montaigne's attention before they met. The friendship that eventuated was "entire" and "perfect"—of a rare sort, unknown, Montaigne thinks, at the time he is writing his essay. "So many coincidences are needed to build up such a friendship that it is a lot if fortune can do it once in three centuries."[8] This is an extravagant and depressing claim, but it seems to follow from Montaigne's reading of Aristotle's dictum that associations based on pleasure, profit, or need are inferior to friendship for the sake of friendship. Certainly, Aristotle and Montaigne agree that the true or highest friendship is rare, few are likely to experience it, and most may never know it at all.

Montaigne distinguishes between common friendship and real friendship.[9] Common friendship is multiple, and one pursues these with bridle in hand, with prudence, and with caution. Real friendship is with one other and you pursue it by throwing caution to the winds.[10] In Montaigne's analysis, real friendship breaks free of the substructure in nature of normal human associations. He identifies the natural, the social, the hospitable, and the erotic as the elements that bind us together by nature. He reviews the typical natural ties that follow and finds that none of them explains the real friendship as he has known it. For example, parents, children, and brothers are kinsmen by nature but they are not, because of that, soul mates. Parents and children are unequal; brothers are naturally competitive. The quality of the associations produced by nature is arbitrary. Relations between husbands and wives may be initially moved by attraction and choice, but they are fulfilled in obligations, law, and practical concerns. In all these cases, full freedom of choice is impossible.

This raises the question whether there can be real friendship between men and women. Montaigne admits that, if it were possible to do so, it might be the best of all because the affinity could be complete in soul and body. But he rejects this on the grounds that, in fact, such relationships will be too scorching and intense, too variable, and too fickle to achieve what he knows friendship to be. Similarly and finally, he considers and dismisses "licentious Greek love" because it is unequal, lacks reciprocity, and is both too dependent on external beauty in the case of the lover, and contingent on the beloved's transposing the relationship based in physical beauty into a quest for the inner beauty of the spirit. At its best it can become philosophic friendship, which in any event is not the highest for Montaigne.

For Montaigne, then, real friendship is most free and most human. We are most human when we are most free from the drives of nature, and thus when we are wrapped in a mystery of encounter:

> In the friendship I speak of, our souls mingle and blend with each other so completely they efface the seam that joined them, and cannot find it again. If you press me to tell why I loved him, I feel that this cannot be expressed, except by answering: Because it was he, because it was I. . . . Our friendship has no other model than itself, and can be compared only with itself.[11]

Common friendship is always practical: "For the familiarity of the table I look for wit, not prudence; for the bed, beauty before goodness; in conversation, competence, even without uprightness. Likewise in other matters."[12]

We can see now the outline of a conversation between ancient and modern ideas of friendship. They have much in common. In both cases, the distinction between utility and affinity is acknowledged. The ancient voice and the modern voice express the range of experiences of a common humanity. Both acknowledge the complexity of the experiences of friendship and the difficulty of holding them together in an intellectually coherent way. In both, we can see the divergence between devotion to the good and devotion to a person. Socrates is a compelling individual whom many sought, and still seek, to befriend. Yet he is an elusive dramatic character, the locus of the fundamental human questions into which he seems to disappear, withholding himself, or being withheld, from the friendship of which Montaigne speaks, perhaps necessarily so if the point is to ascend, by reason alone, beyond ourselves to the eternal things. Montaigne's concreteness, on the other hand, exultant in the value of freedom, individuality, contingency, and mystery in his quest for transcendence within the human realm, leaves the divine at a remove, covered in no less an uncertainty of its own kind than that with which Socratic inquiry leaves us.

Friendship in Political Community, Philosophy, and Liberal Learning

I want to conclude this essay by saying something about friendship in relation to political community, philosophy, and liberal learning. As we learn from Aristotle, justice is the requirement for a political community that cannot depend simply on shared sentiment and mutual affection, but must rely on common advantage. But he also says that the best city will be one in which the citizens can become friends, dependent not alone on the bonds of justice and law. We can reasonably call this the idea of "community."

As we learn from Montaigne, real friendship is unique and not perhaps civic at all. Yet we also know that Montaigne was himself an important and responsible public official whose acceptance of civic duty was widely acknowledged. For him, the political order ideally would not seek to be an Aristotelian community, but would be an association based on a framework of procedural rules that would permit the vast range of human possibilities to express itself, within the rules, and to honor the opportunities for the real private friendships of which he is the preeminent spokesman. To reflect on the alternatives of friendship, then, is to begin also to reflect on what public order is best for us.

Philosophical inquiry is at the heart of the human condition. On one view, it is the best and highest way of life for human beings, exemplary even if it can only be undertaken by a few. On another view, philosophy promotes human pride and a comic claim of self-sufficiency. Perhaps it should be the cure for the human temptation to overreach itself to that which it has itself contributed. In what way, then, is philosophy a friend, or how shall we befriend philosophy? What is the relation of reflection to experience? Considering friendship leads us to these questions, and our authors provide alternatives we cannot ignore in thinking about them.

Finally, as fellow members of the academic community, we have committed ourselves to liberal learning and thus engaged jointly in an historic activity that can trace an unbroken line—admittedly with many permutations—back through Montaigne to Aristotle, Plato, and Socrates. We also find ourselves at a moment when controversies rage about the nature and purpose of education. Much of the controversy is imposed on the academic world by external forces that may or may not understand what we are doing, what we have tried to do for twenty-five centuries in the places we have set aside for undistracted devotion to teaching and learning. This is, of course, not new. Controversy has always raged in some form, both within the academy and outside it. While we must be responsive to our patrons who consider us from outside, it is also incumbent on us to know what it is we stand for and how we should respond to them, respectfully, but with something to say for ourselves. It is, so to speak, a question of how we should seek to befriend them.

One is thus reminded of Montaigne's point that we must find our internal ordering if we are to qualify for friendship with others. Is the place of liberal learning to be a vocational and technical training ground? Is it to foster a love of learning for its own sake on the ground that the possibility of the full flourishing of the human spirit will be otherwise prevented? Is it to be more than one thing? How should teachers befriend their students, and what should students hope for from their teachers? What should we as collegial scholars hope for from each other? Is it not remarkable that reflection on friendship should lead us out into everything we do as a society, as reflective human beings, as teachers and students?

Notes

1. Niccolo Machiavelli, *The Prince,* trans. Harvey C. Mansfield (Chicago: University of Chicago Press, 1985), 66–67.
2. Thomas Merton, *Love and Living* (New York: Farrar, Straus & Giroux, 1979), 34.
3. Michel de Montaigne, "Of Friendship," in *The Complete Essays of Montaigne,* trans. Donald M. Frame (Stanford: Stanford University Press, 1968), 139.
4. This and all subsequent references to Plato's *Lysis* are from *Plato's Dialogue on Friendship: An Interpretation of the Lysis,* trans. David Bolotin (Cornell: Cornell University Press, 1979), 204c.
5. Montaigne, "Of Friendship," 143.
6. Ibid.
7. Ibid., 135.
8. Ibid., 136.
9. Ibid., 140.
10. Ibid., 141–42.
11. Ibid., 139.
12. Ibid., 142.

8

Hobbes on Getting By with Little Help from Friends

Travis D. Smith

With Friends Like These

Hobbes's political thought contains a sustained attack on friendship. At the outset of *Leviathan,* for instance, he draws immediate attention to the problems that friendships present. The book opens with the dedication "To My Most Honour'd Friend Mr. Francis Godolphin, of Godolphin." Hobbes proceeds to concede that this book may not be so well received, for it is likely to offend all interested parties among his contemporaries. Hobbes insists that he is not writing for or about particular men in his own time, but rather about matters political in the abstract. Given that his depiction of human nature suggests that such impartiality must be reckoned extremely rare (L xxvi:21),[1] Hobbes must either be concealing his partialities here or revealing his pride. Aware that the dedicatee may be put in an uncomfortable position as a result of this dedication, Hobbes gives him permission to try excusing himself from the anticipated notoriety of the book (L LD) at the same time that his name is tied to it forever instead of vanishing into relative obscurity. Whether or not this dedication would affect the fortunes of Mr. Godolphin, it alerts the reader to the precariousness of friendship, if the highest honor a friend may bestow threatens to bring its recipient disrepute and danger. Although Hobbes had a roster of enemies, he was also a man blessed with many learned personal friends.[2] It is telling that he does not dedicate this most infamous work of his to any of them. Instead, he praises some of them later in the dedicatory letter of his less overtly political *De Corpore*.

As I am averse to the sort of speculation that endeavors to reduce philosophy to biography, I do not in this essay attempt to draw conclusions regarding Hobbes's arguments based on his personal history and correspondence. I do suggest, however, that the apparent discontinuity between Hobbes's political teaching regarding friendship and his own experience of friendship (and that of most men, arguably [cf. L Intro: 4]) indicates that the present analysis will in part illustrate the extent to which Hobbes distorts the human condition in order to relieve it. It shows how that which is necessary in theory to render politics scientific in the modern sense is not entirely based on observing how men actually live rather than imagining how they should live. The question then becomes whether Hobbes's approach, in which the worst is assumed about every man taken individually in order to design a regime portrayed as an achievable ideal, is not really deeply rhetorical rather than simply ideological.

Reading his political philosophy as a deductive system, as *Leviathan* purports to be, it comes across as if the assault on friendship is something that falls out during the derivation of political science, something that follows from thinking first principles in politics through to their necessary conclusions. But when one considers the preponderance of examples that portray friendship negatively amid his historical reflections—whether pertaining to events in recent English history or to the history of the ancient world; whether recounted at length, as in *Behemoth,* or in the anecdotal references scattered throughout his treatises for the purpose of giving substance to his abstractions—it seems rather that Hobbes's concern for the political problem of friendship is one of the principal motivations behind the construction of the system.

In focusing on the subject of friendship in Hobbes, one can see how both types of knowledge Hobbes recognizes, science and experience, cooperate in the production of his political philosophy. This cooperation is evident in the examples he selects to illustrate the epistemological theory developed in the earliest chapters of *Leviathan*. Hobbes promises to reason systematically to the foundations of a commonwealth from the physical fundamentals of human nature. In the first chapter, having described the basis of Sense according to his materialistic metaphysics, Hobbes criticizes the theory of visible, audible, and intelligible species taught by "the philosophy-schools, through all the Universities of Christendom" (L i:5). His principal target here is not that modified Aristotelian theory or the idea of the university itself. It is the Schoolmen, a fraternity whose members endeavor to secure their own power and advance that of their ecclesiastical superiors and foreign powers through the dissemination of nonsensical doctrines, for the manipulation of professional and political elites and, subsequently, society as a whole. Hobbes does not get through the first chapter without introducing the political problem of subversive associations.

As his epistemological theory proceeds, Hobbes indirectly emphasizes the danger of close personal friendships in politics. His description of the Imagination in the second chapter leads to a discussion of dreams. While explaining the commonplace experience of fearful dreams and visions, he decides to draw on the striking example of Marcus Brutus, Julius Caesar's favorite and murderer, who reportedly experienced superstitious apparitions (L ii:7). Then in the third chapter, while detailing the mechanism of an ordinary unguided train of thoughts, he devises a peculiar example regarding a Roman penny that refers not only to the fate of Charles I, betrayed by the English aristocracy (cf. B 114–15), but also reminds the reader of the treachery of Judas Iscariot (L iii:3). Since the purpose of that chapter is to show how all thoughts, however seemingly unconnected, have necessary connections that could be discerned on reflection, Hobbes here indirectly invites the reader to wonder why his materialistic, mechanistic theory of the operations of the mind should lead him to think of betraying Christ, of all things. To summarize, within the first three chapters, long before he has started to address political subjects directly, Hobbes refers in passing to the two most notorious betrayals of the ancient world and to two of the parties he holds responsible for the sedition and strife of his own time.

Friends, Justice, and Nature

Relationships of justice and injustice and those of friends and enemies constitute categories that interact differently in different political arrangements and situations. The domain of friendship predominates in any society in which patronage relationships are pervasive. Honor is of much greater concern in such a society (L x:48). Hobbes's political philosophy is designed to establish the supremacy of justice, of law, so that considerations of benefit and return, of honor and dishonor, are much diminished as supposed justifications for injustice. Even though he is an outspoken proponent of monarchy, it would be a mistake to suppose that the conventions and institutions of a fully developed Hobbesian monarchy would much resemble those of a traditional European monarchy, given that he seeks to liberate politics, as much as possible, from the kinds of relationships that permeate and sustain the traditional form.[3] Human society cannot sustain itself on the basis of friendship alone without suffering "a great deal of grief," and so men need a power to "over-awe them all" (L xiii:5), to establish and enforce justice while pursuing the common good (L xiii:13, xvii:12; dC i:2; EL xix:4). Still, individuals habitually prefer some goods and some people to others. Partialities among men can be weakened, managed, and monitored, but not eradicated. Hobbes does not identify every act of friendship as illegal, as an injustice, but he is well aware that the love of one's own is the root of injustice.[4] Hobbes's longest sustained discussion of the subject of friendship is found in his *A Brief on the Art of Rhetorick*, when he draws on book 2, chapter 4 of Aristotle's *Rhetoric* to define friends as those who love and are beloved and identify love as that which follows from "The bestowing of *Benefits*" (AR ii:4).[5] Hobbes emphasizes the need for justice because friends act unjustly toward others—another idea he traces to Aristotle's *Rhetoric* (AR i:12).[6] To be sure, in the *Ethics,* Aristotle observes, "if people are friends, they have no need of justice."[7] That observation belongs to a political science oriented toward eudaimonia, in which true friendship is recognized as a human good of a higher rank than justice. Hobbesian political science is oriented decidedly otherwise.

Aristotle claims that there is a "natural friendship" between parents and children, and indeed, among all the members of the human race,[8] whereas Hobbes finds that no two human beings are natural friends. The difference is indicative of the two thinkers' competing conceptions of what is natural, of their disagreement over whether there are final and formal causes in nature. For Hobbes, "life is but a motion of limbs" (L Intro:1), and there really is no such thing as the human race, or any species at all (L iv:6; dC xvii:12). According to Hobbes, when men "seek each other's company and enjoy associating with each other," it is not by nature, "but by chance" (dC i:2). By nature, all human beings are enemies (L xiii:8–9; EL xx:2).[9] With their differing opinions, potent passions, and incompatible strivings, all men are "diverse ways offensive one to another" (EL xiv:4, cf. xiv:11). Even shared passions and pursuits, the very things that could form the basis of partnerships, do naturally instead instigate hostilities (EL xiv:5). By nature men have countless potential legitimate causes of quarrel and no standards of conduct to adhere to on confronting one another. Everyone outside of one's own commonwealth always remains, in principle, an enemy (L xiii:10, xxx:30; dC P 10, i:2 second note, xiii:7), and even after a commonwealth is instituted, vestiges of the old universal animosity remain ever-present among all of its subjects, even within households (L xiii:10, xviii:9; dC P 10–11, vi:9).

What, then, is a friend? Befitting his trademark lack of sentimentality, Hobbes counts friends among "powers instrumental," meaning "means and instruments to acquire more" (L x:2; cf. EL viii:4) in order "to obtain some future apparent good" (L x:1). It is "strengths united," such as would form any faction or league (L x:3). In effect, anyone is your friend if they will do what you want them to do, but only insofar as they will do it without being required to do it by the law, and only so long as they do what you want, or continue to want to do so. Where justice is not being enforced, intentions must be reckoned sufficient

(L xiii:8, xv:36). On Hobbesian grounds, Dale Carnegie's famous title *How to Win Friends and Influence People* expresses a redundancy. Friendships do involve trust, which for Hobbes is only to expect some good from another (EL ix:9), to count on his concern for himself, on his fear of adverse consequences like vengeance or earning a bad reputation. A friend is anyone who endeavors to increase your relative power. The kind of power conferred is irrelevant, as is the character of the person himself or one's own disposition toward him. Aristotelian arguments regarding "complete friendship" between virtuous men, who place the good of their friends above their own, aiming at what is genuinely good, have no place in the Hobbesian scheme.[10]

In their origins, friendships and the societies they develop into begin as "instruments of defence," as a "provision against fear" (dC i:2 second note; cf. dH xi:6; EL xiv:14). Only eventually might friendships contribute to giving a man cause "to compare oneself favourably with others and form a high opinion of oneself," the source of "all the heart's joy and pleasure" according to Hobbes (dC i:5), or develop into one of "the ornaments and comforts of life, which by peace and society are usually invented and procured" (EL xiv:12). Men are directed by the laws of nature and their own "fear of oppression" (L xi:9) to escape the natural condition. Because "no one can live securely without the aid of allies" (L xv:5 [OL], cf. dC i:13), men must join together with others and eventually institute a commonwealth ruled by a sovereign power that ensures the execution of justice.[11] But this transition cannot be effected without men seeking confederates and practicing trust and mutual assistance, trading in the abstract and pervasive vulnerability of the war that renders every man the out and out enemy of every other for the particular and precarious dangers of invariably uncertain friendships.

Men first learned to form a "confederacy," Hobbes suggests, when some two or more agreed to gang up on another who would probably defeat any of them one on one (L xiii:1). In the state of nature, preemptive defenses are not only unobjectionable but entirely necessary, even encouraged. Thus, to say that friendships have as their origins the need for defense is to say they have their origins in going on the offensive, among co-combatants intending to "dispossess or deprive" others of their holdings or their lives (L xiii:3). The aid of others must be sought when peace does not look hopeful (dC i:15), for the sake of waging war well. Unfortunately, "the mutual aid of two or three men is of very little security" (EL xix:3). Before a commonwealth can be created, Hobbes argues, sufficient forces must unite so that together they no longer feel a pressing danger from any other combination of men (L xvii:3; dC v:3). Any multitude of men so allied must continue growing precisely because it must reckon on the continual multiplication of its enemies as well, until they are either beaten or join up (dC i:14). Hobbes furthermore indicates that within such a multitude, even before a sovereign power is formally established, there is likely someone who has "master[ed] the persons" of the others (L xiii:4). Compulsion is a necessary element in any "coalition for defence," otherwise private interests will undermine any hope for mutual assistance (dC v:4). Thus, even though men are reckoned equal in the condition of mere nature, inequalities among them begin to arise as soon as they start combining, even without their formal acknowledgment. Among friends, the rule of the mighty and the obedience of the fearful come to pass well before official authorities are established to institutionalize might as right.

When men, who are enemies by nature and yet commanded by the law of nature to seek peace, seek confederates and a commonwealth results, it is designated by Hobbes something artificial rather than natural. Moreover, mutual assistance cannot be secured without speech (L iv:3), and Hobbes argues that speech is artificial. Arguably, Hobbes's distinction between the natural and the artificial seems itself artificial.[12] Hobbes anticipates this criticism, explaining, "I am not therefore denying that we seek each other's company at the prompting of nature," continuing, "all men ... are born unfit for society; and very many (perhaps the majority) remain so throughout their lives, because of mental illness or lack of training." He concludes, "man is made fit for society not by nature, but by training" (dC i:2 first note). Unfortunately, hitherto, "few in the world ... have learned the rules of civil life sufficiently" (dCorp i:7). These responses raise more questions, however. Is religion the mental illness to which he refers? Could men be rightly trained, so as to become trustworthy and just, or must treachery and injustice be counted on forevermore? Hobbes suggests elsewhere that religion cannot be abolished (L xii:23), presumably because most men will always be ignorant of natural causes, lacking scientific training and the aptitude for it.

The Origins of Friendship

How does one make friends? How does one man get another to do what he wants him to do? He must either give him something first and make his expectations known or ask for something from him and convince him to expect something in return. Here, withholding or alleviating harms count as benefits no less than conferring goods. Either way, Hobbes observes, "of the voluntary acts of every man the object is some good to himself" (L xiv:8, cf. xii:27; dC i:2; EL xvi:6). What one man regards as a benefit to himself is relative to him, to his own appetites, aversions, plans, and circumstances. The relative situation of the beneficiary to his benefactor affects how well a benefit will be received and repaid (cf. L xi:7). There is, however, no objective standard of parity to determine whether or not returns made for benefits given are satisfactory. In the realm of justice, specific duties, entitlements, and punishments may be specified and quantified, but it is up to each person to judge for himself what it takes for someone to qualify as a good friend.

Doing good unto others is always treated by Hobbes as something of a calculation. Relationships of benefit and return can even yield an economy that is beneficial to the common good under one set of circumstances. As Hobbes describes it, "to receive benefits, though from an equal or inferior, as long as there is hope of requital, disposeth to love; for in the intention of the receiver, the obligation is of aid and service mutual; from whence proceedeth an emulation of who shall exceed in benefiting, the most noble and profitable contention possible" (L xi:7). Hobbes does not, however, need to genuinely believe that there is in fact absolutely no incidence of altruism among men.[13] As with several other things that he claims are universal with respect to human behavior, what he really means is that, for the sake of making political science reliable, selfish intentions must be reckoned as if they were universal. If altruism is written out of politics, though it happens to happen from time to time, no harm is done. A political system that depends on any altruism at all, however, will soon meet its ruin. The same holds for the rare man of "generosity" who will keep his promises although he fears no consequences for breaking them. There are such men, but they cannot "be presumed on" (L xiv:31). Hobbes goes so far as to besmirch the generous man as someone concerned with glory or pride. Glory, for Hobbes, is generally vain, and pride is a sin against the law of nature. It would be better for the common good if occasions for private generosity were rare and if men were not so proud and eager to seem magnanimous. Should someone actually do the right thing simply because it is the right thing to do, it should always come as a surprise. It is best to expect people to do what is right only when they can see that they must, or else, and then ensure that effective mechanisms are in place to motivate them accordingly.

Note, however, that it is not only in the domain of justice, of contracts, where it is the same thing as breaking the law, that there is good reason to fear the consequences of breaking one's word. There are often good reasons to fear the consequences of failing to keep one's word in the domain of friendships, too. Friendships are not always nice. To secure "mutual assistance" there needs to be an element of fear (dC v:4). Men in the state of nature who betray their allies probably will not do well for long without the protection of new confederates, supposing them to be reliable (cf. DBT 46). There are perhaps plenty of situations, wherever justice has been established, in which a man has nothing serious to worry about if he does not keep his word when he does not have to, especially where there is a great difference of power between the persons involved. Indeed, one of the great advantages of becoming powerful is that a man may then confidently "ignore a favour-seeker" (dH xi:13). That said, Hobbes generally disapproves of great differences of power between private persons.

Friends are acquired, Hobbes indicates, through the use of a man's natural powers, including his strength, beauty, good birth, experiences, talents, persuasive speech, or the giving of gifts. Friends may also be obtained through mutual friends or through a man's acquisition of wealth, reputation, or "good luck" (which Hobbes calls "the secret working of God") (L x:2). "Riches joined with liberality" is the most convenient means for acquiring both "friends and servants" (the master–servant relationship being a matter of justice), whereas a rich but illiberal man will soon discover that he has effortlessly made many enemies (L x:4, cf. L xv:21; dH xi:7). Ordinary frugality costs a man many opportunities to achieve great things (L xi:15). Lacking riches, the next best route is to combine eloquence and flattery to win many friends (L xi:16). Riches will follow.

On Hobbes's reckoning, the desire for power—and in particular material gain, political power, and reputation (although perhaps also, although less often, knowledge)—is the motor of friendship, as it is the cause of human motivation generally (L x:1–5; cf. B 2–4). Even the barely ambitious person must continue to seek power for the sake of securing what little he has. Even the person who wants to live withdrawn from the world to seek knowledge alone for its own sake still needs food and shelter. He must avoid being perceived as a threat or used as a scapegoat. To this end he should probably prefer a reputation for harmlessness to one for wisdom. Family is a source of friends, or rather a kind of friendship, but its concerns are generally reducible to the aforementioned as well, at least insofar as family matters are politically relevant, which they arguably always are. Sometimes shared ideas are what link friends, but the activity of their friendship will involve considerations of wealth and power soon enough. Religion is but one kind of idea that brings men together.

Friendships that are bought are as good as any other kind. Men try to buy even God's friendship with sacrifices (cf. L xxxi:31; dH xiv:10). Hobbes argues that any agreement made under duress is valid where laws do not exist to say otherwise, because all agreements in such circumstances are made in a state of fear, especially that most important agreement to obey a sovereign (L xiv:27). Similarly, there is a sense in which every benefit given is a purchasing of friendship, for the sake of receiving future benefits in return, or a purchasing of peace, for the sake of averting some harm or to ease hostilities among enemies (EL ix:17). In such cases, there is no formal contract between the persons involved and there is no official, rightful third party to enforce compliance, although there may well be muscle to whom that task is assigned. There is no benefit given without an expectation of return, and the continued survival of civil society depends on reciprocity (L xv:16; dC iii:8; EL xvi:6). Gifts are made, Hobbes explains, "in hope to gain thereby friendship or service from another (or from his friends), or in hope to gain the reputation of charity or magnanimity" (which is tantamount to a hope to gain friends, for that is what such a reputation will bring), "or to deliver his mind from the pain of compassion" (typically accompanied by the desire that the recipient should do the giver the favor of ameliorating his own condition, or at least go away so as to cause him no future pain—for a man may readily feel compassion for the sufferer of misfortune he has encountered but once, yet come to loathe the nuisance whose hardship he is confronted with day after day), "or in hope of reward in heaven" (which is to purchase God's favor) (L xiv:12).

"Benefits oblige" (L xi:7), Hobbes explains. Friendships are not distinguished from contractual relationships by being nonobligatory. A contract is only a formalized and depersonalized exchange of benefits, regulated and enforced by a powerful third party. Benefits oblige because ingratitude is against the law of nature. The laws of nature tell a man what he must and must not do to preserve himself. They outline a man's obligations to himself.[14] Because the natural passions of men tend toward ingratitude, the laws of nature require turning most forms of exchange into legally enforceable contracts. Peaceful coexistence is better secured through legal processes and punishments than feuds and reprisals. The depersonalization of relationships is effective, however, only when people are convinced of the reality of justice, this being a function of its observed success.[15] Impartial justice represents the friendship of the sovereign to all of his subjects, whereas a corrupt justice system reveals only that a network of friends have attained tremendous power.

Being instrumental in nature, friendship is not a good in itself. "Friends are secondary," in that men do not seek friends for the sake of friendship, but for the honor, profit, and other advantages that follows from having them (dC i:2). In general, society as a whole, Hobbes maintains, "is a product of love of self, not love of friends" (dC i:2). The leading passions that bring men together are "fear of death, desire of such things as are necessary to commodious living and a hope by their industry to obtain them" (L xiii:14). Through their own industry, men desire to "nourish themselves and live contentedly" (L xvii:13). Friendships are good insofar as they help men accomplish these goals. They have no value that could be cherished in the absence of the political preconditions that secure these goods, except insofar as they help reestablish them. Men do not enjoy friendships, or have any love for society itself for that matter, except for the safety they afford and the opportunities for success they bring. For "the pleasure [men] take in one another's company," Hobbes argues, "by which men are said to be sociable by nature" is actually but a part of "the joy a man taketh in the fruition of any present good" (EL ix:16). Those, like the Schoolmen, who insist on the natural sociability of men, have their causes and effects reversed.

The Downside of Friendship

Hobbes emphasizes repeatedly how entirely unreliable friendship is. "In a condition of war where every man to every man . . . is an enemy," as Hobbes explains, "there is no man can hope by his own strength or wit to defend himself from destruction without the help of confederates" (L xv:5). Among men who combine, however, some will espy as enemies men whom others among them take for friends (L xvii:5), making all confederacies unreliable mixtures of friends and enemies. Strictly speaking, where every man is an enemy, this in principle would include all of one's confederates. Where justice does not reign, only covenants turn enemies into allies (L xxviii:23), but under these conditions, covenants cannot be reckoned on. Hobbes warns against performing first in any agreement where the other person cannot be forced to fulfill his side of the bargain. Hobbes calls it betraying oneself to one's enemies (L xiv:18; cf. dC iii:27). Put plainly, "everyone is an enemy to everyone whom he neither obeys nor commands" (dC ix:3). Only the fear of adverse consequences convinces a man to keep his word rather than betray his friends, and while there may be good reasons to fear exclusion or reprisal, that fear is much less reliable in the domain of friendship than it is in the realm of justice.

Should the present government be dissolved and the realm of justice along with it, it will not be at all easy to reestablish civil society. Any man who endeavors to dissolve it must realize that none of his confederates can be counted on, either while they operate together as enemies of the present sovereign power or once it has been brought down — even if, or rather, especially if he plans to rule in the next regime. It is far more likely that he will not survive to see what follows, and those who do survive will not thank him for his efforts, proving all of his striving vain and all of his wisdom folly (L xxvii:16). Nothing ruins friendships like the competition for sovereign authority (DBT 42). And it is not easy for the ambitious man to resist feelings of "false glory" from an overestimation of himself, the flattery of others, and trusting too much in his friends and his reputation (EL ix:1). When an ambitious man stumbles or is betrayed, he is usually finished. He cannot count on the assistance of even those who would otherwise remain loyal, for "men usually are content," Hobbes observes, "to be spectators of the misery of their friends" (EL ix:19). After all, they have to look out for themselves. Sacrifices made on behalf of old friends on the way out bring no hope of future reward and often earn one new and recently empowered enemies.

In his delineation of the passions, on the subject of "weeping," Hobbes observes that its frequent cause is the loss of "props of power." Women and children are most subject to weeping, he indicates, because it is they who "rely principally on helps external" (L vi:43; cf. dH xii:7). The reverse of that observation is that a man who depends on friendships too much is like a woman or a child, and though Hobbes does not regard personal courage as a virtue (dH xiii:9), it remains an insult to call a man unmanly or feminine (cf. L xviii:3, xxi:16). When one weeps "for the loss of friends" (L vi:43) he weeps because it is a loss of his own power. Women and men will also weep about "the sudden stop made to their thoughts of revenge, by reconciliation" (L vi:43). That is, when a former friend has withdrawn his friendship, one will so desire to bring him harm in return that it will make him or her miserable to be returned to his favor (dH xii:7). Friendships are so unreliable and adversarial passions are so strong that people prefer to retain former friends as enemies than restore their friendships.

Friendships affect individuals adversely in various ways. The criticism of dependency is part of a broader criticism of the way friendships may corrupt a man's character. It is a mistake to suppose that Hobbes is not interested in shaping the character of the sovereign's subjects. In "familiar company," Hobbes observes, people tend to become both coarser and also more deceitful (L viii:10). Furthermore, to believe or trust or otherwise rely on any other person, to need their protection or their help, is always to honor them (L x:22, 27). As honor is always relative, needing and seeking friends always involves an element of lowering oneself. Meanwhile, to find one's friendship sought out tends to breed vainglory in a man (cf. L xi:12). Everyone also tends to overvalue themselves, and they expect their friends to value them at the same inflated rate. If necessary they will find ways to "extort" that esteem from them (L xiii:5). But people naturally value other men very little (L xviii:5), and so friends will usually disappoint. Mixing pride with wishful thinking, men typically admire only like-minded persons of power and reputation (L xiii:2).

The Hobbesian commonwealth is designed so that every subject should be dependent on the sovereign for his security and prosperity, which his theory of authorization portrays as a kind of indirect dependence on himself. His political philosophy is designed to minimize the dependency of some private individuals on other private individuals, other "props of power," not only to protect the sovereign power, but for their own sake as well. His argument therefore contains a criticism of the dependency of any man on other particular men, introducing an element of individualism designed to be consistent with inhibited ambitions. "Association with others," Hobbes teaches, "does not increase reason for glorying in oneself," because "a man is worth as much as he can do without relying on anyone else" (dC i:2).

The Depersonalized Regime

Having considered conditions in the state of nature and among ordinary subjects in a commonwealth in the abstract, it remains to address the dangers of friendships in the offices and among the officers of the commonwealth. It is a testament to the success of his project that so much of Hobbes's assessment and criticism of friendships in politics is now standard. It is perhaps too easy to forget how relatively novel and unusual it is, taking the whole of human history and the diversity of peoples into account, that we modern Westerners have established a political society where impartial justice and impersonal bureaucrats are expected, even if they cannot be taken for granted. Being friendly to a bureaucrat is like expressing an expectation for special treatment, and there is something amiss when bureaucrats make exceptions or accept gifts for doing their jobs. A bureaucrat's private interest should be satisfied best by always doing his job strictly by the book. Not only are the courts supposed to be neutral rather than respecters of persons, and not only are bureaucrats supposed to be faceless, but there is a constant call to render legislative and electoral processes less susceptible to influence from particular interests. The media too, even where it is a private enterprise, is routinely criticized for exhibiting bias and being a mouthpiece for this or that political prejudice or economic interest. Certainly, advanced liberal democracies are imperfect realizations of the Hobbesian project, but in comparison with traditional regimes of formalized patronage or corrupt nations past or present, despotic, oligarchic, and developing, Hobbes's recommendations for reducing the political power of friendships have proved remarkably persuasive even if they are not always effective, and even if they are something of a ruse.

With respect to the dangers of friendships in politics, I here consider first the sovereign's own friends, then the related subject of counsel, followed by concerns pertaining to the administration of justice, and finally issues in international relations. Afterward, Hobbes's concerns regarding the various sorts of partial associations that form within a commonwealth are addressed.

Whoever represents the artificial person that is the sovereign is also a natural person. When an assembly governs, many natural persons comprise the sovereign. But all natural persons have a tendency to favor their friends and family (L xix:4). It is one of Hobbes's chief arguments in favor of monarchy that this danger is less when one man alone rules, because only then does the private good of the sovereign coincide with the public good. An entire kingdom may be reckoned as something like the king's extended family (cf. L xvii:2, xx:15). Also, his friendship has been directly bought by each subject through those gifts of theirs that established his power (cf. L xviii:4). This is no less true of the sovereign when it is an assembly, but it is arguably more likely that a king, who has been raised to rule, will recognize it, whereas those who rise to power in an assembly are more likely to neglect it and abuse the position they attain (cf. B 181). Of course, it is a long-standing concern that the sovereign will enrich his favorites and their friends or harm their enemies, and the appearance or suspicion of such behavior can be just as damaging as its practice. Hobbes does not pretend that monarchs do not enrich their favorites (cf. B 65), but this is no argument against monarchy, since it is true that the many members of assemblies also use their power to buy friends and benefit their families, multiplying and compounding the problem (L xix:8; dC x:6).

It is important for Hobbes to establish that all titles of honor are gifts of the sovereign, indicating his friendship (L x:52). Aristocrats, where there are any, should know that their privileges are owed ultimately to the sovereign and not simply to their good birth. Noblemen who forget that they are indebted to the sovereign for their station are likely to become his enemies. Likewise, all counselors, ministers, magistrates, and other officeholders ultimately owe their positions to the sovereign (L xviii:13). But it is also best, as far as it is possible, for the sovereign to establish public, impartial rules for the allocation of offices and the conferral of awards, so that they become prizes subjects may compete for and earn rather than opportunities for the corruption that partialities and rivalries invite. The sovereign should limit the number of his direct personal appointments as much as possible. (When Hobbes argues that all Christian sovereigns have the right to baptize, even when they are not ordained, he observes that they generally do not perform baptisms, being much too busy with the business of governing [L xlii:72]. This unpersuasive explanation aside, their abstaining from performing baptisms comports with the idea that sovereigns should avoid designating personal favorites by great public signs. Christ himself, the King of kings, never baptized anyone, and as Hobbes observes, popes and bishops rarely do.) The sovereign's friends and the favorites of men in authority in general are often guilty of the greatest crimes against the common good (L xxx:25). They tend to exploit their position and take advantage of the public. They also like to turn against their benefactors, imagining themselves self-made and deserving of more. Hobbes would remind those who revel in their position among the sovereign's favorites that, even if they do not abuse their position, their position depends on good behavior and is not perfectly safe (cf. B 184). Being in a much envied position should not be too enviable.

The public good is always undermined by bad counsel. Sometimes bad counsel is the result of insufficient or mistaken information and sometimes it is based on poor judgment. Oftentimes it follows from the corrupting influence of the private interests of the counselor. All counselors, including the sovereign's public ministers are "apt to look asquint towards their private benefit" (L xxv:16). The counsel of private individuals or associations is generally always corrupt and deleterious to the public good. Counsel, properly so-called, should attend the benefit of the counseled (L xxv:4). Good counsel follows when the counselor has no private interest contrary to the public good in the matter under consideration, and the best counsel is found under those rare circumstances when the counselor's private interest coincides with the public good (L xxv:11, xxx:25). As a result, Hobbes recommends heeding the express opinions of the public itself (L xxx:27). If impartial opinion polls could be conducted, Hobbes would recommend them to the sovereign, not in all things pertaining to the safety of his subjects, to be sure, but in many things pertaining to their comfort.

When interpreting Hobbes, the reader must discern when he is speaking about what is in principle, in the abstract, according to right or reason, true, and what happens in practice, or will be the case in all likelihood, given experience and the tendencies of human beings. For the most part, Hobbes's political philosophy is well adapted to human realities, and where he hopes to change the way men live, he is well aware that it cannot be done easily or quickly. He must take prevailing tendencies into account. One of the most telling instances where he makes a concession to practice is his lament that "sometimes (as men's manners are) justice cannot be had without money," making it necessary for a man whose private interests are to be effected by an assembly to "hire" as many "friends" as he can from among its members (L xxii:30). It must be assumed that those whose private interests compete with his will endeavor to purchase as many assemblymen as they can too. Hobbes, who teaches that friendship should be removed from politics as much as possible, would deem the infiltration of electoral and legislative processes by special interest groups, corporate lobbies, and other private associations to be damaging, but also typical. Private men may try to sway monarchs, but their bad counsel is collectively much worse where assemblies govern, not to mention where sovereignty is divided (cf. B 114–17), whereupon counselors will have an easier time purchasing the favor of some in ways contrary to the public good and exploiting the ignorance of the rest (L xxv:15–16). According to the Hobbesian teaching, however, the corruption of assemblymen in this fashion is not, strictly speaking, unjust. The sovereign authority has the right to grant or deny any favors or exceptions. Still, it is Hobbes's counsel to sovereigns to keep this to a minimum, since their subjects will interpret favors given to others as unjust and demand special treatment for themselves as their due.

While justice must sometimes be bought, Hobbes specifically restricts the example above to matters debated in the assembly. He does not extend this concession to cases brought before a subordinate judge. (The idea of an independent judiciary with a share of sovereignty would be, to him, madness.) Naturally, he does not want to encourage the purchasing of magistrates. A good judge, Hobbes indicates, practices equity and exhibits "*contempt of unnecessary riches* and preferments" (L xxvi:28), and is therefore difficult to corrupt. Behind his relative silence on the subject may be a recognition that those who pass judgments in courtrooms also need to be bought on occasion (cf. AR ii:5). Judges, like assemblymen, are undoubtedly bound to be expensive friends, but once secured, they are likely to make better friends. After all, an assemblyman is expected to make and break friendships all the time, and does so publicly. A judge is not and cannot. Corrupt magistrates are a greater threat to the commonwealth than self-interested counselors. Whereas it is not, technically speaking, unjust to acquire the friendship of an assemblyman, it is unjust for a magistrate to befriend anyone who appears before him. A corrupt judge is a criminal (EL xxix:6), doubly the enemy of the sovereign for the injustice he commits by contradicting the laws and for betraying the friendship of the sovereign who trusted him to uphold them. A judge that misapplies the laws, even out of pity, Hobbes argues, hastens the dissolution of the commonwealth (dC xiii:17; EL xxviii:6). Special favors and mercies conferred by judges are ultimately paid for by innocent subjects. And when corrupt magistrates punish the innocent—and they will (L xxvi:24)—it represents a violation of the fourth, seventh, and eleventh laws of nature all at once (L xxviii:22). When an innocent man is condemned, the sovereign has not only failed to make the proper return to that man for that gift through which he authorized the sovereign's power; he has made a return of the greatest evil a man can suffer for the greatest benefit a man may rightfully give. A prudent sovereign will not only find reliable magistrates to appoint, he will severely punish those who attempt to corrupt them in order to buy pardon and escape punishment (cf. L xxvii:38, xxvii:13–18 [OL]). Hobbes knows that it is natural for men to forget that they approve of the sovereign's judgments and punishments as soon as they or others close to them are put on trial (dC vi:5).

A sovereign must be wary not only of the corrupting influences of friendships in his counselors, ministers, and magistrates. He must also be wary of alliances among nations, both those among his enemies and those in which he is a member. There is a state of nature among artificial persons in the international arena (L xiii:12; dC xiii:7), and therefore, as with the condition of mere nature among men, the distinction between a friend and an ally is made of nothing more than words, backed up by an uncertain degree of fear. There is no justice among nations, only the exchange of benefits and hostilities.[16] There are no grounds on which to call any war unjust, even a war of preemption, since a war of preemption is merely a war of defense, only sooner. A colony that has been set free of its mother country no longer owes anything more than what an adult owes his parents (L xxiv:14). No commonwealth should be expected to do more than secure and advance its national interest. No country benefits another without the expectation of return. But any nation that a commonwealth has befriended and protected is apt to betray it, or at the very least forget its past friendship, once it perceives that doing so is in its interest. It should not be so surprising if a country that has allied with one nation against a common enemy should form a new union against it soon afterward, or if a once feared enemy, having suffered defeat or collapse, suddenly asks for or offers its friendship. Any league formed among sovereign nations is, on Hobbesian grounds, always unreliable, mostly fraudulent, and just this side of being nothing at all. It is certainly something no sovereign power should recognize as having any rightful authority. A nation should heed its resolutions only insofar as it is in its interest to do so, to the extent that fearful consequences for not following them become manifest. And so, a consideration of international relations illustrates how friendship and justice remain alike. Both treachery and injustice are prevented only through the fear of adverse consequences. Justice essentially involves staying on friendly terms with a supreme power. A sovereign that is truly supreme would be one whom nobody could afford to have as his enemy.

Partial Associations

The twenty-second chapter of *Leviathan* offers a systematization of systems, referring to any partial association within a commonwealth, any combination of men with shared interests or affairs. Some are political, such as territorial governments, bureaucratic entities, and other public institutions. People only ever bother getting involved in politics, Hobbes maintains, for glory, which is generally vain, or to secure advantages for themselves and their friends (dC x:15). Other systems are private, such as sects and corporations. Among private associations, some have regular, formal structures and others do not. Some are lawful and others are not. Any system, private or public, may pose a threat to the security of the commonwealth. Any one of them can become acquisitive and ambitious to the point of practicing injustice, spreading corruption, or engaging in sedition. All systems subordinate to the sovereign are potentially dangerous as it is the nature of men to seek power after power, and men only combine for their mutual advantage, to the relative disadvantage of others. Gradually weakening and diminishing subordinate systems, especially private systems, to render them harmless is among Hobbes's principal long-term objectives. This would be best accomplished by changing men's opinions and directing their appetites toward goods that may be more readily provided for them, so that men feel less of a need to collaborate with each other to get things accomplished and live more contentedly. Hobbes is not so imprudent as to recommend the direct abolition of partial associations, or the revolutionary imposition of new appetites and behaviors.

The family, according to Hobbes's categorization,[17] is but a sort of private system both regular, because it has a leader, and lawful (L xxii:26). Hobbes only suggests that families are in any way "natural" for the sake of lending support to his arguments in favor of monarchy and the traditional line of succession (EL xxiii:16). This preference for hereditary monarchy rests on the convenient way it usually helps to avert much disorder by dissuading friends, favorites, and rivals from disturbing the political order. It is entirely within the rights of the sovereign to determine the nature of a family, its forms, freedoms, privileges, and so forth, since the sovereign has authority over all subordinate systems (dC viii:8; EL xxiii:4), as well as all definitions and doctrines (L xviii:9). Within a family, no obedience is owed beyond what is due according to gratitude and honor (L xxx:11), and perhaps also the fear of consequences. Every mother raises her children under the assumption that they will do what she desires of them (dC ix:3), which requires keeping them enfeebled (cf.

EL xiv:13). Needless to say, mothers always end up feeling betrayed to some extent, supposing that their children do grow up. There is no reason to expect familial relations to be completely reliable, any more than any other friendships. Scripture itself confirms this from the beginning (cf. L xxxviii:2–3). Family has acquired conventional significance, and people with "potent kindred" tend to believe they can act with greater impunity than others (L xxvii:15). But Hobbes would have us understand that families, tribes, nationalities, and races are only accidental, artificial combinations of natural enemies.[18] Group identities are always only expedient fictions invented for the protection or empowerment of their members.

For Hobbes, a faction is any association of men, any "league of subjects" (L xxii:29), with a particular political agenda of its own. All factions are self-interested. There is no such thing as a party of the people (EL xxvii:4), although the leaders of powerful factions often excel at fooling ignorant subjects into thinking that they represent the people (cf. dC xii:12–13; EL xxvii:12–14; L xi:20, R&C:16). Political parties are but one kind of faction that Hobbes declares unlawful (L xxii:32). The main problem with party government in a sovereign assembly is that it institutionalizes the continuing presence of contradictory voices within the sovereign, which properly being but one person artificial should speak to the public with a single voice. Even though disagreements among its members are inevitable, it needs to speak authoritatively and therefore unequivocally. Where an assembly is split into parties, the public is convinced of the legitimacy of minority views voiced within it. Support for them tends to proceed from conscience to word to deed, encouraged by the minority faction through the promise of future benefits. That a political system organized in such a fashion could sustain itself for long, Hobbes doubts. Factions within assemblies engender sedition and civil war, and "the bitterest wars" are those that arise from "different factions in the same country" (dC i:5; cf. x:12, xii:1; DBT 48–49).

Unlawful factions develop outside of the formal institutions of government as well. Some unlawful combinations of men are but "corporations of beggars, thieves and gipsies," whereas others make their chief business "the propagation of doctrines" that challenge the doctrines authorized by the sovereign or the authority of the sovereign itself (L xxii:27). The most dangerous unlawful factions form around men of great wealth or popularity, and democracies in particular breed them much too well (dC x:7, xiii:13). Hobbes is well aware that a popular leader, however traitorous, earns his popularity by acquiring "a reputation of love of a man's country" (L x:6), as if one could be loyal to the commonwealth without being obedient to the sovereign. Popular men tend to presume that they will be able to escape punishment for their wrongdoings because of their great many friends and followers (L xxvii:15, xxvii:13–18 [OL]). The sovereign generally cannot buy off a popular leader, who will welcome benefits from the sovereign not only with ingratitude, but also as proof of the sovereign's fear and vulnerability (L xxx:24). A popular leader also convinces his followers that they too may disobey the law with impunity, as if their safety were his gift to give in exchange for their allegiance, marking a direct usurpation of the sovereign's authority (L xxix:20; dH xiv:8). It is up to the sovereign to teach people not to follow popular leaders (L xxx:8), an effort that is made easier when the sovereign is himself popular (L xxx:29).

Unlike factions led by the rich and the popular, a conspiracy tends to be "irregular" in that it will not have a clearly identifiable public leader (L xxii:28–29), or if it does, he is almost certainly not its real leader. Secret societies in particular are always unlawful (L xxii:29). It must be assumed that they have either the domination of society as their goal or else to profit from its alteration or destruction. Private security forces are also unlawful (L xxii:31). A man who commands a legion of brownshirts has obvious designs. Posses, too, are forbidden (L xxii:34). And although subjects are free to assemble wherever and whenever the law has not specifically forbidden it, any congregation of an "extraordinarily great" number of subjects, for any reason at all, should be reckoned unlawful (L xxii:33). To claim an absolute right to free speech and freedom of assembly is itself seditious (cf. B 16). After all, nobody would propose it unless they had something in mind.

Where Two or Three are Gathered Together

While it is commonly thought that men will form friendships based on shared ideas, especially shared religious ideas, Hobbes takes the view that those friendships are no less instrumental than any other. Moreover, with "scarce two men agreeing what is to be called good, and what evil" (EL v:14), their association is in all likelihood based not on shared ideas—and truly, they never could know if it were—but on the perceived advantages of their association, supposing their ideas to be shared well enough that a profitable alliance may be formed based on their willingness to get along. All of the members of such an association expect some benefit in return for their involvement, although they may not all desire the same good. Whereas some may genuinely desire above all rewards that are strictly intellectual or otherworldly, Hobbes recognizes that the association itself, under the guidance of its leadership, is principally driven by the desire for power, whether political or economic or both. An organization based on scientific ideas is certainly going to be no less political than an organization based on religious ideas. The Royal Society, for instance, is in principle as dangerous as the Roman Catholic Church. Men who reckon themselves possessors of true knowledge tend to question the rightful authorities and deceive people as to the nature of their activities (L xxvii:16). By claiming to know the objective nature of man, the world, and his place in it, natural philosophers assert a claim to rule. Modern scientists furthermore claim a right to manipulate the nature of the world and man without the permission of the sovereign or the consent of other men, for the sake of satisfying their own curiosity, in return for their sponsors' support or in expectation of fame or fortune. Every philosopher harbors a desire to be "a Master," Hobbes candidly reveals (cf. dC i:2).

Given the experiences of Hobbes and his contemporaries, his concern regarding religious associations is understandable. His reflections on religion in particular illuminate his attack on friendship in general. From the scientific point of view, just as there is nothing special about a family, there is nothing special about a church. Even "disciple" and "apostle" are really just fancy words for "friend" (cf. L xli:6–7). Accordingly, when Hobbes expresses support for Christian independency (L xlvii:20), it looks like an attempt to dissolve the power of religious communities by rendering faith a strictly private affair and isolating each believer.

The natural religiosity of man (cf. L xi:17, 23, xii:19) provides frauds and conspirators with lots of material with which to work. Faith is, after all, always reducible to a belief in some man or men, Hobbes argues

(L vii:5, xii:24, xl:6). False prophets, who are legion, seek only "reputation with the people . . . to govern them for their private benefit" (L xliii:1; cf. xxxvi:8). Possibly speaking from experience, Hobbes observes that many men have interpreted Scriptures misleadingly for their own gain (L xliii:24). Of "necromancy, conjuring, and witchcraft," declares Hobbes, they are but "confederate knavery" (L xii:19; cf. xxxvii:10–11). A superstitious confederacy is in the end only a particular kind of criminal activity when conducted on a small scale, with the possibility of becoming a rebellious faction should it win many adherents (L xxxvi:20, xxxix:5). All religion is political, although some religions are more political than others. Hobbes would regard as particularly suspect any religion instituted by a man with worldly wealth and ambition that makes conquest its principal means and domination its foremost objective (L xii:20). Still, even a religion that emphasizes miracles of healing is subject to Hobbes's criticism. There is nothing apolitical about the promise of good health, cures for diseases, long life, or resurrection from the dead. It is plain what is implied when Hobbes writes:

> But if we look upon the impostures wrought by confederacy, there is nothing how impossible soever to be done, that is impossible to be believed. For two men conspiring, one to seem lame, the other to cure him with a charm, will deceive many; but many conspiring, one to seem lame, another so to cure him, and all the rest to bear witness, will deceive many more. (L xxxvii:12)

Hobbes directly confronts the two proven enemies of the English crown who use religion for political purposes, namely, the Roman Church and the Presbyterians. The Roman Church is, straightforwardly, a political enterprise that has as its agenda "setting up unlawful power over the lawful sovereigns of Christian peoples and riches" (L xlvii:17). (The irony contained in the idea of "Christian riches" would not be lost on Hobbes, who uses it with reference to Protestants too.) It is *"a confederacy of deceivers"* that exploits human ignorance to attain *"dominion over men in this present world"* (L xliv:1). In the essay "A Discourse of Rome," Hobbes details how the ranks of the Church are thoroughly corrupt, especially due to quarrels among its many factions, its organization on the basis of relationships of favor, and its dependence on the wealth of great families or the friendship of princes (DR 95–96). He warns Protestant Englishmen, should they find themselves in Rome, to be especially wary because they are in grave danger in that hostile place (DR 99–101). One implication to be drawn is that Rome does not love its enemies. The Presbyterians, according to Hobbes, are "seducers" guilty of "pretending to have a right from God to govern every one his parish and their assembly the whole nation," this being the message they preached from their pulpits (B 2; cf. L xlvii:4). Their agitations were in fact, Hobbes argues, about nothing more than acquiring or securing worldly power and goods (B 63).

These criticisms of the Presbyterians and the Roman Church have continuing relevance, even though neither presbyters nor the pope are presently preparing for conquest. The troubles these two organizations represent are not tied to any particular time or place. There are latter-day Presbyterians who disseminate a militant interpretation of their preferred prophecy in their places of worship and schools, teaching that it is the duty of a believer to struggle against the enemies of the faith in order to subdue the world by any means until it submits to God, which is to say, his best students on earth. There are also many today who speak and act as if their loyalties belong not to their present commonwealth but rather to an imaginary commonwealth, much like the way Catholics preferred a foreign prince in Rome to their rightful king. These latter-day Catholics regard themselves not as subjects of their sovereign, but rather, of the universal regime of perfect peace and justice and equality that history would bring into being if only everyone were dedicated to that righteous goal instead of condoning violence and perpetuating injustice. They are devoted to the future commonwealth of all humankind, where every prejudice will be vanquished and no one has to suffer anymore. Like the Roman Catholics before them, they propound theoretical doctrines and make political pronouncements from the universities that Hobbes would regard as seditious. They influence the professions and manipulate society, turning it against its leaders and itself. They frame debates in terms that have no intelligible meaning, although unlike the Church (cf. L viii:27, xi:18, xliv:1, 3, xlvi:passim), they now regularly admit this and revel in it. Hobbes might have reminded them that "the future [is] but a fiction of the mind" (L iii:7). But Hobbes's own long-term project is perhaps not so different from the distant goals of these dreamers. The prudent Hobbes, however, would have seen that these latter-day Catholics cannot realize their goals so long as the situation with the latter-day Presbyterians remains unresolved.[19]

The Fifth Law of Nature

It should come as no surprise that friendship is nowhere to be found in the Hobbesian catalogue of virtues. No law of nature commands it, just as there is no virtue of giving in the list either. Hobbes offers his reader no reflections extolling friendships among men of virtue, explaining what makes a friendship work, how to know if someone is a good friend, how to be a good friend, who one should befriend, whose friendship one should avoid and how, or anything of the sort. This makes sense not only because friendship is on balance more of a hindrance than a help in the maintenance of peace and security in civil society, even if it is necessary in order to institute a commonwealth, but also because all moral virtue, Hobbes argues, runs contrary to the natural passions of man (L xvii:2). The desire to have other men to do what you want them to do is fully consistent with the natural passions of man (cf. L xvii:1). Partiality toward one's allies in the competitive endeavor to gain an advantage over others is entirely natural to man. In contrast, sociability and working together with the entire community for the collective good is not (cf. L xvii:6–12). For the Hobbesian project to be a success, the natural passions must be overcome, or at least arrangements must be made to render their presence and effects minimal. For instance, civil society should be arranged so that it is very rarely in the interest of any individual to act iniquitously by making an *"acception of persons"* (L xv:24), especially when that individual is acting in an official capacity. Equity in particular—impartial judgment, ceasing to play favorites—is so important to the Hobbesian project that he dedicates in effect three of the laws of nature to it—the eleventh (L xv:23; cf. dC iii:15),[20] where the virtue of equity is specified, and also the seventeenth and the eighteenth, where the principle is the same and only the scenarios to which it is applied change (L xv:31–32, cf. xxx:15; dC iii:19, 24).

Hobbes is not claiming that considerations of justice and equity leave no room for friendships. The liberty of subjects is such that one may form or join any partial association, confer any benefit, hope for any return, and react to the failure to obtain a suitable return as one pleases, so long as it is not done contrary to the law (L xxi:6). Indeed, a philosophy could hardly pretend to teach what a Christian commonwealth is if it did not leave room for charity. Hobbes concedes that the whole of morality is contained in the combination of the civil virtue of justice and the natural virtue of charity (dH xiii:9), but politics requires fully exploiting the greater reliability of the former, rendering the adverse consequences of failing to practice it more certain. So, what is it that remains for Hobbes to call charity? It is distinguished from love, generally speaking, which is simply the name given to the experience of any of the many internal physiological motions interpreted as desires (L vi:3; EL vii:1). It is distinguished as well from the love of particular persons, which is a jealous passion, a species of need described as "lust not condemned" (EL ix:15–16; cf. L vi:33). Equity is a part of charity, Hobbes indicates, for a man must love his enemy, his neighbor, and himself all the same, according to Scripture (dC iv:12; cf. L xxx:13; EL xviii:6, 8, xxix:7). Charity is the "*Desire* of good to another" particular person (L vi:22). It is distinguished from pity, which is compassion aroused specifically by the misfortune of others (L vi:46; dH xii:10), although presumably pity may well inspire charity in some. Charity is good because it wins friends, as people will "adhere unto" a man who would assist them (EL ix:17, cf. ix:21).

In a Hobbesian regime, charity is made into a public concern, something best administered by the state (L xxx:18).[21] It is therefore better labeled a "kindness," using Hobbesian terminology (L vi:30), although it might otherwise be called "welfare."[22] Equitable charity is better ensured by treating everyone according to preestablished, impersonal rules. Furthermore, the sovereign shall thereby increase his subjects' direct dependence on him, if not their gratitude toward him. When charity is left to individuals, it always tends toward injustice, as all "favor and friendship" tends to "break through" the laws (DBT 49). Essentially, Hobbes is asking men not to try to help other people so much, or at least, not directly. It is better to have the state mediate between those who can help and those who need help. While the civil law cannot require that a man should give alms (EL xxix:5), it can confiscate some of his property and redistribute it.

It is a failing proposition to imagine that political society could be based on an expectation of active benevolence (cf. dC i:2). Accordingly, Hobbes modifies the rule of charity, rendering it as the negative rule that a man should not do unto others what he would not want done to himself, instead of recommending the "divine" positive rule that a man should do unto others what he would want for himself (L xv:35; dC iii:26; EL xvii:9). When Hobbes gives scriptural support for his arguments from natural reason, he necessarily references the divine law of positive charity, but only to confirm that it supports the negative natural law (cf. L xiv:5; dC iv:23; EL xviii:9), even though it far surpasses it. Charity is rendered less demanding, less likely to lead to the formation of close personal relationships, and severed from any concern for the salvation of souls. Men should instead learn to leave each other alone. It becomes enough not to harm or hate anyone. The eighth law of nature commands men not to condemn anyone (L xv:20; dC iii:12; EL xvi:11). This does not come naturally to men, who would readily express their hatred for others unless they learn not to do so. Still, to refrain from harming and hating is easier than to love.

In the absence of friendship, however, there is a virtue that Hobbes does recommend in its place. The fifth law of nature commands "complaisance," meaning that "every man [should] strive to accommodate himself to the rest," which is the same as being "sociable" (L xv:17, cf. xv:40; dC iii:9, iv:7; EL xvi:8, xvii:10, 15).[23] Now, as has been indicated above, this too is contrary to man's nature. It is something he must learn. Sociability is constructed. It is the responsibility of the sovereign to educate all of his subjects as to the requirements of the laws of nature and to arrange society in accordance with them, in order to obtain his subjects' compliance with them. The fifth law, on a cursory reading, seems relatively innocuous, apparently recommending only that men refrain from being difficult in their dealings with others. But on closer inspection, there is something much more to it. In the middle of his explication of that law, Hobbes elaborates:

> For as that stone which (by the asperity and irregularity of figure) takes more room from others than itself fills, and (for the hardness)

cannot be easily made plain, and thereby hindreth the building, is by the builders cast away as unprofitable and troublesome, so also a man that (by asperity of nature) will strive to retain those things which to himself are superfluous and to others necessary, and (for the stubbornness of his passions) cannot be corrected, is to be left or cast out of society as cumbersome thereto. (L xv:17, cf. xxix:19; dC iii:9)

This idea belongs to a strong form of socialism, if not communism.[24] Hobbes has already established that men possess no natural right to private property (L xiii:13, xv:3), and he soon establishes that it is entirely up to the sovereign to determine what belongs to whom (L xviii:10; EL xxiv:2) and how to distribute the goods of the commonwealth. He also recommends that goods should be held in common, whenever possible (L xv:25). Accordingly, for the sake of social peace and stability, Hobbes encourages the development of a universal friendliness or camaraderie that will bind the masses of relatively equal, similar, and pliable people together into a society wherein each member lives contentedly thanks to the beneficence of the state. To this end, the state will have to engage in the regulation and redistribution of property in no small way—eradicating any degree of inequality that allows any one person to enjoy some luxury while another has to struggle. Meanwhile, the sovereign must also find ways of taking care of those "irregular" men who resist being "corrected."

Your Friend Thomas

Although it will take time, Hobbes seems confident about the possibility of reeducating human beings and making them behave differently by giving them new opinions and living conditions (cf. L xxx:6, 14). Human nature as Hobbes finds it does not lend itself to the establishment of lasting peace. It will have to be refashioned if that objective is to be accomplished,[25] and that can be accomplished only slowly and indirectly. Hobbes, a lifelong beneficiary of patronage who makes it his personal project to see patronage brought to an end,[26] works to change the human condition while teaching that people should not attempt to change their society (L xxix:13).

Hobbes expects that a properly socialized humanity will be more rational and obedient (cf. L iii:3). The end goal is the everlasting constitution (L xxx:5) and the reconstruction of Babel (cf. L iv:2)—a goal that resembles a rebellion against God and the usurpation of His Kingdom—and Hobbes is pleased to put Scripture to use for the sake of bringing it about. Having examined Hobbes's thought through an investigation into his handling of the subject of friendship, it becomes particularly clear how his project intends the gradual yet certain undermining of not only great private wealth but also family and religion. It requires transforming the state into something impersonal and procedural, not to mention massive. It requires the supervision of all education by public authorities. It emphasizes and intends to provide sufficient means for universal comfortable and commodious living. It has to neutralize the political ambition of capable men, transforming popularity into harmless celebrity. And it intends ultimately to unite all the people of the world without anybody getting too close to anyone else. This legacy is Hobbes's gift to humanity. Its success would constitute his desired return. Not even Hobbes regards all glory seeking as vain.

Notes

An earlier version of this essay was presented at the 2004 annual meeting of the American Political Science Association, on a panel cosponsored by the Eric Voegelin Society. I am grateful to John von Heyking, Horst Hutter, Jeremy Mhire, Julian Schofield, and my research assistant Nina Valiquette for helping me to prepare the final version of this essay in light of their comments, questions, suggestions, and criticisms.

1. The following abbreviations are used in this essay for Hobbes's works:

AR	*A Brief of the Art of Rhetorick*, in *The English Works of Thomas Hobbes*, vol. VI, ed. Sir William Molesworth, 1840
B	*Behemoth, or the Long Parliament*, ed. Ferdinand Tönnies (Chicago: University of Chicago Press, 1990)
DBT	"A Discourse upon the Beginning of Tacitus," in *Three Discourses*, ed. Noel B. Reynolds and Arlene W. Saxonhouse (Chicago: University of Chicago Press, 1995)
dC	*On the Citizen*, ed. and trans. Richard Tuck and Michael Silverthorne (Cambridge: Cambridge University Press, 1998)

dCorp   *De Corpore*, excerpted in *Human Nature and De Corpore Politico*, ed. J. C. A. Gaskin (Oxford: Oxford University Press, 1994)

dH   *De Homine*, trans. Charles T. Wood, T. S. K. Scott-Craig, and Bernard Gert, in Bernard Gert, ed., *Man and Citizen* (Indianapolis: Hackett, 1991)

DR   "A Discourse of Rome," in *Three Discourses*, ed. Noel B. Reynolds and Arlene W. Saxonhouse (Chicago: University of Chicago Press, 1995)

EL   *The Elements of Law Natural and Politic*, in *Human Nature and De Corpore Politico*, ed. J. C. A. Gaskin (Oxford: Oxford University Press, 1994)

L   *Leviathan*, ed. Edwin Curley (Indianapolis: Hackett, 1994)

2. John Aubrey, "The Brief Life," in Hobbes, *Human Nature and De Corpore Politico*, ed. Gaskin, 243.

3. See, e.g., Richard Allen Chapman, "*Leviathan* Writ Small: Thomas Hobbes on the Family," *American Political Science Review* 69 (1975): 77; and Richard Tuck, "The Utopianism of *Leviathan*," in Leviathan *after 350 Years*, ed. Tom Sorell and Luc Foisneau (Oxford: Clarendon Press, 2004), 128–29.

4. The quarrel between justice and friendship is the subject of the opening sequence of *The Godfather*, in the conversation between the Don and the undertaker. The undertaker asks the Don to kill the two boys who assaulted his daughter and is willing to pay him anything. The Don is greatly offended. He does not deal in contract killing—not because he doesn't deal in killing, but rather, because he does not deal in contracts. The Don operates on the basis of an exchange of benefits. His power rests on his reputation for helping his friends and harming their enemies. Should someone refuse to do him a favor on request, he will be treated as someone who has positively harmed him. Nothing illustrates how incomparable his position is like the way he rarely loses out by performing first (cf. L xv:5; EL xv:10). When he informs someone newly indebted to him that on some future day he may be called upon to perform a service for him, you can be sure that it will get done. The Don surely knows that the idea of a contract to do something illegal is folly. But he also knows that contracts, the heart of conventional justice, are really just a means of stripping exchanges of benefits of their personal dimension. While contracts are subject to the law, the law is always open to interpretation, manipulation, and circumvention. Judges, senators, and policemen may be befriended or removed. Unlike Hobbes, the Don openly admits the existence of natural justice, and it is something regarding which he has some expertise. Because the undertaker's daughter is not dead, the murder of the two boys would not be justice, he says. But once the undertaker offers his friendship to the Don in-

stead of his checkbook, the Don promises to exact the "justice" requested of him as "a gift." Of course, justice cannot be a gift, or at least, conventional (Hobbesian) justice cannot be a gift. Does the Don's contempt for the law and conventional justice mean that he is a fool (L xv:4)? Without forgetting that the film is poetic, let us contemplate the fate that befalls the Don's no-good family, especially his beloved Sonny, his loyal friend Luca, the originally angelical Michael, not to mention Michael's daughter and second son.

5. Compare Aristotle, *The "Art" of Rhetoric*, trans. John Henry Freese (Cambridge: Loeb Classical Library, Harvard University Press, 1926), 1381a–82a.

6. Ibid., 1372a–73a.

7. Aristotle, *Nicomachean Ethics*, trans. Terence Irwin, 2d ed. (Indianapolis: Hackett, 1999), 1155a25.

8. Ibid., 1155a15–20.

9. The gloomiest of conclusions do not necessarily follow from this grim statement. Martel understands Hobbes as teaching, "Before we can be friends, we must be enemies. We must respect one another." James R. Martel, *Love Is a Sweet Chain: Desire, Autonomy, and Friendship in Liberal Political Theory* (New York: Routledge, 2001), 211.

10. Aristotle, *Ethics*, 1156b5–10.

11. Oakeshott explains that commonwealths are established when men recognize that they need to combine against their "common enemy (death)" rather than continue to struggle against each other in a never-ending "race for precedence." Michael Oakeshott, "The Moral Life in the Writings of Thomas Hobbes," in *Hobbes on Civil Association* (Indianapolis: Liberty Fund, 1975), 92. Ahrensdorf argues that the plan to keep men united and aligned against that insuperable common foe is unworkable so long as men remain mindful of their personal mortality. Peter J. Ahrensdorf, "The Fear of Death and the Longing for Immortality: Hobbes and Thucydides on Human Nature and the Problem of Anarchy," *American Political Science Review* 94 (2000): 585, 592.

12. Stanlick attempts to show that Hobbes's teaching on friendship exposes Hobbesian man as naturally sociable. Nancy A. Stanlick, "Hobbesian Friendship: Valuing Others for Oneself," *Journal of Social Philosophy* 33 (2002): 345–59.

13. Compare Morton A. Kaplan, "How Sovereign Is Hobbes' Sovereign?" *Western Political Quarterly* 9 (1956): 403.

14. Ibid., 398.

15. Peter J. Steinberger, "Hobbesian Resistance," *American Journal of Political Science* 46 (2002): 864.

16. In *Behemoth*, Hobbes well illustrates the nature of the international situation through the example of the war against the Dutch in the midst of the English revolution (B 169, 173–78). The Rump Parliament, in its first period of

rule, sent envoys to the Netherlands offering friendship, which is to say, to secure recognition of their regime's newly established authority in England, and to assert the continuing dominion of the English over the seas. The ambitious Dutch figured that the English were at this time vulnerable, and decided it was time to challenge that dominion. The Dutch had been testing the English by fishing off their coast contrary to custom. So the "proferred friendship was scorned, and the[ ] ambassadors affronted" (B 174). The war would begin in earnest when the Dutch provoked the English navy by not lowering their flags in the presence of their ships. It was but a ploy, of course, to persuade the English to open fire first. Then the Dutch appealed to the other nations of the world, saying that the English had started the war, in an attempt to rally other nations to their side. The younger character in the dialogue, "B," observes, "as to the gaining of friends and confederates thereby, I think it was in vain; seeing princes and states in such occasions look not much upon the justice of their neighbours, but upon their own concernment in the event" (B 176). The elder character, "A," indicates that England was entirely in the right to defend itself, the provocative behavior of the Dutch being equivalent to having fired first. When England called for the end of hostilities and reiterated its offer of friendship, the Dutch ignored the idea of a league between their states. The offer of friendship must have seemed like an admission of vulnerability. So the war continued, with the Dutch still trying to secure allies from among its neighbors. Naturally, the English retained dominion over the seas.

17. Chapman, "*Leviathan* Writ Small," 80ff.

18. Rousseau observes that according to Hobbes's reasoning, a child "would strike his Mother if she were slow to give him the breast." Jean-Jacques Rousseau, *Discourse on the Origin and Foundations of Inequality among Men*, in *The* Discourses *and Other Early Political Writings*, ed. Victor Gourevitch (Cambridge: Cambridge University Press, 1997), 151.

19. Cf. Leo Strauss, "Notes on Carl Schmitt, *The Concept of the Political*," trans. J. Harvey Lomax, in Carl Schmitt, *The Concept of the Political* (Chicago: University of Chicago Press, 1996), 92.

20. Tuck and Silverthorne translate the law that "forbids favour" in *De Cive* from the Latin as a law of "fairness" that enjoins men not to "discriminate" (dC iii:15). In not discriminating among men, one is like God, Hobbes argues, who does not discriminate between Gentiles and Jews, or between free men or slaves (dC iv:13). Of course, under the old law, God did discriminate between Jews and Gentiles. And under the new law, God still discriminates between repentant and unrepentant sinners. Hobbes's reading of the Christian Revelation, as it pertains to the free gift of salvation, involves rendering repentance unnecessary. Travis D. Smith, "On the Fourth Law of Nature," *Hobbes Studies* 16 (2003): 87 n.7.

21. In Campanella's *The City of the Sun* (1623), the sea captain who has voyaged to the fantastic city after which the dialogue is named reports, "For it is worth the trouble to see that no one can receive gifts from another. Whatever is necessary they have, they receive it from the community, and the magistrate takes care that no one receives more than he deserves. Yet nothing necessary is denied to anyone." Tomasso Campanella, *The City of the Sun*, in *The New Atlantis and The City of the Sun: Two Classic Utopias* (Mineola, N.Y.: Dover, 2003), 51.

22. See John W. Seaman, "Hobbes on Public Charity & the Prevention of Idleness: A Liberal Case for Welfare," *Polity* 23 (1990): 112–15; cf. Tuck, "The Utopianism of *Leviathan*," 136.

23. Tuck and Silverthorne render the corresponding law in *De Cive* as commanding that "everyone should be considerate of others," where "considerate" translates *commodus* (dC iii:9).

24. That communism is incompatible with friendship, see Roger Scruton, "On Loyalty: Is It Ever Okay to Betray a Friend?" *National Review* (5 April 1999): 43.

25. Tuck, "The Utopianism of *Leviathan*," 126–27.

26. On Hobbes's lifelong dependency on patronage, see Lisa T. Sarasohn, "Thomas Hobbes and the Duke of Newcastle: A Study in the Mutuality of Patronage before the Establishment of the Royal Society," *Isis* 90 (1999): 715–37. Sarasohn discerns that freedom of thought does not increase when the age of patronage ends. Because "the validation of one's ideas by a council of peers" is required in order for a scholar to succeed following "the institutionalization of science and thought," the seeker of truth is hardly rescued from concerns regarding friends and enemies. Ibid., 736. Cf. Steven Shapin and Simon Schaffer, *Leviathan and the Air-Pump: Hobbes, Boyle, and the Experimental Life* (Princeton: Princeton University Press, 1985), 333, 337.

9

Social Friendship in the Founding Era

George Carey

The founding era does not yield up any sustained treatment of the role of friendship per se for a properly ordered civil society or for individual fulfillment and well being. Nevertheless, the need for the goods that flow from it—for example, loyalty, trust, understanding, forbearance, empathy—and the extent to which they could be realized in the new and extended republic were matters of utmost concern in light of the political divisions and conflicts leading up to the adoption of the Constitution. Given this contentious political landscape, the political writings of the period are understandably concerned with the attitudes that relate primarily to "social friendship."[1] That is, they are concerned with those beliefs, outlooks, feelings, traditions, interests, and the like that provide the social cohesion necessary for a just and effective national government such as that contemplated under the proposed Constitution. This essay, therefore, centers on those writings that deal most directly with the problems related to social friendship.[2]

There is no secret why concerns surrounding social friendship assumed such an importance during this period. The political universe for Americans was expanding, growing ever larger. This expansion in one sense began even before the Declaration of Independence with the increasing acceptance of the position, advanced most intently by those favoring separation from Great Britain, that America comprised "one people," that is, a people apart from the English. Nevertheless, the enlargement of the political arena that followed independence, particularly the move toward a stronger centralized political union that would come about with the ratification of the Philadelphia Constitution, brought with it very serious questions. These questions arose from the fact that the genius of the American people was republican, and a truism of the time, derived from the classics and echoed by Montesquieu, held that republican governments could survive only over a small territory with a relatively homogeneous population.

On what grounds did this truism rest? At the theoretical level, one case seems obvious enough: the fruits of social friendship are needed to bind or tie a people together, but these fruits can only be had where individuals have the opportunity to interact with one another, which is possible in small, but not extensive, republics. Still another is related more closely to politics and involves the moderation of potentially divisive conflict. The existence of a relatively homogeneous population, for instance, clearly reduces the possibilities of conflicts between antagonistic interests that might produce irreconcilable divisions. Indeed, where there is homogeneity, legislation or any collective action is not likely to have a significant differential impact on individuals. But the attributes of friendship also play a significant and less obvious role in reducing conflict. In a small territory, where the ties between individuals are strong, individuals are in a position to anticipate what issues or policies are likely to create divisions. Conditions, in other words, exist for correct reciprocal anticipation wherein members of the community, having developed close relationships with one another, can accurately anticipate what issues or policies are likely to lead to intense political conflict.[3] Consequently, to preserve the bonds of community and friendship, certain issues may be tacitly avoided or deemed out of bounds in the public discourse. Or, even if such divisive issues do find their way into the political arena, the bonds of friendship—the desire to remain as "one"—may be more powerful and intense than the impulses for disobedience or separation.

The case for the small community has an appealing dimension closely linked with classical political thought and its concern for a well-ordered polis. This appeal, as Jouvenel sees it, arises from "seeing the common good as residing in the strength of the social ties, the warmth of friendship felt by one citizen for another and the assurance that each has of the predictability in another's conduct—all of them, conditions of the happiness which men can create for each other by life in society."[4] That feelings such as these accounted for at least some of the Anti-Federalist opposition to ratification of the Constitution is quite likely. "There is," Barry Shain writes, "persuasive evidence that preceding the Revolution, economic and social practices had already begun to conflict with most Americans' communal normative precepts. Americans were beginning to be torn between dynamic demographic, economic, religious, and social material forces and their static ideational communal norms and expectations."[5] On Shain's showing, a "political localism"—a state of affairs in which largely autonomous communities constituted the political universe for most Americans—prevailed in America through most of the eighteenth century. This localism, as he goes on to remark, "found great support in the thought and practices of reformed Protestantism and its insistent covenantalism" that "demanded local political and religious autonomy to support and foster individual salvation as well as godly and neighborly service."[6] In many respects, then, the teachings and practice of Christianity provided the foundations for the friendship and feelings of unity that prevailed at the local levels.

In the ratification debate, to be sure, the arguments of the Anti-Federalists were seldom cast in terms that emphasized the loss of community norms, much less the "warmth of friendship." The Anti-Federalist Cato (George Clinton, governor of New York), however, does capture the underlying sentiment of many who opposed ratification of the Constitution. Affections and attachments, the bonds of friendship, he holds, are attenuated as we move outward from the center of the "circle," that is, the family or "domestic walls." "The ties of the parent," he writes, "exceed that of any other"; the ties at the center being "small, active, and forcible." Moving outward from the domestic walls, he conceives "the next general principle of union" to be "amongst citizens of the same state, where acquaintance, habits and fortunes, nourish affection, and attachment." But the circle, he warns, can be extended too far, to an extent that individuals lose all "ties of acquaintance, habits, and fortunes" eventually rendering "sameness of species" the only common denominator. In this vein, he asks his readers, will the "inhabitants of Georgia, or New Hampshire . . . have the same obligations towards you as your own, and preside over your lives, liberties, and property, with the same care and attachment?" "Intuitive reason," he maintains, "answers in the negative."[7] This was the answer that virtually every Anti-Federalist would give.

Other opponents of the Constitution made essentially the same point by starting with the conventional wisdom that a republican government over an extensive territory would degenerate, sooner or later, into a tyranny. In so doing, they portray the sacrifices resulting from an enlargement of the political sphere from top down—that is, what they understand to be the incapacity of a remote, impersonal central government to exercise control over an extensive territory consistent with the accepted notions of liberty, due process of law, or the norms of the smaller communities. Such a position is implicit in George Mason's rhetorical inquiries posed at an early point in the Virginia ratifying debates: "Is it to be supposed that one national government will suit so extensive a country, embracing so many climates, and containing inhabitants so very different in manner, habits and customs? . . . Was there ever an instance of a general national government extending over so extensive a country, abounding in such a variety of climates, &c., where the people retained their liberty?"[8] Again, the answers were obvious to the Anti-Federalists. Typical is Aggripa's assertion: "The idea of an uncompounded republick, on an average, one thousand miles in length, and eight hundred in breadth, and containing six millions of white inhabitants all reduced to the same standard of morals, or habits, and of laws, is in itself an absurdity."[9]

Brutus, perhaps the most systematic and effective Anti-Federalist, was equally adamant in arguing that the diversity of the extended republic would eventually pose problems for the central government.

But he went further in showing how this diversity would affect national institutions, primarily the legislature. To begin with, he contends that the "productions," "habits," "manners," "interests," and "laws" of the states not only vary widely, but that they are also often at odds with one another. As a consequence, he believed, the legislature would be marked "by a constant clashing of opinions" with "the representatives of one part . . . continually striving against those of the other." The "heterogenous and discordant principles" that would predominate in the legislative body, he concludes, would impede both the "operations of government" and the realization of the "public good." Brutus comes very close to conceiving the proposed constitutional system in terms of a union of different peoples or even different nations; his concerns, that is, would parallel those who today contemplate the feasibility of an effective world government. What is notable is that neither Brutus nor his Anti-Federalist cohorts believe that the national institutions—and they focus primarily on the legislature—would serve as an effective forum to bridge or to overcome the wide differences between regions and states. In other words, empathy, understanding, cooperation or a willingness to sublimate partial interests for the good of the whole—all qualities associated with social friendship—would be largely absent in the national councils.

The Anti-Federalists's concerns about representation, however, went far deeper than this. In fact, their views on various aspects of representation indicate more clearly than any other the degree to which they believed that trust and loyalty, two of the most fundamental attributes of friendship, would be completely undermined by the proposed Constitution. The views of Melancton Smith, set forth in the New York ratifying convention debates, are perhaps the most elaborate. What disturbs Smith is the small number of representatives (sixty-five) intended initially to constitute the House of Representatives. This means, he maintains, that those elected "will generally be" those of the "first class in the community"; those whom he labels "the natural aristocracy of the country." Acknowledging that there was no aristocracy established by law, he observes that there are classes within all societies: "The author of nature has bestowed on some greater capacities than on other—birth, education, talents and wealth, create distinctions among men as visible and of as much influence as titles, stars and garters."

Smith's point is to emphasize that "those of the middling class of life" will not find a place in the legislature; "that the government will fall into the hands of the few and great." In his view, not only will this render the legislature ill-equipped to understand "the circumstances and ability of the people in general" and to discern "how the burdens" of taxes, duties, and excises "will bear upon the different classes," it will lead to oppressive government. Whereas, Smith asserts, the middling class, being of "middling circumstances," necessarily possess bounded or limited "passions and appetites," the same cannot be said of the natural aristocrats who "fancy themselves to have a right of pre-eminence in every thing."[10] He cautions his compatriots: "We ought to guard against the government being laced in the hands of this class—They cannot have that sympathy with their constituents which is necessary to connect them closely to their interest."[11]

Brutus points to still other dimensions of the Anti-Federalists' displeasure with representation under the proposed Constitution. Again, he is concerned with the smallness of the representative body that, he feels, provides very tenuous connections between the representatives and their constituents. The representative assembly, he writes, will "consist of men, whose names they [the constituents] have never heard, and whose talents and regard for the public good, they are total strangers to." The people, because of this, "will have no persons so immediately of their choice so near them, or their neighbours and of their own rank in life." Nor, Brutus continues, can these representatives "mix with the people, and explain to them the motives which induced the adoption of any measure, point out its utility, and remove objections or silence unreasonable clamours against it." Worse still, he envisions popular mistrust and jealousy developing toward the representatives who will be perceived as having "distinct interests" of their own, resulting in "their laws" being "opposed, evaded, or reluctantly obeyed." In the end, he argues, because the government will not be supported by the "good will" of the people, its laws will have to be "executed by force, or not executed at all" with the inevitable loss of liberty.[12]

For Smith and Brutus, as well as for most Anti-Federalists, the preservation of liberty required that there be a close connection between the people and the representatives. Smith seeks to make this connection by ensuring adequate provision for representatives from the "middling class" along Aristotelian lines: a class, standing between the rich and poor that would constitute a moderating force. With the middling class holding a decisive voice, thereby preventing the rich and poor from exploiting each other, he is convinced liberty would be secure and the public good pursued. He sees "the interest of both the rich and the poor are involved in that of the middling class" and goes so far as to maintain that "[w]hen the interest of this part of the community [middle class] is pursued, the public good is pursued; because the body of every nation consists of this class."[13] Brutus, for his part, is less theoretically oriented and his arguments for a closer connection between the people and their representatives would simply preclude the establishment of an extensive republic; a representative, he insists, should be personally known to his constituents as honest and capable so that they can place "unreserved confidence" in his judgment.[14]

We need not delve further into Anti-Federalist thought in order to see they did not believe there was a sufficiently high degree of social friendship for an extended republic such as that urged by the Federalists. While, to be sure, they do not put the matter in these terms, it is evident from the nature of their objections to key provisions of the proposed Constitution. But, we can profitably ask, how did the Federalists view the landscape? Did they see a sufficiently high degree of social friendship for such an extensive union? Did they feel that the bonds of friendship between different states and sections of the country would strengthen once the new system was set in motion?

The Federalists backed the Philadelphia Constitution precisely because they perceived the government of the Articles of Confederation as incapable of meeting even the most essential needs of union. In Federalist no. 15, Alexander Hamilton pictures the situation under the Articles in the starkest terms: "We may indeed, with propriety, have reached almost the last state of national humiliation. There is scarcely any thing that can wound the pride, or degrade the character, of an independent people, which we do not experience."[15] The basic reason for this state of affairs is well known. As Madison puts it, by way of enumerating the failures of the Articles, "the radical infirmity" was its "dependence ... on the voluntary and simultaneous compliance" with its "Requisitions, by so many independent Communities, each consulting more or less its particular interests & convenience and distrusting the compliance of others."[16] Thus, the Federalists were under no illusion that social friendship by itself was sufficient for an effective political union. Indeed, it seems likely that an overreliance on social friendship—perhaps understandable in light of the revolutionary spirit and temper—was a major reason for the structural and procedural shortcomings of the Articles.[17]

Certain Federalists, nevertheless, did see an underlying desire for union overcoming the centrifugal forces identified by the Anti-Federalists. Chief among them was Noah Webster. Writing as "A Citizen of America," he is "astonished" not only by the conciliation of "so many clashing interests" at the Philadelphia Convention but also by "the many sacrifices made to the *general interest.*"[18] Others, such as "Socius," simply reject out of hand the Anti-Federalist contentions that "we are not, nor ought to be one people" and that state interests would always be at variance from "that of the union."[19] Virtually all who spoke to the issue of representation tacitly assume that the American people have enough sense, fortitude, and integrity not to be enslaved by their chosen representatives.[20] More importantly, those who dealt with the question of representation at any length also assume that the elected representatives under the new system, particularly the senators, would have the integrity and fortitude to advance the national interests over local or regional interests. For Noah Webster such behavior was the key ingredient of the constitutional morality necessary for the system to operate as intended. He grants that a representative had an obligation to express the "true local interest of his constituents," but having done so, he "should act for the *aggregate interest* of the whole confederacy." "The design of representation," according to Webster, "is to bring the collective interest into view" with representatives charged with the solemn responsibility to "act from an impartial regard to the general good."[21] James Wilson, for instance, believes experience to have shown that individuals elected from large districts, which would be the case under the proposed Constitution, would naturally possess these attributes since, in his estimation, "Nothing but real weight of character can give a man real influence over a large district."[22]

Some of those favoring ratification acknowledged divisions that could perhaps block ratification, but they looked on the proposed Constitution as a remedy for these divisions. John Jay, for example, laments that "seeds of discord and danger have been disseminated and begin to take root in America." He acknowledges as well that "unless eradicated," presumably by adopting the Constitution, they "will soon poison our gardens and our fields."[23] In this vein, an anonymous essayist, in agreeing with an Anti-Federalist that the "'habits' of the citizens of America are very dissimilar," contends that this dissimilarity flows "in great measure" from the "discordant principles of the separate Constitutions of the States and the want of a federal Government." He then goes on to a recurrent argument advanced by those urging adoption of the Constitution: "It is vain to expect a national trait in our characters, or a similitude of habits, but as the effect of a national efficient government." Once the Constitution is adopted and the new government begins operations, he envisions that "good laws" will promote virtue and "good habits."[24] "A Foreign Spectator," in many ways the most sophisticated advocate of the Constitution, elaborates on this theme; an extensive republic would eventually serve to strengthen the bonds of friendship and union, while elevating the moral and intellectual character of the citizenry. "If," he contends, "the common object of attachment is interesting, and a sufficient majority has those moral principles, which are the stamina of all rational government; the political union has a tendency to grow stronger—because the selfish passions will necessarily be weakened, or take a better direction; and all the sentiments of integrity, honor, private attachment, and public spirit, will encrease; by the exercise of social duties, by civil habits, and the gradual incorporation of the body politic, which will be finally moulded into a excellent form, and animated by the same generous spirit."[25]

On the whole, it would seem that the Federalists, despite deep discords among the states, felt there was a sufficient bond among the people to support a much stronger central government. Certainly John Jay was optimistic. He writes of the numerous and "weighty" considerations that "advise and persuade the people of America to remain in the safe and easy path of Union." He urges his countrymen "to continue to move and act as they hitherto have done, as a *band of brothers.*"²⁶ John Dickinson, for his part, writing under the pseudonym "Fabius," sets forth a view of the nature of the American people that was implicitly shared to some extent by all Federalists: "the people were so drawn together by religion, blood, language, manners and customs, undisturbed by former feuds and prejudices."²⁷ For him and other Federalists, this cohesion or commonality render an extensive republic feasible, despite the contentions of the Anti-Federalists. Indeed, these shared values, experiences, and traditions were a force that propelled the quest for a closer political union.

Clearly estimates differed about the degree of social friendship that existed during the founding. These differences, in turn, were reflected in the prospects held out for the proposed system to secure order and liberty. At one level the Federalists maintained that there was sufficient commonality and cohesion to overcome the differences emphasized by the Anti-Federalists, primarily with respect to the initial step of adopting the proposed Constitution. In Federalist no. 2, for instance, John Jay makes much of the close ties and bonds among Americans, picturing them as one people united by the "same religion," the "same language," and "common ancestors"—possessing like "manners and customs," being "attached to the same principles of government," and having fought as comrades in arms "side by side throughout a long and bloody war" for their "liberty and independence."²⁸ James Madison makes an even more passionate appeal to the chords of social friendship in Federalist no. 14: "Harken not," he warns, "to the unnatural voice, which tells you that the people of America, knit together as they are by so many chords of affection, can no longer live together as members of the same family; can no longer continue the mutual guardians of their mutual happiness; can no longer be fellow citizens of one great, respectable, and flourishing empire."²⁹

Yet, these assurances of sufficient social friendship for a closer political union did not address a central concern of the Anti-Federalist, which centered around resolution of conflict once the new system began to operate. On this point, the Federalist position, at least as we find it set forth in *The Federalist*, takes an interesting turn. Instead of arguing that, as one big family, these differences could be sublimated or accommodated by those qualities associated with the social friendship that allowed for a stronger political union in the first place, reliance for the peaceful resolution of conflict consistent with the common good is instead placed on competition between interests. The full dimensions of this approach are perhaps best illustrated by examining the theoretical underpinnings of the Constitution as we glean them from *The Federalist*. Here we find that the very characteristic of an extended union, which the Anti-Federalists felt rendered the republican form impossible (that is, its multiplicity and diversity of interest), is taken to be a necessary ingredient for a nondespotic, extensive republic. As Madison puts this in Federalist no. 51, by way of synthesizing his argument in Federalist no. 10, "In the extended Republic of the United States, and among the great variety of interests, parties, and sects, which it embraces, a coalition of a majority of the whole society could seldom take place upon any other principles, than those of justice and the general good."[30] On the other hand, small republics, with fewer interests, he contends would be prone to the injustices of majority factions.[31] Worse still, in his view, are "pure democracies," which had no hooks to grapple with majority factions bent on advancing their partial interests at the expense of the minority. Democracies of this order, he writes, "have ever been spectacles of turbulence and contention."[32] These views of the feasibility of a republican or popular government represented a complete eversion of traditional thought: whereas in traditional thought social friendship was regarded as essential for a republic, which thereby imposed a limitation on both its size and variety of interests, a principal teaching of *The Federalist* is that a stable and orderly republic relies on numerous interests competing with one another, a state of affairs normally requiring geographical extensiveness.

At one level, *The Federalist* is clear that the qualities of moderation, understanding, and forbearance that might be expected from social friendship could not be counted on to prevent republics from degenerating into despotism or even anarchy. In addressing the question of preventing the sovereign majorities within republics from oppressing minorities, Madison cautions that once majorities are organized and feel their strength "neither moral nor religious motives can be relied on" to stay their hand. But such a hard-headed view is not surprising in light of the underlying assumptions regarding human motivation that pervade the essays in *The Federalist*. Richard Scanlan, after careful analysis of the essays, concludes that one of their most important operating assumptions is that "antagonistic passions and immediate interests have greater efficacy than true interests and motives of reason and virtue."[33] If we look more closely at the influence of interest, more specific unarticulated assumptions emerge: individuals will be guided by immediate self-interest, not by the long-term common interest. So strong is the propensity of men to realize immediate interest, they will, more frequently than not, pursue it even at the expense of their own long-term interests.[34]

Without going into detail, the strategy of *The Federalist* centers around using interest to advantage. The multiplicity of interests is seen as the principal factor that makes the formation of an oppressive majority highly unlikely. Likewise, Hamilton and Madison seemed to have accepted the Mandevillian argument as it came to them through Adam Smith and David Hume, that the pursuit of private interest could result in the advancement of the common good.[35] We see this clearly in Federalist no. 51 where Madison contends that the maintenance of the constitutional separation of powers depends on the office holders in one branch using the constitutional means at their disposal to defend their "turf" or institutional interests with which they are connected against encroachments from another. "This policy of supplying, by opposite and rival interests, the defect of better motives," Madison writes, "might well be traced through the whole system of human affairs, private as well as public."[36]

Yet, it must be noted, there are other places in *The Federalist* where we do find recourse, however remotely, to certain attributes that flow from social friendship. Acknowledging that the extended republic is not fool proof, that oppressive majorities might form, Madison sees some hope of forestalling them through delay and deliberation. If the House of Representatives bends to the will of a factious majority, he looks to the Senate "to suspend the blow meditated by the people against themselves, until reason, justice, and truth, can regain their authority over the public mind."[37] Likewise, Hamilton looks to the president to veto measures backed by majorities that are inimical to their interests; "it is the duty of the persons whom they have appointed, to be the guardians of those interests; to withstand the temporary delusion, in order to give them time and opportunity for more cool and sedate reflection."[38]

Clearly, for delay and deliberation to operate in the fashion Madison and Hamilton envision means that majorities—on realizing how adversely their measures would affect the common good, minorities, or even discrete individuals—will sublimate their immediate interests for the well being of others or for the long-range interests of the nation. To even contemplate such restraint suggests the presence of bonds of friendship at least to the extent of a framework of shared values that provides the basis for the meaningful exchange of views about what is best for the whole. So much is intimated in the famous passage that concludes Federalist no. 55—namely, while "there is a degree of depravity in mankind, which requires a certain degree of circumspection and distrust: so there are other qualities of human nature, which justify a certain portion of esteem and confidence."[39] This is a message repeated, albeit in slightly different form, in Federalist no. 76: "The supposition of universal venality in human nature, is little less an error in political reasoning, than that of universal rectitude." There is, we are informed, a "portion of virtue and honour among mankind," sufficient enough to trust that the Senate and president will not conspire with one another to betray the public trust.[40] But the main thrust of *The Federalist*'s appeal is elsewhere—to interests, both immediate and personal, and mainly to those of major economic sectors by way of showing how the proposed Constitution, once adopted, would serve to benefit, advance, or protect their interests.[41]

There are conclusions to be drawn from this brief survey. Looking at the founding era through this prism of social friendship reveals an underlying and unifying concern of the Anti-Federalists that is not immediately apparent in their specific objections to the proposed Constitution; that is, underlying many, if not most, of them is the perceived absence of those conditions and qualities associated with social friendship that were felt to be necessary for a harmonious political order. This observation leads to another. We see the differences that Benjamin Constant points out between the political environment and world of the ancients and that of the moderns, as these are clearly displayed in the positions taken by the Anti-Federalists and Federalists over the proposed constitution and the viability of an extended republic.[42] The two sides, to begin with, entertained two largely different views regarding the requirements for social cohesion and, therefore, they differed as well in what they felt to be the essential tasks of the state. The Anti-Federalists, for their part, were thinking in terms not unlike the ancients; they believed, more specifically, that virtues and states of mind resulting from a high degree of social friendship were requisite for a free and well-functioning republic. The Federalists, on the other hand, could not embrace this view; their new order would require different priorities and conditions because they envisioned a larger, more complex society in which these virtues and attitudes simply could not be nourished to any significant degree. They were, it is clear, aware of the need for social friendship in some degree for the establishment of the proposed political union. But much beyond this, they did not go.

The Federalists have been criticized over the years for, among other failings, not tending to matters such as the cultivation of those virtues that result from or depend on a high degree of social friendship—virtues that, it is believed, would serve to buttress the foundations of the regime and elevate its character. They were, as we have seen, preoccupied in channeling and controlling interest and the acquisitive instinct of individuals, seemingly unconcerned about cultivating behavior and attitudes commonly thought to be necessary for a decent and orderly republican regime, for example, a cooperative disposition, sublimation of self-interest in light of the common good, and attention to civic responsibilities.[43]

Yet—and the matter has not been sufficiently explored in the literature—we can see good reason why these concerns were not explicitly dealt with by the Federalists. As I have remarked, the expansive republic they envisioned simply precluded any hope of securing the blessings associated with social friendship to the degree sought by the Anti-Federalists. This does not mean, however, that the Federalists ignored the need for social friendship. Rather they sought other means to procure what they understood to be a different order or character of friendship. On this score, one thing seems clear: they must have felt that among the economic advantages of a stronger union would be a greater social cohesion resulting from increased commercial activity.[44] Such a conclusion seems entirely warranted since commercial relations have long been regarded as promoting and reinforcing virtues such as trust, loyalty, and a high degree of cooperation as these relations become more complex. Moreover, because these commercial relations knew no political boundaries, because they would be extensive, even spanning the republic in some cases, they would form chords between individuals, groups, and interests that would provide at least greater national cohesion, if not a bonding between individuals and groups.[45]

The nature of friendships cultivated by commercialism are, of course, of a different order from the ideal friendships contemplated by Aristotle or even the more mundane visions of the Anti-Federalists. Yet little more could be expected in an expansive union or from its government; the qualities and virtues resulting from more intimate friendships growing out of close association in daily living within small, relatively stable, local communities simply could not be had at the national level. This realization, as obvious as it seems, carries with it implications highly relevant to our modern political discourse: there is and can be no such thing a "national community" insofar, that is, as we conceive of a community in terms of a high degree of friendship growing out of close personal relationships. Thus, a politics or political understanding based on the premise of a national community with a cohesion founded on the ancient or even Anti-Federalist understanding of friendship is bound to be lacking.

The adoption of the Constitution and with it the creation of an extensive republic in no way affected the smaller communal environments in which more intimate personal friendships could develop and flourish. What is more, even with the adoption of the Constitution, the major responsibilities and functions of government in everyday life were left to the states and localities. Whether today local communities, even the medium-sized and small, can provide such a fertile environment for the development of such deep and lasting friendships is highly questionable. Some, sympathetic to the teaching of Alexis de Tocqueville would argue that the modern welfare state with its highly centralized administrative structure undermines local communities, as well as intermediate associations and institutions through which bonds of friendship and community are established and nourished.[46] Ironically, it may well be that the growth of a commercial society—that which, as we have suggested, perhaps provides the cohesion necessary for a stronger and more expansive political union—now operates to undermine the very conditions necessary for growth of social friendship with smaller communities. Clearly in the world of modern commerce and business, with increasing urbanization and mobility, communities are far less stable and inward looking.[47]

What all this bodes for the future of the American republic is a matter of conjecture. What we do know is that the debates in the founding era reveal profound differences over the character of the nation that fueled equally profound disagreement about the character and degree of social friendship or cohesion necessary for the expansive republic under the forms of the Constitution. The period can be said to have marked a turning point in thinking about these matters, largely in abandoning the classical views and looking to a basic unity of interests within an increasingly commercial society.

Notes

1. The meaning of "social friendship" in the sense I am here using the term is ably set forth by Bertrand de Jouvenel in *Sovereignty: An Inquiry into the Political Good* (Indianapolis: Liberty Fund, 1997). See esp. chap. 8, "Of Social Friendship."

2. There are, of course, other legitimate perspectives for surveying friendship during this era that readily come to mind. One, for instance, could look at the role of friendship among the founders and how this friendship facilitated the move toward a stronger political union or otherwise affected political dynamics. Or one could undertake an examination of friendship within the local communities, perhaps noting how relationships varied among regions. Although approaches such as these would require extensive and time-consuming research, probably beyond the capacity of a single individual, the concluding remarks to this essay propose that the social friendship approach provides greater insight into the foundations and character of the American political order that are relevant even today.

3. The correct reciprocal anticipation to which I refer can be clearly seen in other contexts. Two friends who have known each other for a long time know, so to speak, how to press the other's "button." The same, of course, is true among family members.

4. Jouvenel, *Sovereignty*, 147.

5. Barry Shain, "American Community," in *Community and Tradition*, ed. George W. Carey and Bruce Frohnen (Lanham, Md.: Rowman & Littlefield, 1998), 58.

6. Ibid., 43–44.

7. *The Anti-Federalists: Selected Writings and Speeches*, ed. Bruce Frohnen (Washington, D.C.: Regnery, 1999), 13.

8. *The Debates in the Several State Conventions on the Adoption of the Federal Constitution*, ed. Jonathan Eliot, 5 vols., 2d ed. (New York: Burt Franklin, 1888), III, 30.

9. *The Anti-Federalist*, ed. Murray Dry. An Abridgment of the Complete Anti-Federalist; edited, with commentary and notes, by Herbert J. Storing (Chicago: University of Chicago Press, 1985), 236.

10. Ibid., 340, 341.

11. Ibid., 342.

12. Ibid., 130.

13. Ibid., 42.

14. Ibid., 130.

15. Alexander Hamilton, James Madison, and John Jay, *The Federalist*, ed. George W. Carey and James McClellan (Indianapolis: Liberty Fund, 2000), 69.

16. James Madison, "A Sketch Never Finished nor Applied," in *Notes of Debates in the Federal Convention of 1787: Reported by James Madison*, intro. Adrienne Kock (New York: Norton, 1987), 7.

17. John Jay writing as "A Citizen of New York" put this matter as follows: "It is a pity that the expectations which actuated the authors of the existing confederation, neither have nor can be realized:—accustomed to see and admire the glorious spirit which moved all ranks of people in the most gloomy moments of the war, observing their steadfast attachment to Union, and the wisdom they so often manifested both in choosing and confiding in their rulers, those gentlemen were led to flatter themselves that the people of America only required to know what ought to be done, to do it. This amiable mistake induced them to institute a national government in which a manner, as though very fit to give advice, was yet destitute of power, and so constructed as to be very unfit to be trusted with it." In *Friends of the Constitution: Writings of the "Other" Federalists*, ed. Colleen A. Sheehan and Gary L. McDowell (Indianapolis: Liberty Fund, 1998), 139.

18. A Citizen of America, "An Examination into the Leading Principles of the Constitution," in *Friends of the Constitution*, 404.

19. Socius, "Some Thoughts on the Fears Which Many Appear to Entertain about the Federal Constitution," in *Friends of the Constitution*, 168.

20. Fabius, Letter IX, in answering the Anti-Federalist charge that the representatives would form a cabal to tyrannize the citizens, asks rhetorically: "Is it to be before or after a general corruption of manners? . . . Will a virtuous and sensible people choose villains or fools for their officers? . . . If they should, will not their places be quickly supplied by another choice? Is the like derangement again, and again, and again to be expected? Can any man believe, that such astonishing phenomena are to be looked for?" In *Friends of the Constitution*, 500.

21. A Citizen of America, "An Examination into the Leading Principles of the Federal Constitution," in *Friends of the Constitution*, 383.

22. James Wilson, "Speech in Pennsylvania Ratifying Convention, 7 December 1787," in *Friends of the Constitution*, 204.

23. A Citizen of New York, in *Friends of the Constitution*, 138.

24. Anonymous, "Convention," in *Friends of the Constitution*, 355–56.

25. A Foreign Spectator, "The Principles of Sentimental Political Union" in *Friends of the Constitution*, 427. In this regard, he (Nicholas Collin) perceives American society in terms not unlike most founders, particularly James Madison, and he believes that an increasing multiplicity of interests, which he regards as inevitable given the rapid increase in population, "will improve the general manners by a deeper and more frequent sense of the necessity, propriety, and advantage of an equitable, obliging, and decent conduct." Individuals will soon learn that they can achieve their ends by checking their "rude and selfish passions" (411).

26. A Citizen of New York, in *Friends of the Constitution*, 153. Emphasis in original.

27. Fabius, Letter VIII, in *Friends of the Constitution*, 492.

28. *The Federalist*, 6. Here and elsewhere (see above) Jay comes close to arguing that a firm union is a historical inevitability, that is, it will result from forces, including a high degree of camaraderie and social friendship, set in motion by the movement toward independence. Contrast Jay's view here with those of Hamilton set forth almost at the outset of *The Federalist*: "Happy will it be if our choice should be directed by a judicious estimate of our true interests, uninfluenced by considerations foreign to the public good" (*The Federalist*, essay no. 1, 1).

29. *The Federalist*, 66.

30. *The Federalist*, 271.

31. Madison could readily envision majority factions ruling within the states, but not over the extended republic. As he puts it, factions "will be less apt to pervade the whole body of the union, than a particular member of it" (*The Federalist*, essay no. 10, 48).

32. *The Federalist*, 46. Clearly he did not think friendship or bonds of community would prevent the collapse of pure democracies. He goes on to contend that "[t]heoretic politicians, who have patronized this species of government [pure democracy], have erroneously supposed, that, by reducing mankind to a perfect equality in their political rights, they would, at the same time, be perfectly equalized and assimilated in their possessions, their opinions, and their passions."

33. Richard Scanlan, "*The Federalist* and Human Nature," *Review of Politics* 21 (October 1959): 665.

34. Madison believed the propensity to pursue immediate self-interest was so strong that not even under the direction and control of "enlightened statesmen" could legislative assemblies "adjust . . . clashing interests, and render them all subservient to the public good," when "indirect and remote considerations" had to be taken into account. Such considerations, he writes, "will rarely prevail over the immediate interest which one party may find in disregarding the rights of another, or the good of the whole" (*The Federalist*, essay no. 10, 45).

35. Bernard Mandeville is generally credited with being the first to set forth the notion that "private vices" can lead to "publick benefits" in his *Fable of the Bees* first published in 1714. In more moderate form this understanding permeates *The Federalist*, particularly with regard to preventing tyranny (the concentration of legislative, executive, and judicial powers in the same hands) and majority oppression.

36. *The Federalist*, 269.

37. *The Federalist*, 327.

38. *The Federalist*, essay no. 71, 371.

39. *The Federalist*, 291.

40. *The Federalist*, 395.

41. The argument has been made, and not without merit, that Madison and others saw the major areas of conflict to involve *interests*—not *passions*—in the economic and commercial realm. These interest conflicts, it is noted—unlike those associated with passions—are tractable; they do not involve differences of principle that are difficult or impossible to resolve. Thus, the argument goes, the extended republic is durable precisely because it is dealing with resolvable conflicts between interests. See Martin Diamond, "Ethics and Politics: The American Way," in *The Moral Foundations of the American Republic*, ed. Robert H. Horwitz, 2d ed. (Charlottesville: University of Virginia Press, 1979).

42. See his address, "The Liberty of the Ancients Compared with That of the Moderns," in *Political Writings of Benjamin Constant*, ed. and trans. Biancamaria Fontana (Cambridge: Cambridge University Press, 1988). Constant observes that the modern nation bears little resemblance to the ancient re-

publics in large part because of their size and the growth of commerce. These factors, he points out, have led to a modern understanding and practice of liberty entirely foreign to the ancient world. Likewise, as I contend in the text, there has been an equivalent change with regard to ancient and modern understandings regarding friendship, particularly its function and character.

43. The locus classicus for this point of view is Herbert Croly's enormously influential work *The Promise of American Life* (New York: Macmillan, 1911).

44. They could find respected support for this belief. Montesquieu, for instance, believed that "the spirit of commerce is naturally attended with that of frugality, economy, moderation, labor, prudence, tranquility, order, and rule" (*The Spirit of the Laws,* trans. Thomas Nugent [New York: Hafner, 1949], chap. 5, bk. 2, 46). Even before Adam Smith's *Wealth of Nations,* a widespread belief prevailed that commerce and expanded trade would promote the sciences, arts, civility, toleration, liberty—that is, those conditions and values that would promote social cohesion. See *Commerce, Culture, and Liberty: Readings on Capitalism before Adam Smith,* ed. Henry C. Clark (Indianapolis: Liberty Fund, 2003).

45. As John Courtney Murray points out, the deep religious cleavages in the colonial and founding periods were reduced and even eliminated because of commercial considerations. "The merchants of New Jersey, New York, Virginia, and the more southern colonies were as emphatically on the side of religious freedom as on the side of commercial profits. Persecution and discrimination were as bad for business affairs as they were for the affairs of the soul" (*We Hold These Truths* [Kansas City: Sheed & Ward, 1960], 59).

46. Robert Nisbet is perhaps the best-known modern proponent of this view. See his *Quest for Community* (New York: Oxford University Press, 1953). For a similar view, see Wilhelm Roepke, *The Moral Foundations of Civil Society* (New Brunswick: Transaction Press, 1996).

47. Wilhelm Roepke has explored the difficulties arising from economic centralization in his classic work, *The Humane Economy* (Wilmington, Del.: ISI Books, 1998).

10

It Is Not Good for Man to Be Alone

Tocqueville on Friendship

Joshua Mitchell

The question concerning Tocqueville's understanding of friendship presupposes the question concerning friendship itself, namely: what is its nature; on what occasions does it arise; to whom does it accrue; in what way is it pertinent to the community of men; and so on.

The locus classicus to which historians of political thought return to consider the question of friendship is, of course, Aristotle's *Nicomachean Ethics*. What we find in that compilation, among other things, is the ready distinction between three kinds of friendship: friendships based on pleasure, friendships based on use, and friendships based on virtue.[1] Of these three types, Aristotle tells us, political friendship is the highest and the one that is most needed (even if most unlikely) to gather together a community of men. In our own day, it is usually against the backdrop of this claim—namely, that virtuous friendship is the sine qua non of durable community—that historians of political thought consider the modern manner of "gathering together."[2] Aristotle's typology conveniently suggests to us that the preeminent basis of such gathering in the modern world is friendship based on use, the obvious confirmation of which is the opinion current today that free markets and global trade are what are most needed to produce a durable community. Said otherwise, Aristotle's *Nicomachean Ethics* sets forth a typology that directs our attention to the possibility that the modern understanding of how we may be gathered is largely but not exclusively illuminated by Smith's *The Wealth of Nations*.[3] Man, the market animal; man, the animal who ventures no further than the household, the *oikia*.

While this is certainly an oversimplification, a perusal of any number of seminal works in political philosophy during the modern period confirms that there is little in the way of systematic reflection on the subject of friendship, and a great deal on commerce and market relations. And perhaps more revealing still, when things purportedly political are thought through, they are treated in terms of "contract." Why is this so? What does it mean that friendship *as a philosophical category* scarcely exists in the modern canon? Does it betray a diminution of man? Or does this silence intimate that in the modern period other possibilities for gathering together emerge—ones that Aristotle could not have imagined? Said otherwise, might it be the case that notwithstanding the inability of virtue friendship in Aristotle's sense to take hold of the modern imagination, modern life has its compensations, which more than make up for the absence of what Aristotle purports to be highest in man?[4] Might it be the case that the absence of the category of "nature" makes friendship of the sort Aristotle pondered quite unthinkable for modern, *historical* man? In this essay on Tocqueville's understanding of friendship, I wish to consider these possibilities. If Aristotle's ideal typology is our guide, we will be left to wonder how the modern world has been held together at all. Yet held together it has; and this bald fact leads us to wonder whether Aristotle's typology of friendships can exhaustively comprehend the situation before us. However tempting it may be to claim that the modern world has been based on a philosophical error, a quarter of a millennium is surely long enough to suggest otherwise.

Let me first rename the question before us. Instead of "Tocqueville on Friendship," let us consider "Tocqueville on How We Shall Be Gathered." The latter formulates our problem at the level of the genus; the former, at the level of the species. Friendship, articulated in and through its three subspecies ("virtue," "use," and "pleasure"), is a distinct mode of gathering together, predicated on notions of virtue and of nature—notions that, for better or worse, have little purchase in the modern world. By attending to the larger genus of "gathering together," the absence of the species called "friendship" in modern political thought need not confound us nor lead us to adopt a hostile posture toward that thought, but rather persuade us that other available manners of being gathered together about which modern thinkers write warrant our attention.

As it turns out, the larger question, "how shall we be gathered," rather than the smaller question, "what can we say about friendship in the modern period," is one of the central questions in Tocqueville's *Democracy in America,* especially in the painfully reflective second volume:

> Aristocracy links everybody, from peasant to king, in one long chain. Democracy breaks the chain and frees each link. As social equality spreads there are more and more people who, though neither richer nor powerful enough to have much hold over others, have gained or kept enough wealth and enough understanding to look out for their own needs. Such folk owe no man anything and hardly expect anything from anybody. They form the habit of thinking of themselves in isolation and imagine that their whole destiny is in their own hands. Thus, not only does democracy make men forget their ancestors, but also clouds their view of their descendents and isolates them from their contemporaries. *Each man is forever thrown back on himself alone, and there is danger that he may be shut up in the solitude of his own heart.*[5]

On this account, the historical movement from aristocracy to democracy—itself foreordained by God[6]—reconfigures both human relations and human self-understanding. The easy confidence that human relations are rooted in the stable pronouncements of nature is silenced by the din of an ever more chaotic and contingent world; the assurance that knowledge conveyed by the ancestors is authoritative dissipates as a contingent world redirects attention to the future or, what is more likely, to the instantaneous present—but in either case, *not* to the past. Under such circumstances the democratic age is simultaneously the résumé of an unfolding of a new set of human relations and the emergence of a new modality of human experience, both of which are without bearings. The End of History is disseverance. "This profound saying could be applied especially to me: it is not good for man to be alone," Tocqueville wrote to Madame Swetchine.[7] Tocqueville, the philosopher of loneliness; the philosopher for whom the question of our being gathered together was one of the great questions of the democratic age. Neither nature nor our inheritance binds us. Amid this loneliness, what can gather us together? If man is now a thoroughgoing *historical* animal, what can stand in for that gathering called "friendship," which the absence of *nature* disallows? Friendship is gone, but not the need to be gathered together. In this historical moment as in all others, "it is not good for man to be alone." How is this solitude redressed?

There is much more to be said about the question "How shall we be gathered?" To prepare the way more fully, however, I wish to make some comments first about what I take to be the other imposing question in *Democracy in America,* namely, "What is the measure?" Because addressing this seemingly unrelated question lights the way to the question with which we are more directly concerned here, let us pause here first.

The importance of this question can best be understood against the backdrop of the development that Tocqueville chronicles and that I have already briefly mentioned, namely, the historical movement from aristocracy to democracy. "In aristocracies each man is pretty firmly fixed in his sphere, but men are vastly dissimilar; their passions, ideas, habits, and tastes are basically diverse. Nothing changes, but everything differs."[8] While Tocqueville does not quite put it this way, in the democratic age it could be said that "everything changes and nothing differs." In the democratic age, he says, "all changes are alike."[9] What are we to make of this new situation in which there is relentless change without any real difference? How does this paradox shed light on the immediate question before us? And, to our larger concern, what does this tell us about the manner in which we are gathered together in the democratic age? There are two matters that must be discussed under this heading of collapsing differences: sympathy and money. Let us consider sympathy first.

One of the things that Tocqueville tells us in *Democracy in America* is that in the aristocratic age demarcations within society gave rise to the thought that people from different strata were viewed as different *in kind*. His chilling citation in *Democracy in America* of the late-seventeenth-century letter of Madame de Sévigné to her daughter, in which she dryly notes the quartering of a fiddler amid her cheerful musings about an upcoming wedding,[10] confirms the point: in a highly stratified society there can be no sympathy for the suffering of others unlike oneself. Generosity, yes; but not sympathy.[11] Within the confines of the democratic age, when social distance has more or less collapsed, her letter appears to be evidence of cruelty. Can *we* not imagine the suffering of the fiddler? But Tocqueville tells us that it would be a mistake to think that way. Rather, her letter confirms that in the aristocratic age, the demarcations between social groups were so vast that the suffering of members of one group could not be understood by members of another.

Now in one sense what I have described here points us in the direction of an answer to the question "How can we be gathered?" and to rather breathtaking implications for the community of men of the sort Aristotle could not have imagined. Where the aristocratic age is characterized by rank and the "pathos of distance,"[12] the democratic age is characterized by social equality and "fellow feeling."[13] Each human being is, for the first time, close enough to every other so that all suffering is noticed. The community of men now becomes the whole of humanity. The polis of Aristotle suddenly looks like a quaint gathering of largely like-minded gentlemen. Virtue there may have been; so, too, prudence—but not sympathy. To this let us add that the democratic community of humankind is not held together because of *what is done* in the way of moral or ethical training, but by virtue of what the collapse of social distance *makes possible.* Here the categories of potentiality *(dunamis)* and actuality *(entelecheia)* that are integral to Aristotle's ethical and political project lose their hold on the democratic imagination. The proportionalities of justice, the giving and receiving between equals and unequals that hold community together—these give way before a breathtaking new possibility, namely, *universal man,* dissevered from the heteronymous forces that were the basis of enduring differences in the aristocratic age, and on the basis of which justice was thought through. Here, in the democratic age, it becomes possible to think as Rawls does, viz., of persons without predicates.[14]

This glistening picture, which comprehends the remaining differences between human beings as accidents of history to be overcome, is tarnished by that other emergent fact of the democratic age, namely, the power of money. We may decide, as Marx did, that the emergence of the power of money in the democratic age is a spurious correlation, and that in fact the source of this emergence is the advent of capitalism. We may, that is, decide that history is the tale of economic transformations bringing social transformations in their wake. The account provided by Tocqueville, however deficient it may be in other respects, is able to illuminate, as Marx's is not, the underlying logic that links the advent of generalized sympathy and the emergence of the power of money. On Tocqueville's reading, both of these developments can be explained in terms of democratic social conditions. Said otherwise, Tocqueville's account allows us to make sense of the counterintuitive fact that the Adam Smith who writes *Theory of Moral Sentiments* also writes *The Wealth of Nations.* Sympathy and the inordinate focus on money are coterminous.

On Tocqueville's reading, democratic social conditions not only collapse social distance and, so, yield sympathy; they also destroy the medium by which relations between the different social strata retained the equalibria they did. That medium was honor. It is by now a platitude to say that when the aristocratic age gives way to the democratic age, honor recedes and money becomes the currency that increasingly mediates all relations. Marx tells us that this happens because of the advent of capitalism.[15] Tocqueville suggests that money becomes the single measure in the democratic age because of the collapse of the multiple social rankings of the aristocratic age into one. This does not happen all at once, to be sure; but the power of money grows as proportionally as that collapse occurs.

To understand why this is so, let us begin by asking *where* and *what,* in fact, honor is. In Tocqueville's account, honor is not located *in* a class of people, and so does not, strictly speaking, disappear in the democratic age, as the aristocratic classes succumb. Nor is honor an aspect of a multifaceted soul, in which parts vie for ascendancy, as Plato's *Republic* suggests.[16] Rather, honor is an artifact of societies in which there are *relatively stable* social inequalities. Honor is the currency by which such inequalities are delineated and fortified.[17] In the democratic age, on the other hand, where there is increased social mobility money, not honor, is the currency of choice. "Men living in democratic times have many passions, but most of these culminate in love of wealth or derive from it. That is not because their souls are narrower but because money really is more important at such times."[18] With money, social inequalities are measured, but not delineated. Unlike money, honor cannot exist without relatively stable "social distance." The democratic age brings with it the collapse of the social distance between classes and, therefore, an effective end to the place of honor.[19]

We have, then, something of a paradox in the democratic age with respect to the question "What is the measure?" On the one hand, the collapse of social distance yields sympathy; and on the face of it, we have, through sympathy, a provisional answer to the question "How shall we be gathered?" Because sympathy is generalized, there seems to be a basis, really for the first time in history, for global understanding and, some may presume, global community. On the other hand, however, the same collapse of social distance that makes sympathy possible undermines the apportionments of honor and elevates the currency of money. Honor fortifies the chasm between social strata. It exists in and through the discontinuities that separate one stratum from another. In the "market," however, all are equal and honor can have no place, since what man brings to the "transaction" is not his standing but rather his "currency"—the origin of which word also gives rise to "current," or uninterrupted flow. There can be no real current(cy), no uninterrupted flow, when there are discontinuities between social strata.

Still under the category of the question "What is the measure?" let us turn to the manner in which man measures his world in the democratic age. Tocqueville seems particularly concerned about the shift away from what could be called an "aristocratic mode of knowing," and toward a mode of knowing that is characterized by man's being cut off and unbound. In the democratic age, Tocqueville says, "each man is narrowly shut up in himself, and from that basis makes the pretension to judge the world."[20] The epistemological manifestation of this development we can see already in the thinking Descartes; the theological manifestation in Luther; and the political manifestation in Hobbes.[21] The rejection by Smith of the guild system of production can be seen as evidence of this development in economics.[22] I leave aside important confirmations in the world of art, notably the development of portraiture, where persons are dignified in and through their idiosyncratic features and not insofar as they imitate and intimate long-inherited paradigms. In every domain of life the shift from the aristocratic age to the democratic age evinces the same pattern: dissevered from the links that tied him fast, man now explores the world in accordance with what the authority of his own experience discloses. And he does this not with a view to the majestic authority of the past, which he is to imitate, but with a view to the possibilities of the future, as he himself sincerely imagines them.

Having now briefly assayed the three social facts—sympathy, money, and self-referentiality—that emerge in the democratic age as the aristocratic measure of honor gives way, let us turn more fully to the question of "how shall we be gathered." The first question that was posed—"What is the measure?"—allowed us to consider some of the implications of the collapse of the social stratification found in the aristocratic age. Now, assisted by the knowledge that the democratic age, fully realized, is one without social stratifications, we will ponder the larger question before us, namely, "How shall we be gathered?"

On Tocqueville's reading, the destruction of social stratification pointed in one of two possible directions: either toward equality in servitude or toward equality in freedom. Tocqueville worried a great deal, of course, about equality in servitude. By this he meant a servitude for which there was not yet a name, one wherein citizens lived under a uniform set of rules, thought only of the petty things of life, were saved from expending much effort by the beneficent hand of the State, and felt that they had reached the apogee of well being.[23] Under such conditions the gaze of citizens would be *upward* toward "public opinion" and toward the "single visible power" of the State, rather than *outward* toward each other—they would, that is, be disconnected from each other. These two social facts together would give rise to two distinct "nodes" of experience that would exist simultaneously within each citizen of the democratic age: one corresponding to their disconnectedness; the other corresponding to the immense domain that comes into view once their gaze has shifted from a lateral view of their neighbor toward a vertical view of "the public" and the State that does its political bidding. The former let us call the node of "soliloquy"; the latter let us call the node of "they say."[24]

The psychological confirmation that the "kinder and gentler" tyranny of equality had arrived would come in the form of citizens who, at once, talk incessantly among themselves about sporting events, movies, television series, and the platitudes that pass for political debates, and then return to their enclosed, even if imaginative, worlds at night and rehearse their solitary "narratives" to themselves before falling asleep. In both nodal domains, there is no risk, no *encounter*—about which more shortly.

To understand in a bit more detail what is meant by these nodes, or loci, let us attend briefly to what Tocqueville thinks about the nature of authority in the democratic age:

> [In the democratic age] intellectual authority will be different, but it will not be less. Far from believing that it is likely to disappear, I anticipate that it may easily become too great and that possibly it will confine the activity of private judgment within limits too narrow for the dignity and happiness of mankind. I see clearly two tendencies in equality; the one turns each man's attention to new thoughts, while the other would induce him freely to give up thinking at all. . . . Thus it might happen that, having broken down all the bonds which classes of men formerly imposed on it, the human spirit might bind itself in tight fetters to the general will of the greatest number.[25]

In the aristocratic age, authority was vested largely in intermediary bodies; consequently, truth was not understood as abstract, universal, and discernable by reason, but was rather vested *in a name*.[26] In the democratic age, on the other hand, there are no such intermediary bodies, and so authority and truth change their location and character. They do not, however, disappear.

In the democratic age, the two nodal points where authority and truth lie are, in Tocqueville's words, "private judgment" and the "general will"—what I am calling "soliloquy" and "they say." Americans, he says, naturally suppose two things at once: authority and truth are personal matters, unique to each individual, which are disclosed in the warp and woof of their own soliloquy; and that public opinion—what "they say"—is the final authority and truth. The nodal point of soliloquy accords individuals the freedom to endlessly rehearse and stage their personal narratives without real interruption; the nodal point of "they say" emboldens individuals to rebuff the voice of conscience and condescend to the level of unreflective brutes. Neither one of these nodal points, which the democratic age produces, dignifies humankind, nor renews civilization.

Equality in freedom is the alternative Tocqueville has in mind to equality in servitude. And it is here that we find the rudiments of Tocqueville's answer for historical man to the problem of "gathering together." Psychologically, this amounts to the presence of a nodal point between "private judgment" and the "general will," that is, a coherent locus of human experience that is neither utterly private nor comprehensively public. This locus is generated, sociologically, in the mediational space of associational life, in the face-to-face relations, where human beings must gather together for the purpose of addressing the problems of daily life. "As soon as common affairs *are treated* in common, each man notices that he is not as independent of his fellows as he used to suppose and that to get their help he must offer his aid to them."[27] Here, human beings are drawn out of themselves, gathered together as neighbors, and brought to "self-interest rightly understood,"[28] that sublime achievement of the democratic age that bridges the chasm between soliloquy and "they say." Without this nodal point of common affairs at the intermediate level, new ideas cannot coalesce from the "mental dust"[29] out of which a provisional consensus about authority and truth emerge, and human beings hold fast to the well-worn apparati of personal "narratives" and public platitudes.[30] Only through the mediation of associational life can there be an antidote to the private withdrawal and deference to the public that occurs when equality in servitude prevails. Here "gathering together" of the sort that counts for Tocqueville can occur.

We may ask just how grave is the disease for which Tocqueville purports to find an antidote. I earlier introduced sympathy, money, and self-referentiality, respectively, with a view to disentangling the sometimes contradictory consequences of the breakdown of the social hierarchy of the aristocratic age—and with it, the abandonment of the idea of nature. In Tocqueville's view, all three of these conspire to isolate individuals from one another, and so to guide them without effort toward equality in servitude. Sympathy, of course, *seems* to run contrary to this tendency, but that is not in fact what happens. The sort of sympathy that emerges in the democratic age is *universal* sympathy for the suffering of humanity as a whole, not sympathy for the neighbor who lives next door:

> So people living in an aristocratic age are almost always closely involved with something outside themselves, and they are often inclined to forget about themselves. It is true that in these ages the general conception of *human fellowship* is dim, and that men hardly ever think about devoting themselves to the cause of humanity, but men often do make sacrifices for the sake of certain other men. In the democratic age, on the contrary, the duties of each to all are much clearer, but devoted service to any individual much rarer. The bonds of human affection are wider but more relaxed.[31]

Let us concede, then, that sympathy, money, and self-referentiality conspire to isolate the individual, to elicit the psychological nodal point of soliloquy. Furthermore, let us concede that such soliloquy is part and parcel of the equality of servitude about which Tocqueville worries. What, exactly, is wrong with the mode of "gathering together" that equality in servitude entails? It is, after all, the mode of "gathering together" most likely to occur as in the democratic age. As such, does it not represent the modern answer to Aristotle? Are not universal sympathy, well-ordered States with uniform rules, and individualism the hallmarks of the modern world? Tocqueville thought that they were, but that such a configuration would in no way solve the *historical* problem that preoccupied so many thinkers of the nineteenth century, namely, how in light of impending exhaustion of Western civilization can society be renewed.

Here we come to the central concern that animates Tocqueville's thinking. Recognizing that sympathy, money, and self-referentiality are inscribed into the social condition of democracy, Tocqueville thought it nevertheless possible, indeed desirable, for persons in the democratic age to be gathered together in face-to-face relations. These alone, he thought, could renew a civilization. "Feelings and ideas are renewed, the heart enlarged, and the understanding developed, only by the reciprocal action of men one upon another."[32] Such face-to-face encounters, which disrupt the self-satisfactions of the democratic soul lost in soliloquy or the "they say," should not be confused with what Aristotle or even Plato had in mind. There is no historical consciousness in either Aristotle's or Plato's thought, and so the valence of the term "renewal" is quite different. In Plato's dialogues, as in Tocqueville's writing, there is an attentiveness to the soul, and also an account of the "powerful [public] beast"[33] that is every bit as chilling as is Tocqueville's. To this I would add that Plato is concerned about the human tendency to be self-satisfied and, so, in its own way could be said to be offering the same sort of mediational alternative whereby human beings are drawn out of themselves in face-to-face encounters with others, which rouse them from their slumber. Aristotle, too, could be read this way.

The sort of encounter toward which Tocqueville directs our attention is not, however, a philosophical one. "Nothing is so unproductive for the human mind as an abstract idea," he says.[34] While we may certainly point out that in Plato's philosophy there is no real interest in abstract ideas either (since abstractions are to be found in the world of coming-into-being-and-passing-away), this corrective in no way alters the difference between them: Tocqueville simply did not believe that philosophy was necessary to save democracy.[35] Nor is it the case that Tocqueville thought such face-to-face encounters were for the purpose of grand politics of the sort that provides a forum for human beings to heroically show forth in speech and in deed, against the backdrop of necessity.[36] Tocqueville's view is comparatively ordinary. Face-to-face encounters between human beings in the mediational fora make their world more expansive, broaden their horizons, unleash their energies — all so that they do not withdraw into themselves and broodingly shut out the world. Neither philosophy of the sort Plato's Dialogues invites nor noble politics in the Aristotelian sense captivated Tocqueville's attention. On his reading, unless certain steps were taken, the end of history would be a time of resignation and stupor. Face-to-face relations between human beings, over "common affairs," draw them out of their soliloquies, and renew their lives in and through their relations with those immediately around them.[37] Man *truly lives*, he thought, only in the mediational space between soliloquy and "they say."

What Tocqueville has in mind, then, is not friendship. Indeed, he scarcely mentions the term in *Democracy in America*. Rather, in light of the fact that the collapse of the aristocratic age has disseveared man from nature and from others, Tocqueville thought that the only way forward was to forge a mode of "gathering together" that took full cognizance of that disseverance. Tocqueville worried that man, lonely and isolated, would choose the easier path of equality in servitude, replete with universal sympathy, well-run monied economies, and individualism. But there was another choice, a difficult choice that involved risk, uncertainty, improvisation, trust, and good will. That choice was face-to-face relations. Here the politics that emerges bespeaks not a man who possesses excellence that renders him worthy of praise, as would have been the case for Aristotle, but rather a man whose frailty in a contingent world entails that he reach out to others with an outstretched hand, perhaps akin to the "saying of the peace" at a church service. Here is a mode of "gathering together" that takes as its reference point the impending closure of Western civilization in the democratic age. Here history, not nature, is the lens through which the matter of "gathering together" is thought through. In this interstitial space between soliloquy and "they say," human beings, in face-to-face relations with others, will find a substitute, a replacement, a surrogate, for all that was salubrious in the old category of friendship, but that is no longer available to modern, historical man. History has made man small.[38] But all is not lost. His "heart [may be] enlarged"[39] through that mode of gathering together that is—let us say it—more akin to Christian fellowship than to Aristotelian friendship. Such enlargement occurs in the vicinity of that central figure in Christian anthropology, one absent in Aristotle—namely, the *neighbor*—and takes its cue from that first disseverance from which we must be healed: the fall of man into history, of which historical consciousness is the résumé.

Notes

1. See Aristotle, *Nicomachean Ethics*, in *The Complete Works of Aristotle*, ed. Jonathan Barnes (Princeton: Princeton University Press, 1984), 1156a6–1156b24.

2. The term "gathering together" appears most prominently in the twentieth century in the thought of Heidegger. See, e.g., Martin Heidegger, "The Question Concerning Technology," in *The Question Concerning Technology and Other Essays,* trans. William Lovitt (New York: Harper & Row, 1977), 20. My invocation of the term is not intended to invite comparisons with Heidegger's larger project, not least because his dissatisfaction with a disenchanted world would have struck Tocqueville as yet another confirmation that Europe, unlike America, had yet to understand both the limits and the promise of modernity.

3. See Adam Smith, *The Wealth of Nations* (Chicago: University of Chicago Press, 1976), 17: "[there is a universal human] propensity to truck, barter, and exchange."

4. I leave aside here Aristotle's suggestion in the last several books of the *Nicomachean Ethics* (see 1177a11–1179a32) that while virtue friendship is what is highest in man qua man, contemplation is higher still and discloses the divine in man.

5. Alexis de Tocqueville, *Democracy in America,* trans. J. P. Mayer (New York: Random House, 1969), vol. II, pt. II, ch. 2, 508 (emphasis added).

6. See Tocqueville, *Democracy in America,* Author's Introduction, 12.

7. Letter of January 1, 1856, cited in *Alexis de Tocqueville: Selected Letters on Politics and Society,* ed. Roger Boesche (Berkeley: University of California Press, 1985), 326. See also Wilhelm Hennis, "In Search of the 'New Science of Politics,'" in Ken Masugi, *Interpreting Tocqueville's* Democracy in America (Savage, Md.: Rowan & Littlefield, 1991), 49: "Tocqueville radicalizes this experience [of loneliness] suffered so much more prevalently in modern society by making this oldest pronouncement of our Judeo-Christian conception of human history the basis of his entire political thought."

8. Tocqueville, *Democracy in America,* vol. II, pt. III, ch. 17, 614.

9. Ibid.

10. See Tocqueville, *Democracy in America,* vol. II, pt. III, ch. 1, 563.

11. Ibid., 562.

12. Friedrich Nietzsche, *Beyond Good and Evil,* trans. Walter Kaufmann (New York: Random House, 1966), pt. IX, §257, 201.

13. See Adam Smith, *Theory of Moral Sentiments,* ed. D. D. Raphael and A. L. Macfie (Indianapolis: Liberty Classics, 1982), pt. I, I, ch. I, para. 2–3, 8–9: "By our imagination we place ourselves in [another man's] situation, we conceive ourselves enduring all the same torments, we enter as it were his body, and become in some measure the same person with him.... His agonies, when they are brought home to ourselves, when we have thus adopted and made them our own, begin at last to affect us.... [T]his is the source of our fellow-feeling for the misery of others."

14. Rawls' project, which begins from the vantage point of a "veil of ignorance" (John Rawls, *A Theory of Justice* [Cambridge: Harvard University Press, 1971], pt. 1, ch. 1, 3, 12), and out of which citizens without a socially constituted history emerge, is the resume of a social order without rank.

15. See Karl Marx, "The Communist Manifesto," in *Marx-Engels Reader*, ed. Richard Tucker (New York: Norton, 1978), 475: "The bourgeoisie, wherever it has got the upper hand, has put an end to all feudal, patriarchal, idyllic relations. It has pitilessly torn asunder the motley feudal ties that bound man to his 'natural superiors,' and left remaining no other nexus between man and man than naked self-interest, than callous 'cash payment.'"

16. See Plato, *Republic*, trans. Richard W. Sterling and William C. Scott (New York: Norton, 1985), bk. IV, 439e–441c, passim.

17. See Tocqueville, *Democracy in America*, vol. II, pt. III, ch. 18, 617: "Each of these associations [nations, classes, or castes] forms, as it were, a particular species of the human race, and though they differ in no essential from the mass of men, they stand to some extent apart and have some needs peculiar to themselves. . . . Honor is nothing but this particular rule, based on a particular state of society, by means of which a people distribute praise and blame."

18. See Tocqueville, *Democracy in America*, vol. II, pt. III, ch. 17, 614. See also ibid., vol. I, pt. II, ch. 10, 406: "There is no sovereign will or national prejudice that can fight for long against cheapness"; and ibid., vol. II, pt. III, ch. 17, 615: "In aristocratic nations money is the key to the satisfaction of but few of the vast array of possible desires; in democracies it is the key to them all."

19. Let us also add that the *carrier* of the idea of honor is the father, and his declining standing in the democratic family makes it unlikely that the idea of honor can long survive. See Tocqueville, *Democracy in America*, vol. II, pt. III, ch. 5, 585: "In America the family, if one takes the word in its Roman and aristocratic sense, no longer exists." Consider, in this context, Socrates' observation that democracy is the regime of "boys and women" (Plato, *Republic*, VIII, 557d).

20. Tocqueville, *Democracy in America*, vol. II, pt. I, ch. 1, 430.

21. Tocqueville mentions Descartes and Luther; I have added Hobbes. See *Democracy in America*, vol. II, pt. I, ch. 1, 430–31.

22. See Bernard Mandeville, *The Fable of the Bees* (Indianapolis: Liberty Classics, 1988), pt. II, dialogue vi, 284 [335]: CLEO. "Man, as I have hinted before, *naturally loves to imitate* what he sees others do, which is the reason that savage people all do the same thing: this hinders them from meliorating their condition" (emphasis added). The editor of Smith's *Wealth of Nations* cites the passage immediately before this one in Mandeville's *Fable* as the possible basis for Smith's locution, "the division of labor" (see Smith, *Wealth of Nations*, vol. I, bk. I, ch. I, 7). What is significant here is that Smith understood that attentiveness to the division of labor would cast into relief the "inefficien-

cies" of the guild-apprenticeship mode of production. Marx's response to Smith is that bourgeois civilization reproduces itself in its "own image" ("Communist Manifesto," in *Marx-Engels Reader*, 477). Bourgeois civilization destroys one form of imitation, only to introduce another.

23. See Tocqueville, *Democracy in America*, vol. II, pt. IV, ch. 6, 692.

24. See James Fennimore Cooper, *The American Democrat* (Indianapolis: Liberty Classics, 1956), 233: "'They say,' is the monarch of this country. No one asks '*who* says it,' so long as it is believed that '*they* say it.' Designing men endeavor to persuade the public, that already 'they say,' what these designing men wish to be said, and the public is only too much disposed blindly to join in the cry of 'they say'" (emphasis in original).

25. Tocqueville, *Democracy in America*, vol. II, pt. I, ch. 2, 436.

26. Ibid., 434: "[In the democratic age, mankind has] a very high and often thoroughly exaggerated conception of human reason." See also ibid., pt. III, ch. 21, 641: "For, taking the general view of world history, one finds that it is less the force of an argument than the authority of a name which has brought about great and rapid changes in accepted ideas."

27. Tocqueville, *Democracy in America*, vol. II, pt. II, ch. 4, 510 (emphasis added).

28. See Tocqueville, *Democracy in America*, vol. II, pt. II, ch. 8, 525–28.

29. See Tocqueville, *Democracy in America*, vol. II, pt. I, ch. 1, 433.

30. It is not simply a coincidence that the liberal/communitarian debate occurs in America during the Cold War, and after the New Deal. Both events consolidated federal power and undermined mediational sites, without which we are left with both a caricatured understanding of the individual and a vacuous notion of community. Neither is adequate to the challenges of the democratic age. See Joshua Mitchell, *The Fragility of Freedom: Tocqueville on Religion, Democracy and the American Future* (Chicago: University of Chicago Press, 1995), ch. 5, 258: "Without [associations] we are condemned to oscillate back and forth between . . . an insular concrete personal life that is abstracted from community and a substantive community that abides only as an empty and dangerous, even if imaginative, abstraction; between the solemn impotence of self-enclosure and the euphoric identification with a national forum of politics that promises to fill the void in our souls but simply cannot."

31. See Tocqueville, *Democracy in America*, vol. II, pt. II, ch. 2, 507 (emphasis in original).

32. Tocqueville, *Democracy in America*, vol. II, pt. II, ch. 5, 515.

33. See Plato, *Republic*, VI, 493a–d.

34. Tocqueville, *Democracy in America*, vol. II, pt. III, ch. 18, 617.

35. Consider, among other things, Tocqueville's criticisms of the attempt by European thinkers to found democracy on philosophical ideas (*Democracy*

in America, vol. I, pt. II, ch. 9, 294); and his assessment of the impossibility of plumbing to first principles with philosophy (ibid., vol. II, pt. I, ch. 4, 443–44).

36. Cf. Hannah Arendt, *The Human Condition* (Chicago: University of Chicago Press, 1958), ch. II, §7, 54–55: "if the world is to contain a public space [which gathers men together and relates them to each other], it cannot be erected for one generation and planned for the living only; it must transcend the life-span of mortal men. Without this transcendence into the potentially earthly immortality, no politics, strictly speaking, no common world and no public realm, is possible."

37. I add here that Tocqueville thought that while the idea of rights may have originally had a religious justification, in this troubled time the only way to secure the idea was through the practical experience with political rights at the local level. See *Democracy in America*, vol. I, pt. II, ch. 6, 239.

38. See Friedrich Nietzsche, *Thus Spoke Zarathustra*, trans. Walter Kaufmann (New York: Penguin Books, 1978), Prologue, §5, 16–19.

39. Tocqueville, *Democracy in America*, vol. II, pt. II, ch. 5, 515.

IV

Contemporary Perspectives

11

Zarathustra and His Asinine Friends

Nietzsche and Taste as the Groundless Ground of Friendship

Richard Avramenko

The Turn from Friendship

To ask of Nietzsche sage wisdom regarding friendship seems somewhat misguided—like turning to Henry VIII for marriage advice or to Jean-Jacques Rousseau for tips on parenting. By most accounts Nietzsche was something of a misanthrope, and his biography recounts a litany of failed friendships and long periods of loneliness.[1] In his thought, especially his later work, he repeatedly praises solitude and individualism and takes to calling himself a "free spirit." These free spirits, he says, are "jealous friends of solitude, of our own deepest, most midnight, most midday solitude."[2] But not only does Nietzsche praise solitude, he goes so far as to disparage the company of others: "He who, when trafficking with men, does not occasionally glisten with all the shades of distress, green and grey with disgust, satiety, sympathy, gloom and loneliness, is certainly not a man of an elevated taste *[Geschmack]*."[3] In an even more vitriolic moment, he remarks, "[S]olitude is with us a virtue: it is a sublime urge and inclination for cleanliness which divines that all contact between man and man—'in society'—must inevitably be unclean. All community makes somehow, somewhere, sometime—'common.'"[4]

So what, then, does this misanthropic loner have to add to a discussion of friendship? According to Ruth Abbey, Nietzsche is not always so caustic with regard to friendship. In the middle period of his work, she argues, the issue was a central concern and, though mostly neglected in the secondary literature, here "Nietzsche suggests that there is a close connection between friendship and selfhood, contending that an individual's friendships reflect something about his or her identity."[5] Moreover, in this period, one is able to discern that for Nietzsche friendship lends itself nicely to self-knowledge, that it is not inimical to self-overcoming, that "friendship is a forum in which pity's positive characteristics can manifest themselves," and finally that "solitude need not exclude friendship."[6] Nietzsche, it appears, was not always the misanthrope he is generally considered to be.

There is, then, a disconnect between the younger Nietzsche and the more mature one with regard to the idea of friendship. As Abbey informs us, "there is a gradual enervation of Nietzsche's depiction of friendship and its importance for higher human beings."[7] There is, so to speak, a turn from friendship. And while Abbey is correct that it was a departure from his optimistic view of friendship, there was really nothing gradual about it. In fact, there is a clear and abrupt departure from his middle work to *Zarathustra* and beyond. One is hard-pressed to find anything praiseworthy of friendship after his famous *Incipit tragoedia* at the end of the book 4 of *The Gay Science*.[8] As it were, when Zarathustra left his home and the lake of his home and went into the mountains, so too did Nietzsche. What, then, is the relationship between Nietzsche's literary introduction of Zarathustra and his turn from friendship?

Many commentators point to a thinker's personal life as the impetus for their meditations on friendship. Jacques Derrida suggests this very thing when he claims that "the great canonical meditations on friendship . . . are linked to the experience of mourning, to the moment of loss—that of the friend or of friendship."⁹ While this may be the case for Cicero, Montaigne, and Blanchot, it simply does not apply to Nietzsche. If, as Abbey claims, friendship is a central concern for Nietzsche during his middle period, then this "moment of loss" must have occurred at the end of the so-called first period, or at the beginning of the second. If there actually is any mourning or moments of loss in Nietzsche's personal life, these supposed ruptures begin either near the end of his second period or well into the third. For example, the death of Albert Brenner, the split with his old friend Carl von Gersdorff, the falling out with Richard Wagner, all take place in about 1879—and many of the middle-period thoughts on friendship had been developed and written by this time.

Of the moments of loss in Nietzsche's life, the most important is his break with his friend Paul Rée and the woman to whom he twice proposed marriage, Lou Salomé. This episode had a profound effect on Nietzsche and occupies a central part of his biography. Readers with even a passing interest in Nietzsche are familiar with the photo of Nietzsche, Rée, and Salomé—Nietzsche and Rée are pulling a cart, in the cart is Salomé with a whip. The photo and the friendship between the three, however, was not a time of mourning for Nietzsche. Instead, it was when the friendships were healthy that Nietzsche wrote *Human, All too Human, Assorted Opinions and Maxims,* and *The Wanderer and his Shadow.* But more importantly, it was while on very good terms with Rée and intimate terms with Salomé that Nietzsche introduced Zarathustra in *The Gay Science* and developed the plan for *Thus Spoke Zarathustra.* In other words, both Nietzsche's praise of friendship and his turn to solitude and misanthropy were written while he was on good terms with his friends.¹⁰

It is thus quite evident that Nietzsche's kind words, if we can call them that, regarding friendship do not correspond with any particular moment of loss or period of mourning in his personal life. Similarly, his praise of solitude and more misanthropic writings were not begotten by any moment of loss. Both periods, in fact, begin while he was still immersed in relatively happy friendships. As such, it is necessary to look elsewhere for Nietzsche's change of heart regarding friendship. I would like to suggest that rather than pointing to any biographical progenitor, we look at the great rupture in his thought that stands directly in the middle of these two positions on friendship: the discovery of the "eternal recurrence of the same" and the introduction of the Zarathustra. Together, these two rubrics of his thought stand as the great symbols for the eclipse of what had theretofore been the ground of friendship—Christianity and the nation-state. In what follows, then, I argue that Nietzsche's later period—the period when he is best known for his ruminations on friendship—can be regarded as a quest for a type of friendship that no longer depends on these moribund grounds; as a quest for friendship that can be grounded on a "groundless ground"—a ground that Nietzsche repeatedly refers to as "taste" *(Geschmack)*.

The Eternal Recurrence and the End of Friendship

We must begin with a few words concerning Nietzsche's middle period, which is also often referred to as his "positivistic" period. *Human, All too Human, The Dawn,* and the first four books of *The Gay Science* are the central texts of this period (1878–82). His late, mature works begin with the idea and commencement of *Thus Spoke Zarathustra*. Let us therefore turn to what Nietzsche says about the turning point in his thought:

> Now I shall relate the history of *Zarathustra*. The fundamental conception of this work, the idea of the eternal recurrence, this highest formula of affirmation that is at all attainable, belongs in August 1881: it was penned on a sheet with the notation underneath, "6000 feet beyond man and time." That day I was walking through the woods along the lake of Silvaplana; at a powerful pyramidal rock not far from Surlei I stopped. It was then this idea came to me.[11]

The turn to solitude therefore begins with the advent of Zarathustra, and Zarathustra is fundamentally about the eternal recurrence. It can be added here that this insight occurred to Nietzsche months before he even made his acquaintance with Lou Salomé.

In any case, as Safranski points out, the first three books of *The Gay Science* were written between August of 1881 and the early part of 1882—after the idea of the eternal recurrence had taken hold of him;

after, as he reported to Peter Gast on August 14, 1881, he shed "tears of joy" and his "delight soared into ecstatic rapture" at having solved such a riddle.[12] Thus, insofar as Nietzsche has two contrasting opinions of friendship, the divide between them must therefore fall into the ideas presented in *The Gay Science*, but not just what falls after the literary introduction of Zarathustra in section 342. What comes in the first 341 sections must also be regarded as part of Nietzsche's postpositivistic period and not only licit, but crucial to understanding his general thoughts on friendship.

The Gay Science marks Nietzsche's turn from positivism to what we might call his postrationalism. It is here that he makes the turn from reason to "taste" *(Geschmack).* It is fairly widely agreed that Nietzsche was no great proponent of rationalism, but it is less common to couch his alternative in terms of taste. Moreover, even if we can talk about a contrast between rationalism and taste, it must also be kept in mind that for Nietzsche this turn is not for everyone. Taste, unlike rationalism, has no universal aspirations. In a section titled "The greatest danger," Nietzsche suggests that it is only because the majority of mankind has considered their rationality, or "the discipline of their minds—their rationality," to be a matter of pride and virtue that the human race has not perished. The greatest danger to mankind would be if there was ever "an eruption of madness—which means the eruption of arbitrariness in feeling, seeing, and hearing, the enjoyment of the mind's lack of discipline, the joy in human unreason."[13] Whereas reason is nonarbitrary, taste is completely arbitrary. Taste resides in the abode of the particular, in the abode of what Nietzsche calls madness. Taste is dangerous, uncertain, unpredictable; intellect and reason are safe and, at bottom, aim at certainty and predictability. Nietzsche obviously prefers the former, but he is clear concerning the utility of the latter: "the virtuous intellects are needed—oh, let me use the most unambiguous word—what is needed is *virtuous stupidity,* stolid metronomes for the slow spirit, to make sure that the faithful of the great shared faith stay together and continue their dance."[14] The Madman, the one with a developed sense of taste, is the exception, and "there actually are things to be said in favor of the exception, provided that it never becomes the rule."[15] The exception is uncertain, unpredictable, dangerous. Uncertainty, unpredictability, and danger are good. One must have a taste for the exception. The exception is good. The exception is never common. The common is never good. The Madman has a taste for the exception and a taste for the dangerous. The Madman *is* the exception. The introduction of Zarathustra and the eternal recurrence must be seen as literary turning point between reason on the one hand, and taste on the other.

There is no need, then, to give a reasonable account of the eternal recurrence. The eternal recurrence is a discovery that will be transmitted "tastefully," rather reasonably. Consider the language Nietzsche invokes when he first presents the idea:

> The greatest weight.—What, if some day or night a demon were to steal after you in your loneliest loneliness and say to you: "This life as you now live it and have lived it, you will have to live once more and innumerable times more; and there will be nothing new in it, but every pain and every joy and every thought and sigh and everything unutterably small or great in your life will have to return to you, all in the same succession and sequence—even this spider and this moonlight between the trees, and even this moment and I myself. The eternal hourglass of existence is turned upside down again and again—and you with it, speck of dust!"—Would you not throw yourself down and gnash your teeth and curse the demon who spoke thus? Or have you once experienced a tremendous moment when you would have answered him: "You are a god and never have I heard anything more divine!" If this thought gained possession of you, it would change you as you are or perhaps crush you; the question in each and every thing, "Do you desire this once more, and innumerable times more?" would lie upon your actions as the greatest weight! Or how well disposed would you have to become to yourself and to life *to crave nothing more fervently* than this ultimate eternal confirmation and seal?[16]

The language of weight, of pain, of hearing, of moonlight, of gnashing teeth, of possession is invoked. The idea is not presented as a proof or as an argument. It is a story about a demon and a spider. It stimulates the imagination and the senses, not the rational mind.

In the same section of *Ecce Homo* that Nietzsche describes the irruptive idea of the eternal recurrence he also describes a change in his taste:

"If I reckon back a few months from this day, I find as an omen a sudden and profoundly decisive change in my taste *(Geschmack)*, especially in music. Perhaps the whole of *Zarathustra* may be reckoned as music; certainly a rebirth of the art of *hearing* was among its preconditions."[17] But the change in taste at this time pertained not only to music. In book 3 of *The Gay Science*, in an aphorism called *Against Christianity*, Nietzsche declares another shift: "What is now decisive against Christianity is our taste *[Geschmack]*, no longer our reasons *[Gründe]*."[18] The turn from his positivist period to his third period—from optimism regarding friendship to pessimism—therefore coincides with a shift from reason to taste. While he always rejected Christianity and the old table of values, as he was wont to call it, his objection comes to be couched in the language of taste, rather than reason. The objection, then, must necessarily come from a Madman, and this is precisely on whom Nietzsche calls to deliver his famous declaration of the death of God:

> The madman.—Have you not heard of that madman who lit a lantern in the bright morning hours, ran to the marketplace, and cried incessantly: "I seek God! I seek God!"—As many of those who did not believe in God were standing around just then, he provoked much laughter. Has he got lost? asked one. Did he lose his way like a child? asked another. Or is he hiding? Is he afraid of us? Has he gone away on a voyage? emigrated?—Thus they yelled and laughed. The madman jumped into their midst and pierced them with his eyes. "Whither is God?" he cried; "I will tell you. We have killed him—you and I. All of us are his murderers.[19]

What we know, then, is that Nietzsche's opinion of friendship changed with his discovery of the eternal recurrence. Moreover, the eternal recurrence coincides with the Madman's "tasteful" murder of God. We also know that the eternal recurrence is not just a doctrine of affirmation that comes *ex nihilo*. In fact, it is no doctrine at all, as doctrines rely on reason for their illumination. With the declaration of the eternal recurrence, Nietzsche is turning from all apperceived doctrines. He is (re)introducing uncertainty and unpredictability. It would thus be better to refer to the eternal recurrence as a flavor, one for which we must develop a taste. The eternal recurrence, as Nietzsche well knows, is a bitter medicine to swallow and this is precisely why he calls it "the greatest weight."

The Eternal Recurrence and the End of Christianity

The eternal recurrence did not arise *ex nihilo*. Instead, it must be regarded as patently anti-Christian and part of an older debate. In his *City of God*, St. Augustine himself attacks the proponents of this understanding of time. There are those, Augustine argues, who suggest that humans might be happier if they opt out of the Christian vision of linear time— the vision of time that would have us born, live, then die a mortal death. As a way out of this worldly wretchedness, one might be tempted to repudiate time as process. That is, the unhappiness caused by the awareness of existence as merely a process toward diminution can be resolved by supposing "an infinite series of dissolutions and restorations at fixed periods in the course of ages."[20] In short, one can propose a cyclical theory of time. With this theory one can say that although time may be a process toward death, there is consolation in the fact that one will return to the world in precisely the same manner, an infinite number of times. This alternative theory is therefore one in which time has neither beginning nor end. This position, of course, was the one held by Plato[21] and the Neo-Platonists and appears anew in Nietzsche's eternal recurrence of the same. Augustine calls proponents of this vision "Physicists" and says that in their postulates of periodic cycles

> they asserted that by those cycles all things in the universe have been continually renewed and repeated, in the same form, and thus there will be hereafter an unceasing sequence of ages, passing away and coming again in revolution. The cycles may take place in one continuing world, or it may be that at certain periods the world disappears and reappears, showing the same features, which appear as new, but which in fact have been in the past and will return in the future.[22]

For Augustine this position is cause for even more unhappiness than is supposed to arise from linear time. If the goal is happiness and this goal is achieved through wisdom, then the cyclical theory of time would mean that one could never be happy in either this life or the next.

If we keep in mind that for Augustine happiness is attained when certain desires are satisfied, then the reason for this rejection will be evident. In the Christian formulation, the desire of the soul is satisfied with Truth. Therefore the happy soul will be the soul with wisdom; one must keep in mind, however, that one can never be truly happy if one lives in fear of losing that which satisfies one's desires. One cannot live in fear, Augustine argues repeatedly, and be happy at the same time. Thus the wisdom that satisfies the soul must be eternal and eternally one's own. The problem with cyclical theories of time is that

> they are utterly unable to rescue the immortal soul from this merry-go-round, even when it has attained wisdom; it must proceed on an unremitting alternation between false bliss and genuine misery. For how can there be true bliss, without any certainty of its eternal continuance, when the soul in its ignorance does not know of the misery to come or else unhappily fears its coming in the midst of its blessedness?[23]

Put otherwise, happiness is not true happiness if it is temporary happiness. This is either false bliss or deception and, according to Augustine, no man wants to be deceived. Thus to be happy man requires wisdom that does not change and cannot be taken from him; he requires an eternal, singular, unification with eternal wisdom.

The problem with cyclical theories of time is that they "allow no room for the eternal liberation and felicity of the soul."[24] Since liberation from the original corruption begins with the Incarnation, the intermingling of time and eternity and its concomitant promise of eternal felicity (life), cyclical theories of time must be refuted lest one also accept that Christ will die again and again—lest one accept that Christ himself is subject to eternal suffering. For this reason Augustine says that we must "escape from these false circuitous courses, whatever they may be, which have been devised by these misled and misleading sages, by keeping to the straight path in the right direction under the guidance of sound teaching."[25] The straight path is, of course, the understanding of time characteristic of Christianity. In this view, humans must hold to a progressive movement of time, from a beginning point to a contemplated end, regardless of one's happiness *en route*. For the sound teaching Augustine paraphrases Romans 6:9: "'Christ died once for all for our sins'; and 'in rising from the dead he is never to die again: he is no longer under the sway of death.' After the resurrection 'we shall be with the Lord forever.'"[26] In the Christian understanding, it is at the end of the process toward death that happiness is possible. Unpredictability and uncertainty are unacceptable; one cannot live in fear and be happy—yet Zarathustra has a taste for danger.

The Eternal Recurrence and the End of the Nation-State

That Nietzsche's declaration of the eternal recurrence is not just an alternative to, but a deep repudiation of, Christianity should be quite clear. Not only does he invert the very foundation of Christian theology, he has both the Madman and Zarathustra declare "God is dead." His changed position regarding friendship therefore comes on the heels of this new turn from Christianity. The turn is new here not because Nietzsche suddenly became anti-Christian, but because in his positivist period his opposition came from a more scientific vantage. With the eternal recurrence, however, Nietzsche also abandoned this vantage. This modern, positivist opposition, it occurred to him, was merely another sort of organic cosmology. Like Christianity, these modern mechanistic metaphors of the universe are mere salves for the uncertainty and danger that is natural in the human condition. In other words, the eternal recurrence rejects the Christian cosmic view but at the same time it is not a turn to the great "macrocosmic organism" of the modern rational world. In fact, the eternal recurrence also stands in direct opposition to this world. It presents a new experience on a cosmic level and with it, as Safranski states, Nietzsche is "establishing contact with the colossal vastness of which we are part, [but] it does not mean turning this vastness into a living organism, which would render it too pleasant, anthropomorphic, and reverent."[27] In his notebooks, just a few weeks after the discovery of the eternal recurrence at Lake Silvaplana, Nietzsche wrote: "The modern scientific counterpart to the belief in God is belief in the universe as an organism: I find that revolting" (9,522).²⁸ His intention with the eternal recurrence is to steer very clear of this syrupy, sappy, organic oneness. In Safranski's words, "he ruled out any desire to return to the womb. [He] had not gone to all the effort of liberating himself from a sheltering God just to crawl back into the godlike womb of the universe."²⁹

The eternal recurrence is therefore more than a rejection of the universal God of Christianity—it is also a rejection of universal rationalism and the artificial categories spilling therefrom. We have already seen Nietzsche's invocation of taste, rather than reason, against Christianity. In terms of the artificial categories, his taste therefore also rebels against that most pervasive manifestation of universal rationalism, the nation-state. In Nietzsche's understanding, the nation-state itself grew directly out of Protestant Christianity, which he calls a "peasant rebellion of the spirit,"³⁰ with Martin Luther in the vanguard. It was Luther's rebellion, after all, that replaced the church with the state. At first, this sounds as if Nietzsche laments the end of the Roman Catholic Church; and if we make clear what Nietzsche understands by "church," it turns out that this is so:

> Let us not forget in the end what a church is, as opposed to any "state." A church is above all a structure for ruling that secures the highest rank for the *more spiritual* human beings and that *believes* in the power of spirituality to the extent of forbidding itself the use of all the cruder instruments of force; and on this score alone the church is under all circumstances a *nobler* institution than the state.³¹

For Nietzsche, then, both the church and the state are apparatuses formed for the administration of power. The state, however, is the immanent manifestation of precisely those who have no taste—which is to say, no taste for danger and the exception. The state cannot stomach unpredictability and arbitrariness. The state therefore necessarily becomes the embodiment of the crudely violent application of modern rationalism.

The church's authority, on the other hand, rested on the spiritual superiority of the priestly caste, and this authority was largely derived of the awe and reverence they inspired in the common people. This awe and reverence was in large part thanks to the fact that the priesthood abstained from sexual intercourse. As Nietzsche puts it, "three quarters of the reverence of which the common people, especially the women among the common people, are capable, rests on the faith that a person who is an exception at this point will be an exception in other respects as well."[32] Luther, however, gave women to the Protestant priests, and in so doing removed their spiritual authority. As a result, he also had to take from the priest the confessional, and the confessional is that institution that is a shining example of human beings relating to another human being not through their reason, but through their "taste." Of course, in the confessional the connection is not based on "taste" per se, but rather hearing, and hearing is bound up with the senses and the arts Nietzsche explicitly claims to be reintroducing with Zarathustra: "Luther, having given the priest woman, had to *take* away from him auricular confession; that was right psychologically. With that development the Christian priest was, at bottom, abolished, for his most profound utility had always been that he was a holy ear, a silent well, a grave for secrets."[33]

Out of Luther's Reformation, Nietzsche claims, grew several phenomena. First, when the people lost their taste for the hieratic character of the church, the new formula became "Everyone his own priest." Whereas formerly the priest embodied the higher spiritual type, the everyman-priest became the norm and the practice of associating with others through hearing (which is to say, taste) waned. This he calls the "plebeianism of the spirit" and is marked by the reliance on reason, or "cunning" *(Verschlagenheit)*.[34]

In addition to the erosion of the authority of the church and the atrophy of the art of hearing, Nietzsche points to two other phenomena emerging from Luther's revolt. In general terms he calls them "modern science" and "modern ideas," and the most important manifestation of these is the nation-state and its unholy spawn, nationalism. The attack on Luther and the resulting nationalism picks up steam in *The Genealogy of Morals*. Here, in contrast to the nobility of spirit he sees in many Asian, which is to say, hieratic, cultures, he says,

> one should recall Luther . . . that "most eloquent" and presumptuous peasant Germany has ever produced, and the tone he preferred when conversing with God. Luther's attack on the mediating saints

of the church (and especially on "the Devil's Sow, the pope") was, beyond any doubt, fundamentally the attack of a lout who could not stomach the *good etiquette* of the church, that reverential etiquette of the hieratic taste *[Geschmack]* which permits only the more initiated and silent into the holy of holies and closes it to louts. Here of all places the louts were to be kept from raising their voices; but Luther, the peasant, wanted it altogether different: this arrangement was not *German* enough for him: he wanted above all to speak directly, to speak himself, to speak "informally" with his God.—Well, he did it.[35]

And above all, he did it in German. In short, the Reformation led by Luther effaced the old order—the hieratic order predicated on taste and the "nobility of spirit"—and replaced it with a rational, state-based order. The new basis for divisions in Europe ended up in the Thirty Year War, concluded with the Peace of Westphalia in 1648, and directly led to the birth of the nation-state and what Nietzsche repeatedly calls "petty politics."[36] Luther, he claims, was "calamitously myopic, superficial, and incautious."[37]

So with the discovery of the eternal recurrence and the pronouncement of the death of God, Nietzsche is also pronouncing the end of the nation-state. It is important to recognize that this pronouncement also amounts to a renouncement—a renouncement of nationalism in general, but especially of German nationalism. The founders of nationalism, like Luther, are called "ambitious artists who like to pose as ascetics and priests but who are at bottom only tragic buffoons."[38] Worse than these buffoons, Nietzsche points to the "latest speculators in idealism, the anti-Semites, who today roll their eyes in a Christian-Aryan-bourgeois manner and exhaust one's patience by trying to rouse up all the horned-beast elements in the people by a brazen abuse of the cheapest kind of all agitator's tricks," which deliberately lead to "national constriction and vanity, the strong but narrow principle '*Deutschland, Deutschland über alles*,' and then the *paralysis agitans* of 'modern ideas.'"[39] The eternal recurrence is therefore a boundary—it is a gateway that, once crossed through, closes the door to both Christianity and the nation-state. And Christianity (with its fellowship and love of the neighbor) and the nation-state (with its nationalism and patriotism) had theretofore been the ground for friendship. With the introduction of Zarathustra and the eternal recurrence, the historical ground of friendship was wiped away.

The Groundless Ground of Friendship

In February of 1869, after being appointed assistant professor at the university in Basel, Switzerland, Nietzsche renounced his Prussian citizenship. There is no real evidence to suggest that this was a precondition of the appointment, rather he gave it up out of a sense of duty to his new university. A few months later (April 17), it was made permanent when the Prussian government officially canceled his citizenship. Presumably Nietzsche was going to take Swiss citizenship, but because he never met the residency requirements, he never received it. As a result, he was legally stateless for the rest of his life. When, just over a year later (July 1870) the Franco-Prussian war broke out, Nietzsche was granted a leave of absence from the university to participate in the war. However, because of his association with Switzerland and his lack of Prussian citizenship, he could only participate as a medical orderly. Nietzsche, the stateless philologist, could only work as a stretcher bearer for just over two months, until he fell ill with dysentery and diphtheria. Following this experience, his health deteriorated forcing him to take medical leaves from the university until finally, in 1879, he retired from the university and began what can best be described as a thoroughly nomadic period.

It is from this vantage, then, that Nietzsche writes about friendship. About the time that he discovers the eternal recurrence, he finds himself a stateless man wandering Europe. His best friend is Paul Rée, a Jewish psychologist; he has twice proposed marriage to the itinerant daughter of a Russian aristocrat of Huguenot descent; he has been basically excommunicated by the scholarly world for his *Birth of Tragedy;* and his former friend Richard Wagner has turned to Christianity and anti-Semitism. Prior to the advent of the eternal recurrence, Nietzsche looked at Germany, German music, and German culture in general as nourishment for an elevated and tasteful sort of friendship. After the experience of the Franco-Prussian war, this all changed. Rather than looking at "Germans" and Germany as the ground for friendship, he begins to think of the nation-state as a moribund entity breeding the wrong sort of relationships between people. The new ground for friendship could not be limited by the artificial boundaries of the nation-state and thus Nietzsche begins referring to himself as a "good European." As he puts it:

> European man and the abolition of nations.—Trade and industry, the post and the book-trade, the possession in common of all higher culture, rapid changing of home and scene, the nomadic life now lived by all who do not own land—these circumstances are necessarily bringing with them a weakening and finally an abolition of nations, at least the European: so that as a consequence of continually crossing a mixed race, that of European man, must come into being out of them. This goal is at present being worked against, consciously or unconsciously, by the separation of nations through the production of *national* hostilities.[40]

This "artificial nationalism" as he calls it, is the product of certain princely dynasties and businesses that can profit from such artificial boundaries. Once the source of these hostilities and their artificiality are recognized, "one should not be afraid to proclaim oneself a *good European* and actively work for the amalgamation of nations."[41]

It is quite clear that for Nietzsche, then, the very category of the nation-state had ceased to be the ground from which friendship can grow. The proclamation of the eternal recurrence is therefore as much a declaration of the death of God as it is a declaration of the death of the nation-state. Killing God and the nation-state, however, does little to cultivate a new ground for friendship. Instead, it forced him to declare, as early as *Human, All too Human*, "how uncertain is the ground upon which all our alliances and friendships rest, how close at hand are icy downpours or stormy weather, how isolated each man is!"[42] Without the church as the ground for "tasteful" relationships between man and man, without the nation-state as the proving ground for friendship, Nietzsche is stymied as to where he can turn.

It is in this light that the second part of the Madman's declaration of the death of God becomes clearer. The Madman, we recall, says we have killed God, that all of us are his murderer. But by killing God we have poisoned the soil out of which the nation-state grew. With neither God nor the nation-state, we must ask:

> [H]ow did we do this? How could we drink up the sea? Who gave us the sponge to wipe away the entire horizon? What were we doing when we unchained this earth from its sun? Whither is it moving now? Whither are we moving? Away from all suns? Are we not plunging continually? Backward, sideward, forward, in all directions? Is there still any up or down? Are we not straying as through an infinite nothing? Do we not feel the breath of empty space? Has it not become colder? Is not night continually closing in on us? Do we not need to light lanterns in the morning? Do we hear nothing as yet of the noise of the gravediggers who are burying God? Do we smell nothing as yet of the divine decomposition? Gods, too, decompose. God is dead. God remains dead. And we have killed him.[43]

Without God, without the nation-state, we are without our customary horizons.[44] We simply have no anchor, no fixed point around which our friendships can revolve. We are, quite plainly, homeless, and friendship is left to teeter on uncertainty and unpredictability.

One of the most important (and neglected) passages in *The Gay Science* is titled "We who are homeless." It is here that Nietzsche begins searching for an alternative ground for friendship. He writes: "Among Europeans today there is no lack of those who are entitled to call themselves homeless in a distinctive and honorable sense: it is to them that I especially commend my secret wisdom and *gaya scienza*."[45] These proud and homeless ones, he claims, must be content in their homelessness. They must reject the manifold tasteless ideas being flung from the marketplace. They must reject both the conservatives on the right and the leftist reformers:

> We "conserve" nothing: neither do we want to return to any past periods; we are not by any means "liberal"; we do not work for "progress"; we do not need to plug up our ears against the sirens who in the market place sing of the future: their song about "equal rights," "a free society," "no more masters and no servants" has no allure for us.[46]

In other words, he knows well that this sort of friendship can grow neither from the moribund past nor from the ground of equality. Those who talk in these terms are just vendors screaming the slogans of petty politics.

In addition, just as these homeless must reject the "religion of pity" and humanitarianism, they must, in no uncertain terms, reject the growing tide of nationalism and petty politics of the most tasteless sort:

> No, we do not love humanity; but on the other hand we are not nearly "German" enough... to advocate nationalism and race hatred and to be able to take pleasure in the national scabies of the heart and blood poisoning that now leads the nations of Europe to delimit and barricade themselves against each other as if it were a matter of quarantine. For that we are too openminded, too malicious, too spoiled, also too well informed, too "traveled": we far prefer to live on mountains, apart, "untimely," in past or future centuries, merely in order to keep ourselves from experiencing the silent rage to which we know we should be condemned as eyewitnesses of politics that are desolating the German spirit by making it vain and that is, moreover, petty politics.[47]

And finally, these homeless must also reject the Christian alternative:

> We have also outgrown Christianity and are averse to it—precisely because we have grown out of it, because our ancestors were Christians who in their Christianity were uncompromisingly upright: for their faith they willingly sacrificed possessions and position, blood and fatherland. We—do the same. For what? For our unbelief? For every kind of unbelief? No, you know better than that, friends! The hidden Yes in you is stronger than all Nos and Maybes that afflict you and your age like a disease; and when you have to embark on the sea, you emigrants, you, too, are compelled to this by—a faith![48]

The secret wisdom in *The Gay Science* is therefore a declaration of a new ground for friendship. It commends a Yes-saying type of statelessness. It praises the type of man who, without Christianity, without a state, maintains his spirit and spiritedness. As Nietzsche puts it, "we are, in one word—and let this be our word of honor—good Europeans, the heirs of Europe, the rich, the oversupplied, but also overly obligated heirs of thousands of years of European spirit."[49]

The secret wisdom Nietzsche is sharing in *The Gay Science* is his Yes-saying wanderer, Zarathustra.

Zarathustra's Teaching of Friendship

With Zarathustra, Nietzsche gives us the teacher of the eternal recurrence.[50] He gives us the figure who both gives an emphatic Yes to The Greatest Weight and shows others how to do the same. He gives us a figure who epitomizes the hidden Yes—the Yes to the ring of existence. Zarathustra is the quintessential example of a man freed from the tastelessness of (Lutheran) Christianity and who has overcome such "modern ideas" as universal rationalism. However, in giving us this figure, Nietzsche also presents us with a "fugitive from all fatherlands and forefatherlands."[51] Zarathustra, because he says Yes to the eternal recurrence, must also be saying no to the nation-state and Christianity. The whole of *Thus Spoke Zarathustra* can thus be understood as Zarathustra's quest for a type of friendship that can grow out of this groundless ground—that can grow after the discovery of the eternal recurrence, the death of the Christian God, and the eclipse of the nation-state. Zarathustra the Godless is a friendless, uprooted wanderer; the words of his shadow might well be spoken by himself: "'I am a wanderer, who has already walked far at your heels: always going but without a goal and without a home: so that, truly, I am almost the eternal Wandering Jew, except that I am neither eternal nor a Jew.'"[52] Zarathustra, even more than he is the teacher of the eternal recurrence, is the wandering teacher of postmodern friendship. As Zarathustra puts it, "I do not teach you the neighbor but the friend."[53]

In this vein, some insight might be had from considering Jacques Derrida's reading of Nietzsche on friendship. According to Derrida, no one has "broken more radically than Nietzsche with the Greek or Christian canon of friendship"[54] Both the Greek and Christian canons associate friendship with the hearth, or the household, and thus there is always an underlying theme of brotherhood, or fraternity. For Derrida, this ground necessarily leads to an exclusionary type of friendship. It means that while it may be open and friendly to anyone who falls inside this range of fraternity, it is particularly hostile to those outside it. It is hostile to the "other," and this includes the linguistically different, the racially different, the ethnically different, and, importantly, women. Thus in appropriating Nietzsche and his Zarathustra, Derrida thinks he has found a ground for "a friendship without hearth, of a *philía* without *oikeiótes*. Ultimately without presence, without resemblance, without affinity, without analogy. Along with presence, truth itself would start to tremble. . . . Is an *aneconomic* friendship possible?"[55] For Derrida, like Zarathustra, the task is to find a groundless ground for friendship.

Where Derrida departs from Zarathustra, and we should be very clear on this, where he departs from Nietzsche in general, is in his search for a universal and all-inclusive friendship. Derrida would like to construe friendship in *Zarathustra* as a

> friendship to come and friendship for the future. For to love friendship, it is not enough to know how to bear the other in mourning; one must love the future. And there is no more just category for the future than that of the "perhaps." Such a thought conjoins friendship, the future, and the *perhaps* to open on to the coming of what comes—that is to say, necessarily in the regime of a possible whose possibilization must prevail over the impossible.[56]

The friendship of the future is grounded on contingency and uncertainty. With this, Nietzsche would agree. The major departure is Derrida's contention that because of this contingent uncertainty, we must be open to whosoever may come. Derrida's friendship of the future includes being open to any mendicant wanderer who may knock at our door. Like his postmodern brethren, he seeks to destroy all boundaries, to deconstruct all barriers. Nietzsche, on the contrary, seeks to destroy only the tasteless boundaries.[57]

Moreover, in this description of friendship of the future, of a "perhaps" friendship, one detects a sort of enthusiasm, in its most literal sense. In it, one almost hears parousiastic whispers. One would almost think that Derrida's "friendship to come" is imbued with messianic undertones. If we look to the concluding line of Derrida's original essay on friendship, this suggestion becomes less of a suggestion. There he says that Nietzsche calls "the friend by a name that is no longer that of a neighbor, perhaps no longer that of a man."[58] John Caputo also reads

Derrida in this way, stating that "the Nietzsche we find in *Politics and Friendship* ... is a very *messianic,* somewhat Jewish Zarathustra ... a Dionysian rabbi, a kind of 'Abraham of Paris,' a very heteromorphic figure of a Dionysus wrapped in a tallith unfurling a sacred scroll."[59] Friendship as being open to any mendicant wanderer who may knock at our door is thus bound up with both the Greek and Jewish tradition of hospitality. In the Greek tradition, one must be hospitable to the stranger because it might actually be a god in disguise. In some Jewish traditions, at Passover seders the door is opened and a cup of wine is poured for Elijah for similar reasons. In this tradition, or at least in the folklore tradition, there are tales of poor strangers coming to Passover seders who turn out to be angels, or messengers of God. Thus in the course of the proscribed seder, Jews state that anyone who is hungry should join them that night, not just for the sake of offering hospitality to any stranger sent by God, but because every visitor, particularly on Passover, may be godly or God-sent.[60]

That Zarathustra wanders statelessly (like Nietzsche) with his shadow is clear. That Zarathustra rejects the neighbor (which is to say, Christianity) as the source of friendship is clear. That Zarathustra seeks a groundless ground for friendship is also clear. But it is not so clear that Zarathustra either seeks or waits for a messiah. The messianic vision, like the Christian Parousiastic vision, contradicts the cyclical understanding of time found in the eternal recurrence. Soteriology, be it Christian or Hebraic, entails an End Time, which is precisely the closed, limited ground from which Nietzsche is departing. These messianic practices (if they can both be called that) may appeal to Derrida, but they also depend on a virtue—namely, pity—from which Nietzsche is departing.[61] Closedness and pity are simply not to Zarathustra's taste.

Zarathustra's Asinine Friends

In saying that the future friend is perhaps no longer a man, Derrida might well be onto something else—one might also consider Zarathustra's animals. Zarathustra, we know, left his fatherland when he was thirty and went to live in solitude in the mountains. There he lived with his friends, the eagle and the serpent, for ten years until his cup began to overflow with wisdom. As Zarathustra says, "Behold! This cup wants to be empty again, and Zarathustra wants to be man again."⁶² While his friendship with animals is salubrious for a time, it comes to pass that the wise man will need to be amid those who will listen to him. The animals, it would seem, are not capable of eating the honey he has to offer; they cannot drink from the cup he has filled. The eagle and the serpent do not share his taste and it is precisely this—a friendship based on taste—that Zarathustra seeks. As he puts it a little later, "one day solitude will make you weary, one day your pride will bend and your courage will break. One day you will cry: "I am alone!"⁶³

When this happens to Zarathustra, he wanders down from his mountain looking for friends. On his way to the nearest town (called The Pied Cow—not coincidentally, a herd animal), he crosses paths with the holy hermit. The hermit, who also lives apart from other humans, has not heard the news that God is dead. That he is still clinging to this moribund Christian category disqualifies him from being Zarathustra's friend. So Zarathustra moves on to The Pied Cow where he finds a marketplace full of potential friends. There he declares himself to be the teacher not of the eternal recurrence, but of the Superman: "*I teach you the Superman.* Man is something to be overcome."⁶⁴ The scene resembles closely the Madman's declaration in *The Gay Science*. There, however, the Madman goes into the marketplace and declares the death of God. Here, Zarathustra goes into the marketplace and declares the Superman. The usual way of reading this is that Zarathustra is teaching that the current consciousness of mankind needs to be overcome; that should the people in the marketplace heed his advice, the human race will catapult into a new era of more highly evolved individuals. This reading is not altogether inaccurate, but there is another way to understand this teaching. When Zarathustra announces the Superman, he is actually teaching the way to a new mode of friendship. He is teaching the people a different mode of articulation.

We know that after the discovery of the eternal recurrence, the nation-state and Christianity no longer suffice as the ground for friendship—that the sort of friendship Nietzsche is seeking cannot be predicated on reason or Christian virtue (pity). Instead, he suggests that taste is the best way to describe the groundless ground for friendship. We also know that taste is arbitrary, that taste resides in the abode of the Madman, that the Madman has a taste for the exception, that the Madman is the exception. Now, listen to what Zarathustra says:

"Behold, I teach you the Superman: he is this lightening, he is this madness!"⁶⁵ When Zarathustra enters the marketplace in The Pied Cow, he is teaching taste! He is asking them to "hear" him. He is teaching friendship not based on reason, not based on virtue, but rather on taste, that most dangerous, uncertain, and unpredictable mode of human articulation:

> What is the greatest thing you can experience? It is the hour of the great contempt. The hour in which even your happiness grows loathsome to you, and your reason and your virtue also.
>
> The hour when you say: "What good is my happiness? It is poverty and dirt and a miserable ease. But my happiness should justify existence itself!"
>
> The hour when you say: "What good is my reason? Does it long for knowledge as the lion for its food? It is poverty and dirt and a miserable ease!"
>
> The hour when you say: What good is my virtue? It has not yet driven me mad! How tired I am of my good and my evil! It is all poverty and dirt and miserable ease!"⁶⁶

The people in the marketplace, of course, do not understand and his failure forces him to announce "the most contemptible man: and that is the *Ultimate Man*."⁶⁷

Tracy Strong suggests that Zarathustra fails in the marketplace because the crowd does not share the same experiences. Teaching, he claims, "is an activity that can only meet with success when there is already a community of experience. One can't teach or tell someone something unless the other person would be in a position to ask for that particular thing. Unless there were a preexistent community (of the unquestioned), telling something to someone, or trying to teach him virtue, is likely to be an expedition on the wrong path."⁶⁸ If Strong is right, Zarathustra's failure is a problem of epistemology; to say that the crowd does not have the experience to understand is to say that they lack data. To experience is, at bottom, to gather data, and data provides the grist for comparing and contrasting what is known to what is unknown. To learn by way of experience is therefore to employ controls. It is, in modern parlance, to be empirical and it betrays a particular epistemological relation to one's world and one's community.

If we keep in mind that experience, empirical, empire, and imperial all grow from the same Greek root, this will be clearer. The Greek root is *peras,* which means end, or limit, or boundary. What Zarathustra—the teacher of the eternal recurrence, the teacher of the "madness"—teaches is a friendship that defies these limits. It resides outside the artificial boundaries begotten of pity and reason. The problem in the market place, contrary to what Strong would have us think, is not one of epistemology. The problem is that the crowd lacks taste. They lack taste for the exception, for what is different. They yearn for certainty and predictability. As Zarathustra puts it, they are the herd, and "everyone wants the same thing, everyone is the same: whoever thinks otherwise goes voluntarily into the madhouse."[69]

The herd of Ultimate Men cannot have had the same experience as Zarathustra. They simply do not have an ear for Zarathustra's song. They look, but cannot hear, prompting Zarathustra to say, "There they stand (he said to his heart), there they laugh: they do not understand me, I am not the mouth for these ears."[70] He knows they have ears. He knows they can hear. But they look at him and can only blink. To found the friendship Zarathustra is seeking they must hear with their eyes. They can only relate to him as a friend if they somehow invert their senses. They must elongate their ears. They need to open their eyes and hear him. The traditional association of knowing with seeing must be shattered. As Nietzsche puts it in *The Gay Science,* their senses must work vicariously: "'Our eyes are also intended for hearing,' said an old father confessor who had become deaf; 'and among the blind he that has the longest ears is king.'"[71]

So Zarathustra finds himself in The Pied Cow amidst a herd of Ultimate Men. For him, the people are like animals, but not like the proud and wise animals he left at his cave.[72] Zarathustra leaves his solitude to teach a new type of friendship. He comes into the marketplace to teach the crowd how to hear the "hidden Yes" that lies in them. He comes to teach them to say Yea to the eternal recurrence. Instead, they say Yea to the Ultimate Man: "'Give us this Ultimate Man, O Zarathustra' so they cried—'make us into this Ultimate Man! You can have the Superman!'"[73] They say Yea, but do it like the animal with the longest ears, the jackass.

In what is perhaps the funniest joke in *Thus Spoke Zarathustra,* Nietzsche invokes the ass. In German, the "Yes" Zarathustra's teaching is supposed to invoke is *Ja*. The braying of an ass is rendered *I-A*, a virtual homonym. In the Hollingdale translation *Ja* is "yea," and *I-A* is "ye-a." The herd of Ultimate Men are portrayed as a mostly contented lot, happy with their "miserable ease." Their capacity for friendship with Zarathustra comes more fully to light when he states:

> Truly, I dislike also those who call everything good and this world the best of all. I call such people the all-contented.
>
> All-contentedness that knows how to taste *[schmecken]* everything: that is not the best taste *[Geschmack]*! I honour the obstinate, fastidious tongues and stomachs that have learned to say "I" and "Yea" and "No." But to chew and digest everything—that is to have a really swinish nature! Always to say Yea—only the ass and those like him have learned that.[74]

The herd at The Pied Cow is neither bovine nor porcine. They are Zarathustra's asinine friends. They are animals, but not like the proud and wise animals waiting for him at his cave. They have tongues, but they have no taste. They have long, asinine ears, but they hear nothing. They may have left Christian virtue behind, they may have abandoned the nation-state as the ground for their friendships, but they do not hear the Dionysian song of Zarathustra. They simply have not the taste for what Zarathustra feeds them—the possibility of a higher form of friendship. Their asinine ears are inadequate, which reminds us of the tradition of frustration Dionysus has finding friends sharing his taste:

> "O Dionysus, divine one, why do you pull me by my ears?" Ariadne once asked her philosophic lover during one of those famous dialogues on Naxos. "I find a kind of humor in your ears, Ariadne: why are they not even longer?"

Notes

1. For an excellent account of Nietzsche's personal life as it develops with his thought, see Rüdiger Safranski's *Nietzsche: A Philosophical Biography*, trans. Shelley Frisch (New York: W. W. Norton, 2002). Other good accounts

include Curtis Cate, *Friedrich Nietzsche* (Woodstock, N.Y.: Overview Press, 2005); Alexander Nehamas, *Nietzsche: Life as Literature* (Cambridge: Harvard University Press, 1985); and Ronald Hayman, *Nietzsche: A Critical Life* (New York: Routledge, 1999).

2. Friedrich Nietzsche, *Beyond Good and Evil*, trans. R. J. Hollingdale (New York: Penguin Books, 1990), 73.

3. Ibid., 57.

4. Ibid., 214

5. Ruth Abbey, "Circles, Ladders and Stars: Nietzsche on Friendship," in *The Challenge to Friendship in Modernity*, ed. Preston King and Heather Devere (London: Frank Cass, 2000), 51. Nietzsche's "middle period" is generally thought to include *Human, All too Human* (trans. R. J. Hollingdale [Cambridge: Cambridge University Press, 1986]) (which includes *Assorted Opinions and Maxims* and *The Wanderer and His Shadow*); *Daybreak* (trans. R. J. Hollingdale [Cambridge: Cambridge University Press, 1982]); and the first four volumes of *The Gay Science* (trans. Walter Kaufmann [New York: Vantage Books, 1974]). In other words, everything after his fascination with Schopenhauer and Wagner up to the introduction of Zarathustra. Nietzsche himself divided his work into three periods, which he called "The Road to Wisdom." Eric Voegelin insightfully observes how to understand the tripartite division of Nietzsche's work: "One cannot and should not dispense with it, but one should be aware that a too exclusive adherence to it is apt to obscure certain traits of Nietzsche's thought that remain permanent throughout the three periods" (*Collected Works of Eric Voegelin*, vol. 25, *The New Order and the Last Orientation*, ed. Jürgen Gebhardt and Thomas Hollweck [Columbia: University of Missouri Press, 1999], 251).

6. Abbey, "Circles, Ladders and Stars," 54–56, 56–59, 60–61, 62.

7. Ibid., 66.

8. *The Gay Science*, #342, 274.

9. Jacques Derrida, "The Politics of Friendship," *Journal of Philosophy* 85 (1988): 643.

10. For an excellent account of this "intellectual ménage à trios," see Safranski's chapter "Lou Salomé and the Quest for Intimacy," in his *Nietzsche*, 221–75. An interesting account of the intellectual rift that developed between Nietzsche and Rée from the Salomé affair can be found in Brendan Donnellan's "Friedrich Nietzsche and Paul Rée: Cooperation and Conflict," *Journal of the History of Ideas* 43(4) (October–December 1982): 595–612. Irvin D. Yalom, in *When Nietzsche Wept* (New York: Basic Books, 1992), has written a fictive account of the psychological fallout Nietzsche suffered from the end of this friendship.

11. Friedrich Nietzsche, *Ecce Homo*, trans. Walter Kaufmann (New York: Vintage Books, 1989), 295.

12. As cited in Safranski, *Nietzsche*, 235.

13. Nietzsche, *The Gay Science*, #76, 130.
14. Ibid., #76, 131.
15. Ibid.
16. Ibid., #341, 273–74.
17. Nietzsche, *Ecce Homo*, 295.
18. Nietzsche, *The Gay Science*, #132, 186.
19. Ibid., #125, 181. Book 3 of *The Gay Science* opens with Nietzsche's first iteration of this famous proclamation: "*New struggles.*—After Buddha was dead, his shadow was still shown for centuries in a cave—a tremendous, gruesome shadow. God is dead; but given the way of men, there may still be caves for thousands of years in which his shadow will be shown.—And we—we still have to vanquish his shadow, too" (#108, 167).
20. Augustine, *City of God*, trans. Henry Bettenson (New York: Penguin Books, 1972), XII, xii, 475.
21. Cf. *Timaeus*, 39d; *Laws*, 677a–680b.
22. Augustine, *City of God*, XII, xiv, 487.
23. Ibid.
24. Ibid., XII, xv, 489.
25. Ibid., XII, xiv, 487–88.
26. Ibid., XII, xiv, 488–89. A bit later Augustine reiterates this point: "So let us keep to our straight way, which is Christ, let us take him as our guide and saviour, and turn our minds from the absurd futility of this circular route of the impious, and keep instead to the way of faith" (ibid., XII, xxi, 500).
27. Safranski, *Nietzsche*, 226.
28. Cited in ibid.
29. Ibid.
30. Nietzsche, *The Gay Science*, #358, 310.
31. Ibid., #358, 313.
32. Ibid., #358, 311–12.
33. Ibid., 312.
34. Ibid.
35. Nietzsche, *The Genealogy of Morals*, trans. Walter Kaufmann (New York: Vintage Books, 1989), 145.
36. Nietzsche, *Beyond Good and Evil*, 138.
37. Nietzsche, *The Gay Science*, #358, 312.
38. Nietzsche, *Beyond Good and Evil*, 158.
39. Ibid., 158–59.
40. Nietzsche, *Human, All too Human*, #475, 174.
41. Ibid. For more on "good Europeans," see *Beyond Good and Evil*, #241; *The Gay Science*, #357; and *Genealogy of Morals*, 161.
42. Nietzsche, *Human, All too Human*, #376, 148.
43. Nietzsche, *The Gay Science*, 125, 181.

44. In the section immediately preceding "The Madman," Nietzsche discusses the "Horizon of the infinite." Here he exhorts us to sail into the infinite sea of uncertainty, to leave the land, and thus the familiar horizon, behind us. Cf. *Daybreak,* #117.

45. Nietzsche, *The Gay Science,* #377, 338.

46. Ibid., 339.

47. Ibid., 339–40.

48. Ibid., 340.

49. Ibid.

50. Nietzsche, *Thus Spoke Zarathustra,* trans. R. J. Hollingdale (New York: Penguin Books, 1969), 237.

51. Ibid., 221.

52. Ibid., 284. Shadows can never be eternal—at noon, or at "the great noontide" as Nietzsche is fond of saying, the man stands in the bright light of the day but he loses his erstwhile friend, his shadow.

53. Ibid., 87.

54. Jacques Derrida, *Politics of Friendship,* trans. George Collins (New York: Verso, 1997), 34.

55. Ibid., 155.

56. Ibid., 29.

57. As Nietzsche puts it in *The Gay Science,* #204: "*Beggars and courtesy.*—'There is no lack of courtesy in using a stone to knock on a door when there is no bell'; that is how beggars feel and all who suffer some sort of distress; but nobody agrees with them."

58. Derrida, *The Politics of Friendship,* 644.

59. John D. Caputo, "Who Is Derrida's Zarathustra? Of Fraternity, Friendship, and Democracy to Come," *Research in Phenomenology* 29 (1999): 192.

60. This Jewish tradition, commonly referred to as "Elijah's Cup," is part of the Haggaddah that constitutes the set order and sayings in the Passover seder: "This cup of Elijah we have set aside. Why? On this night of our ancient deliverance from Egypt, the barriers to redemption are at their weakest. While any season may see the arrival of Elijah the Prophet, to help us find lasting reconciliation and peace, tonight his arrival is imminent. So in addition to the four cups we drink tonight, to recall the four promises fulfilled in our past liberation, we have a fifth cup made ready. When Elijah arrives, we will drink it to celebrate the fulfillment of a fifth promise, the promise of a world returned and healed. Century after century we have prepared this cup and left it untasted, yet tonight we have filled it again. Stubbornly, we continue to bear witness to the promise of a Day when all oppression and war shall cease, as it's written (Isaiah 19): 'None shall hurt, and none shall do harm, in all My holy mountain; For the land shall be as full of the knowledge of God, As the waters cover the sea.'"

61. According to Ruth Abbey, attention to Nietzsche's ideas about friendship in his middle period will necessitate "a revision of the common interpretation that he is unremittingly skeptical about pity and other forms of fellow-feeling" ("Circles, Ladders, and Stars, 51). Attention to *Daybreak*, #132–42, and *Assorted Opinions and Maxims*, #68, both middle period works, might disabuse Abbey of this position. In this regard, Paul van Tongeran is perhaps more accurate when he rejects this sort of view, along with Derrida's "utopian reading of Nietzsche," in favor of the more traditional reading. For van Tongeran, "Nietzsche sees not only politics, but human beings themselves as being constituted by a violent act of submission, and characterized by an ongoing struggle for power" ("Politics, Friendship and Solitude in Nietzsche: Confronting Derrida's Reading of Nietzsche in *Politics of Friendship*," *South African Journal of Philosophy* 19[3] [2000]: 209). For example, Zarathustra teaches that "Pity is importunate—be it the pity of a god, be it human pity: pity is contrary to modesty. And unwillingness to help may be nobler than that virtue which comes running to help" (*Thus Spoke Zarathustra*, 277). Nietzsche goes even so far as to say that God himself choked to death on pity (ibid., 272).

62. Nietzsche, *Thus Spoke Zarathustra*, 39.

63. Ibid., 89.

64. Ibid., 41.

65. Ibid., 43. One is also here reminded of the light that comes to Paul on the road to Damascus; or, as at John 1:4, "the light that shines in the darkness."

66. Ibid., 42.

67. Ibid., 45.

68. Tracy B. Strong, *Friedrich Nietzsche and the Politics of Transfiguration* (Berkeley: University of California Press, 1988), 174.

69. Nietzsche, *Thus Spoke Zarathustra*, 46.

70. Ibid., 45. The line is repeated almost verbatim at 49.

71. Nietzsche, *The Gay Science*, #223, 211.

72. When Zarathustra sends the Ugliest Man to his cave, he says, "And first of all and above all speak with my animals! The proudest animal and the wisest animal—they may well be the proper counselors for both of us!" (279).

73. Nietzsche, *Thus Spoke Zarathustra*, 47.

74. Ibid., 212.

12

Friendship, Trust, and Political Order

A Critical Overview

Jürgen Gebhardt

The Evil of Politics

The strong man is most powerful when he is alone. (Schiller, *Wilhem Tell*, I, 3)

It is appropriate to begin with the question: Does friendship count in modern politics? At first glance there are reasons for an answer in the negative, as the following reflection on the modern political discourse seems to suggest.

Politics and friendship rarely go together. As President Truman used to say, "If you want a friend in Washington get yourself a dog." German politicians subscribe to the following degree of comparison: enemy— deadly enemy—fellow party member *(Feind—Todfeind—Parteifreund)*.

At best the power game of politics might allow for friendships of utility. Political friends do not love each other in themselves, but only insofar as some benefit accrues to them from each other as Aristotle had already observed. Based on the notion of the quid pro quo, a blend of trust and distrust is required to complete a successful bargain. This friendship of utility shows in political logrolling and lasts as long as it promises common political gain. But if the chips are down and the power game turns into serious struggle for power, the friend of today might become the foe of tomorrow. "From this perspective, friendship can be seen to lead to an injustice akin to nepotism in public life, while political calculations can lead to betrayals in private life." This modern view of friendship, as Julian Haseldine indicates, brings forth an overriding concern with the "distorting, even corrupting, influence of the personal and internal on the political and external." Thus the institution of friendship is denied any ordering function in the political and social life of modern society.[1] "Friendship is supposed to be strictly private."[2] This position lends reason to the opinion that the world of power that is the modern state knows just a semblance of friendship among rulers and subjects, and that politics is built on the expectation that most people are to be distrusted. From the vantage point of the modern Hobbesian we cannot but face the "evil of politics":

> The ubiquity of the desire of power which, besides and beyond any particular selfishness or other evilness of purpose, constitutes the ubiquity of evil in human action. . . . To the extent in which the essence and aim of politics is power over man, politics is evil. . . . For here the *animus dominandi* is not a mere admixture to prevailing aims of a different kind but the very essence of the intention, the very lifeblood of the action, the constitutive principle of politics as a distinct sphere of human action. . . . The evil that corrupts political action is the same evil that corrupts all action, but the corruption of political action is indeed the paradigm and prototype of all possible corruption.[3]

Under the particular conditions of the modern state the scope of this corruption has been broadened and its intensity strengthened. As the ultimate manifestation of power, the modern state expands the "corruption of the political sphere both qualitatively and quantitatively."[4] Morgenthau does not denounce political ethics but it is an ethics of doing evil in that "its last resort . . . is the endeavor to choose, since evil there must be, among several possible actions the one that is least evil."[5] If this choice is guided by political wisdom and moral courage man might reconcile his political nature with his moral destiny without, however, escaping the evil of politics.[6]

Morgenthau had dissociated himself from Carl Schmitt for moral and political reasons early in his German days. However, they enunciated the very same Weberian concept of state- and power-centered politics. The political defined in terms of the ultimate struggle for power is void of any ethically grounded political agency in society that rests on the notion of human fellowship, because it pits political collectivity against political collectivity in a life-and-death battle thus constituting the fundamental distinction between enemy and friend. In the last analysis the *animus dominandi* reveals itself in the antithesis of war, "whereby men could be required to sacrifice life, authorized to shed blood, and kill other human beings."[7] Schmitt does not distinguish between war in general and civil war. Civil war decides the future fate of a disintegrating political entity "and this is particularly valid for a constitutional state, despite all the constitutional ties to which the state is bound." So it should be noted that Schmitt denies the constitutional state's capacity for peaceful conflict resolution. Quoting from Lorenz von Stein, he states that as soon as the constitution is attacked, "the battle must then be waged outside the constitution and the law, hence decided by the power of arms."[8] The disjunction of enemy and friend emerges from combat in an existential sense in that it defines the substance of the political. But who is the friend with whom we are here concerned? It is the comrade in arms whom I have to trust because I rely on him as he relies on me for survival. The collective ethos of political community emerges from the combatant's experience.

Morgenthau left open the question of how community springs from the evil of politics in the modern state. Schmitt responds with the argument that all human beings are symbolically combatants and that any political community destined for political survival in the world of power must constitute itself as a fraternity in arms bound by the spirit of soldiery, and last but not least by the authority of the decisionmaking power that is again, in an existential sense, in command of the fraternity. Schmitt thinks through what Weber worked into his discursive exegesis of the power- and domination-centered idea of politics. The political community possesses the coercive power over life and death of its members and their actions are ultimately dictated by the threat of physical force to the point where "the serious demand is made upon the individual to suffer death in the service of common interest. This imparts the political community its specific pathos and creates its enduring emotional foundations. Shared political destinies, i.e., above all the sharing of political life and death battles, bring about communities bound by shared memories which often have a deeper impact than the ties of merely cultural, linguistic, or ethnic community in that they are the ultimate constituent of 'national consciousness.'"[9] The crucial point is that this political fraternity of a human group welded together by the shared experience of war devalues the fraternal ethics of religion in that now politics creates the emotional basis of the coercive community that is the modern state.[10] This is reflected in the politics of modern mass democracy, which rests on the emotional bond between the charismatic leader and his mass following that puts its trust in the leader who in turn steers the masses by means of demagogic manipulation. From the fraternity in arms emerges the political order of plebiscitarian caesarism.

A final remark is in order: Schmitt denounces any anthropologically based vision of a common humanity of human beings that would allow for an ethically grounded political community guided by the mutual trust among citizens, including the rulers and the ruled. Neither Schmitt nor Weber can deal with what the classics and the modern neoclassics call "civil friendship." When they think in terms of communal traditions they have in mind the Christian idea of fraternity and its modern revolutionary varieties. To Weber the modern age is marked by the marginalization of ethics of Christian fraternity, and to Schmitt it has become a liberal deceit. Both, however, hold the Christian notion of a universal fraternity to be in principle apolitical in the face of modern politics. Their point of view is misleading insofar as it downplays the impact of historically metamorphosed Christian ideas of community on the diverse modes of political modernity.

The semantics of the power-centered paradigm does not entail a conception of friendship and of its precondition, namely trust, as stated above, nor does power-focused political science. A politician's mixing his friendships with his politics may be a probable moment of the power game, but not a determining element of political order. This also holds true for the concept of trust, which until recently was treated as a psychological or moral concept in European political discourse.[11] So runs the argument of Germany's leading sociologist:

> Trust has never been a topic of mainstream sociology. Neither classical authors nor modern sociologists use the term in a theoretical context. For this reason the elaboration of a theoretical context, one of the main sources of conceptual clarification, has been relatively neglected. Furthermore, empirical research—for example research about trust and distrust in politics—has rather relied on general and unspecified ideas, confusing problems of trust with positive and negative attitudes toward political leadership or political institutions, with alienation . . . , with hopes and worries, or with confidence.[12]

This might hold true so far as mainstream social science is concerned, but by and large this statement is off the mark because it neglects the great tradition of "political trusteeship" in Anglo-Saxon political thought and practice that made "trust" a key concept of political discourse in the English-speaking world in contrast to continental European political semantics. It speaks for itself that a recent German publication on *Vertrauen* refers to Hobbes of all people as the thinker who laid out in his *Leviathan* the basic model for dealing with the problem of trust.[13]

This observation points to the crucial point of this inquiry. The state-centered notion of power politics portrays the modern political world from the vantage point of the continental European experience. Its political paradigm of the modern state was not and could not be modeled on the civil polity of democratic constitutionalism that has become the hallmark of political order in the course of modern history. Anglo-Saxon political science emerged from a citizen-centered civil polity but succumbed to a degree to the paradigm of power politics in spite of the above mentioned fact that traditionally the semantic complex of "trust" is politically coded in English-speaking political cultures.

But there remains still the question to be answered whether the overall view of politics as outlined by the Weberian paradigm does not in fact present us with an accurate portrayal of global politics in the modern age. It reflects indeed the pervading disorder of our age without, however, probing into the cause of the deplorable state of affairs that is characterized by the fundamental contradiction between longing for the good life in society and suffering under harsh domination. The explanatory force of the assumption that public order springs from power is limited or more precisely deficient in theoretical and empirical terms. Modern state building, whether revolutionary or not, involves in effect power and force, and the activities of fraternities in arms are instrumental in this enterprise. They provide the political nucleus of the emerging public order; but the fraternity in arms, once it is in power, creates systems of domination that lack stable foundations and fail to live up to the aspirations of their citizens in terms of life, liberty, and prosperity. The world abounds in miscarried state and nation building.

That is where the concepts of friendship and trust come into the picture when the question of political stability, and in particular of the stability of the constitutional regime, is raised by a theorist who argues from the unspoken premises of civic politics. Such a theorist is John Rawls. His *A Theory of Justice* introduces rather casually the notions of civic friendship and mutual trust as factors stabilizing a just scheme of cooperation in order to counter the Hobbesian recourse to sovereignty: "One may think of the Hobbesian sovereign as a mechanism added to a system of cooperation which would be unstable without it.... Now it is evident how relations of friendship and mutual trust, and the public knowledge of a common and normally effective sense of justice, bring about the same result.... Of course, some infractions will presumably occur, but when they do feelings of guilt arising from friendship and mutual trust and the sense of justice tend to restore the arrangement."[14] Neither here nor in the follow-up work *Political Liberalism* is the quasi self-evident notion of civic friendship closely inspected. In *Political Liberalism* it is tied to the "ideal of democratic citizens trying to conduct their political affairs on terms supported by public values that we might reasonably expect others to endorse. The ideal also expresses a willingness to listen to what others have to say and being ready to accept reasonable accommodations or alterations in one's own view. This preserves the ties of civic friendship and is consistent with the duties of civility. On some questions this may be the best we can do."[15] Rawls' "scheme," Gianfrancesco Zanetti comments, "entails a civic friendship, public values; respect for an existing reasonable pluralism is coupled with the need for *one* particular *ethos,* that of Rawlsian political liberalism." Rawls "exhibits a strong sense of political friendship, it is not surprising that a third of *A Theory of Justice* aims ultimately to develop a uniform consensus that will create (political) stability on the basis of a compound of justice and friendship distinctly reminiscent of Aristotle."[16] A close reading of Rawls, hailed as the high priest of modern liberal contractualism, uncovers a commitment to an idea of trust grounded in civic friendship operating as the binding force in political life and sustaining the ideal of democratic citizenship in constitutional regimes.

From the perspective of modern democratic constitutionalism as exemplified by Rawls, it is highly problematic exclusively to consider friendship in terms of the subjective, informal, and personal in private relations notwithstanding the fact that this view dominates modern discourse in general and power-centered politics in particular. At the present moment the "Western tradition of thought" that regarded the idea of friendship "the major principle in terms of which political theory and practice are described, explained and analysed" might indeed have "receded into the background" as Hutter and other students of the subject claim.[17] But "[the] problem which friendship presented to ancient thinkers, and which in turn seemed quite a natural starting point . . . to their medieval successors" seems not to be (as Haseldine assumes) so much of a different nature as far as the modern constitutional theoretician is concerned: "[H]ow does the institution of friendship form and regulate human society?"[18]

The Politics of Civility

As there is a degree of depravity in mankind which requires a certain degree of circumspection and distrust, so there are other qualities in human nature which justify a certain portion of esteem and confidence. Republican government presupposes the existence of these qualities in a higher degree than any other form. (*Federalist* no. 55)

The *Federalist* refers here to the quintessence of constitutional government that was summarized in *Cato's Letters*: "What is government, but trust committed by all, or the most, to one or a few, who are to attend upon the affairs of all."[19] The message of the early modern constitutional revolutionaries is that any legitimate public order is built on trust. It is the starting point of an ongoing discourse on trust that is in some way a follow-up of the discourse on civic friendship that began in Greek—Roman antiquity and resurfaced in the citizen-centered political science of the democratic regime that, however, blended into and occasionally succumbed to the prevalent power-centered paradigm of politics. A basic outline of the current trust discourse is called for in order to show how it connects implicitly or explicitly with the grand theme of friendship and civility.

Surveying the phenomena of political order and political decay in the global world, Samuel Huntington points out that "the degree of community in a complex society ... depends upon the strength and scope of its political institutions. The institutions are the behavioral manifestation of the moral consensus and mutual interest."[20] "A society with weak political institutions lacks the ability to curb the excesses of personal and parochial desires." Its politics is a "Hobbesian world of unrelenting competition among social forces."[21] "A government with a low level of institutionalization is not just a weak government; it is also a bad government." It "lacks authority, fails to perform its function and is immoral in the same sense in which a corrupt judge, a cowardly soldier, or an ignorant teacher is immoral." Thus, political institutions entail structural as well as moral dimensions. The morality of the institutional makeup requires trust, which in turn "involves predictability; and predictability requires regularized and institutionalized pattern of behavior."[22] There is a dialectical interplay between political culture and public institutions that Huntington explains by referring to Bertrand de Jouvenel: community means "the institutionalization of trust" and the "essential function of public authorities" is "to increase the mutual trust prevailing at the heart of the social whole." The "climate of mutual trustfulness" that is conducive to the pursuit of the common good depends even in modern complex societies on a modicum of "social friendship."[23] "Social friendship is strengthened when all are aware of one and the same framework of loyalties—a framework built of the most complex materials, with as many small rituals as large symbols. The construction of this framework is effected by life in common, it derives from lessons and experiences which all have shared alike"; it denotes the "culture of the people."[24]

Societies that lack stable and strong political institutions are, according to Huntington, "also deficient in mutual trust among their citizens, in national and public loyalties, and in organization skills and capacity." In other words social friendship is missing. These political cultures are "marked by suspicion, jealousy, and latent or actual hostility toward everyone who is not a member of the family, the village, or perhaps the tribe."[25] In sum: stable and effective political institutions depend on mutual trust among the citizens and the cultural force of social friendship generates this trust. Adam Seligman generalizes this sociopolitical function of trust albeit without explicating the specific nature of the trust-generating quality of human relations: "The existence of trust is an essential component of all enduring social relationships. . . . Power, dominance, and coercion, in this reading, become a temporary solution to the problem of order and the organisation of the division of labour therein, but they will not in themselves provide the basis for the maintenance of said order over time."[26]

The foregoing considerations of trust derive from a broad range of empirical studies of the subject. Practitioners of empirical trust research distinguish between "social trust" and "political trust." The first refers to the interpersonal dimension of social life. It entails the "expectation that arises within a community of regular, honest and cooperative behavior, based on commonly shared norms, on the part of other members of the community."[27] The latter connotes "trust in government or other social institutions." "Trust in other people is logically quite different from trust in institutions and political authorities,"[28] but "[a]cross individuals, across countries, and across the time, social and political trust are, in fact, correlated, but social scientists are very far from agreeing why."[29] The answer to this question would require a reflection on the moral constitution of human being that allows for the mutual recognition of trustworthiness because "[t]rustworthiness, not simply trust, is the key ingredient."[30] However, such an anthropological reflection moves beyond the theoretical horizon of normal social science. In the following, the subject of this rough outline will be explored in depth.

The sociohistorical context of trust must be clarified in order to understand the meaning of the ongoing trust discourse stretching from undertheorized empiricism to overtheorized system building à la Luhmann. There are three interrelated aspects to be considered.

First, it is foremost the self-understanding of the American republic that preserved the idea of public or political trust as the self-evident constituent of public order. That all rulership is political trusteeship was an unquestioned and generally shared conviction as evidenced by public discourse from the founding era onward. All power is fiduciary power granted by the citizens to their representatives. "The institution of delegate power" remarks *Federalist* no. 76, "implies that there is a portion of virtue and honour among mankind which may be a reasonable foundation of confidence."[31] This quasi Lockean legacy (to be discussed presently) shaped the American concept of political legitimacy in a way that distinguished it from the state-centered paradigm of politics

Second, as the *Federalist* asserted, entrusting officeholders with power involves the assumption of a mutual trust that places officeholder and citizen under a reciprocal moral obligation. This raised the issue of trust in general terms: Does the democratic order depend on the presence of trust among the citizenry? "If one cannot trust other people generally, one can certainly not trust those under the temptation of and with the powers that come with public office. Trust in elected officials is seen to be only as a more specific instance of trust in mankind."[32] Trust, however defined and measured, is considered to be an indicator of the strength or weakness of the civic culture in the United States and elsewhere. The link between political trust and the legitimacy of government is thus reinforced. From this point of view, trust—social and political—turns into the moral foundation of democratic political order. Political trust articulates the belief "that the government is operating according to one's own normative expectations of how government should function. The concept is closely related to the notion of legitimacy, a statement that government institutions and authorities are morally and legally valid and widely accepted." The democratic order rests on political trust; "when that trust is undermined, the whole system of government is threatened."[33] Since, however, political trust is contingent on trust among people, it is social trust that is at stake: "[P]eople who trust others are all-around good citizens, and those more engaged in community life are both more trusting and more trustworthy. Conversely, the civically disengaged believe themselves to be surrounded by miscreants and feel less constrained to be honest themselves."[34]

Third, the political, intellectual, and scholarly debate of trust sprung from American political experience and, as a consequence, the American republic was considered the paradigmatic case of a "culture of trust," at least as far as the concensus school of American social science was concerned.[35] And it referred with good reason to the specific "associative characteristics," the persistence of which in American history has been pointed out by American and foreign observers since Tocqueville.[36] The associational trust Tocqueville found in America resurfaces in modern trust discourses in two different modes: (1) conceptually, in that trust was recognized as a crucial ingredient of community formation in political culture sustaining regime stability, and (2) in terms of rich empirical research in that the development of survey research methodology in the 1930s made trust research into a scientific instrument for the measurement of the levels of trust and distrust present among citizens. Trust scientifically measured became an indicator of political stability and societal well being and trust research mutated into a collective self-analysis of the body politic in times of political crises because decline of trust meant in this view that "[t]he heritage of trust that has been the basis of our stable democracy is eroding."[37] The more trust research seems to uncover symptoms of trust decreasing the more trust discourse turns into a crisis discourse: a jeremiad about the "strange disappearance of civic America." Americans are bowling alone: "At century's end, a generation with a trust quotient of nearly eighty percent was being rapidly replaced by one with a trust quotient barely half that. The inevitable result is a steadily declining social trust, even though each individual cohort is almost as trusting as it ever was."[38] Be that as it may.

The crucial point is that trust research and trust discourse are contingent on principles of political order that in themselves are never elucidated in spite of the fact that American political science has universalized the assumptions underlying trust research and has made the trust–distrust disjunction a functional determinant of political culture in general as demonstrated by Huntington. Almond and Verba, the godfathers of modern comparative politics, inform us that trust signifies the "sense of community" of political culture: "Political cultures are built either upon the fundamental faith that it is possible to trust and work with fellowmen or upon the expectation that most people are distrusted.... Each political culture differs according to its pattern of trust and distrust, its definitions of who are probably the safe people and who are their most likely enemy, and its expectations about whether public institutions or private individuals are more worthy of trust."[39] Verba and Almond pioneered this new approach of survey research based on comparative study of democratic political culture that started with the civic culture project in the late 1950s. They integrated the trust complex into their paradigm of political culture that was widely accepted by international social and political science.[40] Only since then has trust research been carried on in non-American democratic polities. There it is still marked by the vexing problem that it clashes with Weberian politics where political trusteeship and the modalities of trust never figure prominently.

The political culture approach still begs the question as to the nature of this community building "fundamental faith" that is held to be the warrant of political stability. It is obviously considered the most important sociomoral resource a civil polity possesses and it is supposed to shape social life whose main features are those "networks, norms, and trust that enable participants to act together more effectively to pursue shared objects."[41] This sociocultural complex that permeates political culture was recently defined as "social capital." In fact it fits Jouvenal's concept of "social friendship." Neither Putnam nor the Straussian Fukuyama nor any other author resorts to the semantic of friendship, in spite of the fact that at least Putnam has an inkling of the anthropological moment involved: "Social capital is closely related to what some have called 'civic virtue.' The difference is that 'social capital' calls attention to the fact that civic virtue is most powerful when embedded in a dense network of social relations."[42] Indeed it is—and this network of social relations theoretically analyzed denotes civic or political friendship. As an aside, it should be mentioned that trust analysts never refer to the Rawlsian notion of civic friendship. Social capital is a "value free" descriptive term that nevertheless treads over normatively loaded issues, and in the latter sense it points to the anthropological ground of civic morality and its formative force of community creation. But even the most theoretical attempts at conceptionalization of trust fail to come to grips with this problem.⁴³ It remains to be stated that mainstream political science in spite of its devotion to trust research has neither developed a conceptual apparatus nor a theoretical frame for analysis of the principles of order as expressed in the historical vision of a civil polity that was to evolve into the Western form of political order. American normative political science runs into difficulties in this respect because it is fixated on the symbols of self-interpretation couched in scientific language with a claim to universality. It is rarely aware of the distinction between theory and civil theology, settling for a more reflective self-interpretation instead of theoretical and historical discourse.

The Politics of Tradition: The Lockean Hypothesis

> Since then those, who liked one another so well as to joyn into Society, cannot but be supposed to have some Acquaintance and Friendship together, and some Trust one in another. (John Locke, *The Second Treatise of Government* §107)

The critical discussion of political culture research as it was outlined above evokes some historical observations and comments that provide the subject of the following reflection. First of all, civic culture, the key concept of this approach, tacitly presupposes the citizen-centered communitarian notion of the political. It originated in the ancient citizen-polis, was interpreted and explicated in terms of a discursive paradigm of order by the philosophers, and received into Western Christian culture to be reinterpreted, revised, and adapted to the cultural exigencies of their time. In the form of a Christian neoclassical blend, this paradigm of politics informed the *idée directrice* of an emerging public order committed to the republican principle of self-government of free citizens. The principle of civic self-government that is explicitly emphasised in all modern democratic theory and empirical political culture research only makes sense on the condition of the rational and spiritual nature of the citizen-man, which is the source of ordering spirit among cooperating citizens evoking community. This vision of civil politics originated in the seventeenth-century crisis of postreformatory civil wars in response to the ascendancy of the continental monarcho-confessional state and it brought forth the constitutional state in the late-eighteenth-century Atlantic revolutions.

The Greek polis found its reflexive exegesis in Plato and Aristotle, Rome in Cicero, the Christian republic in Thomas, and the monarchical state in Bodin. For the constitutional state we are at a loss in this respect. We might refer to Harrington, Locke, the Federalist, or Tocqueville—even Kant—Kant for theoretical illumination, but none is *the* philosopher of the constitutional state who discursively separates theory from symbolic self-interpretation that is civil theology. Notwithstanding this caveat all these thinkers have expounded to a degree the principles of order that ground civil politics. John Locke is certainly not the spiritual godfather of Western liberalism—a misreading of his part in the history of the modern political mind that owes much to American self-interpretation and its impact on the social sciences at large. But in one respect Locke is important in that he contributes to our understanding of the principles underlying the notions of trust and friendship in a civil polity.

In his study of American political culture, Donald J. Devine contends that "a consensual political culture has existed in the United States, essentially unchanged in its entire history. It roots are in the republican principles of Locke and were reinforced and adapted to American circumstances by Madison and the other 'founding fathers' of the constitution."[44] Devine's inquiry reflects the "liberal tradition" thesis that had been proposed by Louis Hartz in the 1950s.[45] "The political culture of the United States is conceived as being composed basically of Lockean values, which can be called the liberal tradition."[46] This "Locke hypothesis" guides his analysis of American culture. In the meantime, American historiography has come to disregard this *nihil praeter* Locke approach to American intellectual history in favor of the "republican synthesis." It refers to a republican paradigm of order that blends neoclassical civic humanism with the radical Protestant republican biblicism and fits Locke into the overall republican interpretive frame of analysis sketched out in the foregoing paragraph.[47] The "Lockean hypothesis" works if limited to the issue at hand, as pointed out as far as the modern trust discourse is concerned.

In the following I confine myself to what I think are the key concepts in a theoretical analysis of friendship, trust, and the civic polity.

Whatever we think of Locke philosophically, he discussed the fundamental question "What is the bond of human society?" in a way that proved to be historically effective in that it became constitutive for the institutional and symbolic form of the civic polity. His "trust-discourse" is motivated by the classical idea that a commonwealth is established for peace, security, and "common friendship."[48] His arguments may be guided by tradition and informed by the constitutional debates of seventeenth-century England and by widely held tenets of the neoclassical republicanism, but he formulates a concept of common friendship whose centerpiece is the idea of trust, which is the foundational morality of political order. Locke's conception of political trusteeship builds first of all on the analogical legal figure of trust developed in the constitutional conflicts since the early 1600s: "We . . . find two main forms, with some minor varieties: first, the idea that the king, or the executive, is a trustee for the people governed, and second, that the members of parliament are trustees of the electorate."[49] Thus, the concept of political trusteeship had become an established mode of thought by the middle of the seventeenth century and it "reached Locke in a well-developed form, and . . . he did no more than receive and apply it."[50] This is correct as far as Locke considers all legitimate power fiduciary power entrusted to the legislative to act for certain ends. But the doctrine of political trusteeship as presented in *The Second Treatise of Government* involves the well-known conclusion that the power reverts to the people whenever the legislative acts are contrary to the trust reposed in the members of society. In legitimate civil societies ruler and ruled are morally bound by mutual trustworthiness—the root of all political agency—and society in itself is conceived as an enterprise of cooperative agency operating on the assumption that "[t]rust is both the corollary and the safeguard of natural political virtue."[51]

In his early *Essays on the Law of Nature* Locke denounces the Hobbesian law of nature that men are in a state of war: "So all society is abolished 'et societas vinculum fides.'"[52] The term "fides" means trust as well as faith, and in this sense it refers back to medieval political thought and practice: fides defines the feudal relationship between lord and subject as well as the religious relationship between God and the Christian believer. Either relationship involves mutual trust. Locke's anthropology and Socinian theology is dubious, but we are concerned with the politicoreligious part of it. The virtue of fides is the virtue of keeping one's promises: "Trustworthiness, the capacity to commit oneself to fulfilling the legitimate expectations of others, is both the constitutive virtue of, and the key causal precondition for the existence of any society. It is what makes human society possible. . . . The duty to be trustworthy is primary because moral conventions and positive laws depend on it."[53] Trust springs from human beings' natural sociability, but it is safeguarded by the comprehensive order of the divine laid down in the *lex naturae*. Human trust and trust in God are intrinsically joined together in the sense of the biblical tradition. Human trust is premised by trust in God: "Those are not at all tolerated who deny the being of God. Promises, covenants, and oaths, which are the bond of human society, can have no hold upon an atheist. The taking away of God, though but even in thought, dissolves all."[54] In an addendum to the final draft of his 1667 *Essay on Toleration* Locke explains "that the belief of a Deity is not to be reckoned amongst purely speculative opinions for it [represents] the foundation of all morality, and that which influences the whole life and actions of man, without which a man is to be counted no other than one of the most dangerous sort of wild beasts and so incapable of all society."[55] "To be rationally and consistently trustworthy, for Locke the human being must fear the wrath of God."[56] Common friendship is guaranteed by the reverence for and fear of God. They alone lastingly ingrain the true principles of the law of nature, the foundation of morality in the heart of people.

To Locke the *obligatio moralis* is contingent on the sensual apperception of the well-ordered universe, the contemplation of which leads the mind by its discursive faculty that is reasoning to acknowledge God as the creator of everything and the author of the *lex naturalis:* "Hence it appears clearly that, with sense-perception showing the way, reason can lead us to the knowledge of a law-maker or of some superior power to which we are necessarily subject"—insofar God "has a just and inevitable command over us."[57] Once the nature of this command is more closely inspected it is clear that this God is not the God of the philosophers, not the God of the Deists, but a kind of Christian God as revealed in Locke's *The Reasonableness of Christianity*. The labors of reasoning produced only an inconsistent modicum of morality. The law of nature in its entirety gave Jesus Christ the authority of God in the Gospels: "Where was there any such code, that mankind might have recourse to, as their unerring code, before our Saviour's time. . . . We have from him a full and sufficient rule for our direction, and conformable to reason."[58] Locke extracted from the Gospels a Christian core doctrine, similar to the radical Protestant biblicism that expounded a primordial Christianity: the acceptance of Christ as the Messiah, the belief in the one God, and genuine repentance and the submission to the law of Christ. "In his last major work . . . Locke sets out a clear and simple account of how for an English Christian in 1695 trust may be more confidently and securely disposed."⁵⁹

But there is more to this ethics of belief. This reading of the Gospels authorized Locke's religiopolitics. Since the coming of Christ, God's command, the law of nature, is known to be the fundament of morality and this commits one to the reverence of God. Genuine "religion" combines piety and peacefulness, and the salvation of the soul is beyond the jurisdiction of the magistrate, which is to tolerate all religions believing in God and animated by the fraternity among human beings. This includes all Christian denominations that agree on the minimal dogma as laid down in the Gospels, and Muslims, Jews, and pagans so far as they do not deliver themselves to the protection and service of another prince as Catholics to the pope of Rome and Muslims to the mufti of Constantinople. Nobody who confesses to the belief in God should be excluded from civil rights of the commonwealth on account of his religion.⁶⁰ This political conception of public morality anchored in monotheism is a nonconformist Protestant version of the Roman concept of *religio* that had been reanimated and reformulated by neoclassic humanism albeit without raising the matter of trust in any particular way. Religion in the sense of reverence for the divine emancipated the spiritual dimension of politics from doctrinal Christian orthodoxy and delegitimized the political power of the church. Locke dissociated the public sphere from the church-dominated spiritual sphere, but he committed the whole society to political monotheism. This ordering faith of the commonweal was separated from the saving faiths of the warring denominations. This concept of a more or less nondenominational Protestant public religion unfolded its full efficacy in revolutionary republicanism to become the religiopolitical framework of the American republic. All American founders and in particular the early presidents Washington, Adams, and Jefferson subscribed to this ordering faith, making it the civil religion of the republic.

From the trust discourse of Lockean politics emerges the unique Anglo-Saxon conception of government of political trusteeship. Only in English thought were the legal concepts of trust and trusteeship transferred into the political sphere. The Weberian semantics of domination does not admit a concept of government in terms of trusteeship, nor is there a people that exerts this fiduciary power in terms of self-rule on the admittedly precarious basis of common friendship. The Lockean espousal of an order grounded in trust represented a paradigm of the political less fixated on the reason of state as Dunn explained: For Locke "the political primacy of *fides* is certainly not a matter of the priority of private rights over public utility. What divided him on this score from . . . exponents of the claims of state authority . . . was not any lack of sensitivity to the *rationes status*. . . . Rather, it was a more disabused and less alienated conception of the state. For him the state was only an organizational system through which some human beings are enabled to act on behalf of (or against) others."[61] This conclusion oversimplifies the matter in that Locke, like his neoclassical contemporaries, expounds the idea of a civic community unified by public virtue and committed to a "Higher Law" "promulgated by the Deity." Implied in Locke's conception of community was the notion of civism that animates cooperative civic agency and that Locke himself, on account of his specific theological individualism, was unable to articulate. It was the concept of reason, in that Locke differed from the neoclassic paradigm that was to absorb his politics of trust in turn.

The crucial point of this theological epistemology is that it eclipses reason as the constituent of humanity in terms of the ordering center of humans' personal existence in society. This has to be viewed in connection with the further observation that Locke did not develop a notion of citizenship. The alleged father of modern liberalism speaks of the "citizen" neither in his political tracts nor in his draft of the constitution for Carolina. All political and intellectual factions of this era envisioned the "free man" to be the pivot of civil politics, but it fell upon the neoclassic followers of Harrington to elevate the "free man" to "citizen" in the civic humanist tradition. "[T]he difference between *civis* and *servus* is irreconcilable; and no man, whilst he is a servant, can be a member of a commonwealth; for he is not in his own power, cannot have a part in the government of others."[62] This credo of republicanism inspired by the Greco-Roman legacy, however, affirmed the essential rationality of human nature and made it the *condicio sine qua non* of the citizen's political agency. This premise provided Locke's trust discourse with a more specific political rationale: "common friendship" reveals itself as "civic friendship" based on the common sense of rational human beings. The trust discourse justified the right of revolution and legitimized regime change, but Locke "is not at all explicit about what actually happens when people find themselves at liberty to entrust new hands with the government."[63] It was the republican legacy of 1649 that filled this lacuna with the republican paradigm of civic self-government grounded on the principles of reason and common sense. Moreover, it was easily entwined with the Lockean concept of political monotheism and the privatization of church establishment. Setting aside the complex history of emergent Anglo-American republicanism, and at the risk of simplifying the story, the following brief comment might suffice in order to indicate how the moment of political rationality came to play a crucial role in the revolutionary trust discourse of the founding era of the American republic.

The salient point is, in brief, that Locke's highly individualistic political ontology was cleansed from the subjectivist implications of his anthropology by the Scottish philosophy of common sense that became an intellectual force in late-eighteenth-century America. It supplied the Lockean idea of common friendship with a philosophical grounding of the kind that objectifies ontologically the civil-theological precepts of the Lockean idea of political community. Thomas Reid's philosophy of common sense restates the rationality of human nature and, consequently, of the citizen as the prudent man of common understanding that activates his moral sense. It enables him to make right judgements on private and public affairs. Common sense is the symbolic expression of the bond of community in that the common sense of the individual coincides with the *sensus communis* of interacting people. It is the constituent of the common world of human agency. Therefore, it is to be distinguished from the discursive faculty of reasoning (Locke's definition of "reason"), because it denotes that degree of reason that is necessary "to our being subjects of law and government . . . it is this reason, and this only that makes a man capable of managing his own affairs and answerable for conduct toward others; this is called common sense, because it is common sense to all men with whom we transact business or call to account for their conduct."[64] It installs a regularity of human conduct that inspires confidence in the action of fellowmen: "If we had no confidence in our fellow-men that they will act such a part in such circumstances, it would be impossible to live in society with them. For that which makes men capable of living in society, and uniting in a political body under government, is, that their actions will always be regulated, in a great measure, by common principles of human nature."[65]

Reason allows for judging of things self-evident and apprehending first principles of order. Common sense in this understanding "coincides with reason in its whole extent" and is an "inward light or sense ... given by heaven to different persons in different degrees" and it is "this degree that entitles them to the denomination of rational creatures."[66] The public world of common sense emerges from reason as the source of order—it is the order articulated in common friendship among citizens. It rests on "public spirit, that is an affection to any community to which we belong.... Without it, society could not subsist." If this affection of belonging is dominated by private concerns, public spirit is weak; but when it is "under the direction of virtue and reason, it is the very image of God in the soul."[67] Needless to say, Reid, like many of his intellectual confreres in the late eighteenth century, insists on the nation's duty to "honour God by stated acts of devotion and piety," "rational piety being the most powerful motive to virtue."[68] And he even proffers with reference to Locke the idea that a state may be well governed without an established religion, as in the case of Pennsylvania.

The concept of common sense is central to this understanding of the modern version of friendship in the civic polity because "it is the habit of judgement and conduct of a man formed by ratio" as Eric Voegelin indicates. But contrary to Voegelin's assertion, Reid was aware of the fact that "common sense is a civilizational habit that presupposes noetic experience." He would agree with Voegelin that the citizen of common sense need not himself possess "differentiated knowledge of noesis. The civilized *homo politicus* need not be a philosopher, but he must have common sense."[69]

The civic culture of civil polity, I conclude, presupposes political friendship and political friendship rests on the community of existentially formed *homines politici*. This Anglo-Saxon view of government has been so instilled into the political mind of the moderns that it has become a self-evident doctrine of democratic civil theology without, however, any interest paid to the underlying political ontology. However, as Eric Voegelin indicates, "A theory that insists on discussing politics in terms of Anglo-Saxon democracy can not deal adequately even with the Western national states, and not at all with the political organization, e.g., of Asiatic civilizations. It will, therefore, be . . . a problem of political philosophy to separate the essential from the historically contingent and to break with the habit of treating the institutions of a particular nation state at a particular time as if they truly manifested the nature of man."[70]

Such a systematic and reflexive account of the essentials of the political friendship discourse as distinguished from the modalities of its historical form is not an easy task for several reasons. First, it is inextricably bound up in the doctrine, thought, and institutional practice of Anglo-Saxon democracy, and its understanding of political trusteeship. In this regard it is a product of experiences engendered by historical situations, and effectively interpreted in terms of sets of symbols that were, as pointed out, an ideational amalgam coming to fruition in the modern constitutional state. Second, to reflect theoretically on the essence of this complex of ideas, sentiments, and behavioral attitudes requires penetrating to the formative principles and the underlying experiences at the root of the political friendship discourse in order to make sense of its modern modalities. This reflexive that is the philosophical approach to this discourse entails necessarily a recurrence to its ancient beginnings of a political reading of friendship and trust, because it emerged from a philosophical reading of citizen politics that set the ground base of the discourse that continues to resound in the modern era.

The Reflexive Politics of Friendship: Ancient and Modern

> Friendship is so eminent a republican virtue. (Hannah Arendt, *Denktagebuch*, I, 12)

Hannah Arendt's lifelong theoretical endeavours aim at a reconceptualization of citizen-related politics that would bring this classical idea of civic community to fruition in modern political discourse. This she accomplishes by reanimating the concept of friendship as the key to understanding the authentic meaning of the political. In contrast to the power-centered notion of politics, her reconstruction of the political realm reasserts the dignity of the political that in terms of the "practical truth of politics" is a politics of friendship. Arendt's theorizing on politics is set to retrieve anamnetically the spirit of civil politics and to instil a modicum of civility into the apolitical manner of modern political life.[71] This entails an Aristotelian meditation of kind. She refers to Aristotle's explanation that "community is not made out of equals, but on the contrary of people who are different and unequal." The community comes into being through equalizing in economic and political terms. The political noneconomic equalization is friendship. The equalization in friendship, Arendt argues, means that the friends become "partners in a common world—that they together constitute a community." And she brings to the fore the crucial point of her analysis: the political element in friendship is that in truthful dialogue each friend can understand the truth inherent in the other's opinion.

More than his friend as a person, one friend understands how and in what specific articulateness the common world appears to the other, who as a person is forever unequal or different. This understanding is "the political insight par excellence." This understanding and action inspired by it brought about without the help of the statesman would mean for "each citizen to be articulate enough to show his opinion in its truthfulness and therefore to understand his fellow citizen."[72] Republican friendship binds together the citizens of good judgment communicating their mutual judgments on the basis of truthfulness. This common understanding of friendship allows for leadership in politics but not for domination. The virtue of judgment is prudence, the virtue of the mature citizen (the Aristotelian *phronimos*). The commonality of prudence articulated in civic interlocution and interaction brings forth the common sense of political society. This Arendtian approach to civic culture illuminates to a degree the notion of the model citizen and the modality of community conducive to civic self-government in terms of friendship that is the unspoken prerequisite of all democratic political theory. Arendt recognizes the significance of the prudent citizen's capacity for judging for the common realm of political interaction but she does not raise the question whether it requires some existential quality inherent in judging that makes its persuasiveness into an active force of order among the people.

To Arendt the truly political realm is constituted by the plurality of human beings whose quality of being citizens blunts the temptation for domination on the part of the despot, be it even the philosopher. Arendt's Heidegger-induced anti-Platonism causes her to underestimate the theoretical relevance of Plato's reflexive critique of "normal" polis politics. He follows Thucydides in analyzing the destructive impact of power politics on a citizen-community—not constrained by a communal spirit:

> Where offices of rule are open to contest, the victors in the contest monopolize power in the polis so completely that they offer not the smallest share in office to the vanquished party or their descendants; and each party keeps a watchful eye on the other, lest any one should come into office, and in revenge for the former troubles, cause a rising against them. Such *politeiai* we, of course, deny to be *politeiai*, just as we deny that laws are true laws unless they are enacted of in the interest of the commonweal *(koinon)* of the polis. But where the laws are enacted in the interest of a few, we speak of *stasioteiai* rather than of *politeiai*.[73]

Also, "a polis ought to be free and wise and in friendship with itself, and ... a lawgiver should legislate with a view to this."[74] Plato's radical antidote to a *stasioteia* riddled by brutal interest and power politics was a *politeia* where there is observed the old Pythagorean maxim that "friends have all things really in common" meaning that there is "a community of wives, children, and chattel as well as all other private things *(idia)*."[75] We no longer have such a succinct terminology at our disposal as suggested by the *stasioteia–politeia* disjunction in order to distinguish a civil society based on trust and consensus from that one derailed into pure interest and power politics. The problem itself has been a vexing one in civil polities ever since, and Locke's trust discourse is just one case in point.

To Aristotle as well as to Arendt, and—as should be noted—to the "constitutional" tradition at large, the Platonic price was much too high since with the *stasioteia* the citizen polis altogether would have to go: "It is clear from this consideration that it is not an outcome of nature for the polis to be a unity in the manner in which certain persons say that it is, and that what has been said to be the greatest good in the *poleis* really destroys *poleis.*"[76] "For in one way the Polis as its unification proceeds will cease to be a Polis, and in another way, though it continues a Polis, yet by coming near to ceasing to be one it will be a worse Polis, just as if one turned a harmony *(symphonia)* into a unison *(homphonia).*"[77] For the polis is by nature a plurality of persons, and it consists of persons differing in kind.[78] Against Plato's friendship of a guardian class engineered by a community of wives, children, and property, his student Aristotle opts for a friendship of civic integration: "We think that friendship is the greatest blessing of the Polis, because it is the best safeguard against lapsing into *stasioteia (stasiazein).*"[79] "Friendship." Aristotle asserts, "appears to be the bond of the Polis,"[80] and a *politeia* of free citizens requires "that all citizens shall be equal and shall be good, so that they all rule in turn and all have an equal share in power; and therefore the friendship between them is also one of equality." "For where there is nothing in common between ruler and ruled, there can be no friendship between them either, any more there can be no justice."[81] This is "political friendship" the substance of societal concord *(homonoia).* "Therefore *homonoia* exists when there is the same purposive choice as to ruling and being ruled—not each choosing himself to rule but both the same one."[82] In passing it should be noted that this conceptualization sums up the Philosopher's analysis of polis politics. Neither the historians nor the orators speak of *philia* as a political concept in the Aristotelian sense. When friendship and friends were mentioned, they referred to personal relations among associative ties based on family, regional, and cultic networks and their working together or against each other in the political process.[83]

Arendt's concept of republican friendship builds on Aristotle's political friendship and she follows Aristotle in that not the rule of the philosopher, but friendship among citizens is the proper response to the crisis of democratic order. The Arendtian conception of republican friendship unfolds its theoretical potential only on the condition of including the constituent element of human rationality, because according to Aristotle friendship among citizens reflects the modality of "primary friendship" among good human beings that is a loving meeting of rational spirits united in mutual trust *(pistis)*. Primary friendship is the epitome of friendship that is "the ultimate substance of all human relations, the bond of feeling, varying in color, intensity, and stability according to the things which are felt to create the community in the concrete case." Primary friendship figures as the source of order in human relations "in so far as a perfect community will be achieved between men who have the order of the nous in common."[84] Political agency in the citizen polis rests on political friendship that is *homonoia* or like-mindedness in that it requires citizens to be of one mind or spirit in regard to subordinating their interests, plans, and actions to the common weal: political friendship determines whether concord or discord rules in society. The concord—discord disjunction corresponds to the trust—distrust junction of political culture research. The first, however, brings the problem of the substance of order into the picture, the second does not.

Arendt's anti-Platonism lets her repudiate Plato's anthropological principle that God is the measure of all human things by emphasizing Aristotle's statement that the measure for everybody is virtue and the good man: "The standard is what men are themselves," she claims, "when they act and not something which is external like the laws or superhuman like the ideas."[85] But the political truth attained by prudence is the truth of the good life that provides the measure of a well-ordered political life. According to Aristotle we arrive at it by induction that is the living experience of the good man who practices the life of reason: "Not in virtue of his humanity will a man achieve it, but in virtue of something within him that is divine."[86] This seems to fly in the face of the modern's humanistic belief. It might well be that this is the reason for Arendt's eclipsing this existential that defines the essence of the citizen's humanity. The Arendtian conception of political friendship has Aristotelian implications that must be explicated in order to confront it with so-called modern conceptions of community. Both are deficient in that they avoid acknowledging the anthropological premises of the Western idea of civic community as mentioned above, notwithstanding the historical fact that the modern constitutional form of public order, its institutions and symbolic form, derives from a paradigm of order that made human nature the base of self-government. So it may come much to the surprise of the practitioner of political science that this notion of human nature's spirituality became the centerpiece of the emerging citizen-centered vision of a civic polity in early modernity in that it accounted for the legitimacy of republican self-government, as demonstrated by a close reading of Locke's trust discourse and of Reid's common sense philosophy.

This statement necessitates further comment. Arendt's paradigm of republican friendship provides the modern friendship discourse with a near-Aristotelian theoretical grounding but she misses the "religious" moment involved. If we compare her vision of friendship to the civil theological thinking on friendship, this drawback becomes obvious. This idea of civic friendship was religiously connoted insofar it fed on a trans-denominational nonconformist version of Christian communalism. The community under God that is the national commonwealth blends the political notion of civic friendship with the Gospel's postulate of fraternity. Thus was the Christian vision of like-mindedness in Christ's body transferred to the body politic in the course of the "spiritual closure of the national cosmion."[87] From the outset this whole complex of ideas represented a politicocultural provincialism whose claim to universal validity was evoked by the new revolutionary regimes of Western constitutional democracy. In this respect the Christian ethic of fraternity was not marginalized as Weber claimed but metamorphosed in modernity. Weber is only correct in his analysis where he is concerned with another modern outgrowth of Christian fraternity: the eschatologically loaded project of a fraternity of revolutionary comrades in arms recreating the political world in their own image. "The relationship between Christian and pagan reflections on *philia/amicitia* is a complex one" in antiquity and even more so in the Middle Ages.[88] The presence of friendship in discourse and variegated modes of social practice in the Latin West is beyond the scope of this inquiry.[89] But an understanding of the revolutionary evocation of fraternity in modernity is contingent on its backdrop in terms of the evocation of the spiritual community of Christ. It was eschatologically coded insofar as it allowed for friendship with God (being denied by the pagans) to be perfected in a world to come:

> The very last, and perhaps most defining, novelty of the Christian theories of friendship—defining because all other elements lead up to it—was the inherent link forged between friendship and the life of heaven.... Aelred of Rievaulx brought his *De Amicitia Spirituali* to

a close with the following words . . . : The sting of death, which now afflicts us and makes us grieve for one another, will be destroyed. And then, in complete security, we shall rejoice for the everlasting existence of the Highest Good, when this friendship to which on earth we admit but view, will be extended to all, and by all will be extended to God, since God will be all in all.[90]

Once the Christian paradigm of a sacred history was transformed into a speculation on the meaning of the intramundane historical processes leading up to a terrestrial paradise, the promise of true fraternity was relegated to an open horizon of human perfection: a *democratie à venir* is the imagined place where the quest for true friendship comes to rest, as Jacques Derrida argues in his *Politiques de l'amitie.* Derrida's meandering speculation on the politics of friendship sets the counterpoint to Arendt's republican friendship and "deconstructs" the civil theological tradition in general. From his vantage point the political discourse on trust and friendship in past and present is under the spell of a political world marked by the Schmittian friend—enemy disjunction. The deconstructivist hermeneutics revolves around an apocryphal saying of Aristotle: "He who has friends can have no (true) friend" or "O friends, there is no friend."[91] Derrida operates with an erudite sleight of hand. He follows Plato and Aristotle in their philosophical understanding of primary friendship and hyperbolizes it in a twofold way: all modes of friendship are exclusive and therefore "politically" connoted (family, gender, nation) and the telos of friendship par excellence, universal and freed from any social fetters, is unattainable either because the pursuit of friendship is infinite or because the nature of friendship in itself is incomprehensible.[92] Thus, whenever people befriend each other they miss the all-inclusive universality of a true human intercourse—at least for the "political" time being. This reading destroys the ontological underpinnings of any politics of trust and friendship as well as it neglects the empirical reality of civil politics. This done, there is only one question left: "Is it possible . . . to think and to live the bittersweet rigor of friendship, the law of friendship with the experience of a certain inhumanity, in the absolute separation, on this or that side of the commerce between gods and men? And which politics could one still base on this friendship which exceeds the measurement of the man without becoming a theologeme?"[93] Neither man nor god is the measure: Who is left but Derrida? His imagined point of reference is a parousia: the "*democratie à venir.*" It appertains to the time of promise, and it remains in all future times "in coming": "Is it possible to open with the 'coming' of a certain democracy that is no longer an insult, which has the friendship with which we try to think beyond the homofraternel and phallogocentric scheme?"[94] In the last analysis Derrida acts the French Jacobin turned prophet, passing judgment on the lapsed people of democratic common sense.

The Western discourse on trust and friendship is a theoretical and practical discourse on the human condition of political order and as such it is an inherent element of Western self-understanding from its origins in the Greco-Roman world onward. But the semantics of friendship connotes foremost the highly personal moment of the face-to-face encounter of individuals and defines the optimal mode of human intercourse. In this respect it is correct to say: "The language, ideas, and lived experience of friendship are common place in human society,"[95] because this personal friendship is a transcultural phenomenon that can be studied in terms of equivalent modes of expression. The crucial point is, however, the "political" understanding friendship: it refers to the public sphere of common meanings sustaining a common reference world that signifies common purpose, action, and aspiration of the members of society. They live together by virtue of the binding force of trust. Its social efficacy results from a public ethics of trust. It links the personal habitus of trusting and trustworthiness to an image of human personality that serves as the ordering principle of society. It envisions the existentially engaged participation in the life of community on account of the common reason present in all citizens that signifies the theomorphy of human being's humanity. This linking of friendship to the public order was dependent on the citizen politics of Western antiquity, and following suit the evocation of the spiritual Christian community. From a theoretical point of view the political symbolism of trust and friendship entails a paradigm of order emerging from a specific mode of Western experience. The symbolism welds the historical contingent to the essential inherent in the political form of order: the constitutional state. This became obvious in the course of the global spread of this political model: the outward institutional form founders on the lack of community-creating substance because no ordering experience has materialized and become socially effective in the process of societal and political "Westernization."

In effect, any theoretical reflection on political friendship is in principle limited insofar as it is bound up with the Western form of order. The theoretical quest for the essential involves the study of symbolic and structural equivalent modes of evoking a political unit, a "cosmion of order" (Voegelin), into existence by acts of imagination in accordance with an ordering idea of human existence in society in intercivilizational perspective. The reflexive politics of friendship is in this respect a case study of human nature's potential for creatively ordering its existence in societal form.

Notes

1. Julien Haseldine, "Introduction," in *Friendship in Medieval Europe*, ed. Julien Haseldine (Gloucestershire: Sutton Publishing, 1999), xii.

2. Horst Hutter, *Politics As Friendship: The Origins of Classical Notions of Politics in the Theory and Practice of Friendship* (Waterloo, Ont.: Wilfred Laurier University Press, 1987), 1.

3. Hans J. Morgenthau, "The Evil of Politics and the Ethics of Evil," *Ethics* 56(1) (October 1945): 14.

4. Ibid., 15

5. Ibid., 17.

6. Ibid., 18.

7. Carl Schmitt, *The Concept of the Political*, trans. George Schwab (Chicago: University of Chicago Press, 1996), 35.

8. Ibid., 47.

9. Max Weber, *Wirtschaft und Gesellschaft*, ed. Johannes Winkelmann (Cologne: Kiepenheuer & Witsch, 1956), 658. My translation.

10. Max Weber, *Gesammelte Aufsätze zur Religionssoziologie*, vol. 1 (Tübingen: J. C. B. Mohr, 1972), 548–49.

11. Niklas Luhmann, *Vertrauen* (Stuttgart: Kohlhammer, 1989), v.

12. Niklas Luhmann, "Familiarity, Confidence, Trust: Problems and Alternatives," in *Trust*, ed. D. Gambetta (Oxford: Blackwell, 1988), 94.

13. Martin Hartmann, "Einleitung," in *Vertrauen*, ed. M. Hartmann and C. Offe (Frankfurt: Campus, 2001), 10.

14. John Rawls, *A Theory of Justice* (Cambridge: Belknap Press, Harvard University Press, 1973), 497–98.

15. John Rawls, *Political Liberalism* (New York: Columbia University Press, 1996), 253.

16. Gianfrancesco Zanetti, *Political Friendship and the Good Life: Two Liberal Arguments against Perfectionism* (Boston: Kluwer, 2002), 96.

17. Hutter, *Politics of Friendship*, 2.

18. Haseldine, "Introduction," in Haseldine, ed., *Friendship in Medieval Europe*, xvii.

19. *Cato's Letters, Or, Essays on Liberty, Civil and Religious, and Other Important Subjects*, vol. 1, ed. Thomas Gordon, Ronald Hamowy, and John Trenchard (Indianapolis: Liberty Fund, 1995), 267.

20. Samuel Huntington, *Political Order in Changing Societies* (New Haven: Yale University Press, 1968), 12

21. Ibid., 24.

22. Ibid., 28.

23. Bertrand de Jouvenel, *Sovereignty: An Inquiry into the Political Good* (Chicago: University of Chicago Press, 1957), 123.

24. Ibid., 131.

25. Huntington, *Political Order in Changing Societies*, 28.

26. Adam Seligman, *The Problem of Trust* (Princeton: Princeton University Press, 1997), 13.

27. Francis Fukuyama, *Trust: The Social Virtues and the Creation of Prosperity* (New York: Free Press, 1996), 26.

28. Robert Putnam, *Bowling Alone: The Collapse and Revival of American Community* (New York: Simon & Schuster, 2000), 137.

29. Ibid., 466.

30. Ibid., 136.

31. Alexander Hamilton, James Madison, and John Jay, *The Federalist Papers* (Harmondsworth: Penguin Books, 1987), 431.

32. Robert E. Lane, *Political Life: Why People Get Involved in Politics* (New York: Free Press, 1959), 164.

33. Arthur H. Miller, "Rejoinder to 'Comment' by Jack Citrin: Political Discontent or Ritualism?" *American Political Science Review* 68(3) (September 1974): 989, 1001.

34. Putnam, *Bowling Alone*, 137.

35. D. J. Devine, *The Political Culture of the United States* (Boston: Little, Brown, 1972) 47.

36. Ibid., 98.

37. Robert N. Bellah et al., *The Good Society* (New York: Knopf, 1991), 3.

38. Putnam, *Bowling Alone*, 141.

39. Lucian W. Pye, "Introduction," in *Political Culture and Political Development*, ed. Lucian Pye and Sidney Verba (Princeton: Princeton University Press, 1969), 23.

40. Gabriel Almond and Sidney Verba, *The Civic Culture: Political Attitudes and Democracy in Five Nations* (Boston: Little, Brown, 1965), 239.

41. Putnam, "The Strange Disappearing of Civic America," *American Prospect* 24 (Winter 1996): 34

42. Putnam, *Bowling Alone*, 19.

43. For example, Fukuyama, *Trust*; Seligman, *The Problem of Trust*.

44. Devine, *The Political Culture of the United States*, 47–48.

45. Louis Hartz, *The Liberal Tradition in America* (New York: Harcourt, Brace, 1955).

46. Devine, *The Political Culture of the United States*, 61.

47. Jürgen Gebhardt, *Americanism: Revolutionary Order and Societal Self-Interpretation in the American Republic*, trans. Ruth Hein (Baton Rouge: Louisiana State University Press, 1993), 65–67; Gebhardt, "The Transformation of Classical and Religious Elements in the Creation of the American Republic," in *Negotiations of America's National Identity*, vol. 1, ed. R. Hagenbüchle and J. Raab (Tübingen: Stauffenberg Verlag, 2000), 259–79; Mark Noll, "The Contingencies of Christian Republicanism: An Alternative Account of Protestantism and the American Founding," in *Protestantism and the American Founding*, ed. Thomas S. Engeman and M. P. Zuckert (Notre Dame: University of Notre Dame Press, 2004), 225–56.

48. John Locke, *The Works of John Locke*, vol. 6 (Darmstadt: Scientia Verlag, 1963), 20.

49. J. W. Gough, *John Locke's Political Philosophy: Eight Studies* (Oxford: Clarendon Press, 1950), 142–43.

50. Ibid., 163.

51. John Locke, *Two Treatises of Government by John Locke*, ed. Peter Laslett (Cambridge: Cambridge University Press, 1960), 112.

52. John Locke, *Essays on the Law of Nature*, ed. W. von Leyden (Oxford: Clarendon, 1954), 212.

53. John Dunn, "The Concept of 'Trust' in the Politics of John Locke," in *Philosophy in History: Essays on the Historiography of Philosophy*, ed. Richard Rorty et al. (Cambridge: Cambridge University Press, 1984), 286–87.

54. Locke, *The Works of John Locke*, vol. 6, 47.

55. Locke, quoted by Dunn, "The Concept of 'Trust,'" 287.

56. Ibid., 294.

57. Locke, *Essays on the Law of Nature*, 155.

58. John Locke, *The Works of John Locke*, vol. 7 (Darmstadt: Scientia Verlag, 1963), 142–43.

59. Dunn, "The Concept of 'Trust,'" 298.
60. Locke, *The Works of John Locke,* vol. 6, 46, 52).
61. John Dunn, "Trust and Political Agency," in *Trust,* ed. D. Gambetta (Oxford: Basil Blackwell, 1988), 87.
62. Algernon Sidney, *Discourses concerning Government,* ed. Thomas G. West (Indianapolis: Liberty Fund, 1990), 103.
63. Locke, *Two Treatises of Government by John Locke,* 114.
64. Thomas Reid, *The Works of Thomas Reid,* vol. 1, ed. Sir William Hamilton (Edinburgh: James Thin, 1895), 422.
65. Ibid., 451.
66. Ibid., 425.
67. Ibid., 564.
68. Thomas Reid, *Practical Ethics,* ed. Knud Haakonssen (Princeton: Princeton University Press, 1990), 255–56.
69. Eric Voegelin, *Collected Works of Eric Voegelin,* vol. 6, *Anamnesis: On the Theory of History and Politics,* trans. M. J. Hanak, ed. David Walsh (Columbia: University of Missouri Press, 2002), 411; Reid, *The Works of Thomas Reid,* vol. 2, 791.
70. Eric Voegelin, *Collected Works of Eric Voegelin,* vol. 16, *Order and History, Volume III: Plato and Aristotle,* ed. Dante Germino (Columbia: University of Missouri Press, 2000), 25.
71. Hannah Arendt, *Was Ist Politik?* (Munich: Piper, 1993), 41.
72. Arendt, "Philosophy and Politics," *Social Research* 57(1) (Spring 1990): 83–84.
73. Plato, *The Laws,* trans. W. R. M. Lamb (Cambridge: Loeb Classical Library, Harvard University Press, 1967), 715a–b.
74. Ibid., 693c.
75. Ibid., 739c.
76. Aristotle, *Politics,* trans. H. Rackham (Cambridge: Loeb Classical Library, Harvard University Press, 1959), 1261b79.
77. Ibid., 1263b34–35.
78. Ibid., 1261a 24–25.
79. Ibid., 1262b 8–9.
80. Aristotle, *Nicomachean Ethics,* trans. H. Rackham (Cambridge: Loeb Classical Library, Harvard University Press, 1962), 1155a23–24.
81. Ibid., 1161a 27–28; 33–35.
82. Aristotle, *Eudemian Ethics,* in *The Athenian Constitution, Eudemian Ethics, On Virtues and Vices,* trans. H. Rackham (Cambridge: Loeb Classical Library, Harvard University Press, 1971), 1241a32–34.
83. Morgens Herman Hansen, *The Athenian Democracy in the Age of Demosthenes* (Oxford: Blackwell, 1991), 283.
84. Voegelin, *Order and History, Volume III: Plato and Aristotle,* 320–21.

85. Aristotle, *Nicomachean Ethics*, 1176a17; Arendt, *Was ist Politik?* 89–90.

86. Aristotle, *Nicomachean Ethics*, 1177b26.

87. Eric Voegelin, *Collected Works of Eric Voegelin*, vol. 24, *History of Political Ideas, Volume VI: Revolution and the New Science*, ed. Barry Cooper (Columbia: University of Missouri Press, 1998), 73.

88. James McEvoy, "The Theory of Friendship in the Middle Ages," in Haseldine, ed., *Friendship in Medieval Europe*, 34.

89. Haseldine, ed., *Friendship in Medieval Europe*.

90. McEvoy, "The Theory of Friendship in the Middle Ages," 36.

91. Diogenes Laertius, *Lives, Teachings, and Sayings of Famous Philosophers*, vol. 2, trans. R. D. Hicks (Cambridge: Loeb Classical Library, Harvard University Press, 1950), 465.

92. Jacques Derrida, *Politiques de l'Amitié: Suivi de l'Oreille de Heidegger* (Paris: Galilée, 1994), 249–50. My translation.

93. Ibid., 326–27. My translation.

94. Ibid., 339–40. My translation.

95. P. Hatlie, "Friendship and the Byzantine Iconoclast Age," in Haseldine, ed., *Friendship in Medieval Europe*, 137.

Contributors

Richard Avramenko
is assistant professor at the University of Wisconsin-Madison, where he teaches political science and integrated liberal studies.

George W. Carey
is professor of government at Georgetown University, where he teaches American political theory. He is author of *The Federalist: Design for a Constitutional Republic* and editor emeritus of *The Political Science Reviewer*.

Timothy Fuller
is Lloyd E. Worner Distinguished Service Professor and professor of political science at Colorado College. Most recently he has published "The Idea of the University in Newman, Oakeshott and Strauss"; "Eric Voegelin on the Idea of Law"; *The Intellectual Legacy of Michael Oakeshott,* coedited with Corey Abel.

Jürgen Gebhardt
is emeritus professor of political science at Friedrich-Alexander University, Erlangen-Nürnberg, and director of the Bavarian-American

Academy, Munich. He has published extensively on political theory, history of political ideas, and comparative politics. His most recent book is *Politik, Hermeneutik, Humanität*.

Thomas Heilke
is professor of political science and associate vice provost of International Programs at the University of Kansas. He has published a variety of books and articles on a range of topics, including political ideologies, the political thought of Friedrich Nietzsche, Eric Voegelin, the Radical Reformers, and classical political thought. His current work is primarily in the area of political philosophy and religion.

John von Heyking
is associate professor of political science at the University of Lethbridge in Alberta. He is the author of *Augustine and Politics as Longing in the World*, along with articles on just war, deliberative democracy, Islamic political thought, Nicholas of Cusa, and religious liberties under Canada's Charter of Rights and Freedoms. He coedited volumes 7 and 8 of the *Collected Works of Eric Voegelin*.

Joshua Mitchell
is professor, and former chair, of the Department of Government at Georgetown University. He is the author of *The Fragility of Freedom: Tocqueville on Religion, Democracy and the American Future*. His most recent book is *Plato's Fable: On the Mortal Condition in Shadowy Times*.

Walter Nicgorski
is professor in the Program of Liberal Studies and concurrent professor in the Department of Political Science of the University of Notre Dame. He is editor emeritus of *The Review of Politics* and has written on Cicero, Leo Strauss, as well as on liberal and character education.

James M. Rhodes
is professor emeritus of political science, Marquette University. He is the author of *Eros, Wisdom, and Silence: Plato's Erotic Dialogues* and *The Hitler Movement: A Modern Millenarian Revolution*. He is a winner of the Pere Marquette Faculty Award for Teaching Excellence.

Stephen Salkever
is Mary Katharine Woodworth Professor of Political Science at Bryn Mawr College. He is the author of *Finding the Mean: Theory and Practice in Aristotelian Political Philosophy,* and a number of articles and chapters on ancient and modern political philosophy.

Jeanne Heffernan Schindler
is a member of the Department of Humanities at Villanova University and an affiliate professor in the Villanova Law School. Trained as a political scientist, Professor Schindler's primary research field is political theory, though her interests are interdisciplinary. She has lectured and published articles on Christian political thought, democratic theory, and faith and learning. She has recently edited a volume on Christianity and civil society to be published shortly by Lexington Books.

Travis D. Smith
is assistant professor of political science at Concordia University in Montreal. His 2005 dissertation on the role of medicine in the founding of the modern project, "On the Generation of New Natures," received the Robert Noxon Toppan prize for that year's best essay or dissertation on a subject of political science at Harvard University.

Index

agape, 49, 140, 144, 145, 147, 151, 155, 156
Alcibiades, 21, 33
Anti-Federalists, 250–54
anxiety, 21, 72, 123, 209
Aquinas, St. Thomas, 5, 6, 7, 9, 185–86, 187, 328
   on Aristotle, 146–49, 156n7, 157n8
   on civic friendship, 153–55
   friendship with enemies, 149–50
   friendship with God, 148, 154, 156
   on political authority, 151, 153, 154
Arendt, Hannah, 14, 73–75, 78n16, 117–18, 120, 121, 131, 284n36, 335–41
arête. See virtue
aristocracy, 71, 216, 252, 270, 271
Aristotle, 2, 4, 5, 8, 9, 12–15, 22, 27, 44, 50n13, 84, 91, 127, 140, 141–42, 143, 146–49, 153, 156n7, 158n28, 163, 164, 169–72, 174, 183, 186, 187, 197, 209, 211, 217, 218, 262, 268–69, 272, 278, 279, 280, 316, 321, 328, 336, 337, 338–39, 341
   and *endoxa* (widespread opinions), 54–55, 63, 71, 72
   and *epieikeia* (equity), 59, 68, 69
   homonoia (civic concord), 170, 338
   Nicomachean Ethics, 58–61, 141–42
   on the *phronimos* (practically wise person), 58, 336
   on *pleonexia* (greed), 65, 66, 70
   prohairesis (thoughtful choice), 54–55, 58, 59, 61, 78n14, 78n17
   — on the *prohairetic* life, 63–70

Aristotle (*cont.*)
   and the *spoudaios* (the serious person), 67
   style and substance, 56–63
   on teleology, 57
   on *thumos* (spiritedness), 55
association, 10, 96, 99, 165, 177, 184, 208–11, 216, 227–34, 236, 240, 262, 263, 277, 282n17, 283n30, 325
Augustine, 5, 7, 8, 9, 15, 101, 145, 150, 152, 164, 171, 185
   against cyclical theories of time, 294–96
   on analogical method, 116
   Confessions, 122–25
   conversation as friendship, 118, 119, 124, 126–31
   conversion, 123
   eros and friendship, 126, 128
   on justice, 130
   On the Trinity, 125–32
   and *populus* (political community), 120, 121, 129
   on unrolling (*evolvi*) as friendship, 116, 128–29, 132

Basil, 145
benevolence, 147, 160n40, 183, 241

Calvin, John, 5, 6, 9
   concord as friendship, 177
   on discipline, 186
   on government, 184
   on virtue, 181–83
caritas, 6, 7, 9, 98, 99, 101, 109n30, 158n27
charity, 11, 142, 178, 179, 223, 240, 241
Christ, 127, 143, 148, 158n27, 175, 176, 180, 182, 183, 187, 217, 229, 295, 296, 331, 340. See also Jesus
Chrysostom, John, 145
Cicero, 115–17, 119, 120, 122, 133, 143, 171, 185, 289, 328
   consensio (agreement), 94
   De Amicitia, 122
   — affinities with *De Re Publica*, 86–89
   — setting of, 87–88
   — suppression of Greek in, 90–91
   De Re Publica
   — affinities with *Amicitia*, 86–89
   — differences with *Amicitia*, 89–92
   — history of, 85
   — setting of, 87–88
   and *imbecillitas* (weakness), 95
   and pirates, 119
   and *sapientia* (wisdom), 94
   Scipio's Dream, 88–89, 105
   and the Stoics, 91, 97, 99–100, 103, 107n16
civil society, 4, 80n26, 223, 225, 239, 248, 337
common sense, 14, 35, 36, 333–34, 336, 340, 342. See also *sensus communis*
compassion, 4, 6, 223, 225, 240. See also pity
conversation, 27, 46, 57, 69, 71–75, 86, 86, 93, 118, 119, 124, 126–31

Declaration of Independence, 249
democracy, 2, 4, 5, 12, 13, 14, 21, 26, 71, 72, 133, 134, 143, 169, 228, 235, 258, 318–22, 324–27, 334, 335, 336, 338, 340, 341, 342
Derrida, Jacques, 6, 44, 72, 288, 304–6, 314n61, 341–42

Descartes, Rene, 275
Dickinson, John, 257
Dion of Syracuse, 48
Diongenes Laertius, 72
dishonor, 55, 166, 217. *See also* honor
dogs, as best friends, 3, 98, 315
domestic walls, 250–51

endoxa, 54–55, 63, 71, 72
enemy (and enemies), 6, 15, 82n42, 98, 120, 140, 149–50, 162n61, 183, 202, 215, 217–26, 229, 231–34, 237–38, 240, 244n4, 247n26, 245n11, 315, 317, 326, 341
Epic of Gilgamesh, 165–66, 168, 185
Epicureans, 95, 100–101, 110n31
equality, 12, 13, 63, 72, 133, 143, 144, 147, 148, 156n7, 166, 187, 189n10, 228, 266, 270, 272, 275–78, 280, 303, 338. *See also* inequality
equity, 59, 68, 179, 231, 239, 240
erastes (lover), 26, 44–46, 52n29
eromenos (lover), 44–46, 52n29, 82n43

factions, 12, 21, 74, 103, 105, 127, 218, 234–35, 237–38, 258 265n31, 332
family, 54, 56, 63, 64, 69, 71, 75n1, 76n2, 80n26, 85, 98, 109n28, 143, 168, 183, 223, 233, 234, 236, 243, 250, 257, 258, 282n19, 323, 338, 341
Federalists, 254–60 322, 324
fellowship, 13, 127, 147, 149, 176, 180, 278, 280, 299, 317
fraternity, 216, 304–5, 317, 318, 320, 331, 340–41

freedom, 2, 10, 11, 13, 29, 30, 72, 82, 199, 210, 211, 233, 235, 275, 277. *See also* liberty

gifts, 148, 180, 222, 223, 227–29
glory, 8, 37, 103, 117, 174, 221–22, 225, 227, 233, 243. *See also* vainglory
grace, 9, 145, 148–53, 158n27, 175, 177, 179–84, 187
Gregory of Nazianzus, 145

Hamilton, Alexander, 254, 259, 260, 265n28
Heidegger, Martin, 54, 281, 337
Hobbes, Thomas, 5, 6, 11, 12, 14, 15, 62, 78n15, 82n42, 275, 316, 319, 320, 322, 329
 against the Schoolmen, 216
 and altruism, 221
 on Aristotle's *Rhetoric*, 217–18
 on factions, 218, 234–35, 237–38
 on family, 223, 233, 234, 236, 243
 friendship defined, 218
 on gifts, 222, 223, 227–29
 and glory, 221–22, 225, 227, 233, 243
 on hiring friends, 230
 and justice, 217–25, 227, 230, 231, 232, 233, 238, 240, 244n4
 on Laws of Nature, 219, 224, 231, 239, 241
 on nature, 217–20
 on religion, 220
 on religious associations, 236–39
 and the "state of nature," 219, 222, 227, 232
 and vainglory, 226, 243
Homer, 36, 151, 167–68, 169, 185
homoerotic love, 44–46, 52n29

homonoia (civic concord), 170, 192n61, 338, 339
honor, 12, 34, 58, 59, 68, 165, 172, 174, 175, 215, 217, 224, 226, 229, 233, 256, 273–75, 282n19, 302, 303. *See also* dishonor
household, 30, 31, 64, 69, 138n36, 160n40, 174, 218, 269. *See also* oikos/oikia
human nature, 12, 22, 44, 57, 63, 65, 99, 102, 199, 214, 216, 220, 242, 260, 321, 332–34, 339, 343. *See also* nature
Hume, David, 259
humility, 144

Icarus, 208
imagination, 10, 102, 127, 207, 216, 269, 272, 281n13, 292, 343
inequality, 220, 242, 274. *See also* equality
injustice, 167, 258, 316. *See also* justice

Jay, John, 256, 257, 264n17, 265n28
Jefferson, Thomas, 2, 331
Jesus, 140, 143, 149, 160n40, 174, 330. *See also* Christ
justice, 130, 152, 153, 157n17, 159n32, 170, 171, 179, 182, 211, 217–25, 227, 230, 231, 232, 233, 238, 240, 244n4, 258, 272, 273, 320–21, 338. *See also* injustice

Kant, Immanuel, 2, 6, 23, 45, 46, 54, 62, 64, 66, 70, 71–72, 76n3, 82n42, 140, 328
Kierkegaard, Søren, 144–45

lex naturalis (laws of nature), 330. *See also* Hobbes, Thomas, on Laws of Nature
liberalism, 2, 3, 7, 152, 321, 328, 332
liberty, 2, 12, 30, 240, 251, 253, 254, 257, 267n42, 320, 333. *See also* freedom
Locke, John, 5, 11, 14, 82n42, 324, 327–35, 337, 340
loneliness, 2, 10, 16nn5–6, 133, 271, 281n7, 287, 288, 292. *See also* solitude
loyalty, 73, 248, 253, 262
Luther, Martin, 5, 6, 9, 178, 187, 275, 297–99
    on government, 184
    rejection of Aristotelian teleology, 172–74
    on virtue, 172–76

Machiavelli, 7, 102, 109n30, 118, 185, 199–99
Madison, James, 254–55, 257, 258, 259, 260, 265n25, 265n31, 266n34, 328
Mandeville, Bernard, 259, 282n22
Manicheanism, 125
Marx, Karl, 82n42, 273
memory, 83, 117, 124–28, 132, 134
money, 12, 21, 33, 162n61, 174, 230, 272–78, 282n18. *See also* wealth
Montaigne, Michel de, 5, 9, 11, 13, 14, 15, 54, 70, 72, 199, 205, 289
    "common" and "real" friendship compared, 209
    friendship between men and women, 210

friendship with Etienne de la
  Boetie, 206, 207, 209
 on the limits of reason, 208
 and public order, 211
 romantic view of friendship, 207

nature, 8,, 12, 23, 41, 43, 57, 61,
  62–63, 67, 69, 71–73, 78,
  79n23, 8242, 84, 85, 89,
  94–96, 100–103, 105, 117, 148,
  150, 151, 178, 198, 209–10,
  217–20, 224, 232, 242, 252,
  269–71, 278, 280, 337, 338.
  See also Hobbes, Thomas, on
  Laws of Nature; human
  nature; *lex naturalis*
neighbor, 4, 7, 31, 50n13, 82n44,
  115, 118, 121, 129, 132, 149,
  150, 172–76, 178–79, 201, 240,
  250, 276–78, 280, 299, 304–6
Nietzsche, Friedrich, 6, 13, 15,
  82n42, 128, 188n8
 "eternal recurrence of the same"
 —and Christianity, 294–96
 —discovery of, 290
 —and friendship, 290–94
 —and the nation-state, 296–300
 on Europe, 300–301
 and the "last man," 71, 308, 309
 on love as *Habsucht*, 43–44
 on Luther, 297–99
 on reason, 291
 Zarathustra, 304–10

Odysseus, 42
oikos/oikia, 69, 269, 305. See also
  household

patronage, 11, 217, 228, 242
Paulus of Nola, 144

philonikia (love of victory), 37
phronesis (practical wisdom), 30, 31,
  50n10, n12
pity, 4, 76, 231, 240, 288, 303, 306,
  307, 309, 314n61. See also
  compassion
Plato, 3, 5, 7, 8, 10, 13, 14, 55, 57,
  58, 60, 68, 73, 85, 90, 91, 97,
  100, 163, 169, 274, 279, 294,
  328, 337–41
 Apology, 33, 54, 204
 Gorgias, 47
 hermeneutics of, 24–25
 Lysis, 25–43, 199–206
 —friendship as utility, 200
 —image of the hunter in, 201
 —and the "in-between," 203
 —and trust, 201
 Menexenus, 26
 Phaedrus, 40, 45–46
 Republic, 25, 30, 54, 73, 169, 274
 Seventh Letter, 22, 24, 47
 Symposium, 39, 40, 46–47
 Theaetetus, 24
 on writing, 24
pleasure, 5, 23, 31, 54, 62–68, 70, 71,
  74, 95, 133, 141–43, 146, 149,
  170, 172, 175, 182, 209, 219,
  224, 268, 270, 303
pride, 28, 208, 212, 215, 222, 227,
  254, 291, 307
property, 28, 29, 30, 174, 180, 198,
  241, 242, 251, 338

Rawls, John, 2, 273, 320–21
Reid, Thomas, 14, 333–34, 340
rights, 2, 180, 233, 266n34, 284n37,
  302, 331, 332
romance, 3, 198
romantic, 70, 207

Rousseau, Jean-Jacques, 5, 6, 7, 54, 70, 71, 74, 246n18, 287

Schmitt, Carl, 6, 13, 317–18, 341
sensus communis (common sense), 333–34. See also common sense
Smith, Adam, 11, 117, 259, 269, 273, 275, 282n22
sociability, 153, 225, 239, 241, 330
Socrates, 14, 15, 54, 73, 88–89, 91, 100, 198, 200–206, 209, 211, 212
    as midwife, 24, 25, 31, 32, 126
    on beauty, 24
    and the *Agathon*, 118
solitude, 3, 129, 270, 271, 287–90, 306, 307, 309. See also loneliness
Sophocles, 168
Stoicism, 117, 178, 187. See also Cicero, and the Stoics
suicide, 16n6, 167
sympathy, 4, 12, 253, 272, 273–75, 277–78, 280, 288

Theognis, 168
Thucydides, 73
Tocqueville, Alexis de, 4, 5, 117, 133, 134, 262, 325, 328
    on honor, 273–75, 282n19
    on money, 272–78, 282n18
    and associational trust, 325
    and "social distance," 272–74
trust, 5, 11, 13, 14, 104, 167, 172, 201, 203, 219, 220, 226, 231, 248, 252, 260, 262, 280, 316–42

utilitarian, 3, 7, 10, 13, 23, 27, 31, 32, 34, 44, 50n14, 79n18, 98, 121, 175, 177, 181, 186, 188, 191n57, 198
utilitarianism, 23, 32, 42
utility, 5, 9, 10, 14, 24, 34, 35, 38–43, 45, 67, 96, 100, 120, 134, 141–43, 146, 170, 172, 174–75, 182, 198–205, 208, 210, 253, 291, 298, 316, 332

vainglory, 37, 152, 226. See also glory; Hobbes, Thomas, and glory
virtue, 5, 6, 8, 9, 11, 15, 22, 24, 25, 26, 46–48, 58–62, 116, 118, 120, 121, 141, 142–45, 147, 149, 150, 151, 153–55, 158n28, 160n40, 161n43, 161n48, 170, 171, 172–76, 181–83, 184, 187, 226, 239–41, 256, 259, 260, 261, 262, 268, 269, 270, 272, 288, 291, 306–08, 310, 324, 326, 329, 333–36, 339, 342
Vlastos, Gregory, 22, 25, 27, 28, 32, 33, 35, 45–46, 50n9
Voegelin, Eric, 14, 311n5, 334–35, 343

wealth, 33, 96, 222, 223, 235, 237, 238, 243, 253, 270. See also money
Webster, Noah, 255
welfare, 154, 155, 159n32, 240, 262
Wilson, James, 255
women, 3, 147, 210, 226, 282n19, 298, 305

Xenophon, 91

www.ingramcontent.com/pod-product-compliance
Lightning Source LLC
Chambersburg PA
CBHW050429240426
43661CB00055B/2319